AF072620

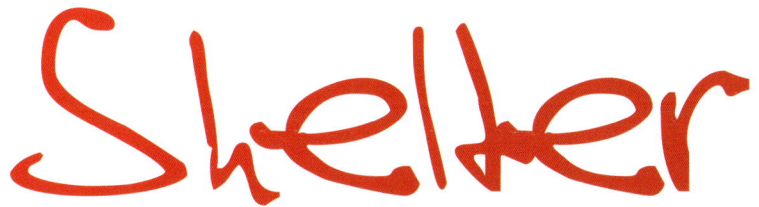

# Shelter

## Lucky S.Michaels

**TROLLEY**

# Sylvia's Place

## New York City's Emergency Shelter for LGBTQ Youth

**It was cold outside, I remember that; and we were marching to City Hall, back in the days when activists still marched on City Hall. Whether by accident or divine engineering, I suddenly found myself walking next to Sylvia Rivera, the legendary mother of the Queer rights movement in the United States.**

I'd read several accounts of the revolution that began late one night in June of 1969, in a "sleazy bar", as Duberman put it, off Sheridan Square; a bar called Stonewall. I'd read varying accounts of the named characters involved. Listening to Sylvia talk about that night and STAR {Street Transvestite Action Revolutionaries originally}, and things like "fingers for Jesus" and who could be trusted to help Queer people, especially the Trans community; listening to all the stories of kids on the streets that she'd met and taken care of in some way, shape or form, stirred something in me. It felt like Gospel --- like I was walking in the presence of a holy incarnation that previously I'd only read stories about and studied theological reviews of. Sylvia Rivera had a passion for human life, for celebrating and saving life.

Sylvia had a passion for kids --- Queer kids --- especially Queer homeless kids trying to survive in the only ways available to the young who've been abandoned.

I don't know how long the demonstration lasted or how long we talked. I left her with my card, and invited her to Church, though she'd been more than clear about her feelings, opinions, stances and actions against "the Church."

Eventually, Sylvia came to Church --- to Metropolitan Community Church of New York, a church of the LGBTQ community, open to all. She was hailed as the revolutionary she'd always been --- a hero --- someone who lived the answer to the only question the Scriptures we revere say will ever be asked of us: What did we do for those in need? {Matthew 25}

Eventually, I hired Sylvia to serve as the Director of our Food Pantry Ministry. She'd been trained as a kitchen service worker, and took to both the service and the people immediately. The crowds lining up for a bag lunch or groceries grew as rapidly with Sylvia at the helm, as did the range of humanity suddenly finding its way to this tiny church on West 36th Street. Children and young people were quickly sizing up the joint and deciding that if Sylvia worked here, they were probably safe and welcome.

It was hard when she fell ill --- noticeably ill in October of 2001, a little over a month after "September 11th." Sylvia neither wanted to acknowledge the stark realities of liver cancer rapidly eating away at all the feistiness and frenzy, nor allow anyone else to even suggest that something was very wrong. She came to work every day; many, many days after she probably should have been in a hospital. Even when finally left with little choice but to check herself in, she ran the food pantry from her sickbed, barking orders for others to carry out.

It was during her last hospitalization that she took a firm hold of my arm and said in that inimitably raspy voice, "Well, are you going to do IT or not?"

We both knew what IT was. No elaboration was necessary. For some time we'd both been talking about, fuming about, lamenting about {and in my case at least, praying about} the need for a safe emergency shelter space for homeless Queer youth in New York City. At that point, early 2002, unofficial estimates suggested as many as 8,000 homeless LGBTQ youths were living on our streets in this one city alone.

I'll never forget the feel of her grip on my arm or the question, "Are you going to do IT or not?" She was dying and she knew it --- I knew it. It was her passion --- truthfully, a passion we shared. It's hard to say no to a dying person; it's even harder to say no to the living. That's how Sylvia's Place was born --- living, human need met passion and a torch being passed on.

Every night, seven nights every week any LGBTQ kid who comes to our doors is received. Some stay for seven days, some for ninety or more. Everyone gets a safe space to rest for the night, a shower, a good meal that night and a hearty breakfast the next morning. Volunteers donate clothing, support and time. Staff spend the night, mostly listening and encouraging. --- A very high percentage of those abandoned to the streets have parents or other guardians alive and well. It's the Queer thing that has made the adults in these kids' lives abdicate both their responsibilities and what would have doubtless been their blessings. That's all it has ever been for the community of faith at 446 West 36th Street, Hell's Kitchen, New York --- a blessing.

Our current efforts are directed not only at keeping Sylvia's up and running, but also at expanding our services and inspiring other communities of faith to join us in providing safe and homelike environments for children and youth.

- 30,000 kids --- that's how many some studies say call the streets of New York home.
- 40% of all homeless youth are Queer-identified.
- 40% of all homeless Queer youth have attempted suicide.
- 4-10% of the juvenile "justice" population are LGBTQ.

Those are some of the cold, hard facts behind the shelter ministry. The faces you will see in this book are the heart and soul of Sylvia's Place. May she rest in peace. May all her children sleep peacefully every night of their young lives.

The Rev. Pat Bumgardner, Pastor
Metropolitan Community Church of New York

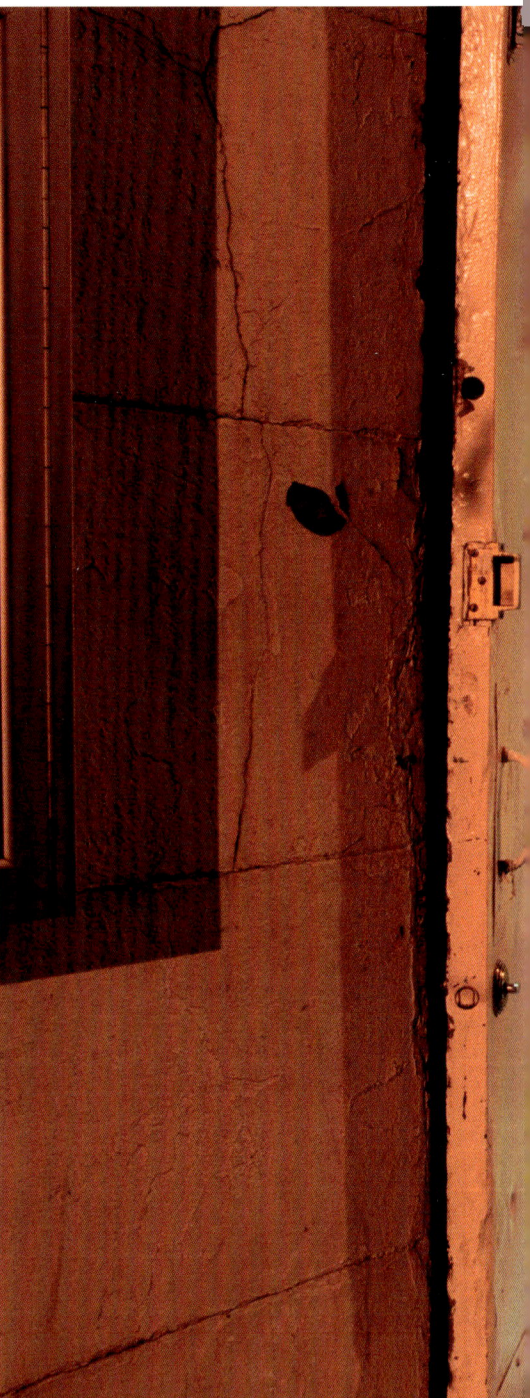

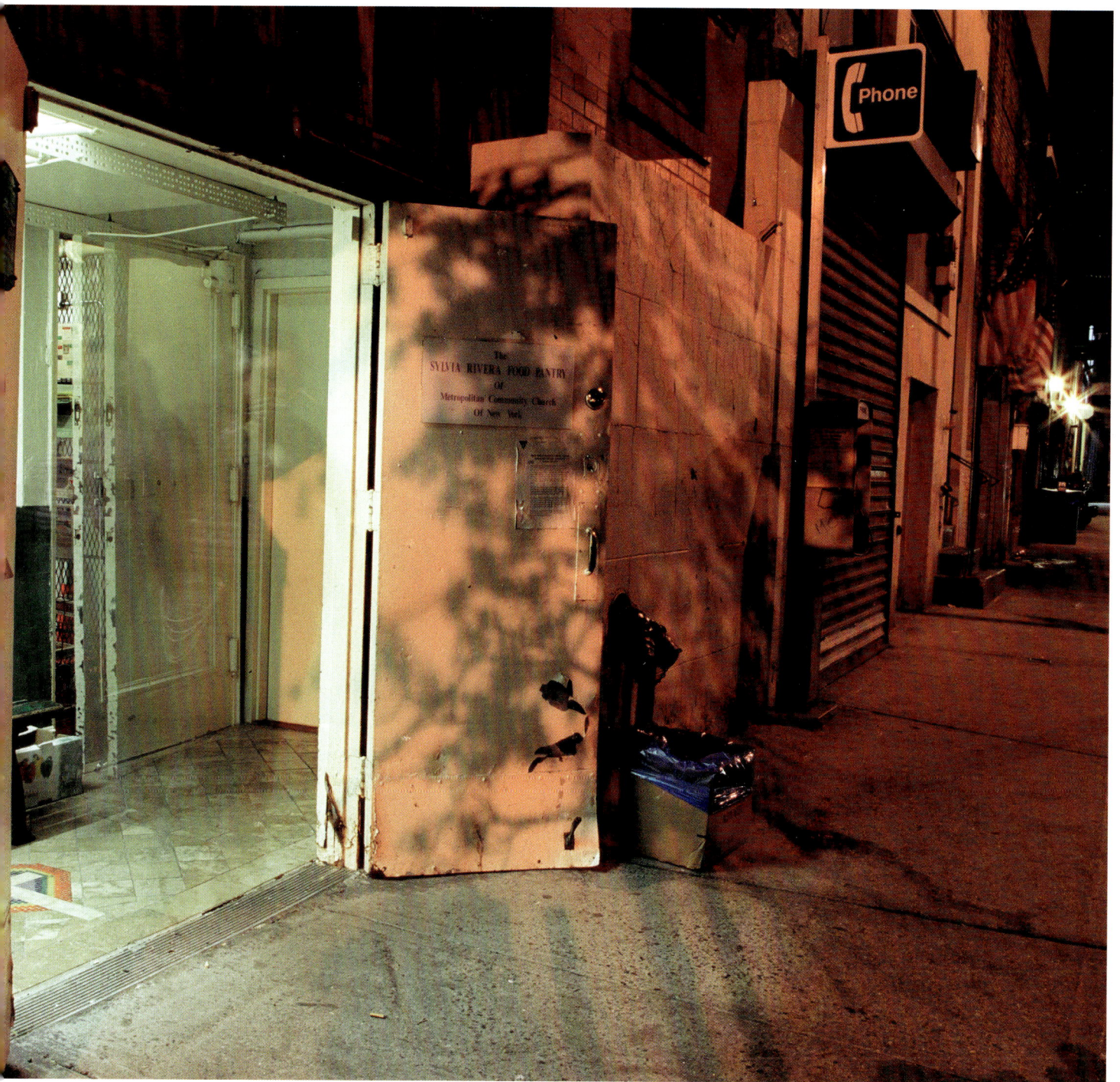

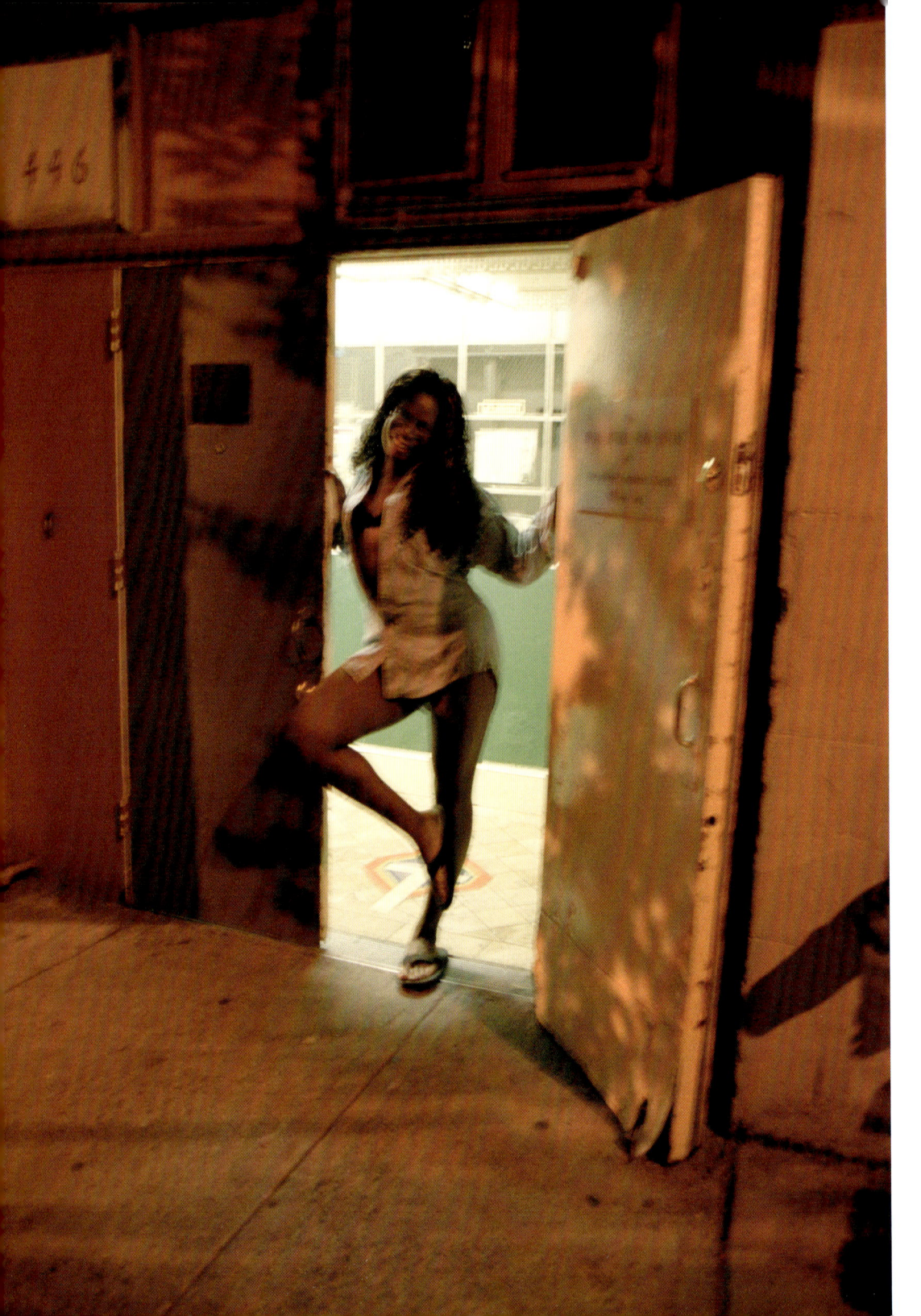

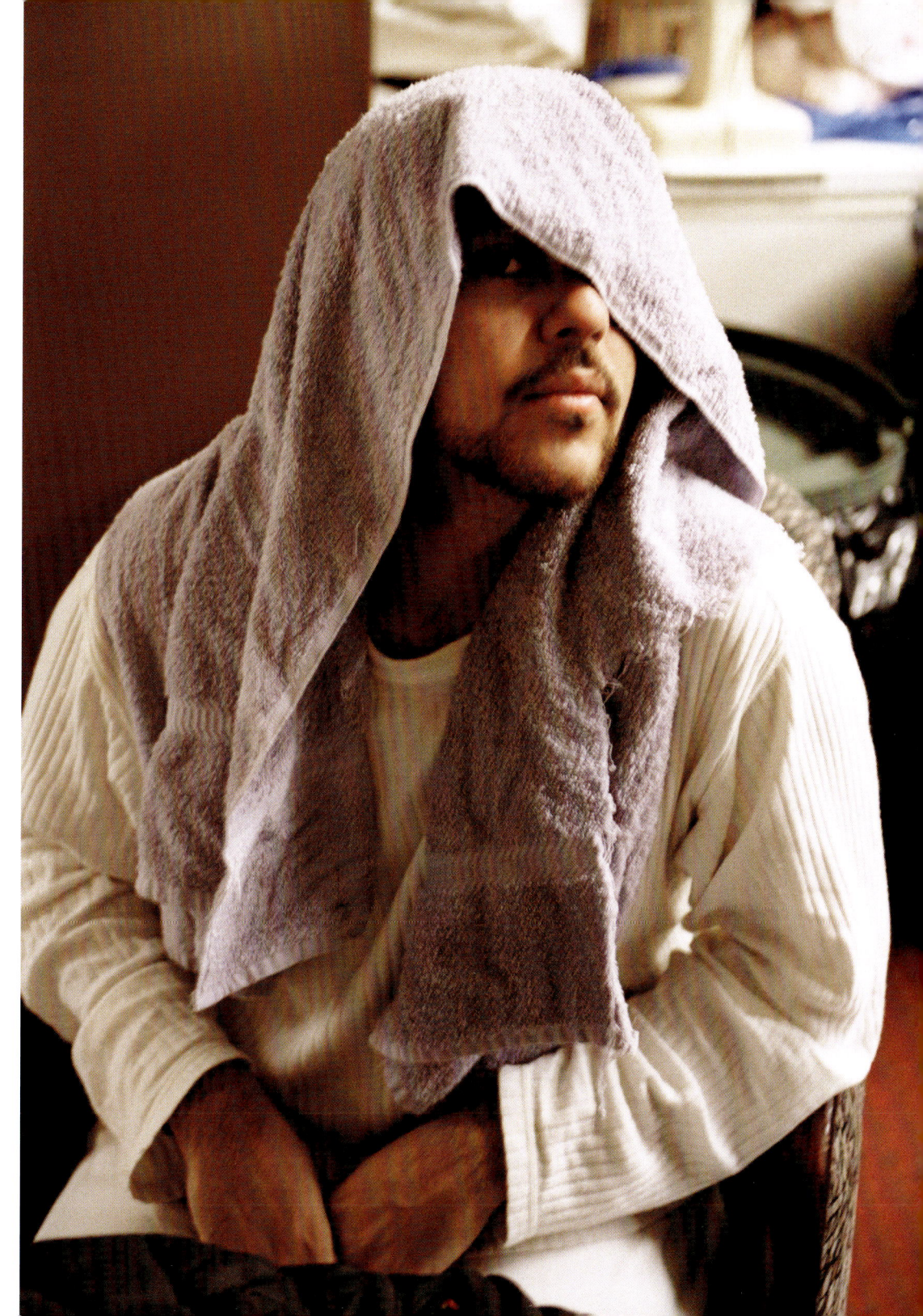

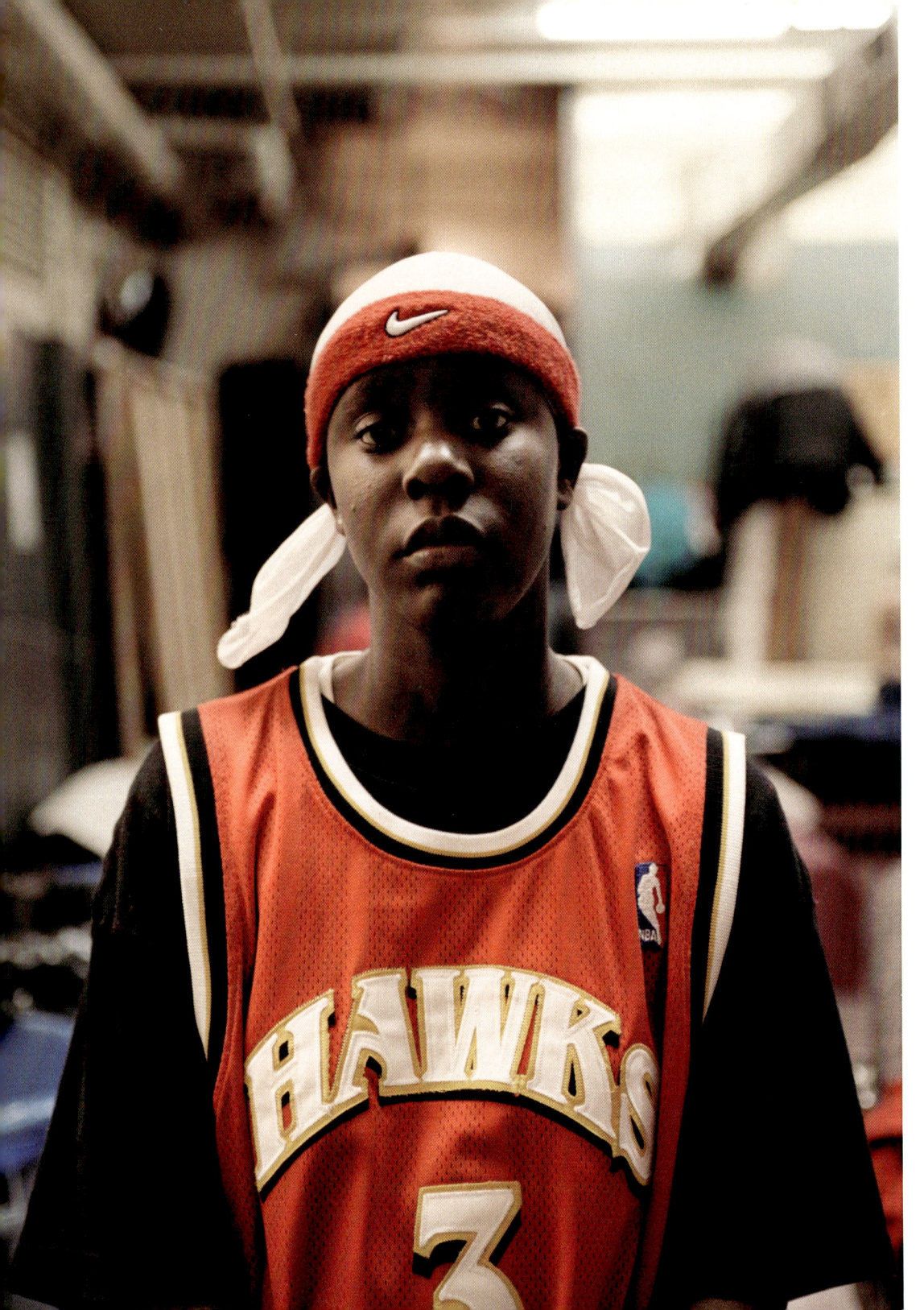

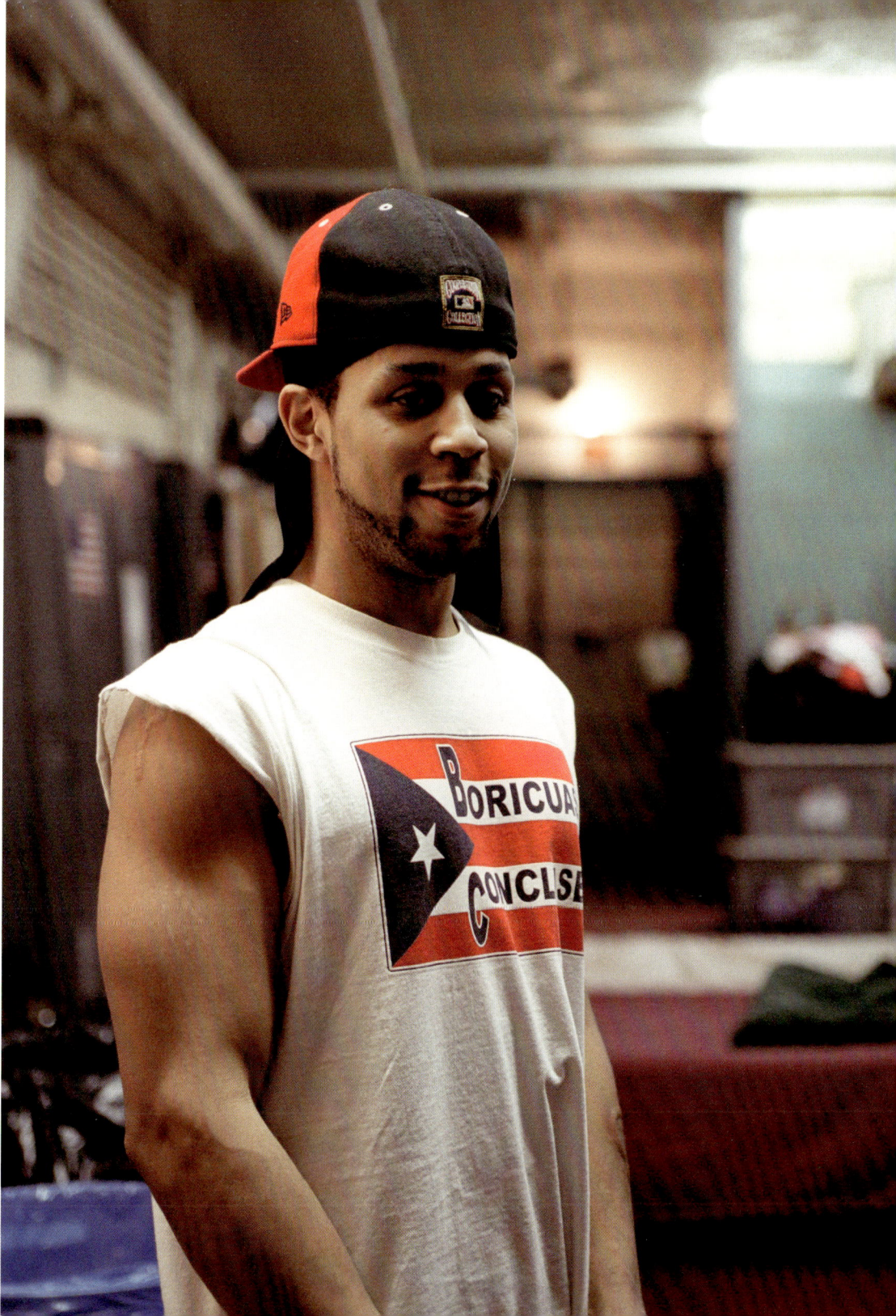

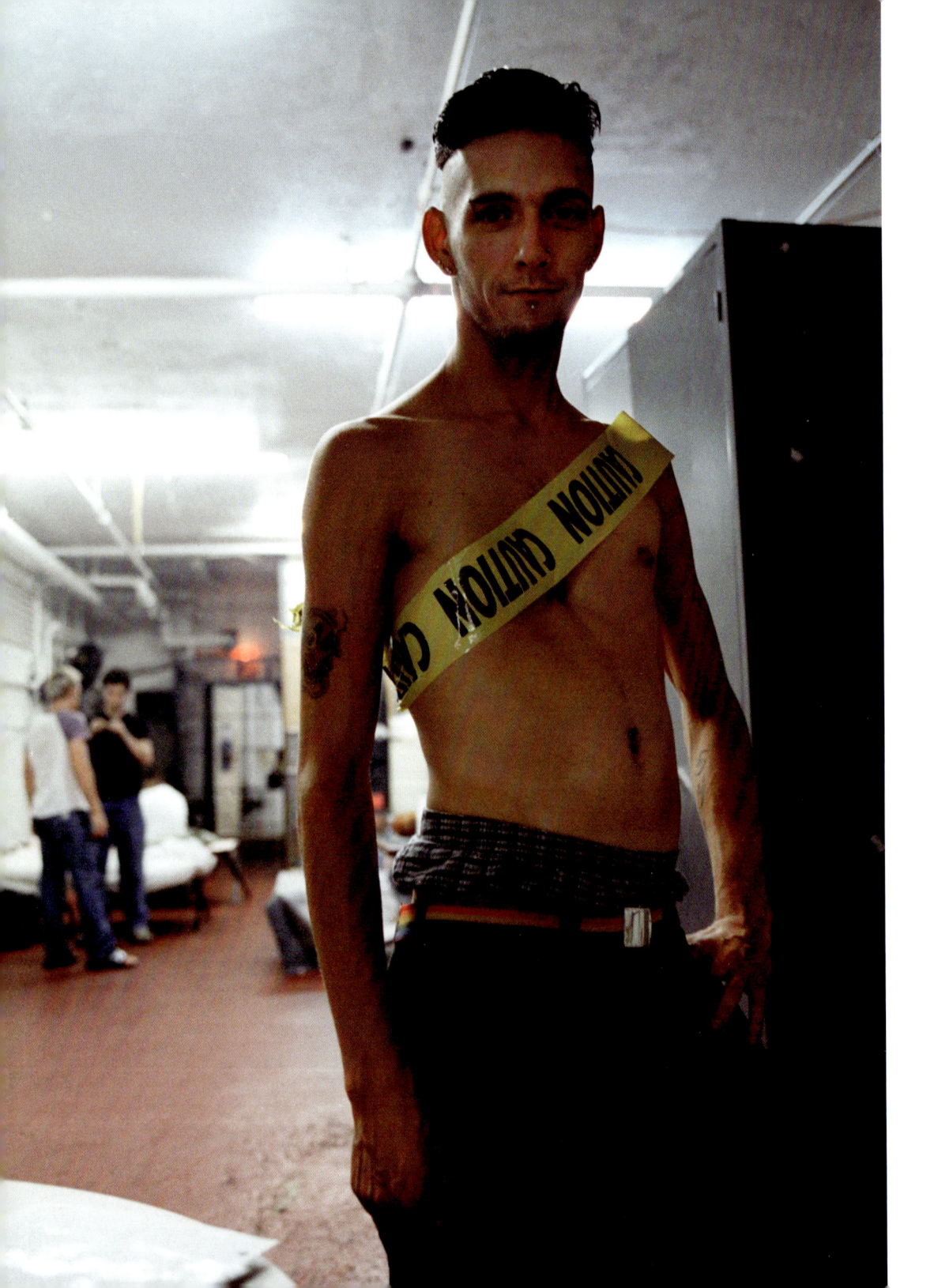

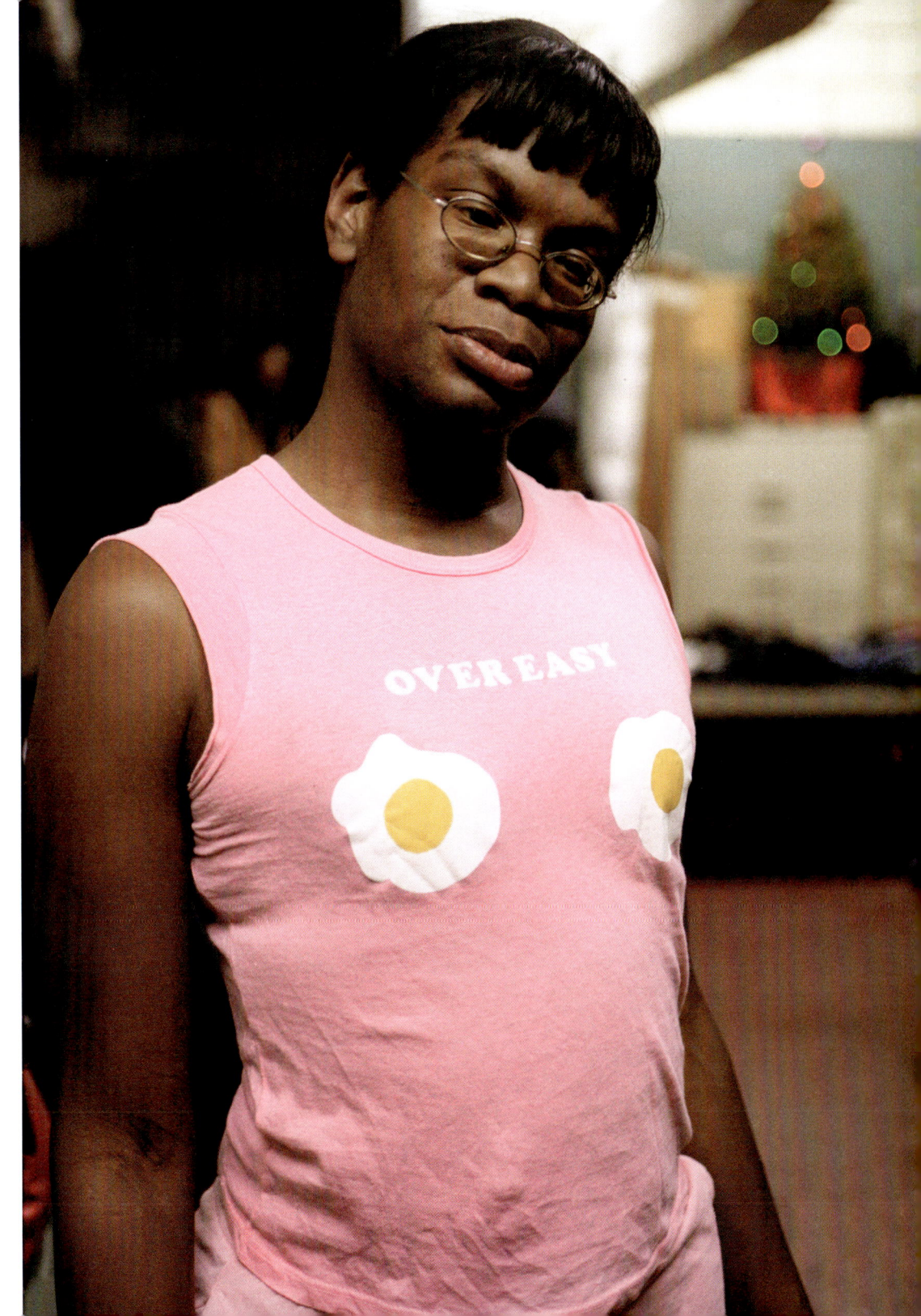

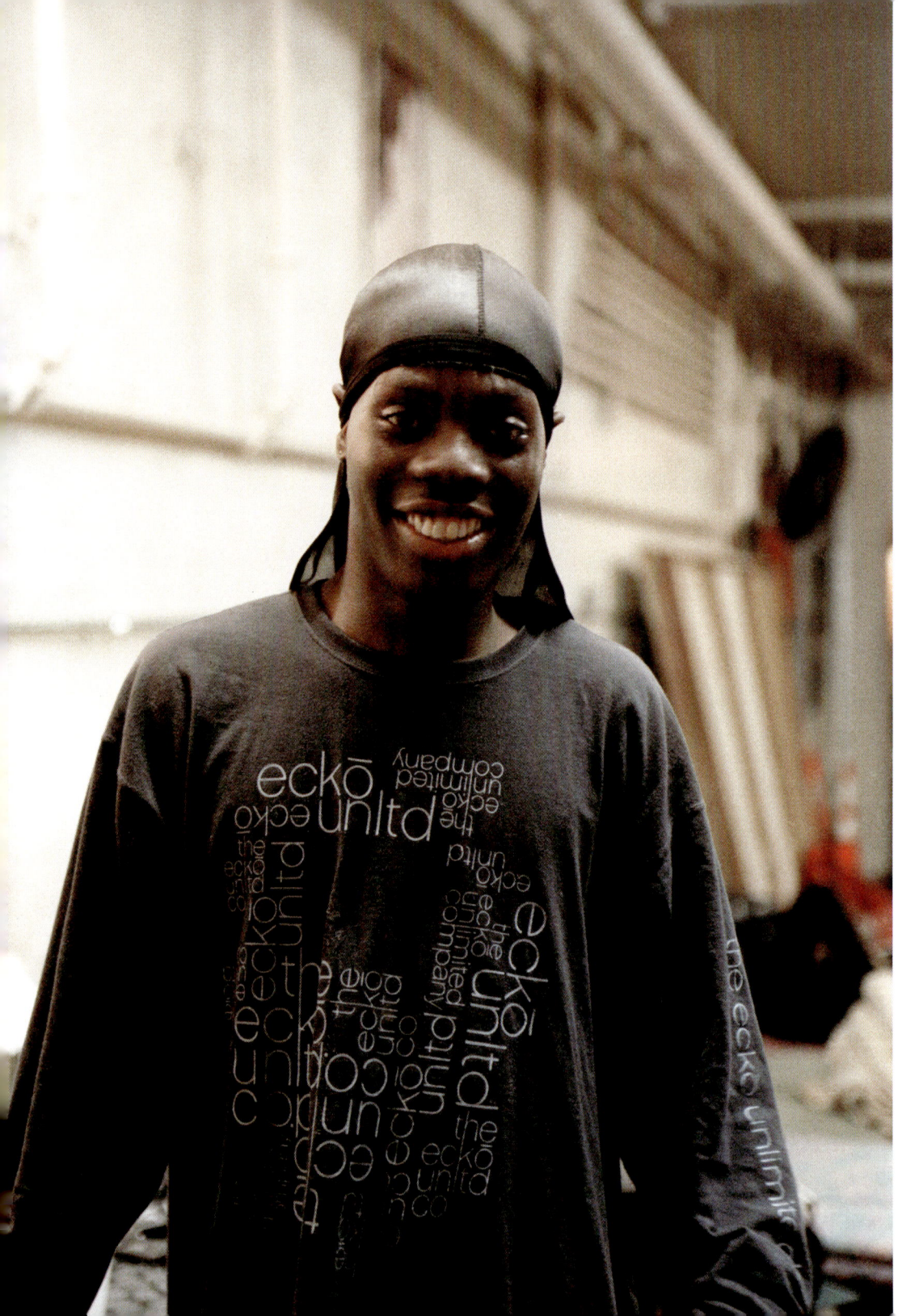

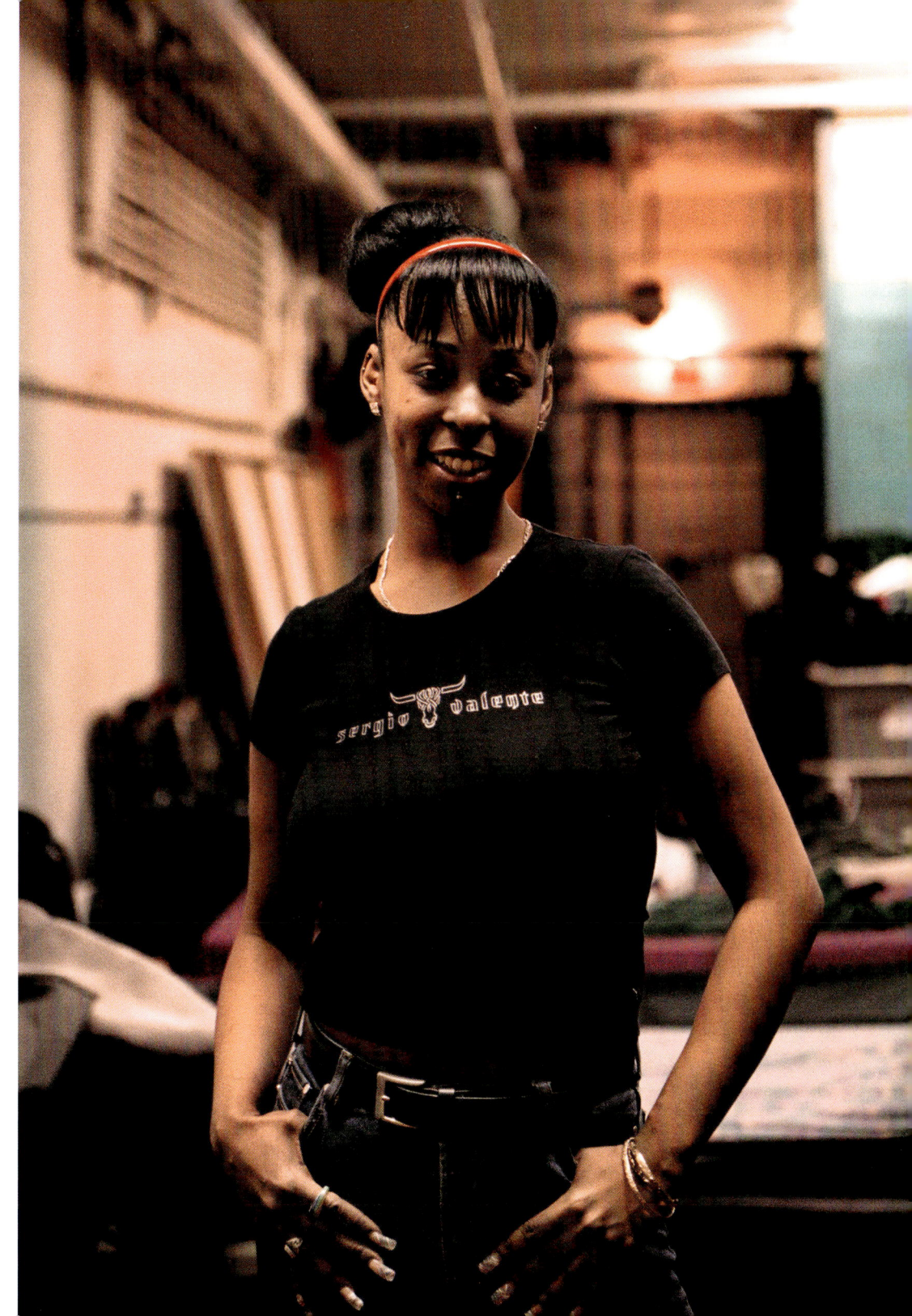

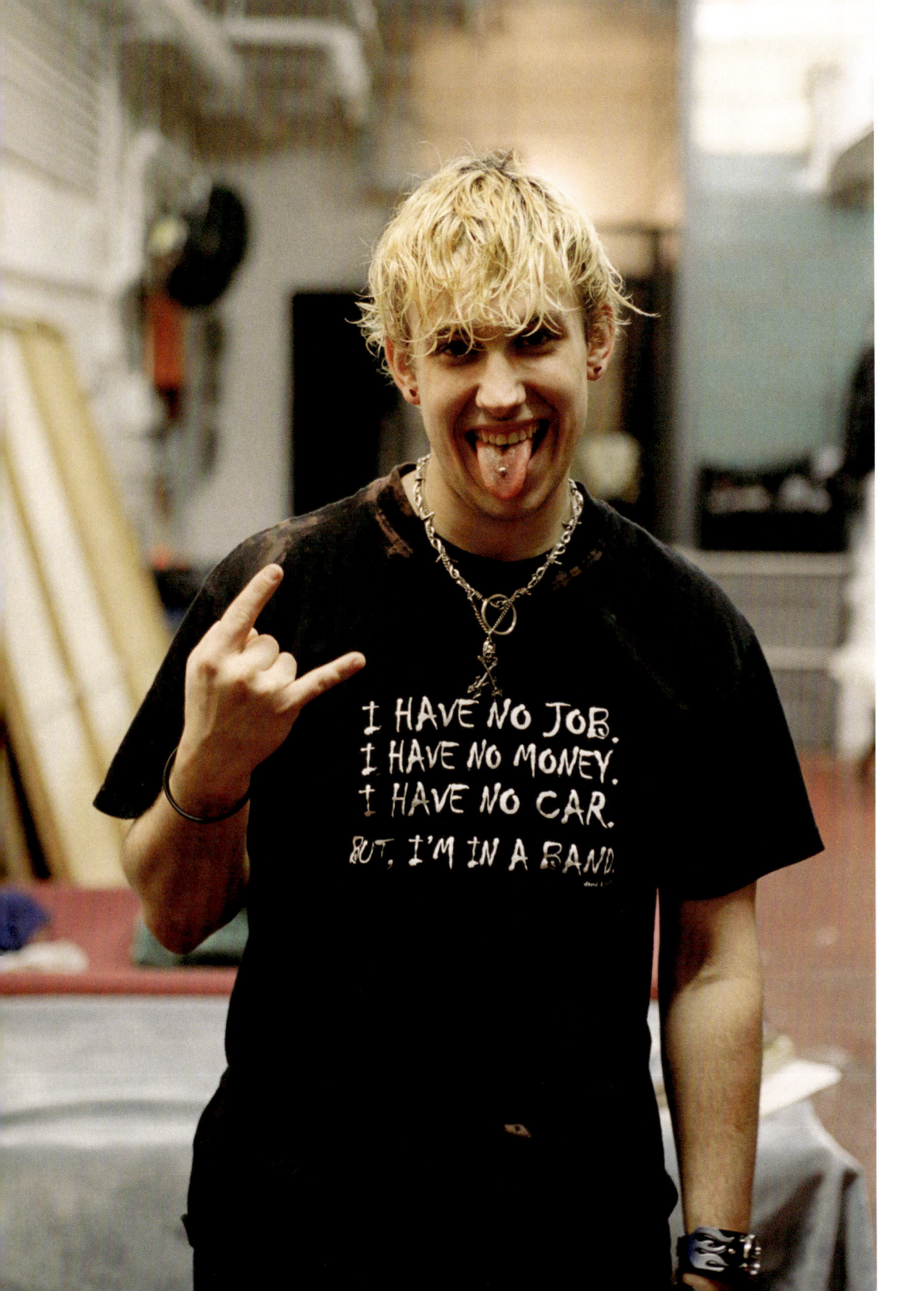

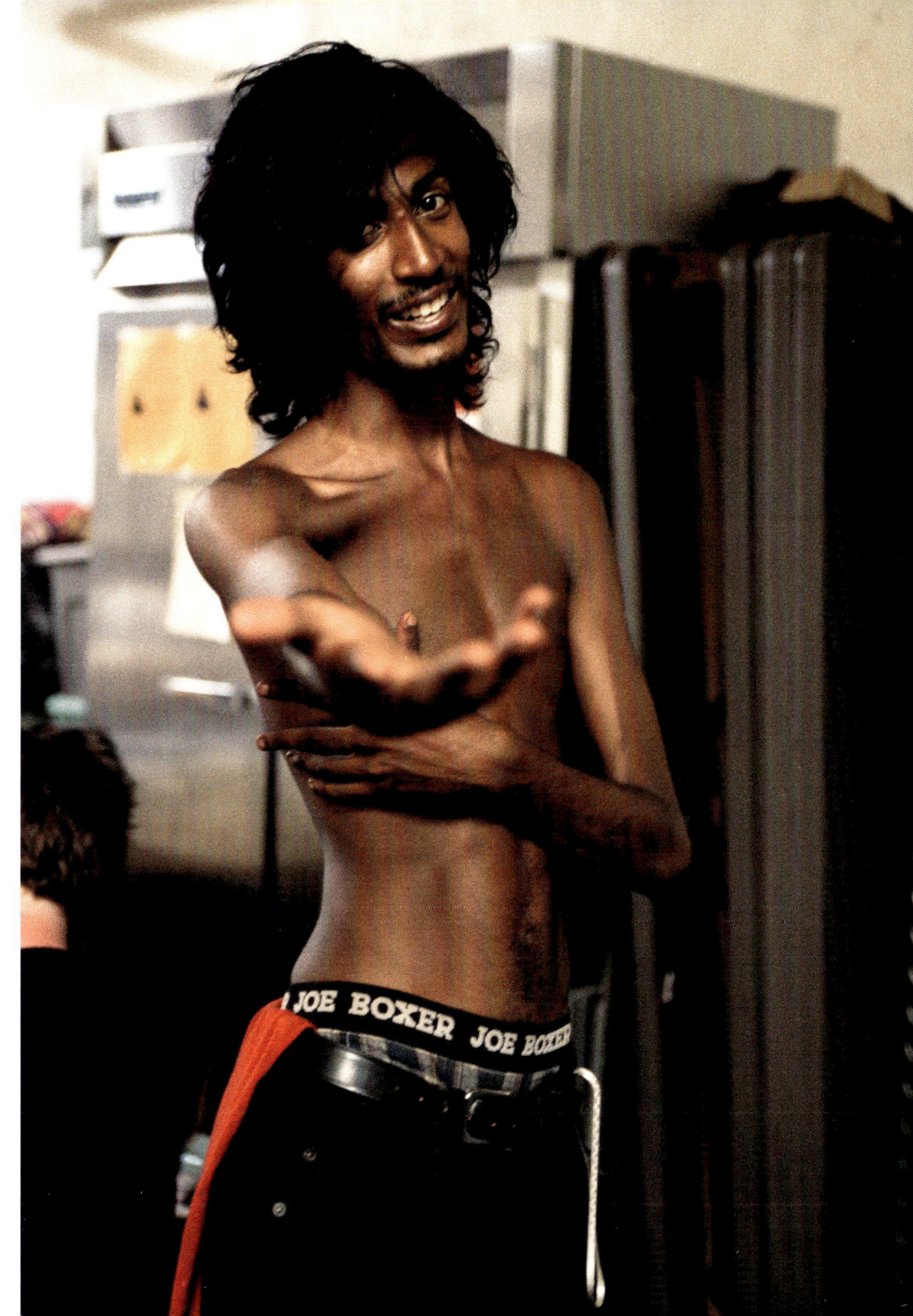

# Fact

As many as 35% of all homeless youth identify as lesbian, gay, bisexual or transgender.

March 31st 2003, Sylvia's Place opens its doors once again and becomes NYC's emergency shelter for homeless LGBTQ youth.

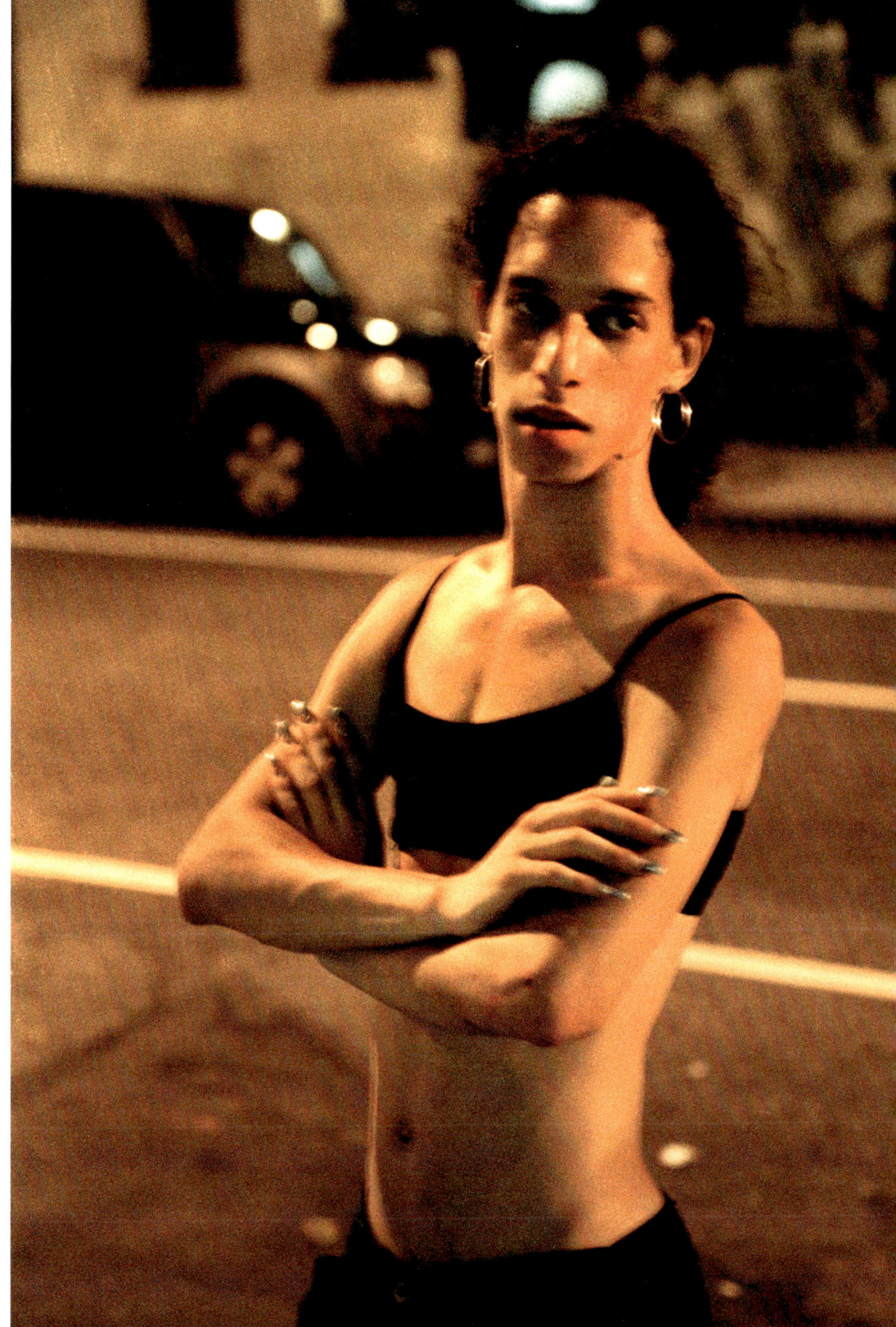

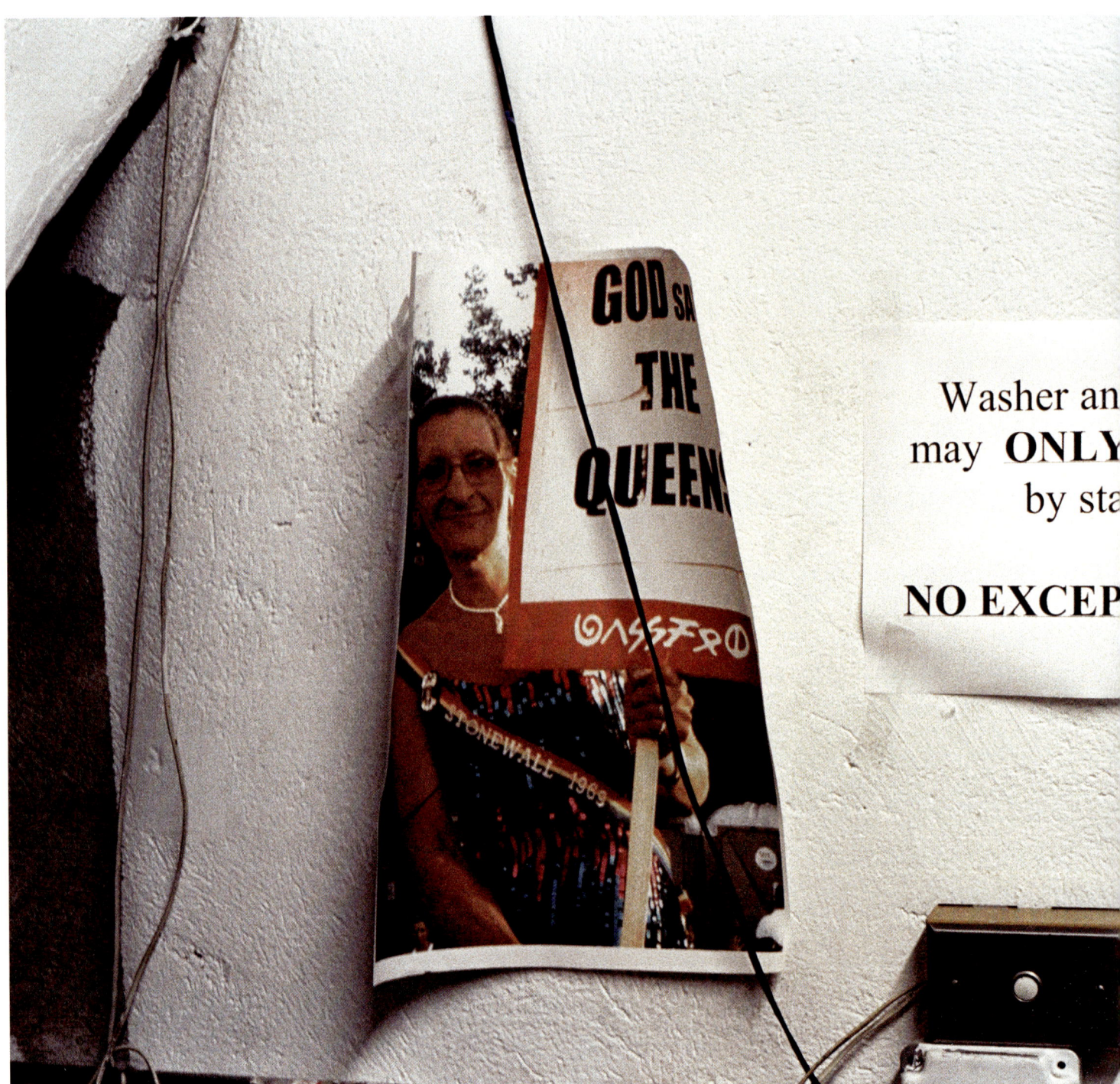

Dryer
be used
f.

TIONS!!

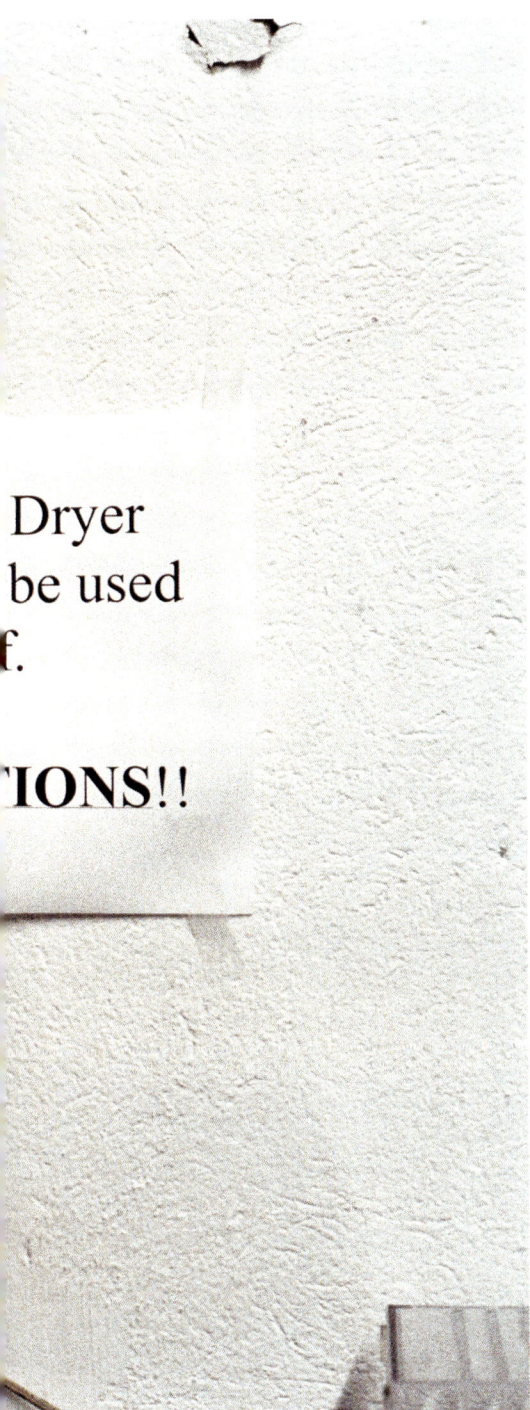

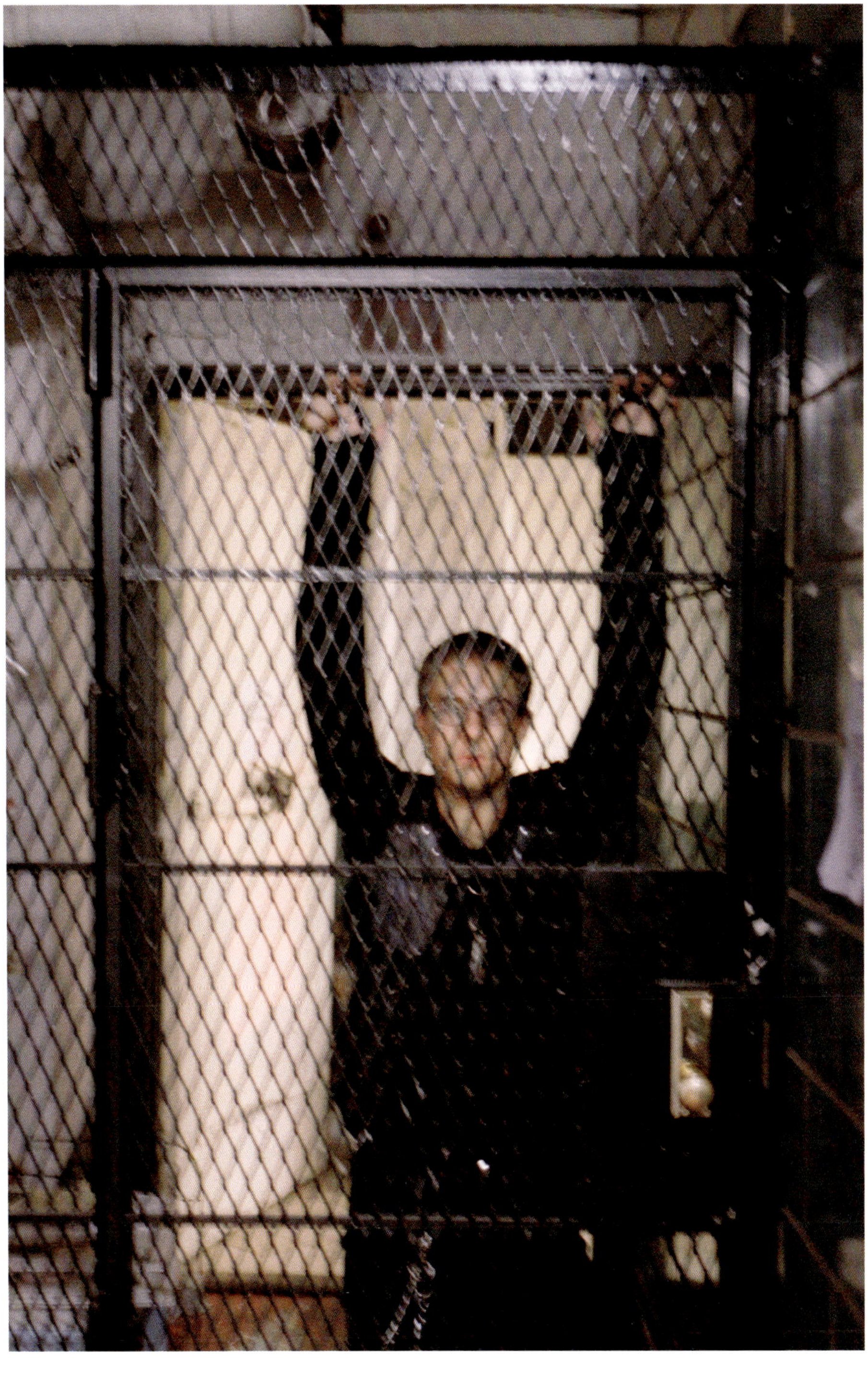

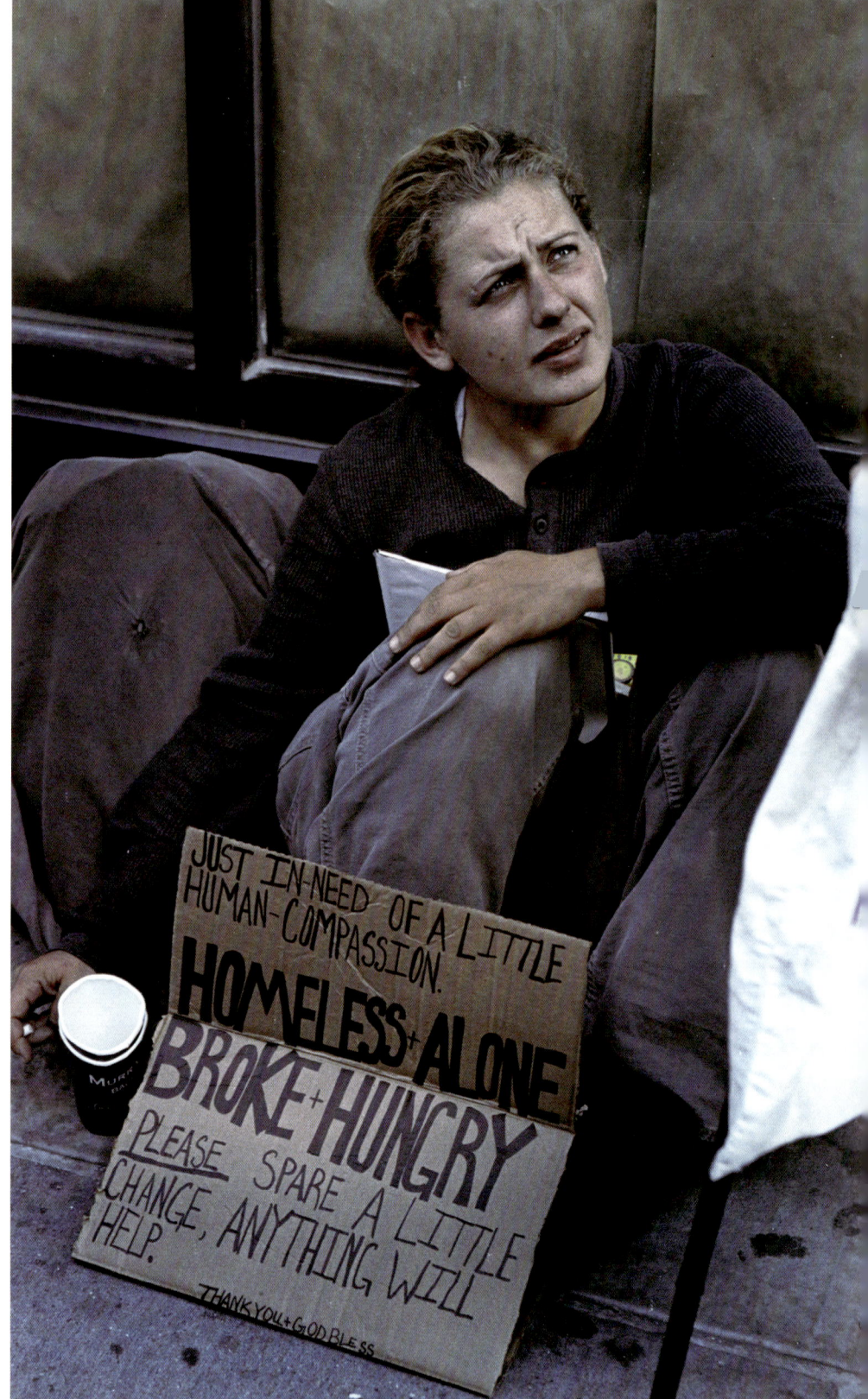

# Fact

In 2001, the National Runaway Switchboard estimated that 1.3 million youth live on the streets of America every day.

Within the 5 boroughs of NYC there are an estimated 30,000 homeless youth.

# Malice

He walked up to the black metal gate of the newly opened shelter, a humble space empty except for a counselor sitting at a table in the back of the room. He had been on the streets all day, hanging out with his crew at Astor Place in the East Village. In his hand, he held a crudely printed business card for Sylvia's Place and over his shoulder hung a backpack filled with everything he owned. He walked into the shelter and sat at a small round table across from a young counselor who had never done this before. The counselor asked if he goes by his real name, or if he had a street name that he likes better.

*Yeah. It's Malice. Malice of Hell. Wanna hear my slogan? Life's a bitch and then you die, so fuck that shit, lets all get high.*

Malice was happy to be off the streets that night. He had been at other shelters before, lived on the streets, slept in Central Park. As far as he was concerned, they had never been this bad. He had money once, and he would again.

*When Sylvia's first opened, this was better than having a house. I swear to God living in Sylvia's was better than having a house. Why? Because every single person that came near this spot was my best friend. As soon as Malice walked in, everybody would come running to me, hug me, kiss me, shake my hand, say hi and we'd start the night. The residents of Sylvia's*

*when this place first opened was amazing. I knew every single person that stayed here.*

His look defined him. He was proud of the pants he bought down on St. Mark's Place. They were black and baggy. They had chains and straps hanging from every loop. He was wearing his favorite vest, with thick plastic plates outlined by metal spikes. The marks of old piercings outlined his face. He stayed up most of the night, happy to be inside recounting a version of his life story. He had said he didn't need to stay at the shelter very long. Only until he got a job and saved up enough money for an apartment. He was planning to apply to work at the Intrepid Museum.

*I came here in April and didn't get my own house until around November or December. I had a job at the Intrepid Museum and I was making good money.*

The job didn't last and Malice couldn't pay his rent anymore, so he ended up back at the same black gate that he found the year before. Most of the faces changed, but not all of them. He felt comfortable at Sylvia's. It became his safe haven. The rules were hard for him to follow and he could have done without the chores, but at least he had a place to sleep and food to eat. And Malice loved the people here. He called them his family. More like a family than his real one. He didn't see his father very much at that

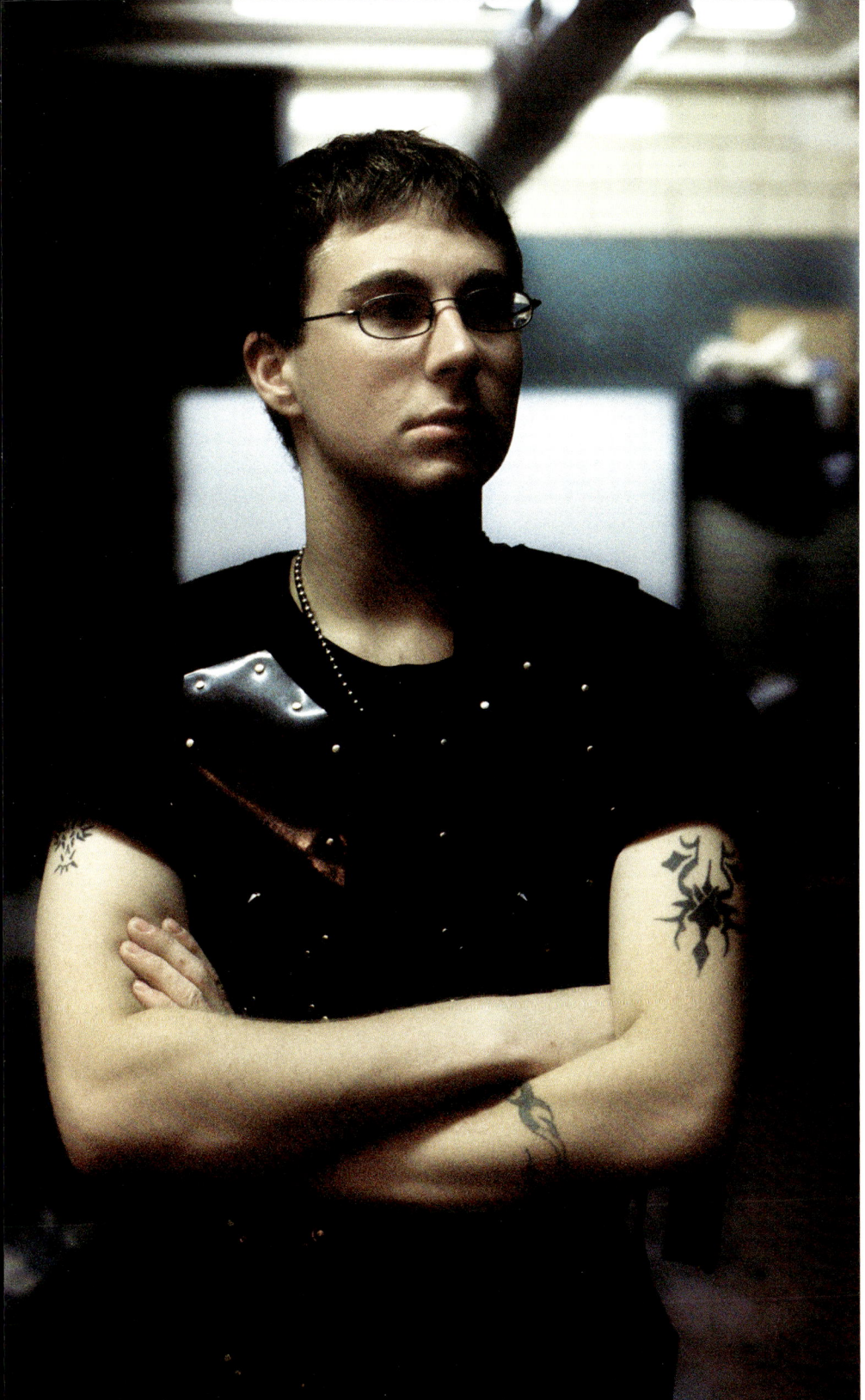

point in his life. Malice stole from him once and got thrown into juvy jail. They still talk sometimes and Malice goes to see him once in a while, but he doesn't trust him. They don't trust each other. His mother lives in Florida. But what really mattered to Malice was making the money to have his own place and do his own thing.

*I went from the Intrepid Museum to working at a Deli. It was a grocery store-type place. I was basically sweeping, mopping, stocking stuff up, taking cash. You know, I was a cashier every once in a while. I actually cooked food sometimes. And that was $11.75 an hour, so that was making me money, so I went and got another house. And I lost my job and I lost my house. After I lost that job at the Deli, I started selling drugs, because I had the money saved and everything and I figured, you know what? I don't have a job, I have no way to get money, I need money, so I'm gonna do this. And I started selling drugs and I started making mad money. I stayed at Sylvia's while I was dealing, because I wanted to save my money. I wanted my money to build up. I wanted to get more money in my pocket.*

When Malice moved out of Sylvia's for the second time, he had his own place. Actually, he says he had three places. He was selling drugs and making a lot of money. He could afford whatever he wanted. But what he really wanted was to turn his life around. He wanted to quit selling and go legit. Malice was almost ready to do it. It was all going to be different from here on out. He was finally going to leave his old life behind.

Sylvia's Place would see him again. Malice's life would take him in directions he never expected and the shelter would become a bigger part of his life than he could have ever known.

The residents of Sylvia's when this place first opened were amazing. I knew every single person that stayed here. They were not assholes, they were not dickheads, they weren't people that would talk shit to you and be fucking assholes to you. Malice

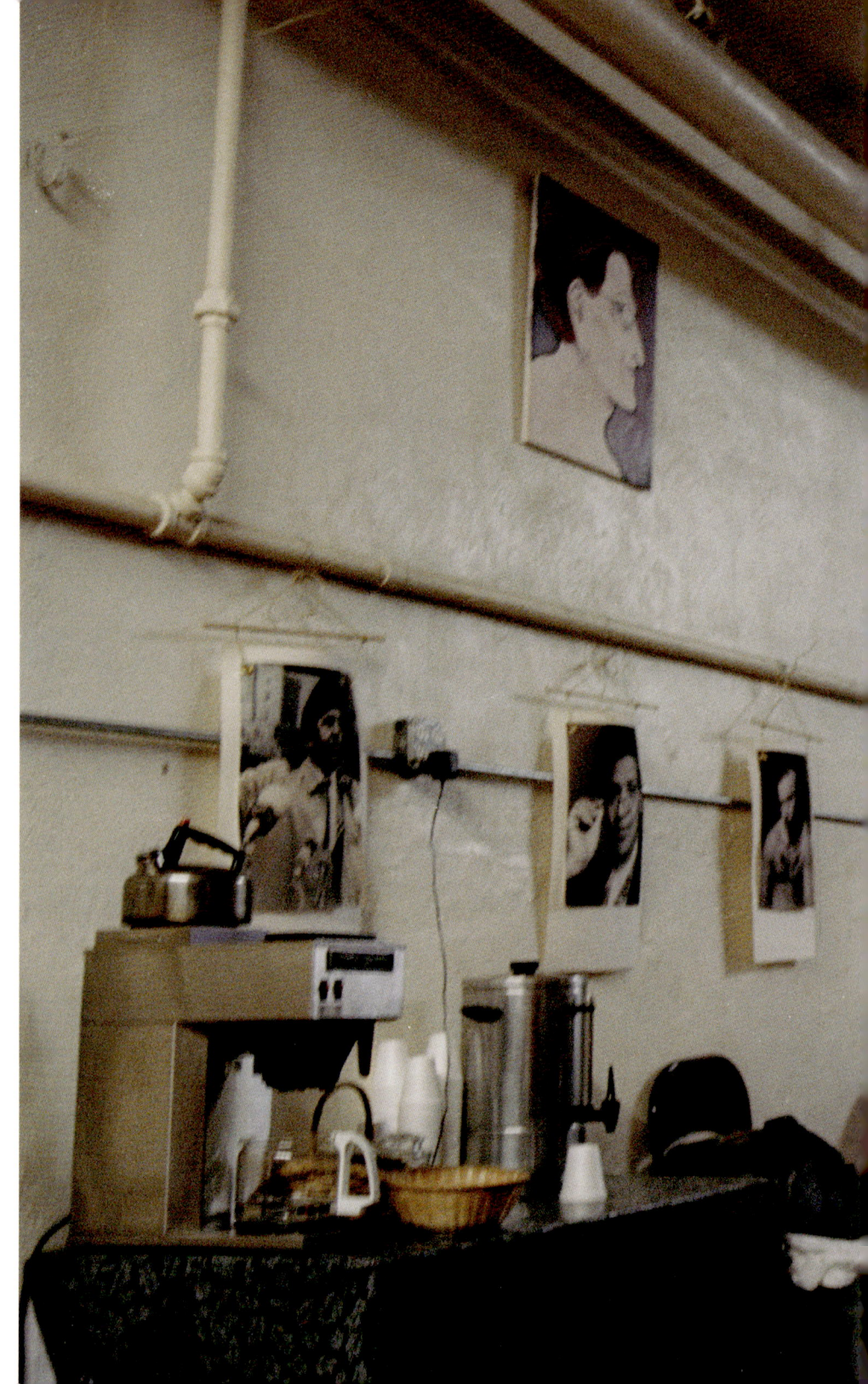

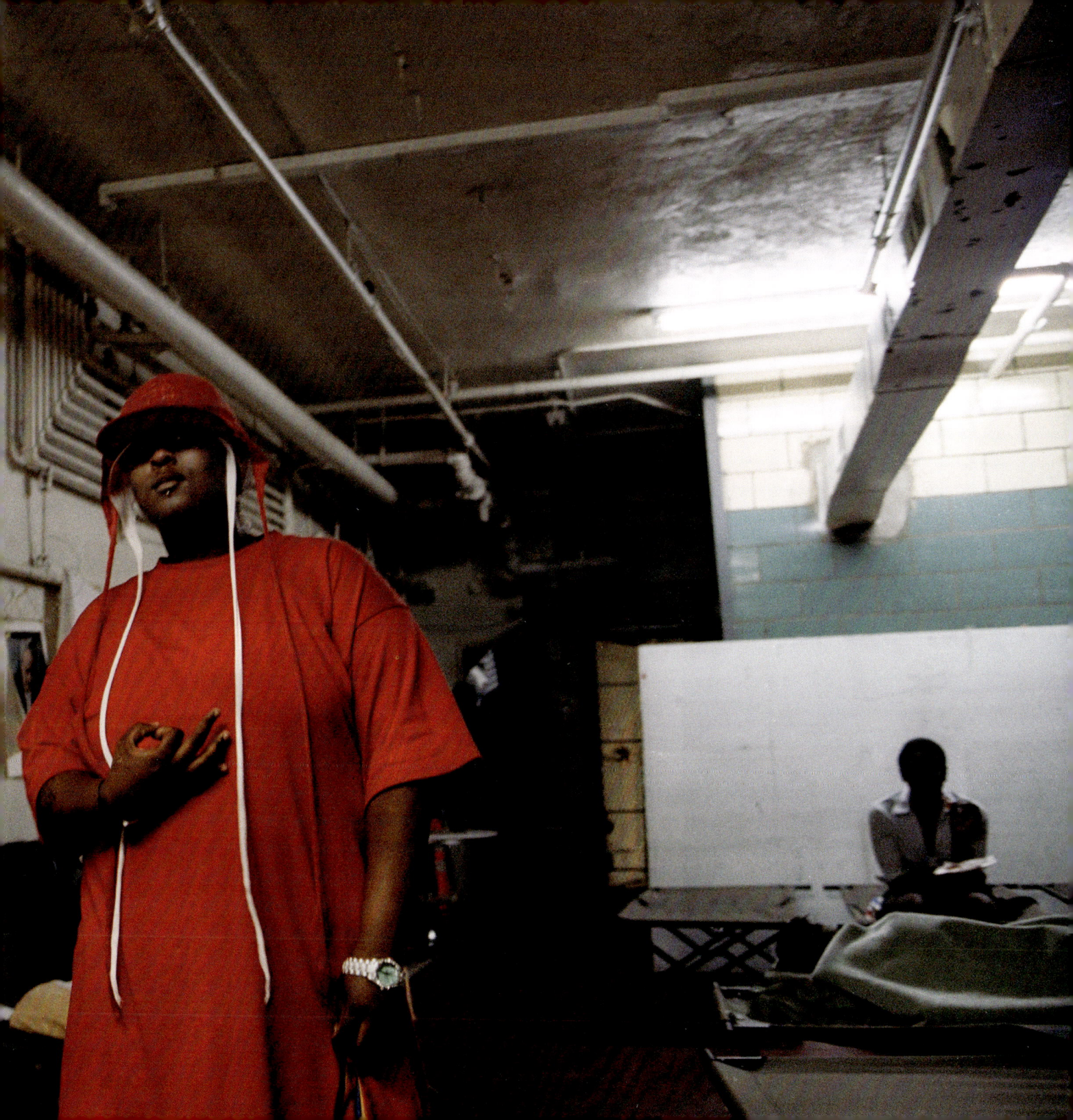

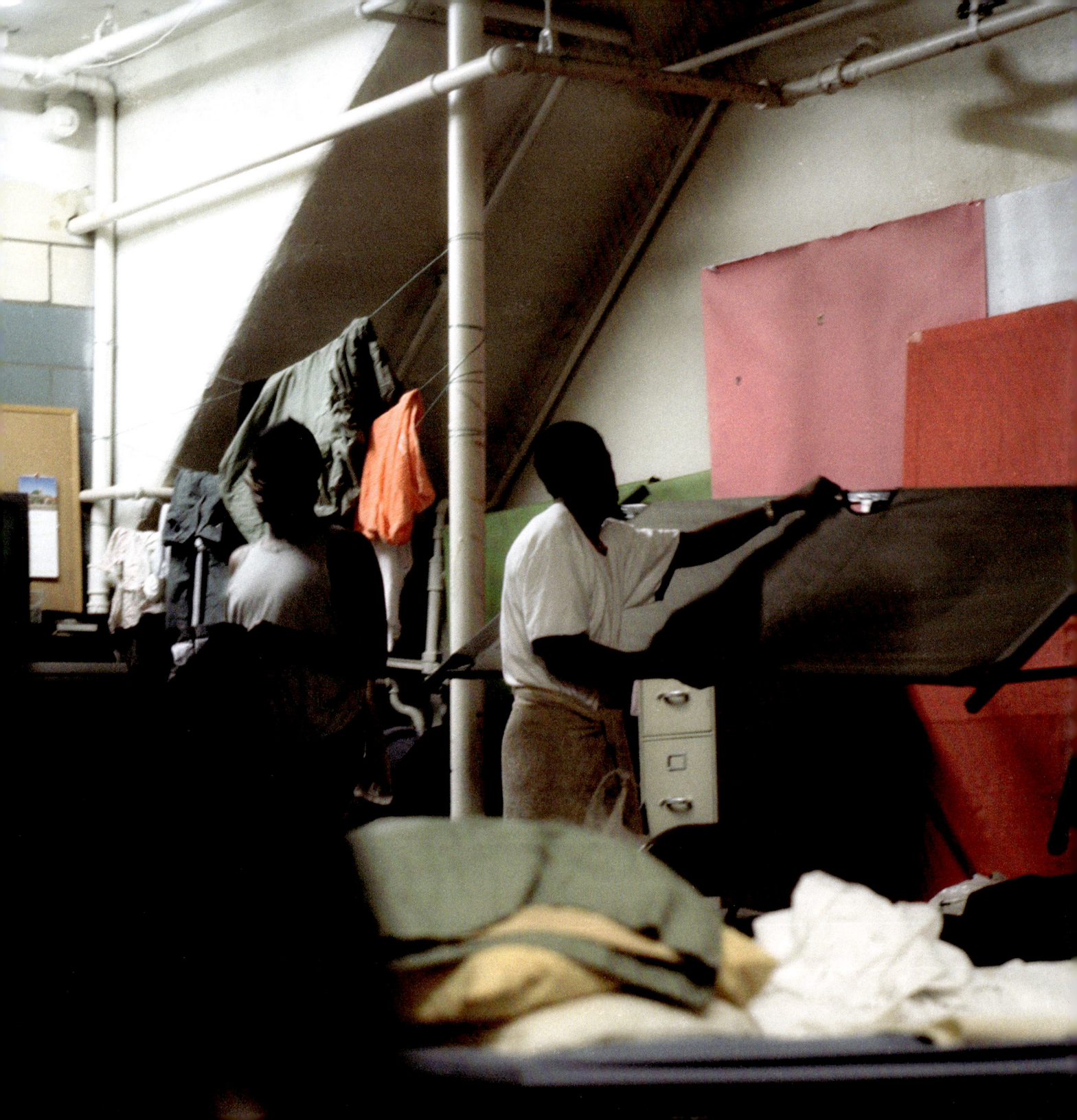

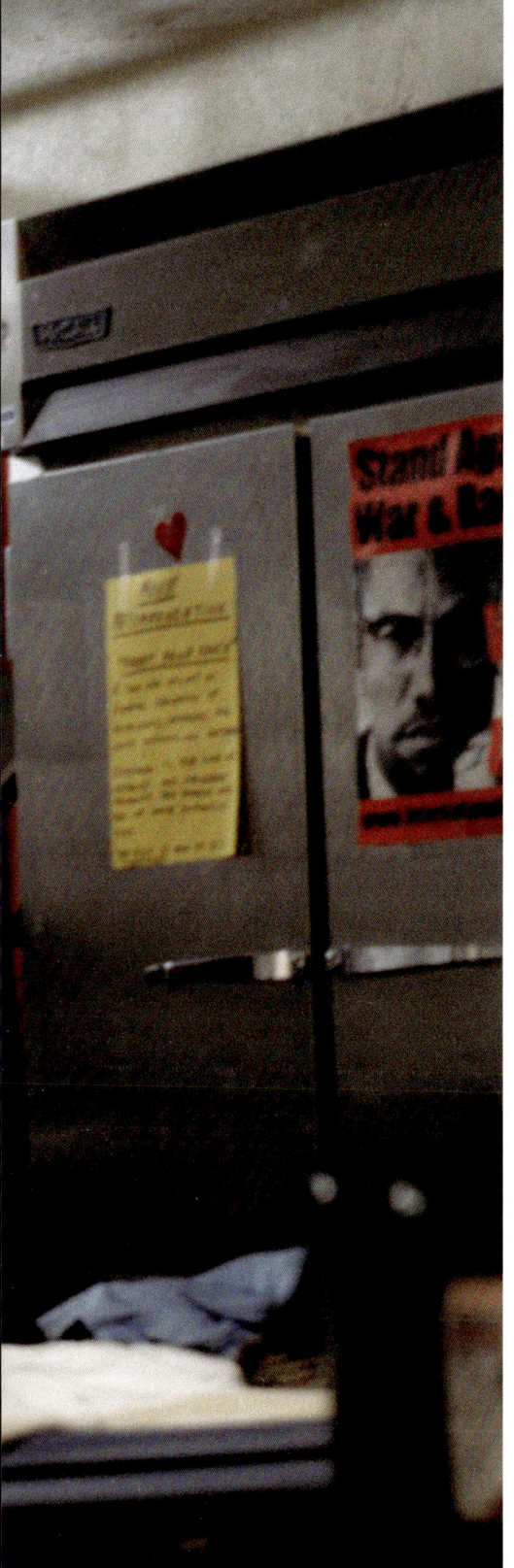

The first day was good, 'cause I got to meet some of my cool people, like Eternity. I love Eternity. She was very welcoming, so after I met her, we became friends. We just clicked. Charlene

# Fact

Homeless LGBTQ youth suffer from higher levels of violence, trauma, HIV infection, substance abuse problems, and have more mental health issues than their straight counterparts.

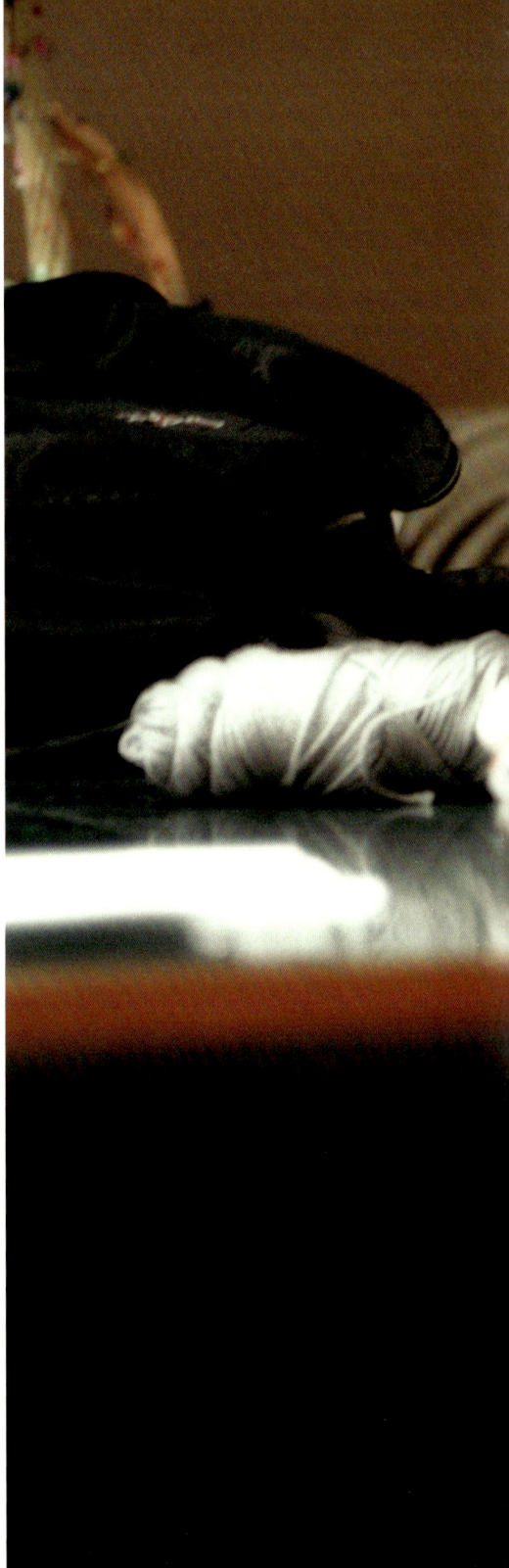

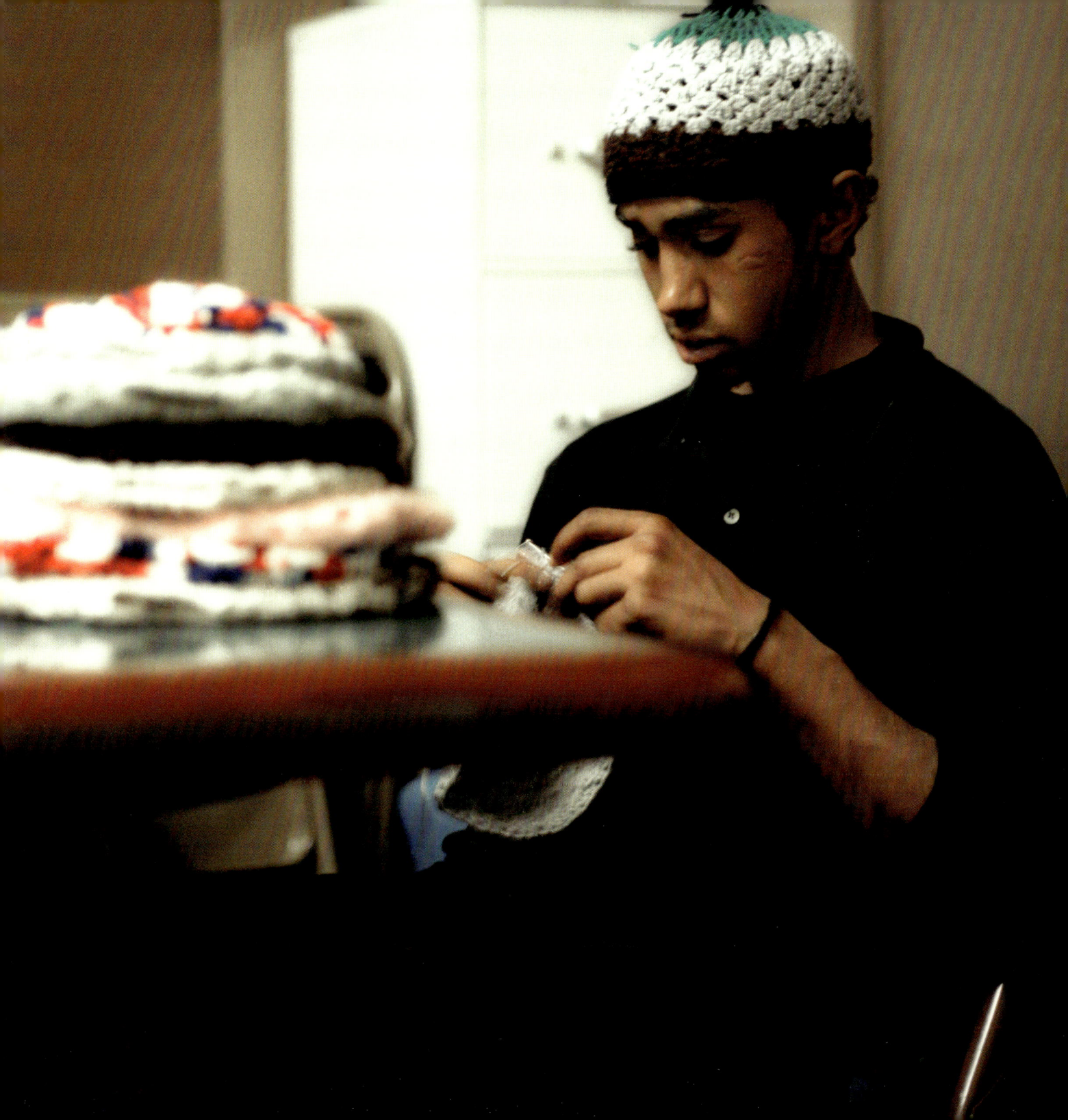

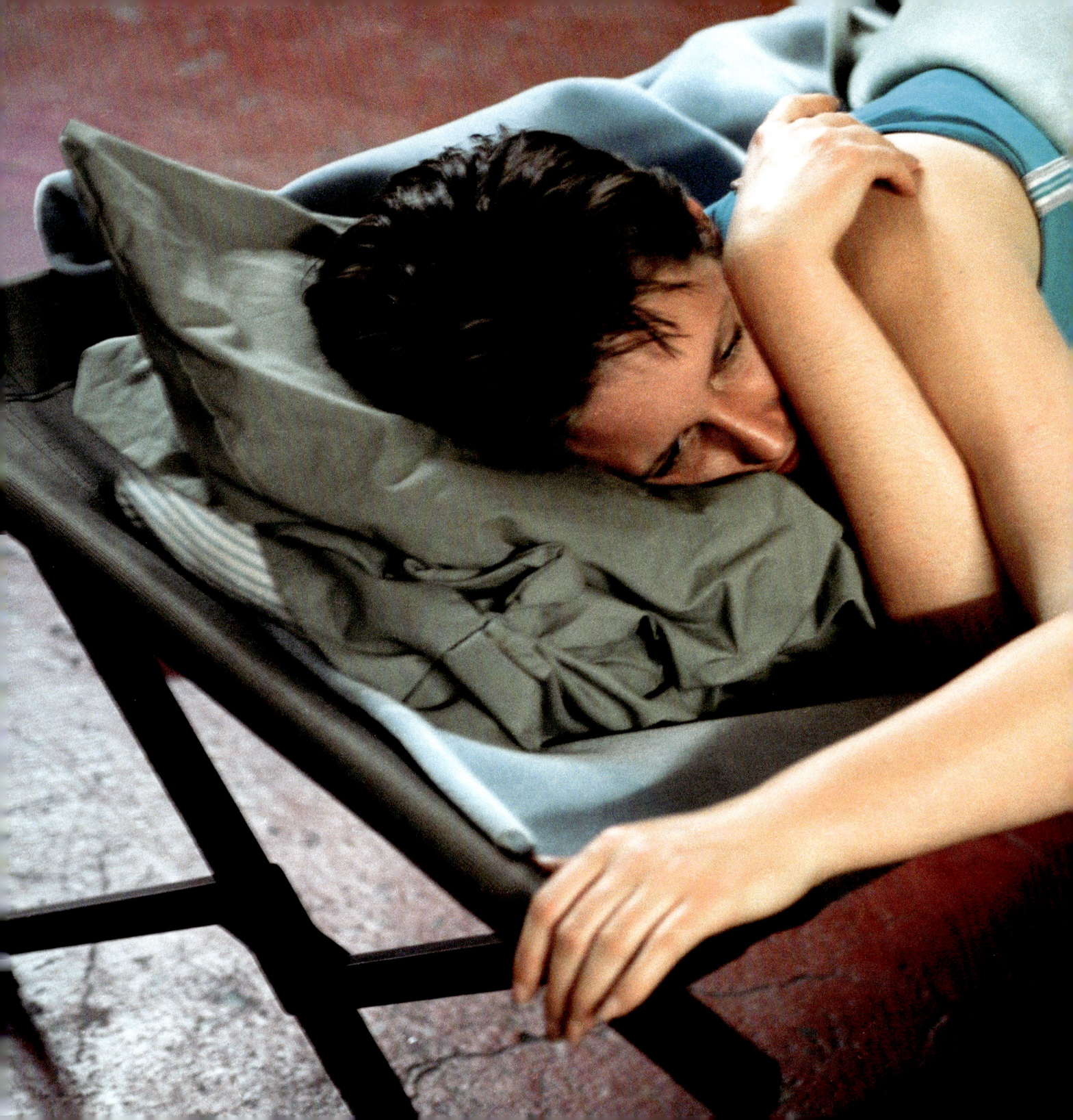

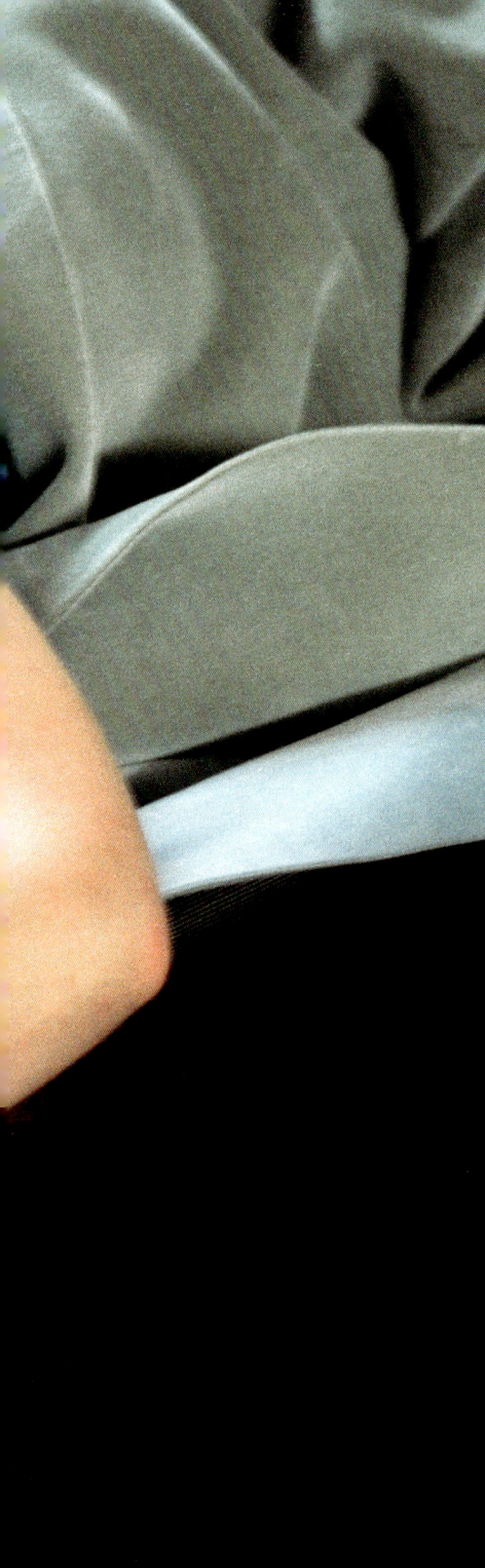

Just two months after Sylvia's opens its doors, one young woman had a psychological breakdown at the shelter. A recent addition to the shelter family, she had a tragic history of sexual assault, serious physical abuse, and teen pregnancy. Her presence at the shelter was one of pronounced solitude; distancing herself from other clients and confiding, only occasionally, in one of the counselors.

On this particular night, she quietly set up her cot in the front of room and laid down absently staring at the wall, perhaps recalling one of uncountable troubled memories. Without warning, she got up from her cot and adopted an alternate personality, passionately yelling and preaching to the other residents. Her eyes glossed over as she began denouncing the sins of everyone in the room. Curses and biblical threats were hurled at both the clients and the counselor, stunning residents and staff alike. Hidden in her tirade were years of repressed memories of a past filled with tragic abuse. The residents begin to fear her next moves as she called the police. When the police decided that they could not offer any assistance, she was discharged for the evening in an effort to protect the other clients. She returned the next day with no recollection or explanation of the previous night's events. She collected her belongings and left on a bus out of New York City. Sylvia's Place has never heard from her again.

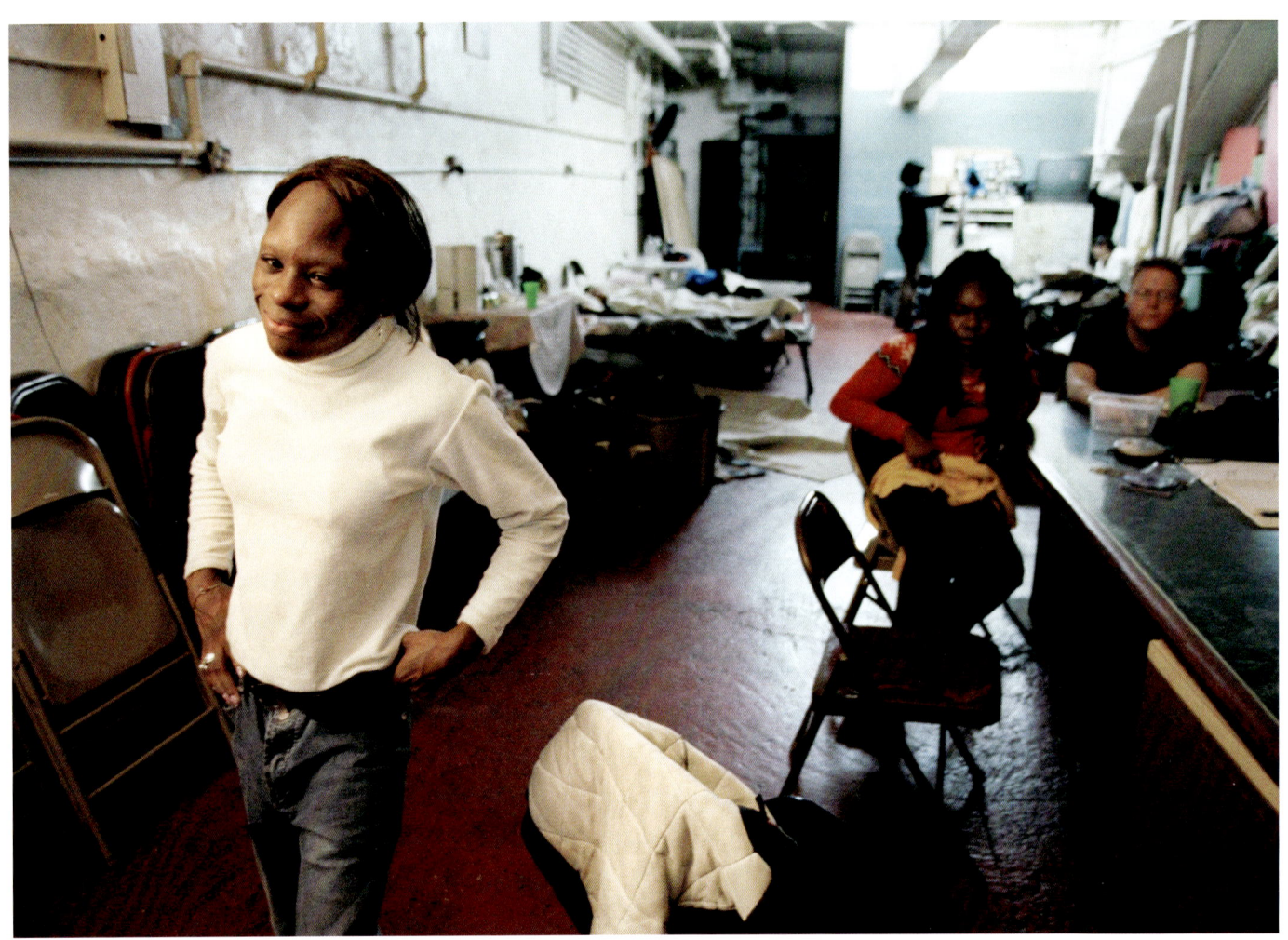

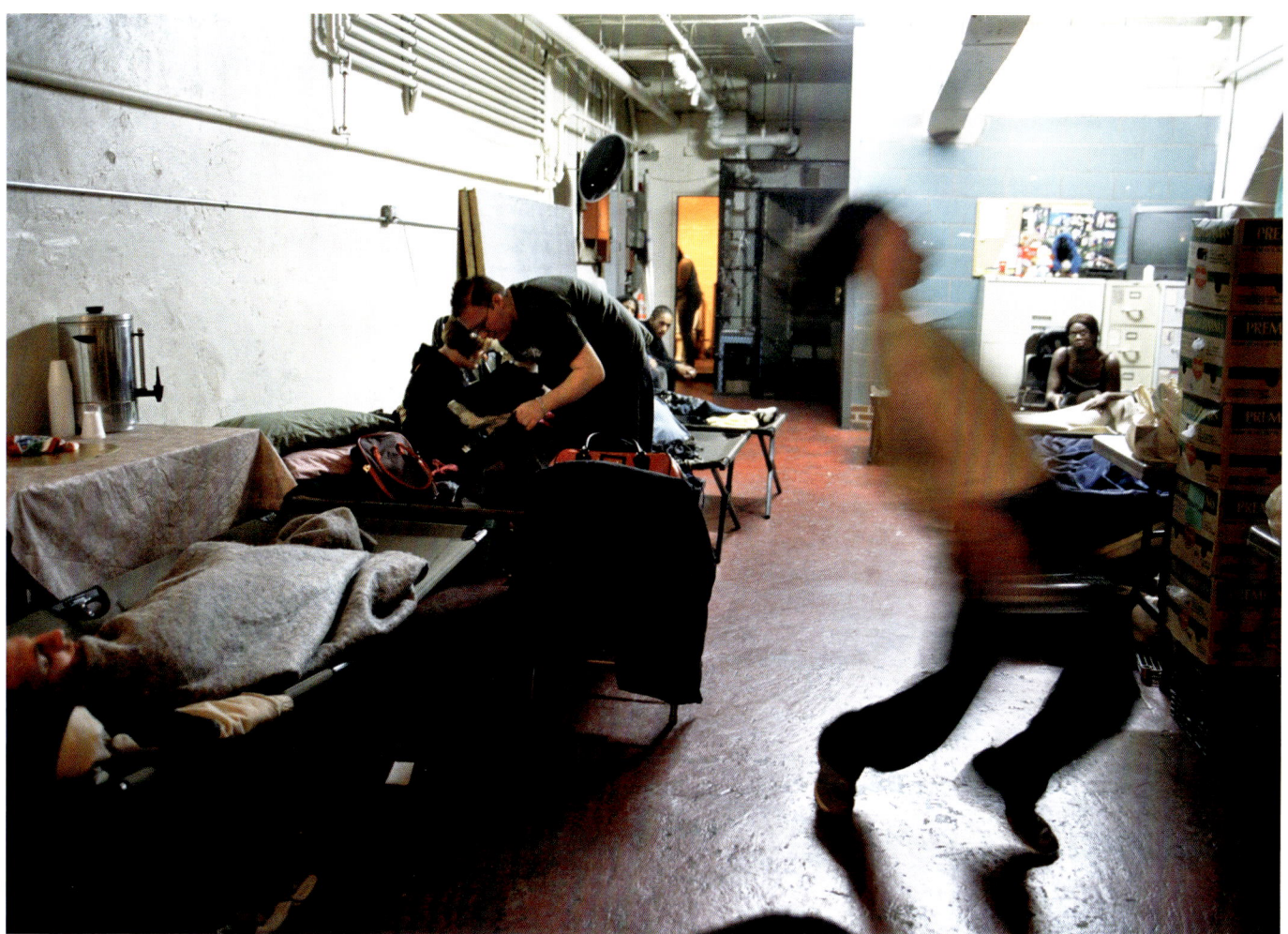

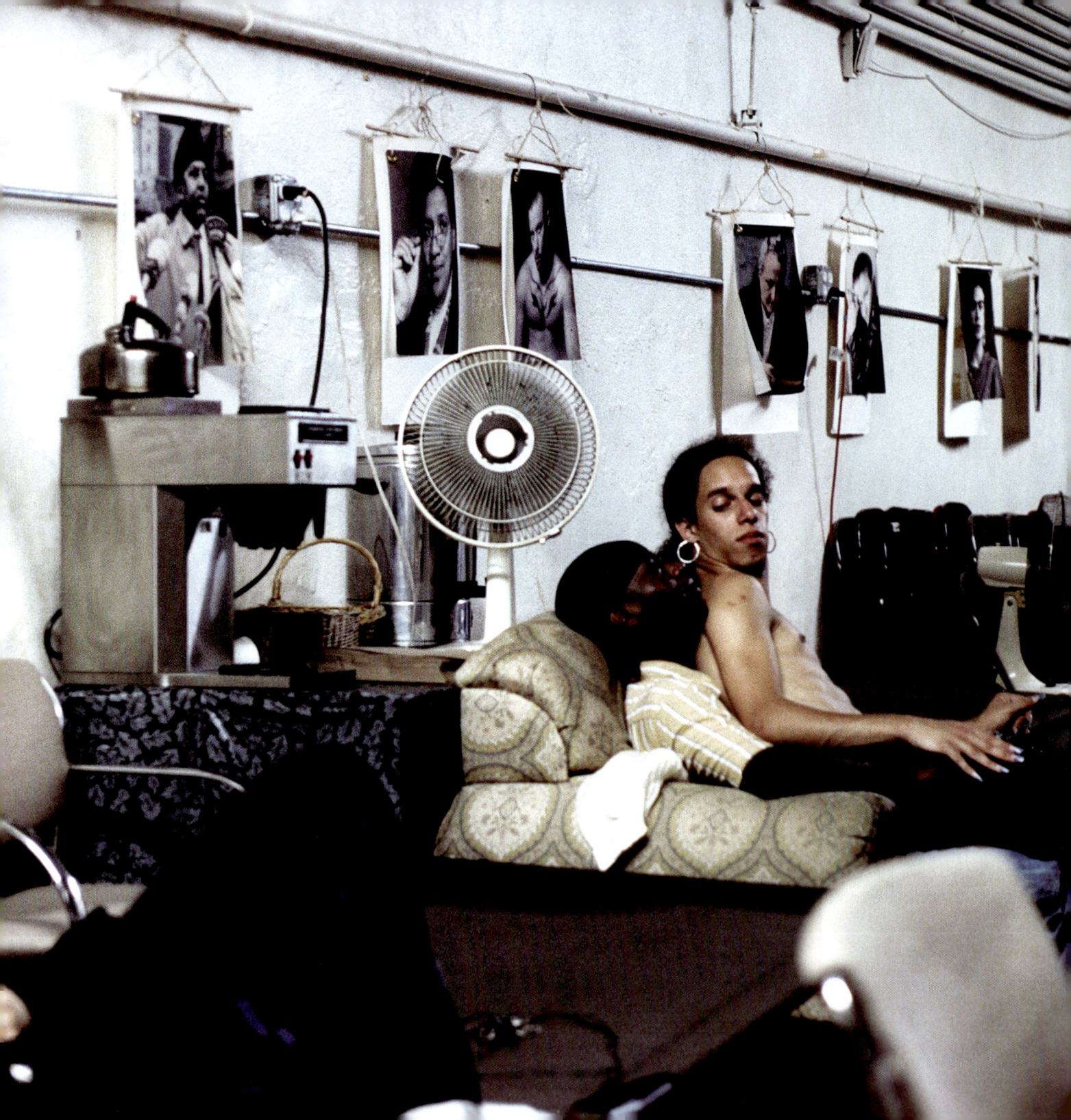

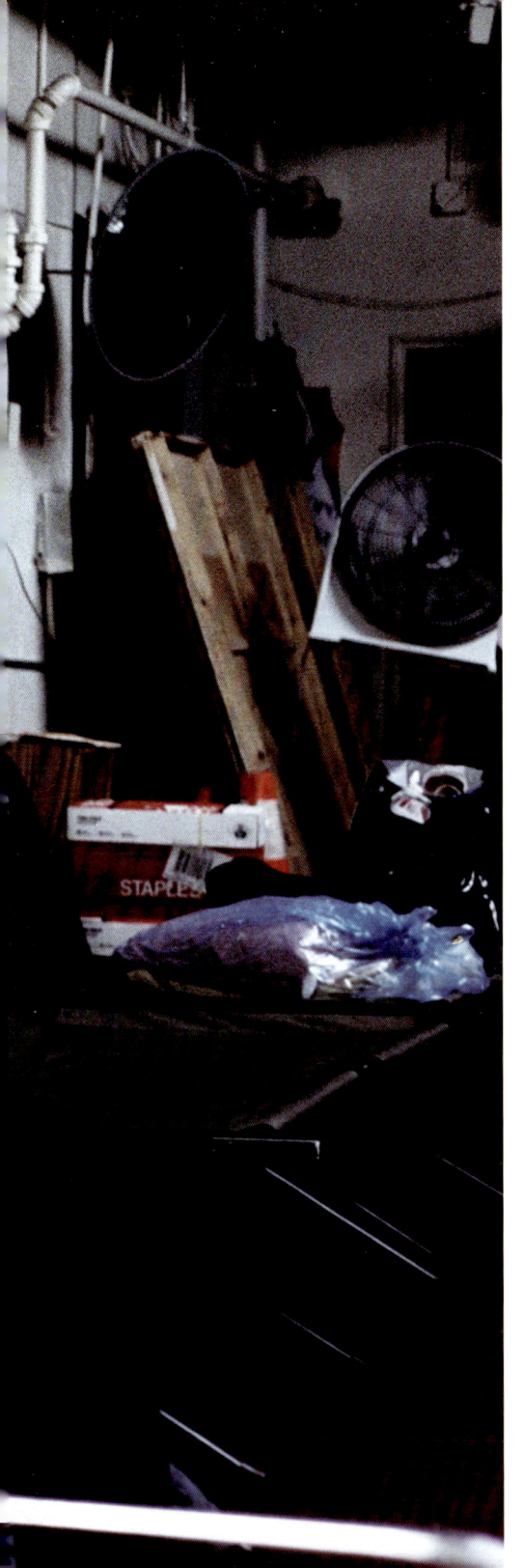

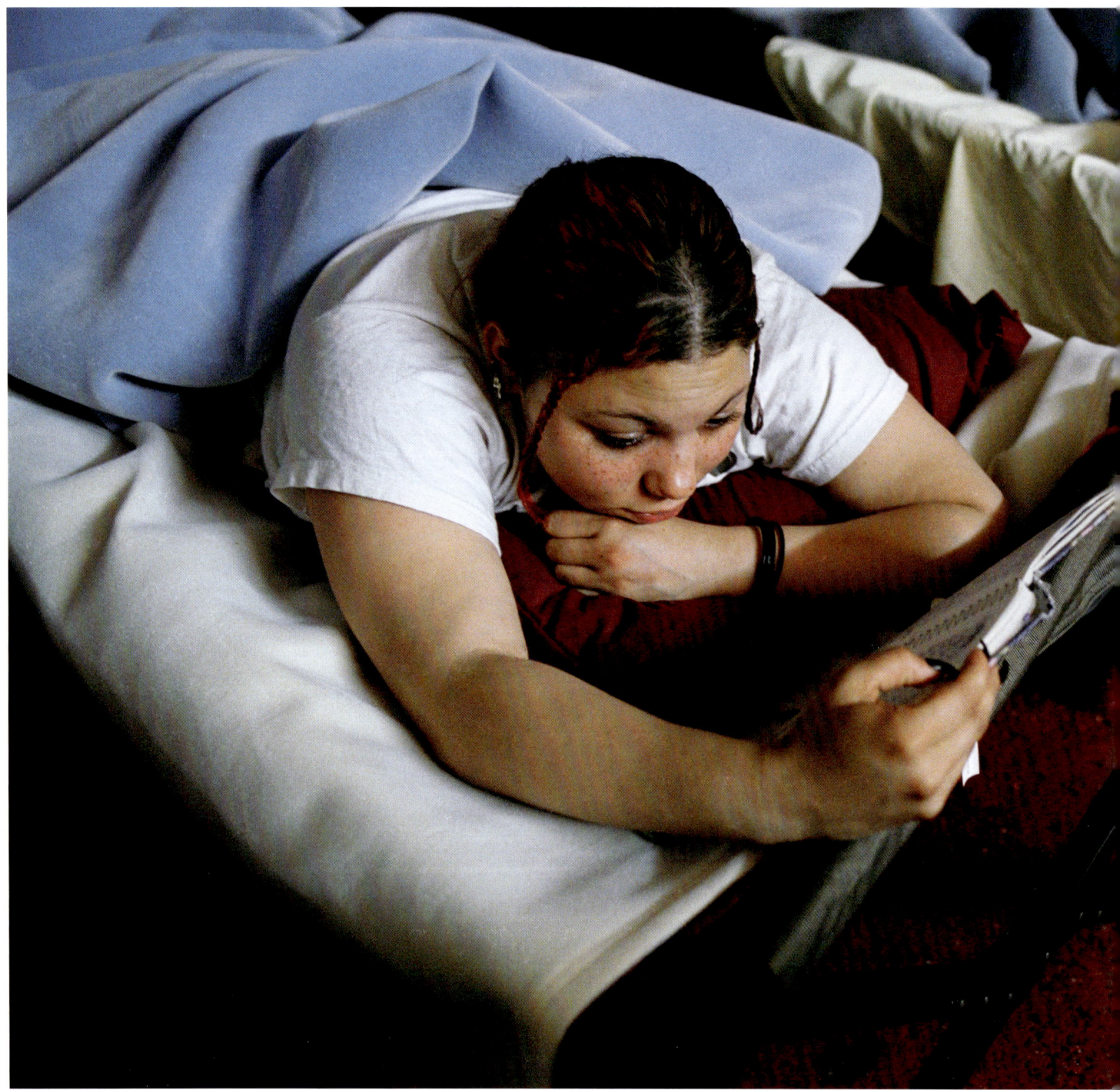

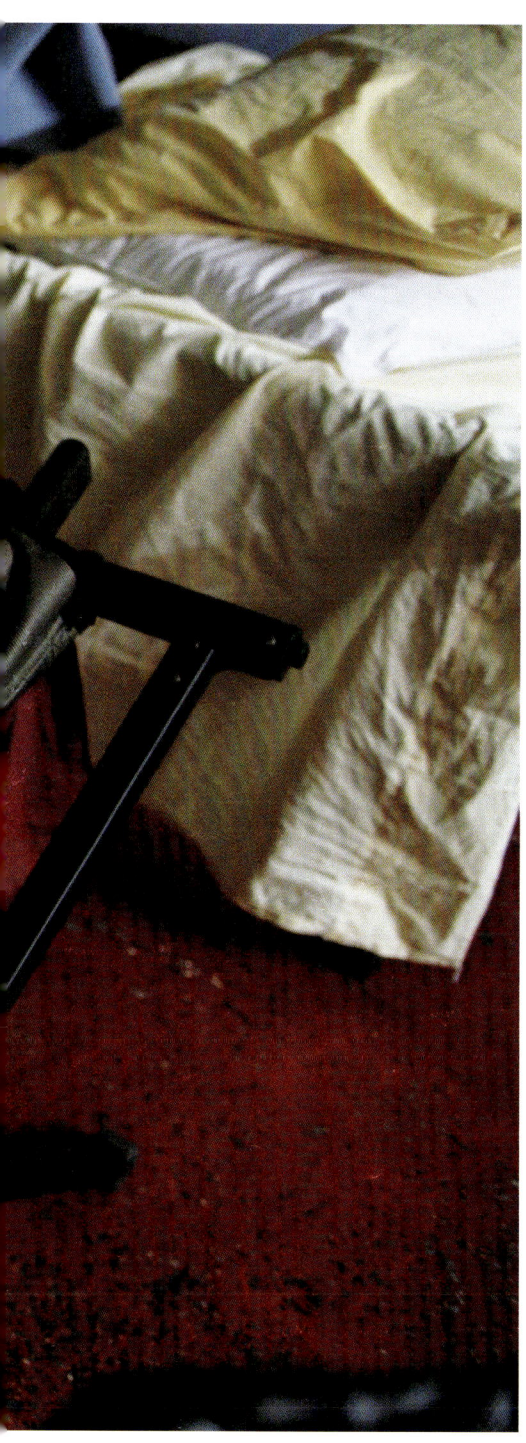

I also had a habit of not wanting to talk to my mom. Yeah, I think I have a problem with not wanting to talk period. I don't know, I guess I feel sometimes that when I do have something to say, no one wants to listen. So, why should I even bother telling you anything. That's my whole thing. That's why I like to write, 'cause you have no choice but to read it, 'cause it's in your face.

My writing is more about my tragedy. I don't consider what I've been through experience. I refuse to believe that. I refuse for anyone to call it that. Or for anyone's life for whatever they've been through. Don't call the tragedy that you've been through an experience. An experience is something you enjoy or something that you wanted to go through. I'm pretty sure that whatever bullshit that other people went through or what I went through... I know for a fact I didn't want that. I know for a fact that I didn't enjoy any of it. So, when I write, I basically just write about my tragedy. Eternity

# Eternity

When Eternity came through the gate at Sylvia's Place, she carried with her a tortured history and a shelled emotional exterior. She has a thing for wearing lots of chains, spiked bracelets and black lipstick.

*I like to dress weird on purpose... well, not weird, 'cause I don't think I'm weird. I think I'm strange. I like to wear things that would scare people away, so they don't talk to me. I'm not a real people person. So, I figure, if I wear all this stuff that looks scary, maybe they won't want to talk to me. But, it's not working, because people still want to talk to me.*

She's not in the habit of letting people get too close. But, despite Eternity's attempt to scare people away, she found a family at Sylvia's Place unlike any she had experienced before. Her mark on the shelter's history is profound and her unique story echoes in the lives of so many of the residents who have come since.

*That's like the only place I ever called home. 'Cause living with my mom way back then, and living with my sister, and bumping around from friend to friend, that didn't really feel like home. It didn't feel like a place of solace. It was more of a relief, knowing I could lay down, not really go to sleep, but just close my eyes and think that I'm not going to get hurt. No one was going to want to hurt me.*

By the time Eternity showed up at Sylvia's door, she had learned how not to sleep. Since she was a child, there were always monsters in her life making sure that she never felt safe with her eyes closed.

*I was six years old. And there was this guy and I was really scared of him. The guy with the nails and the brown hat that I won't name, that's Monster #1. I was scared of him already. That year for Halloween, I didn't see Charlie Brown. Instead I was tied down to a chair in front of that movie, and my mother's loving son decided to hold my eyelids open. So, I was basically stuck there for I don't even know how many hours watching that guy kill people in their sleep. After that, I basically grew to fear him. That's the only thing I fear, because he gets you when you're sleeping. Which is probably why I don't like sleeping.*

Freddy wouldn't be the only monster in Eternity's life, and unfortunately the others weren't bound inside a television set. When Eternity was 11 years old, her mother's son raped her. At that moment he became Monster #2.

*I didn't know any better. I didn't know that brothers weren't supposed to do that. And when I realized that they're not supposed to, I stopped talking for two years. He only did it once. My mom took me to a bunch of psychiatrists and stuff. And I wouldn't say anything. They didn't get it. They just said that something apparently traumatic must have happened to me to make me stop talking. They didn't get it. So all the diplomas that they had were for nothing. If they couldn't get that, they were for nothing.*

By the time Eternity had reached her teenage years, she was desperately searching for something to help take the pain away.

*When I was 13, that was the first time a knife had cut me, 'cause I had picked up a knife, I was doing dishes, and a knife slipped out of my hand and it cut me, and I didn't feel anything. I didn't feel no pain and I wasn't upset anymore about anything. After that is when I found out that cutting made me feel better. So I got into cutting, but it wasn't until I was 15 that I started cutting heavily.*

*I started cutting my wrists. From there I went on to my legs. You know, places that most people wouldn't really look at, especially since I'm always wearing bracelets. I never cut and then put my bracelets on because I was ashamed of what I was doing, I was never ashamed of my cutting. It was just, more or less, that I didn't want to hear what other people had to say, 'cause I couldn't care less.*

While she had lived far more trauma than any girl should, Eternity's hell was only just beginning. Monster #3 entered into her life in the summer of her 16th year when she went to stay with her sister and her husband.

*That was when everything went to hell and I couldn't do anything about it. It was when I was 16, and it was during the summer, when Monster #3... that's my sister's husband, had asked me, "Why is it that monster #2 is a monster?" And I told him. I trusted him. He used to call me his little sister. A week or two later he started touching me while I slept. I would wake up and have weird dreams and I would tell him about it and he wouldn't say anything about it. I just thought they were weird dreams, until I woke up one day really, really soaked down there and he said, "I have a secret to tell you."*

But her sister became pregnant and had a little boy. Eternity's nephew became her everything. It was the first person she felt genuine love for and she cherished him. But, spending time with her nephew came at a horrible price.

*I didn't want to leave my nephew. So, I sacrificed myself some more and more and more. I just loved being around my nephew, playing with my nephew. Because I loved my nephew so much, I figured all of this was worth it. Little by little, I learned how to basically not feel it when it was happening. I learned how not to sleep. Seeing as how Monster #1 could get me in my dreams or I could just be sleeping and not dreaming and Monster #3 could still get me.*

The cutting got worse.

*I would go into my sister's bathroom and actually lock the door and break one of her razor blades, and I would just use those... until I started carrying around my own razor blade in my mouth. Then I found out about other ways of hurting myself without it showing, So, I started banging my head against the wall whenever I was really, really upset or really, really sad, whichever one, I would bang my head against a wall until I passed out. And then I would throw myself down a flight of stairs. I was trying to find out different ways that I could hurt myself without it being on my wrists.*

*And it's not like I never tried to tell my sister anything. I told her what he was doing to me while she was sleeping... you know, she would kind of brush it off, brush it off like she didn't care. I learned how to just shut up, unless my nephew was around. Living with her, I felt like a ghost most of the time. That didn't work out. That really didn't work out at all.*

Tired of bouncing around the couches of different friends, Eternity found the directions for Sylvia's Place on the back of a condom that was handed to her on the streets. After doing her intake, she tentatively put her cot together and let her shelter journey begin.

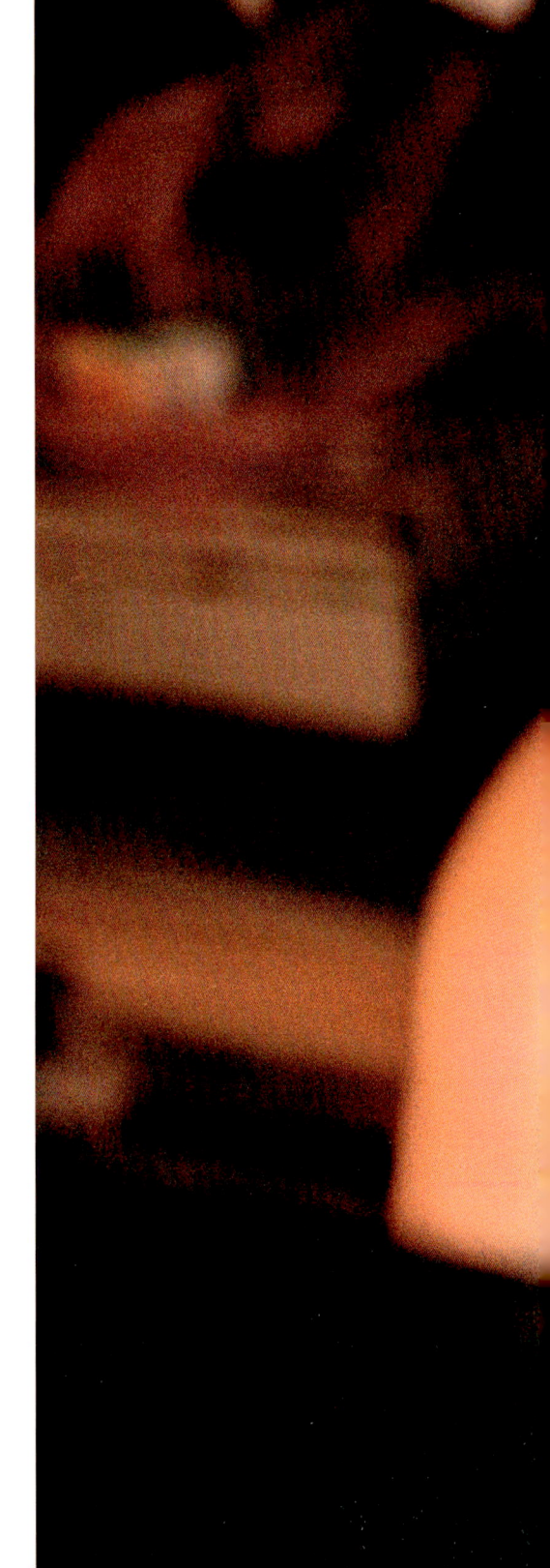

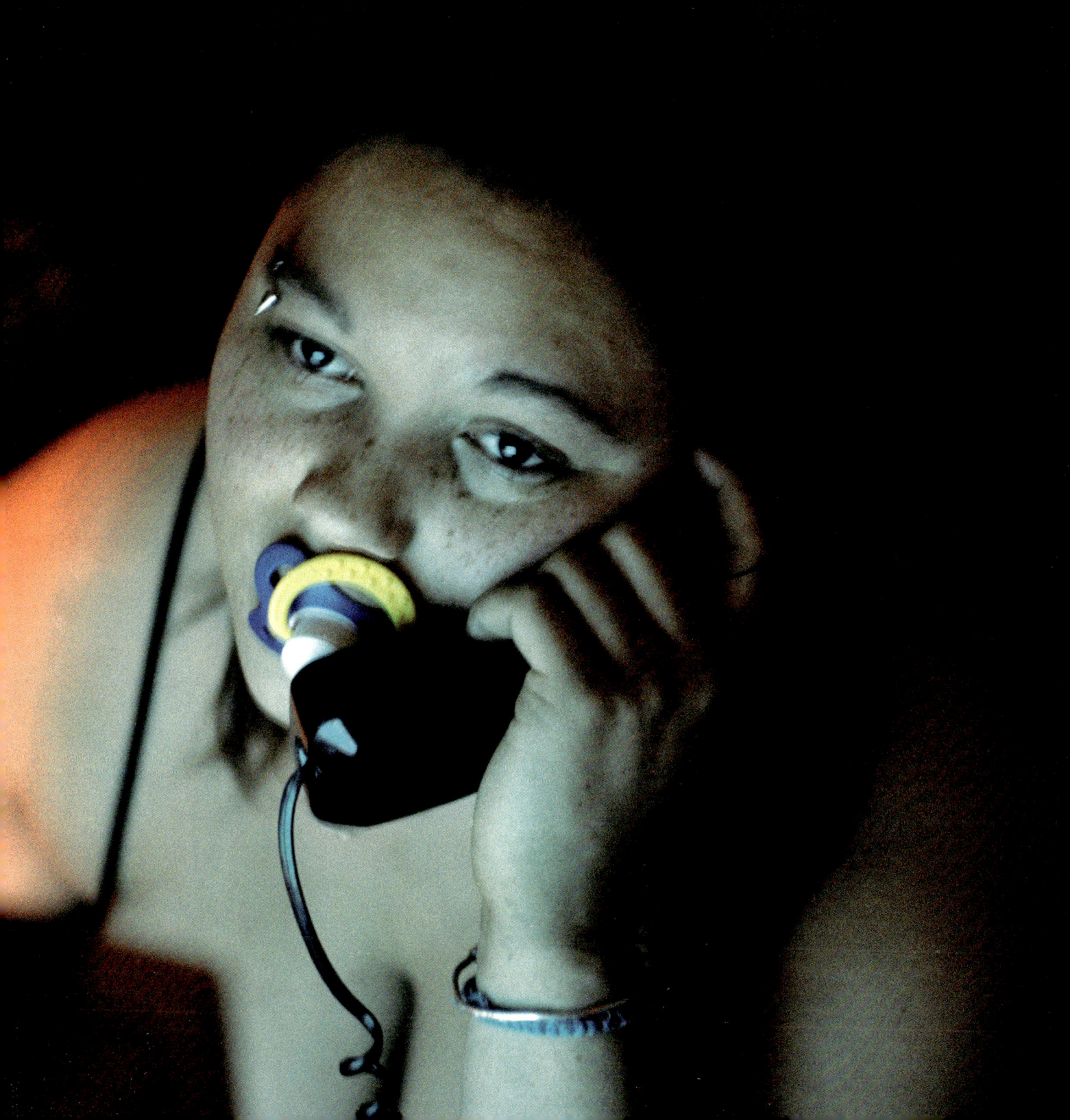

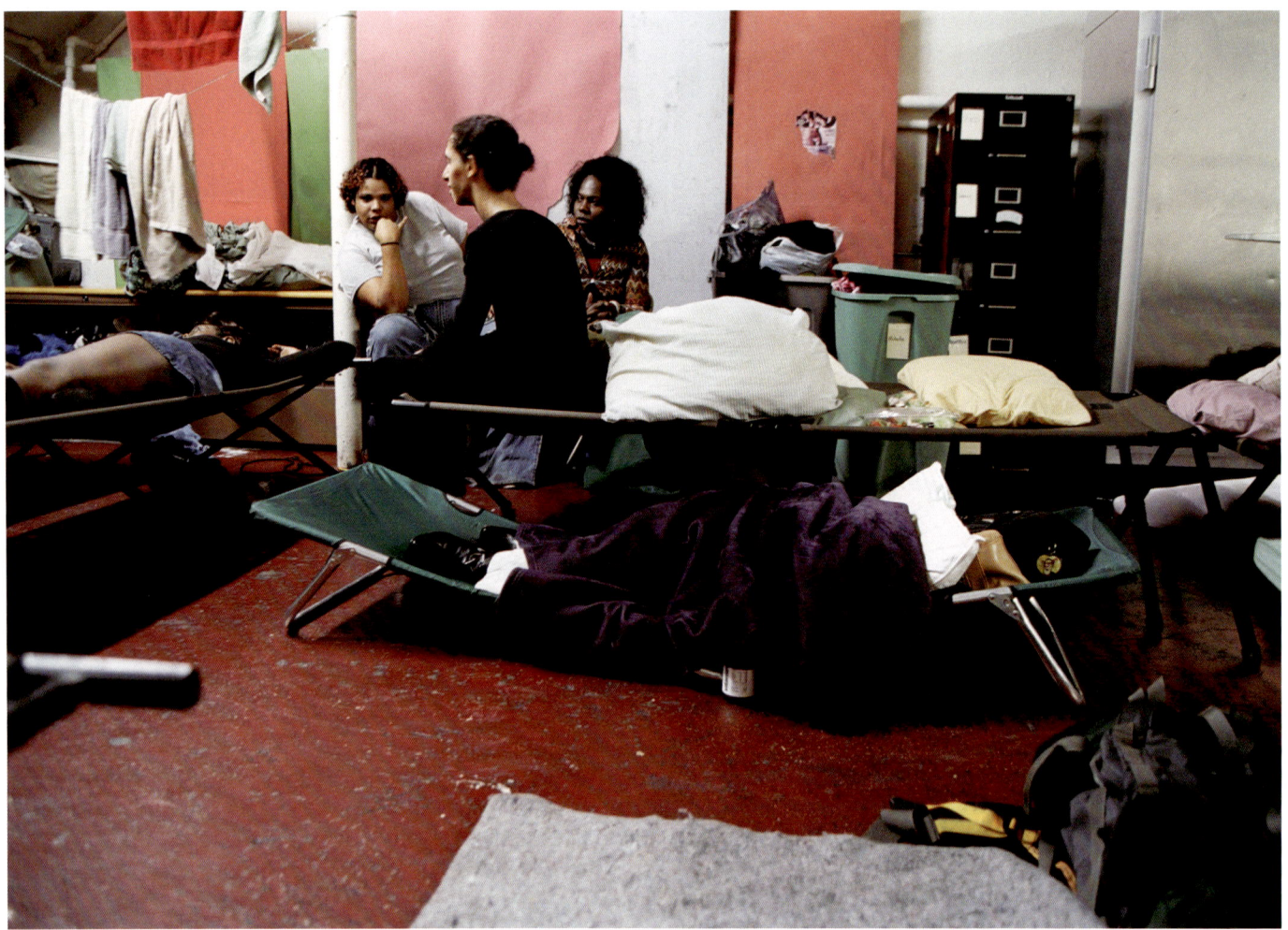

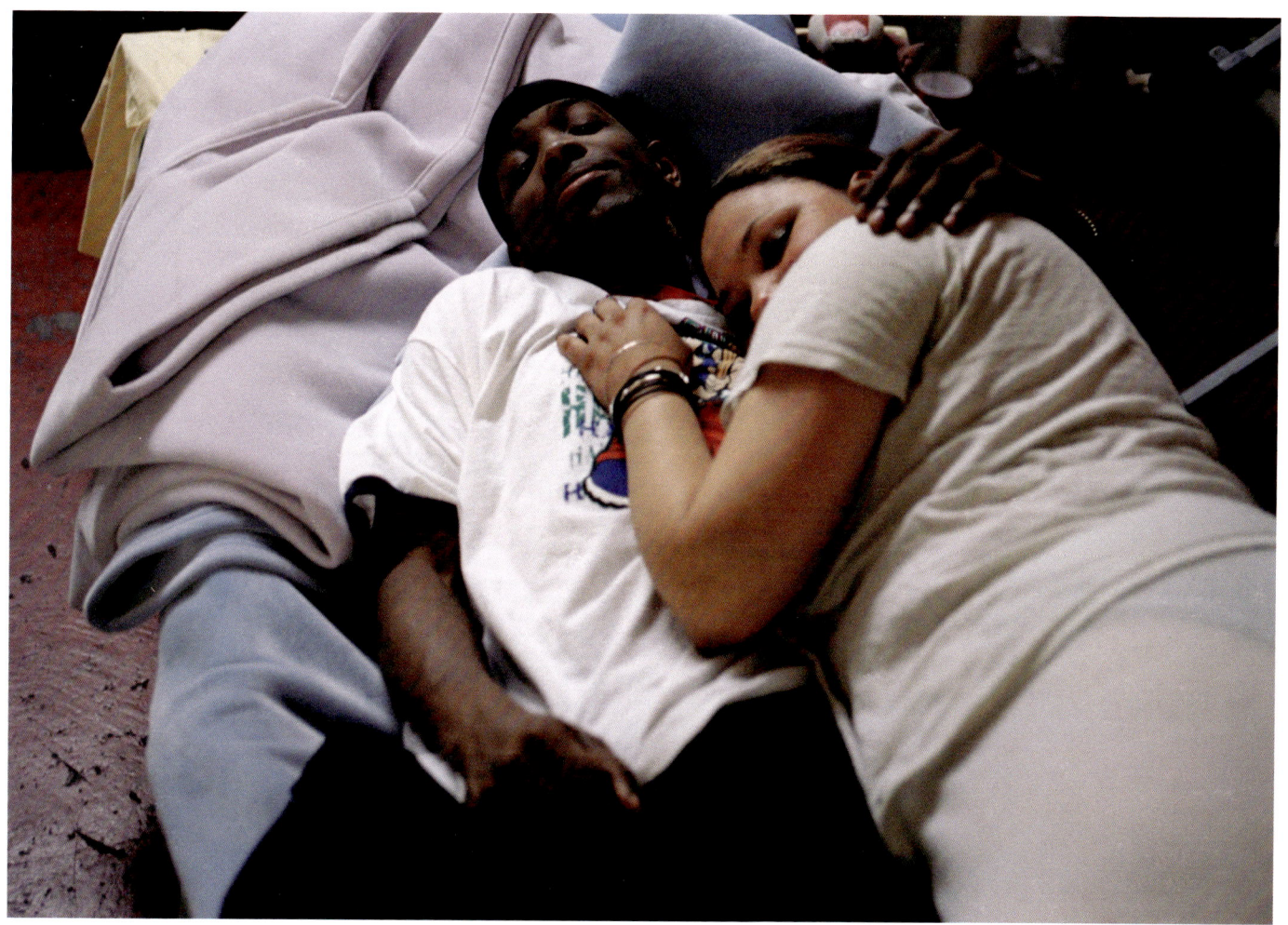

# Charlene

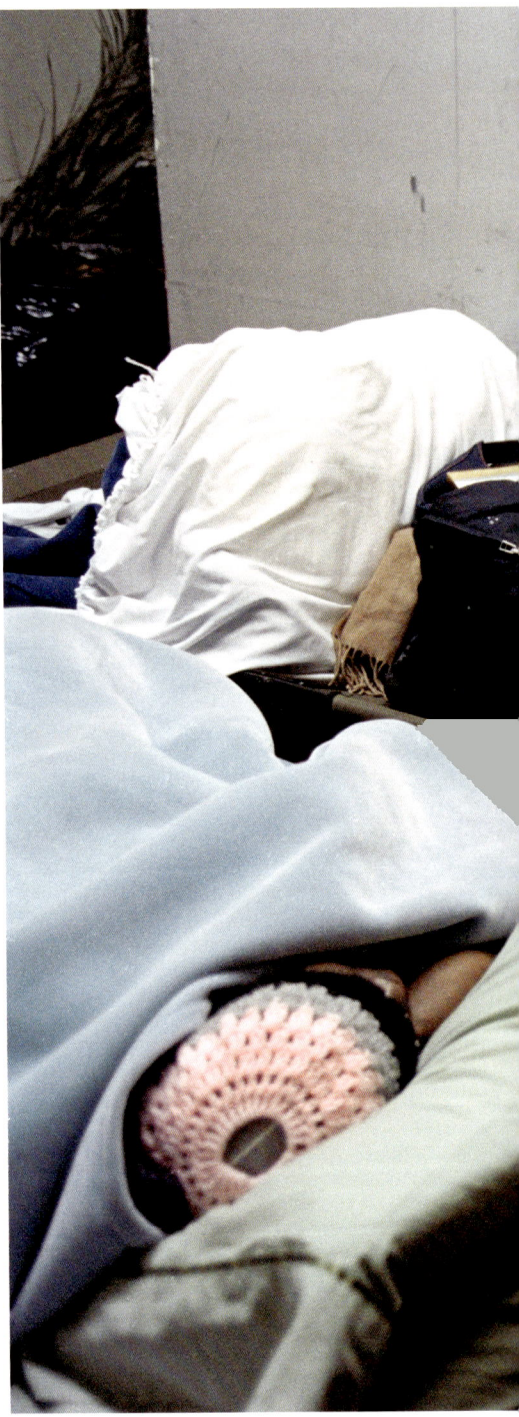

*Being a transsexual, you're always going to get that question, "How much?" No matter where you go, no matter what time of day it is. I guess it's just the idea of a person having the parts of both a man and a woman. It's a beautiful thing, I guess. You feel like a female, but you have male parts.*

Being gay or lesbian, young and homeless is more of a challenge than any of the young people at Sylvia's should ever have to face. For many of those who have come through the door of Sylvia's, navigating homelessness and being transgender has been their reality. Charlene was the first transgender youth who laid her head down within these shelter walls. Her stay would echo over the next several years for the multitude of transgender men and women who found a temporary home at Sylvia's Place.

Charlene came to Sylvia's under a different name. She's had several over her lifetime, and each name has represented a part of her vibrant personality. Sometimes, she presented as a boy, but mostly as a girl. When she first arrived, her name was Janet.

*You know I was Janet, because Janet Jackson was my favorite person. Actually, in Covenant House, I was Jennifer. I had changed it, because I didn't really look like a Jennifer. I didn't like Jennifer. I liked Janet. I'm black. So, I went with Janet. Then I happened to see Bringing Down*

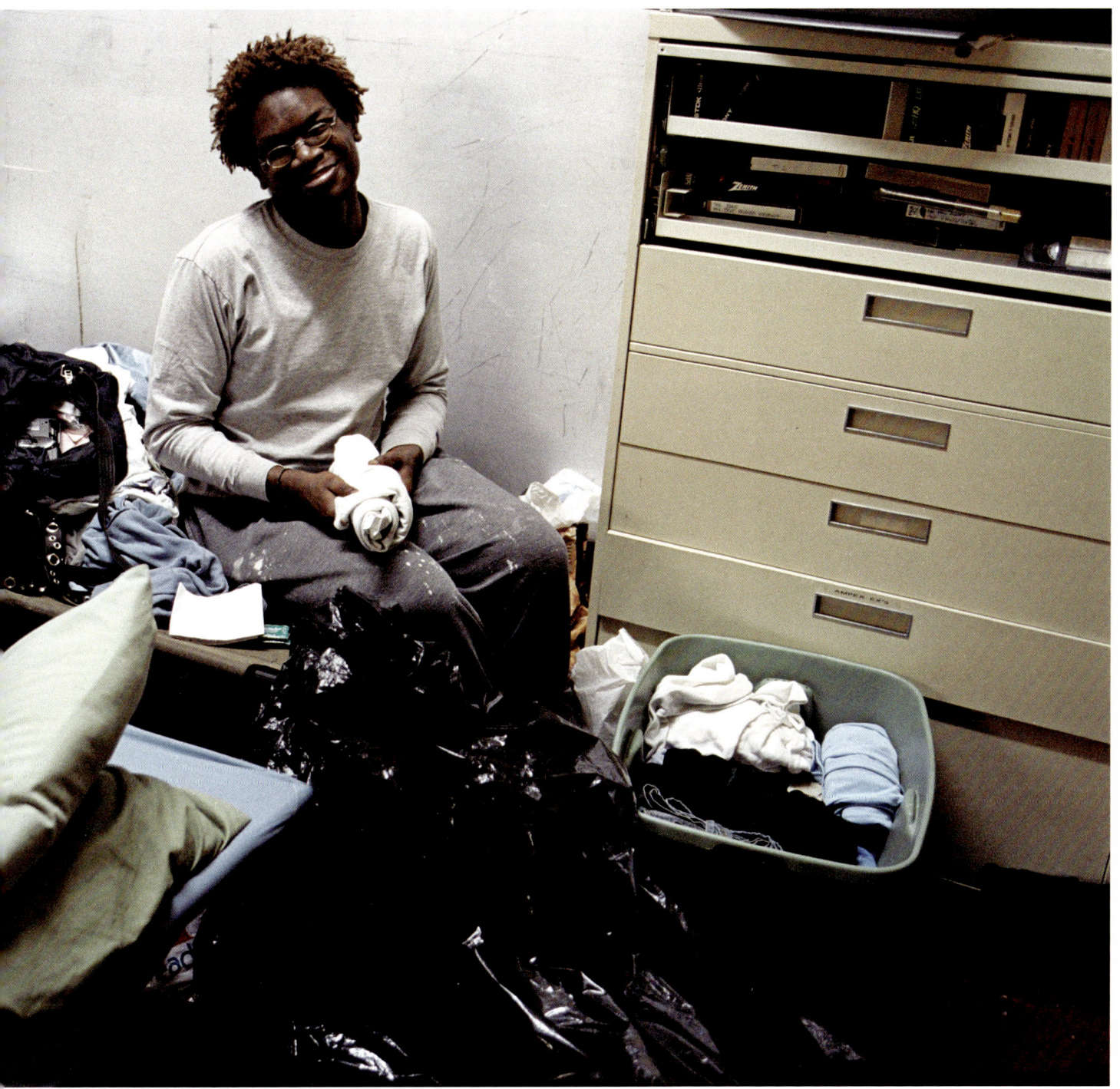

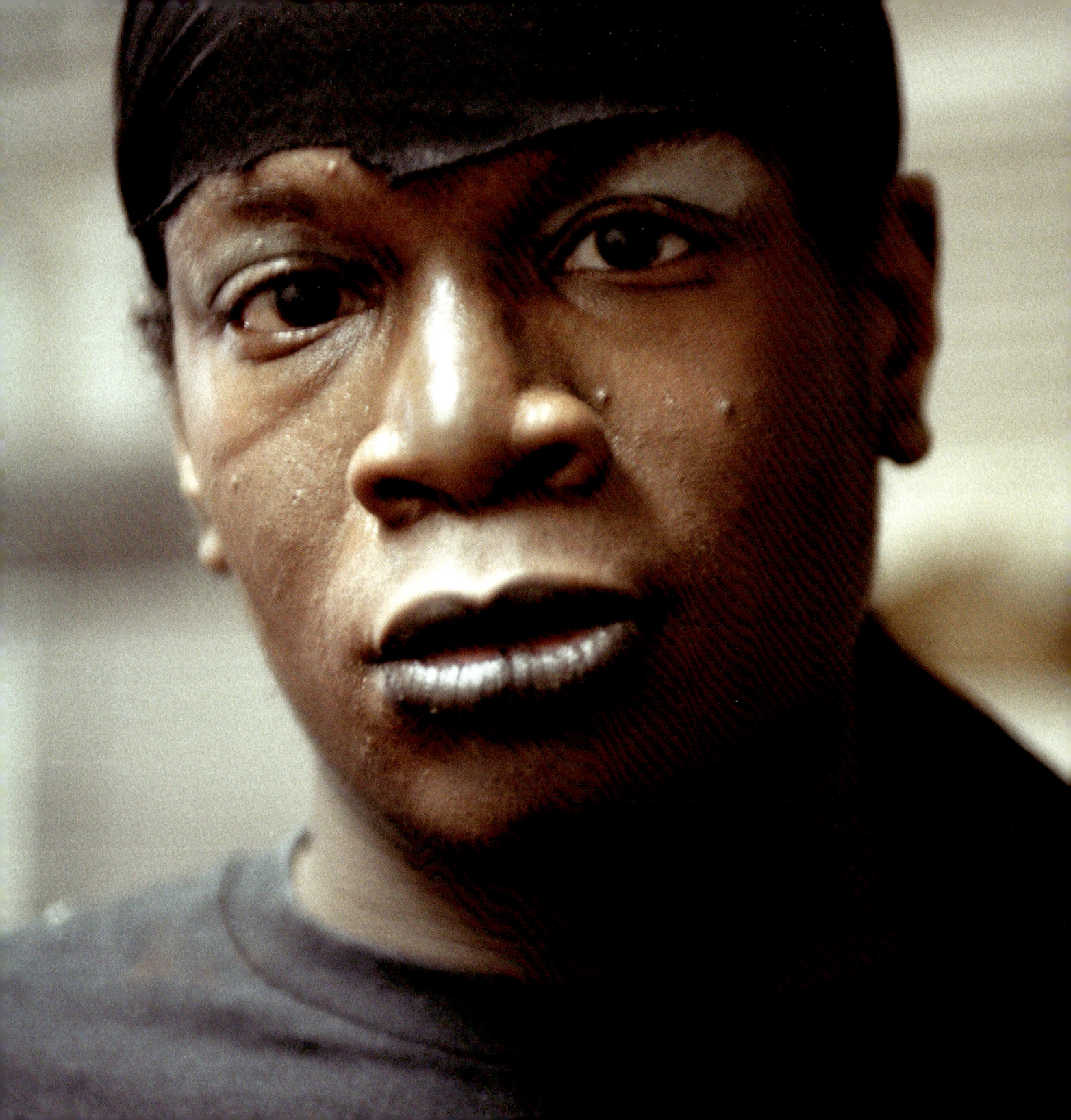

the House. The main character, who was played by Queen Latifah, my favorite person in the world, was named Charlene. So then I thought, Charlene sounds better. So, I've been Charlene for a couple of years now. I was just like the character. Ghetto. Very ghetto.

*Ray-Ray is my alter ego. He's like the He-man, like the big brother. Charlene's like the little sister, and Ray-Ray is the big brother. Ray-Ray's not nice. He's not very compassionate. He's not very eager to hear other people's side. He's very one-sided. It's pretty much his way or the highway. Charlene is a lot more understanding.*

Like many of the residents, Charlene was surprised to find herself homeless. She had not grown up in a house of hardship. Her parents were good to her and she never had to live in poverty.

*I was spoiled. Yeah, I was spoiled. I got everything I wanted. You know, my parents raised me to the best of their ability. They both worked. They were both hard working people. I have no regrets about my parents. I have nothing negative to say about my parents. I've never seen them fight in front of me.*

But her life changed when her father died. His death put the family in disarray and she would find herself homeless for the first time.

*My father had passed away. We had the house for a little while, until the September of 2001. My mother had lost her job and couldn't afford the rent no more. The landlord was selling the house, 'cause he couldn't afford the mortgage no more. So there was a big ol' mess, because the people who bought the house didn't want us living there, so me and the downstairs neighbor had to move out. My mom went to live with my sister and I was going to live with my sister, but my sister has kids, so it was really not good to be in the house with those two kids. And I was doing my drugs back then, so it wasn't good. So that's how I became homeless. Running the streets, doing whatever, sleeping with whoever, partying wherever.*

*I slept on buses, I slept on trains, I slept in parks. I picked the lock on someone's car one time and I was sleeping in the car. I'd sleep anywhere. Because I had a pride about myself, and I'm such a diva, I was not trying to go to anybody's shelter. I come from a family where my mother was working, my father was working, so I never really experienced welfare, and I never really experienced a shelter, so I was not going to one. I had my high standards about it.*

Eventually, she did find herself in a shelter. The first stop for many homeless youth is Covenant House, and often it's not the last. Sometimes, life is easier on the streets.

*When I finally got there, I was staying at Covenant House. I tried to come out, being bisexual. It didn't work. I was gay bashed in Covenant House the first night. They hit me with batteries; they beat me up. I went to security, and they was like, "We don't know what happened. We didn't see nothing." But there were cameras right there, right where it happened. That was my last night I spent there. I thought I was never going to a shelter again. But somehow I found out about Sylvia's.*

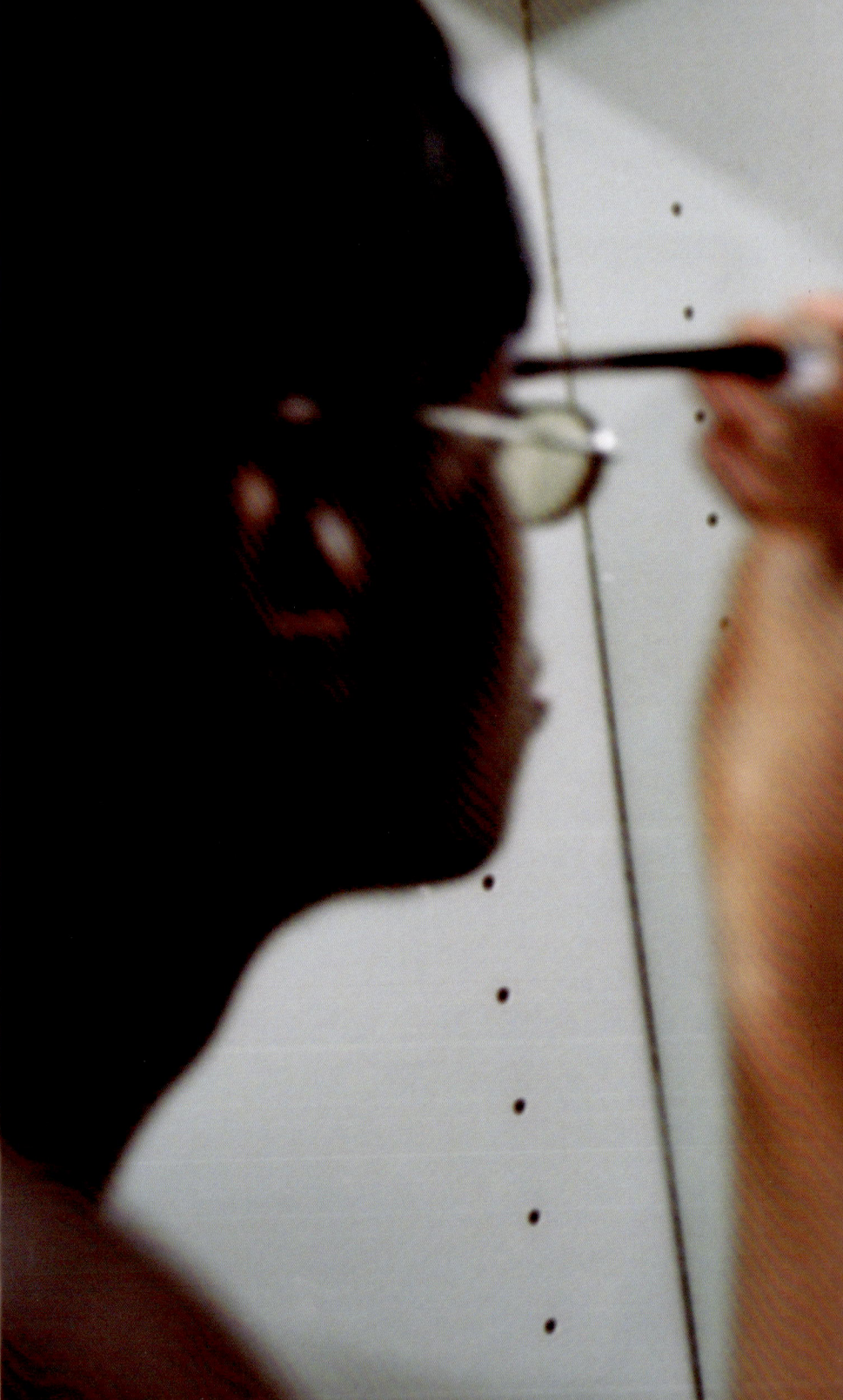

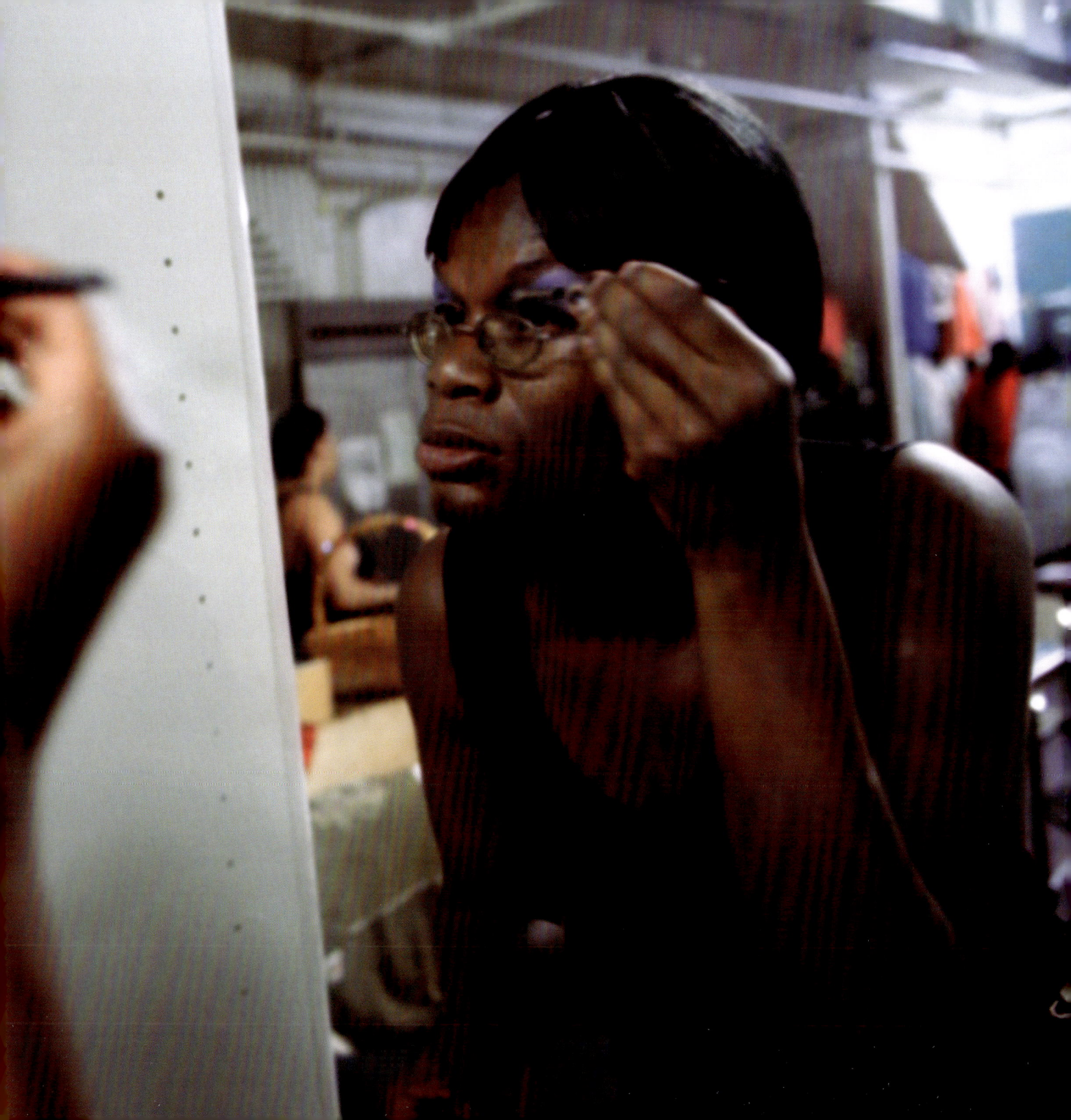

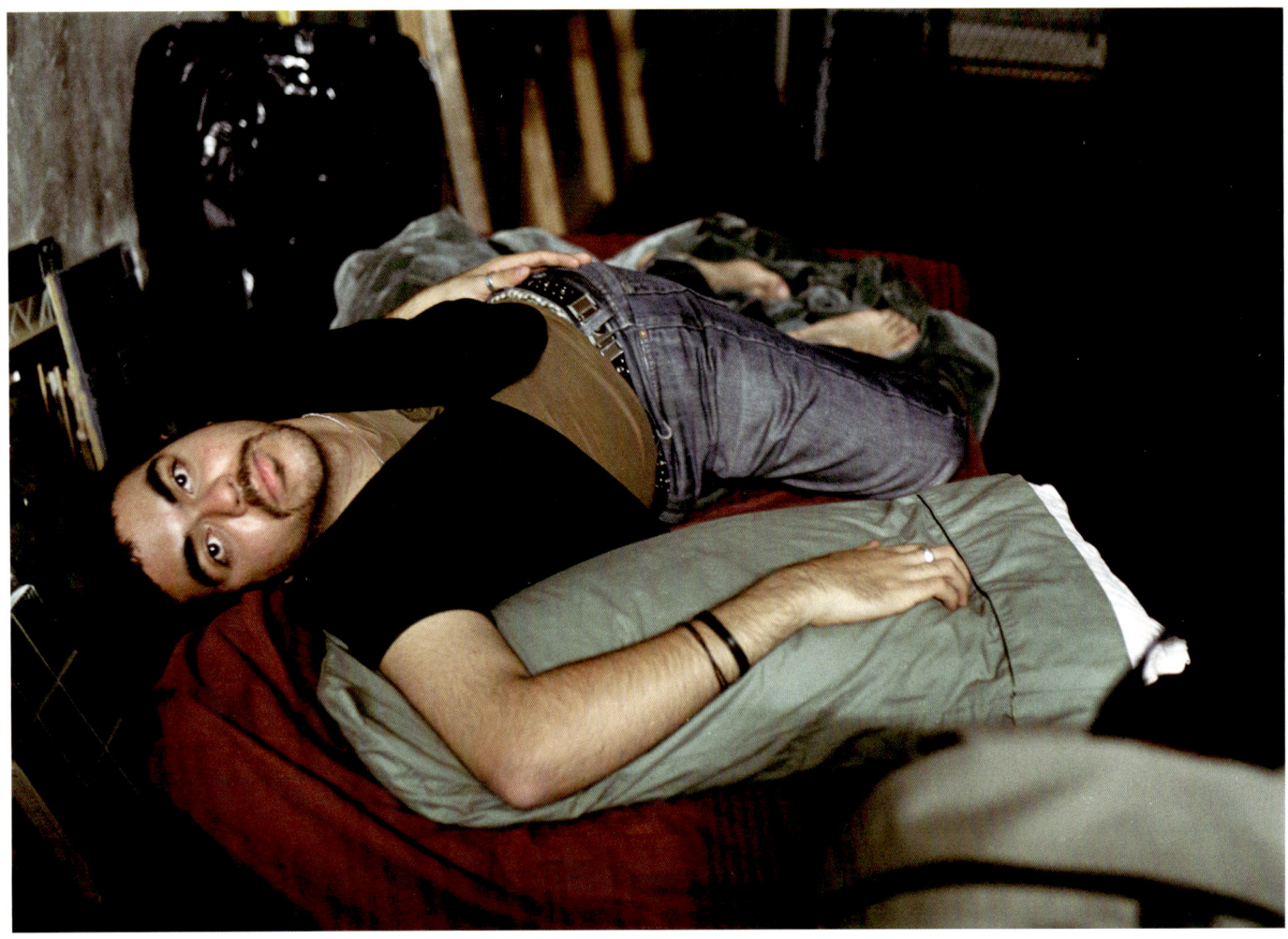

Shelter 54

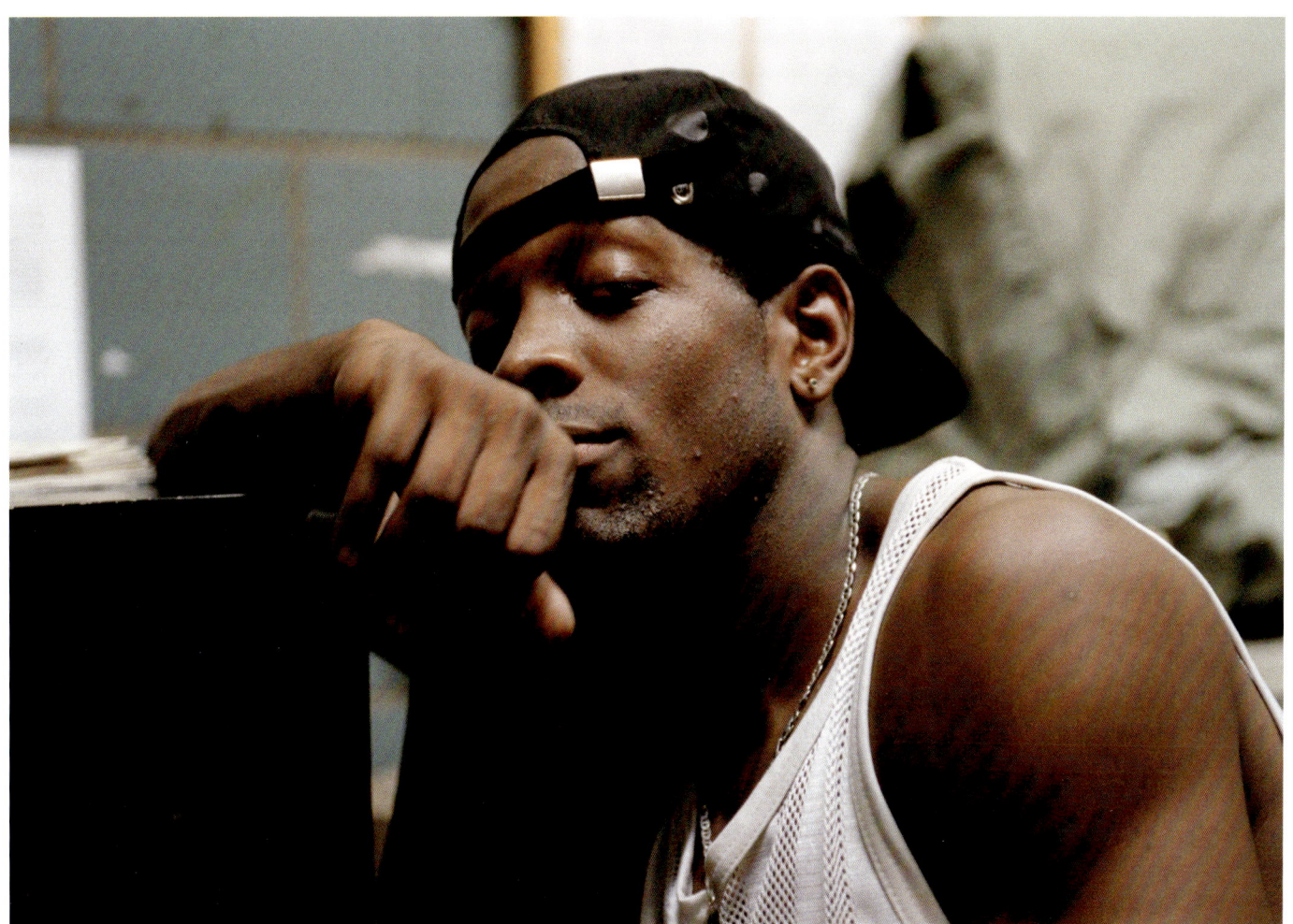

On a spring night when two counselors, Lucky and Tanino, were helping to get the shelter set up for the night, one resident arrived at the shelter dangerously drunk. He was faltering in and out of the back bathroom, occasionally attempting to eat something, and mostly unaware of his surroundings. When Lucky noticed him disappear into the front bathroom, he decided that something must be very wrong. He saw a pool of vomit in front of the bathroom and followed the trail in. The scene inside was a frightening one. There was vomit in all corners of the bathroom. A completely naked body was passed out on the toilet, with his head resting on a shelf. Lucky tried to rouse him awake and get him to eat bread to avoid alcohol poisoning, and managed to keep him safe. With Tanino keeping the other clients busy, Lucky saw to his safety and used a generous amount of bleach to clean up the mess in the bathroom. The next morning, Our client had no memory of the previous night's events.

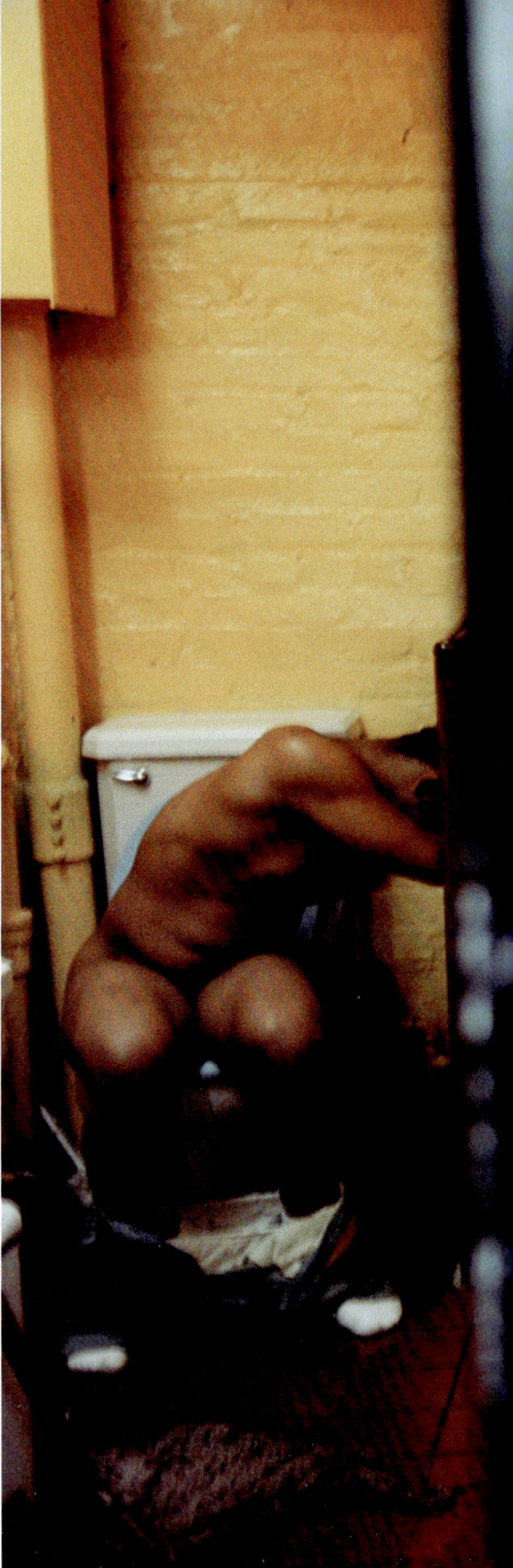

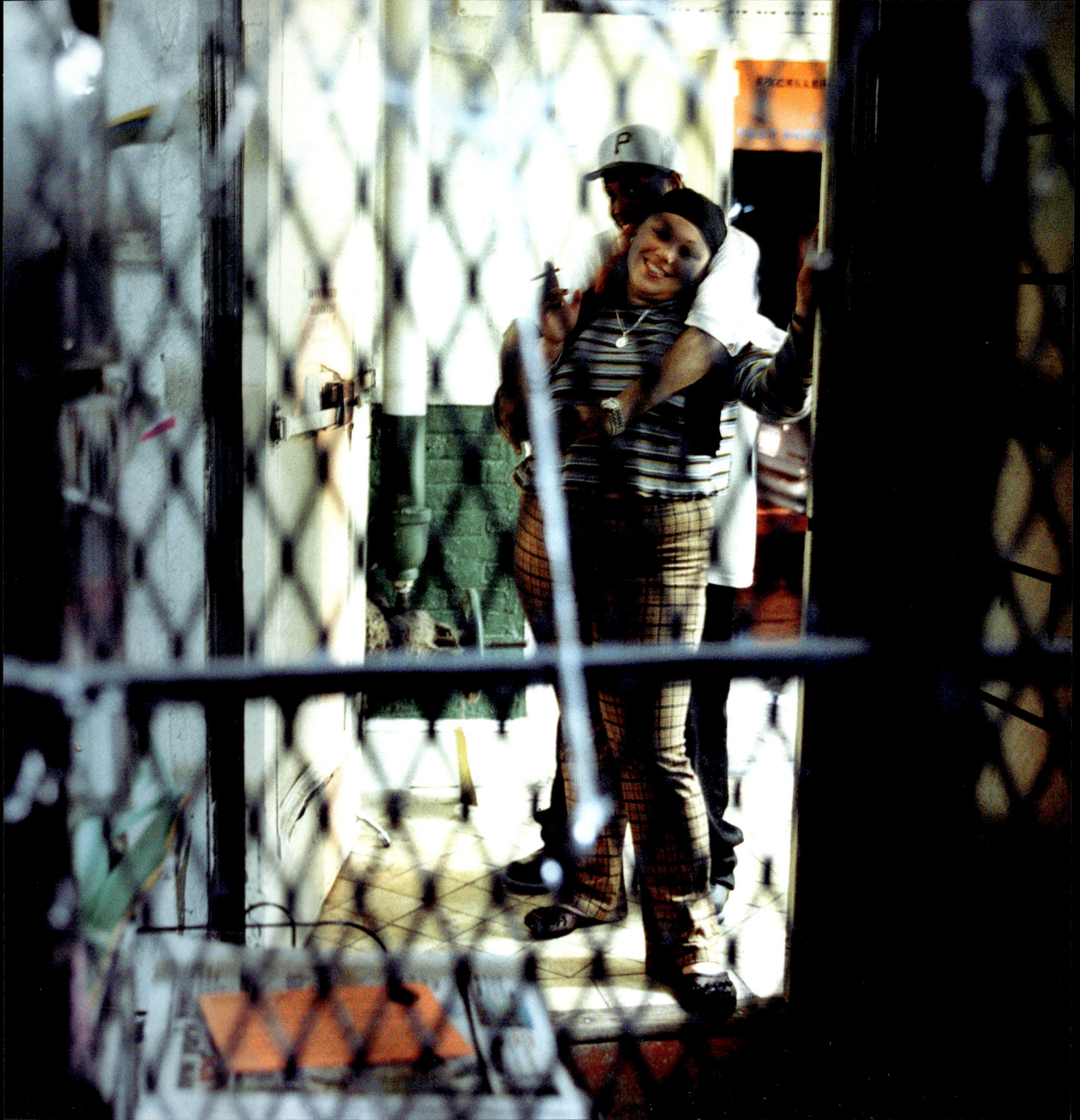

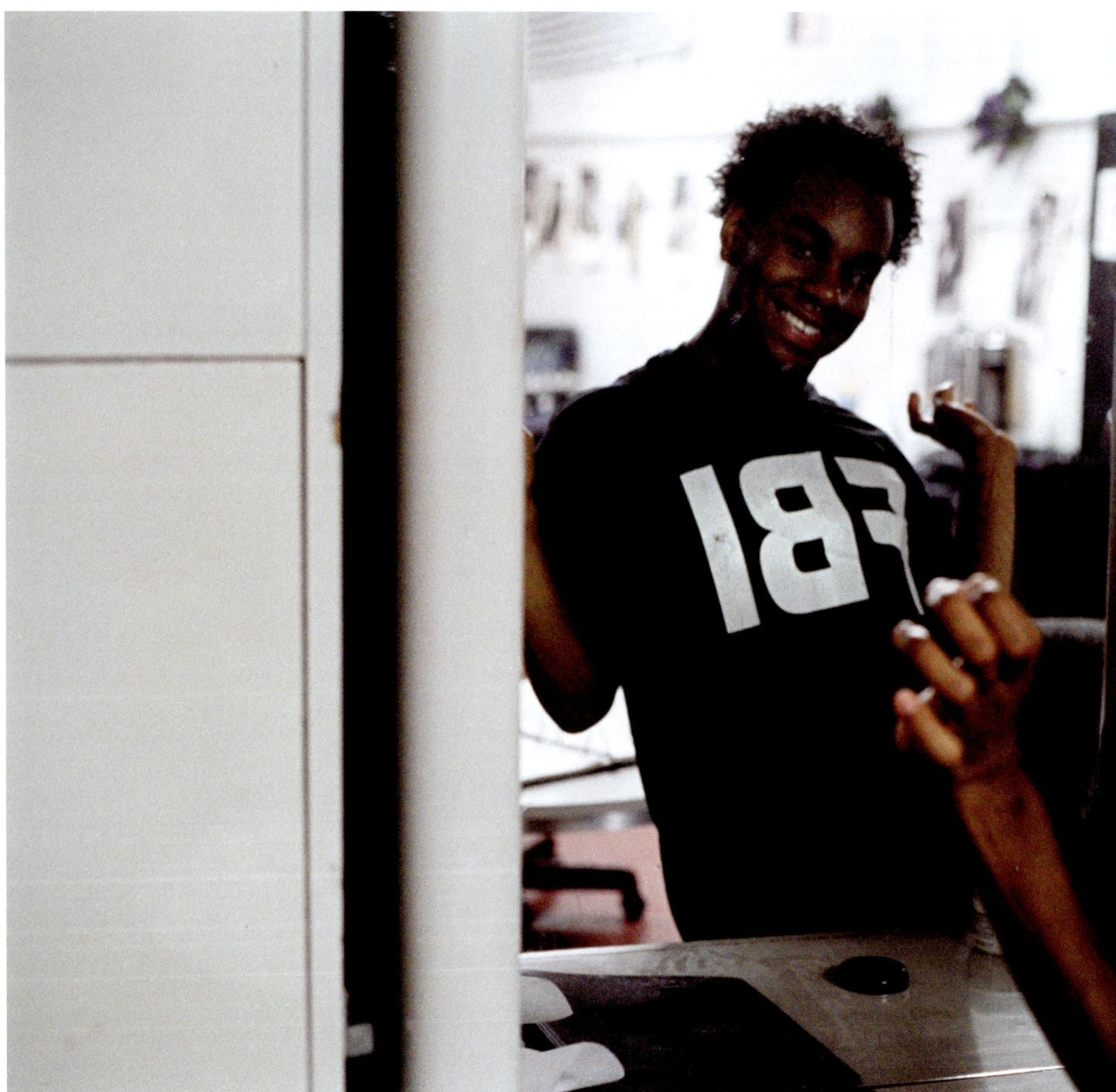

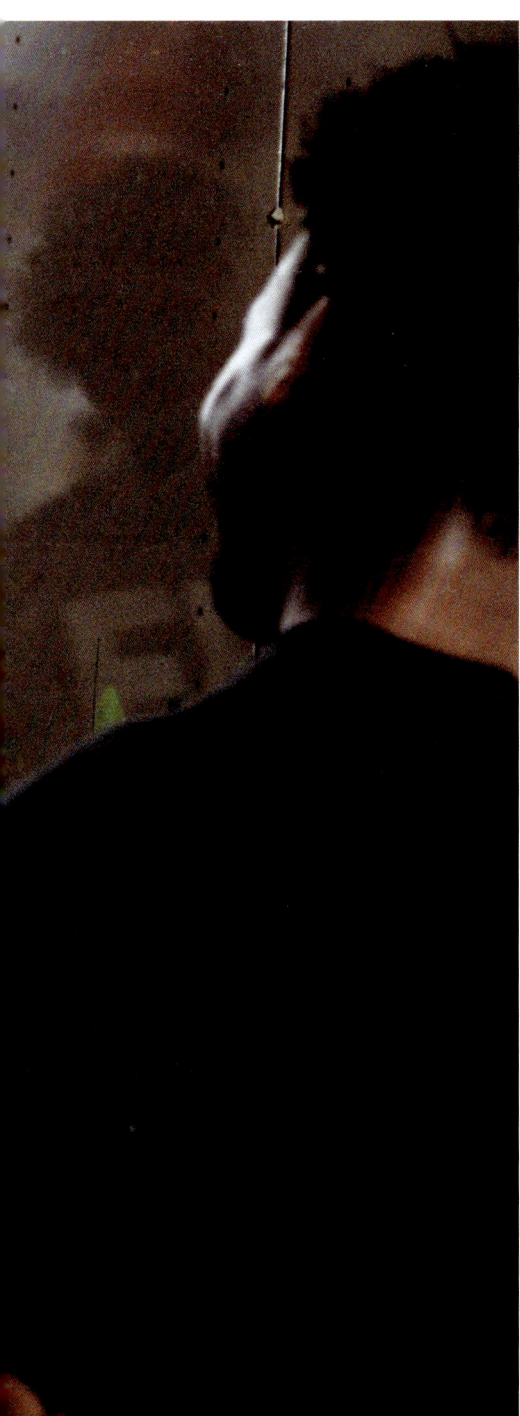

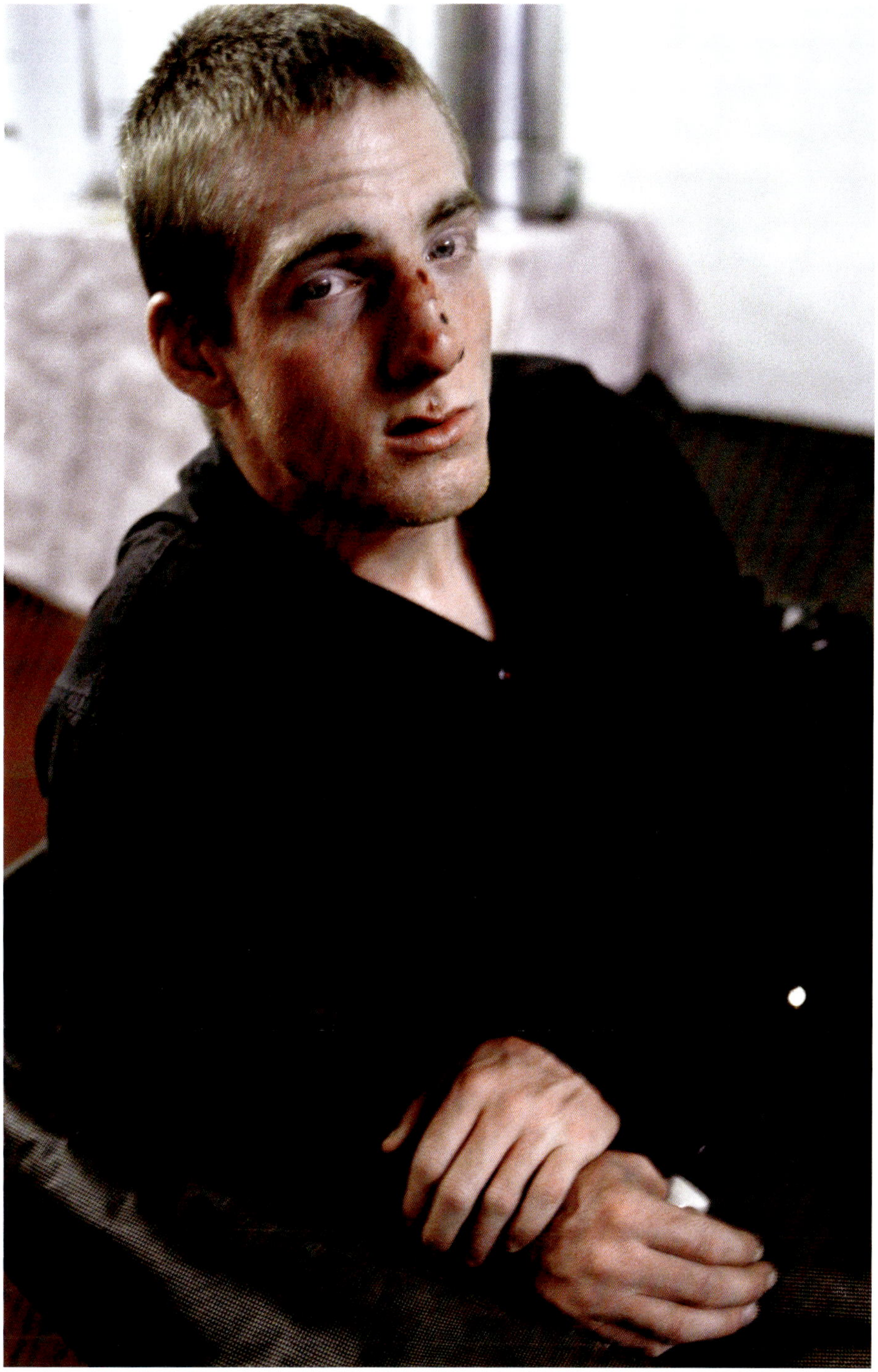

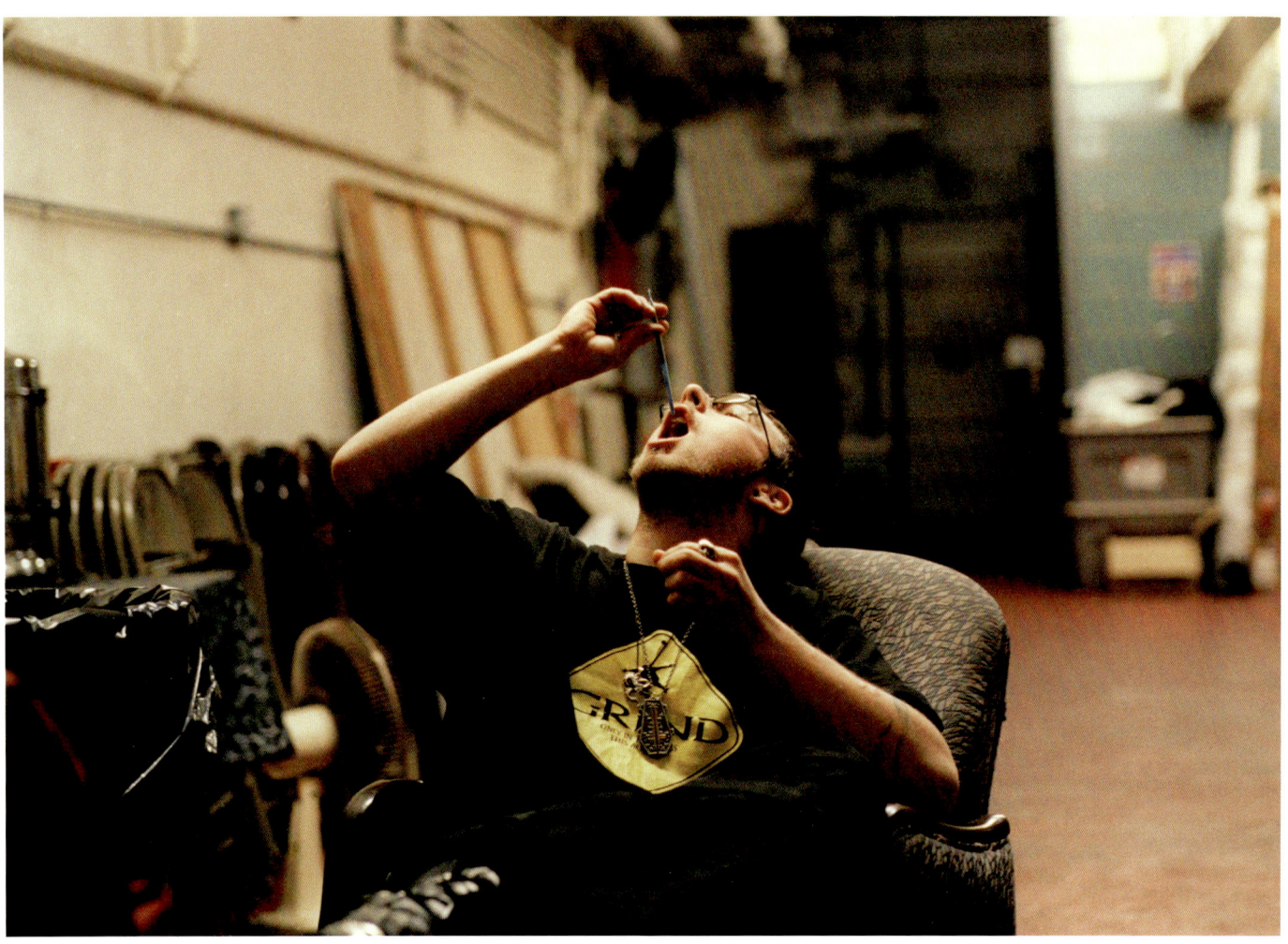

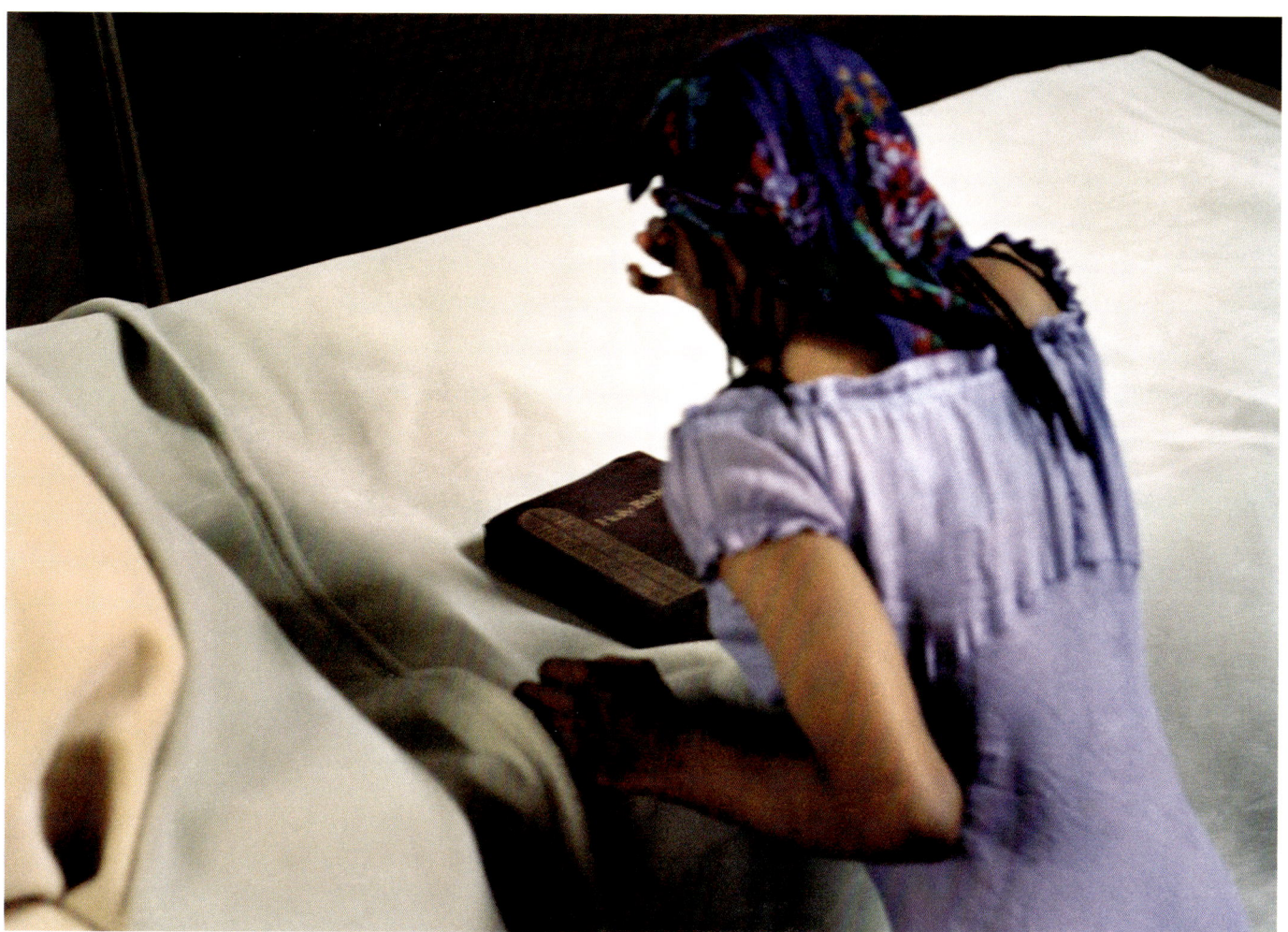

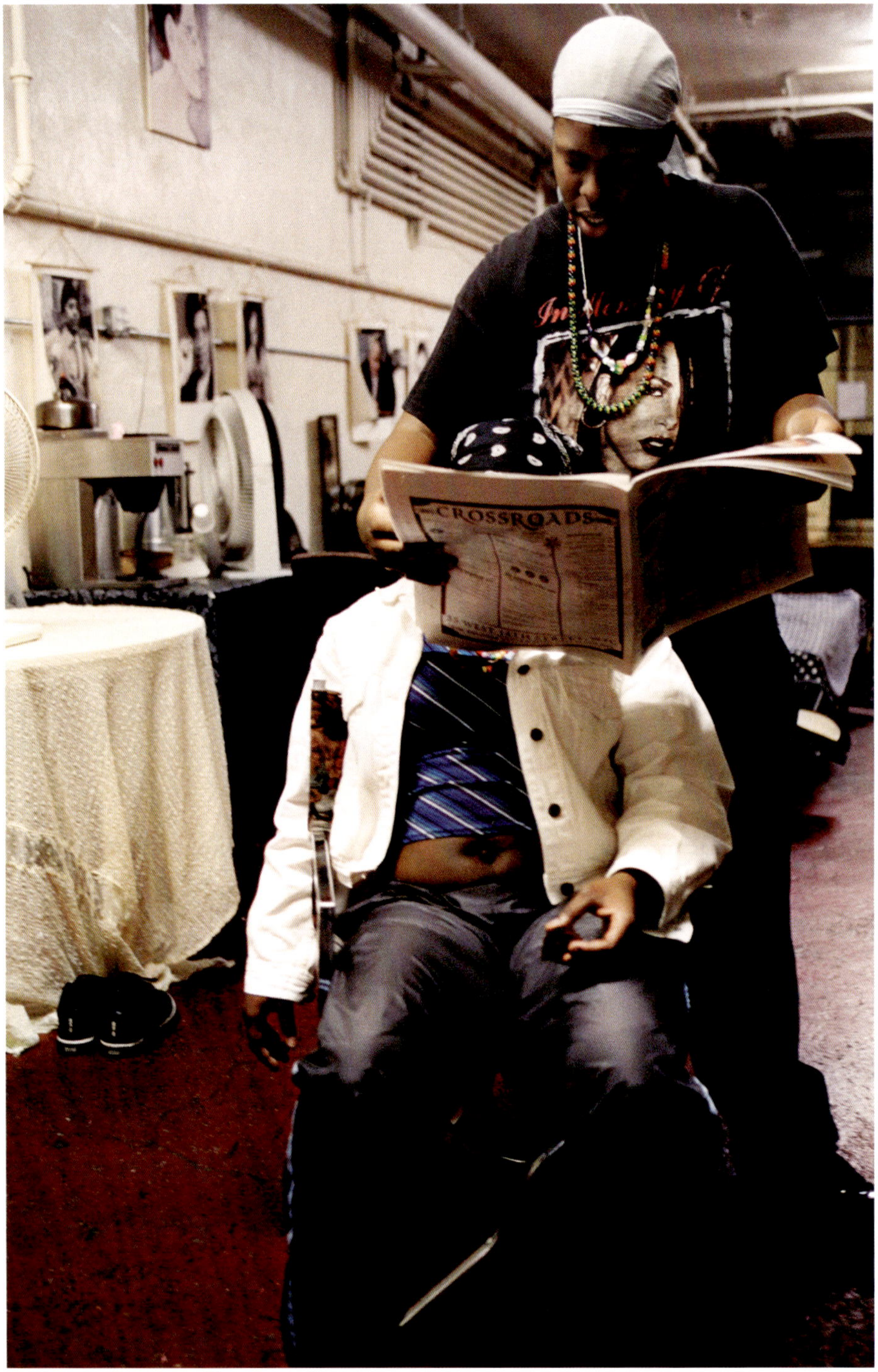

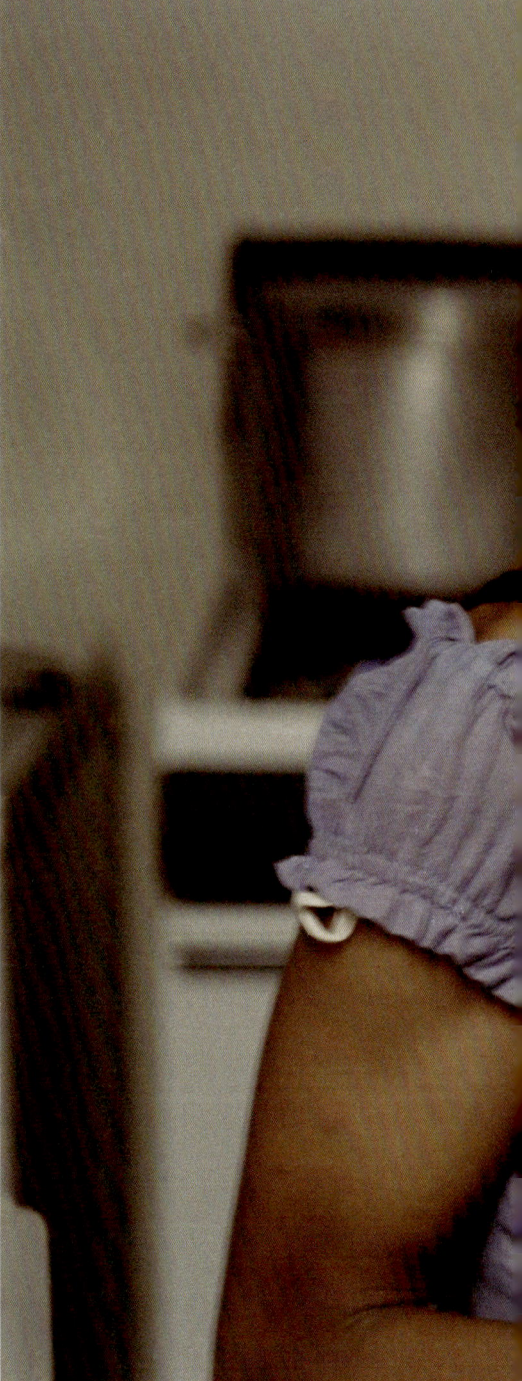

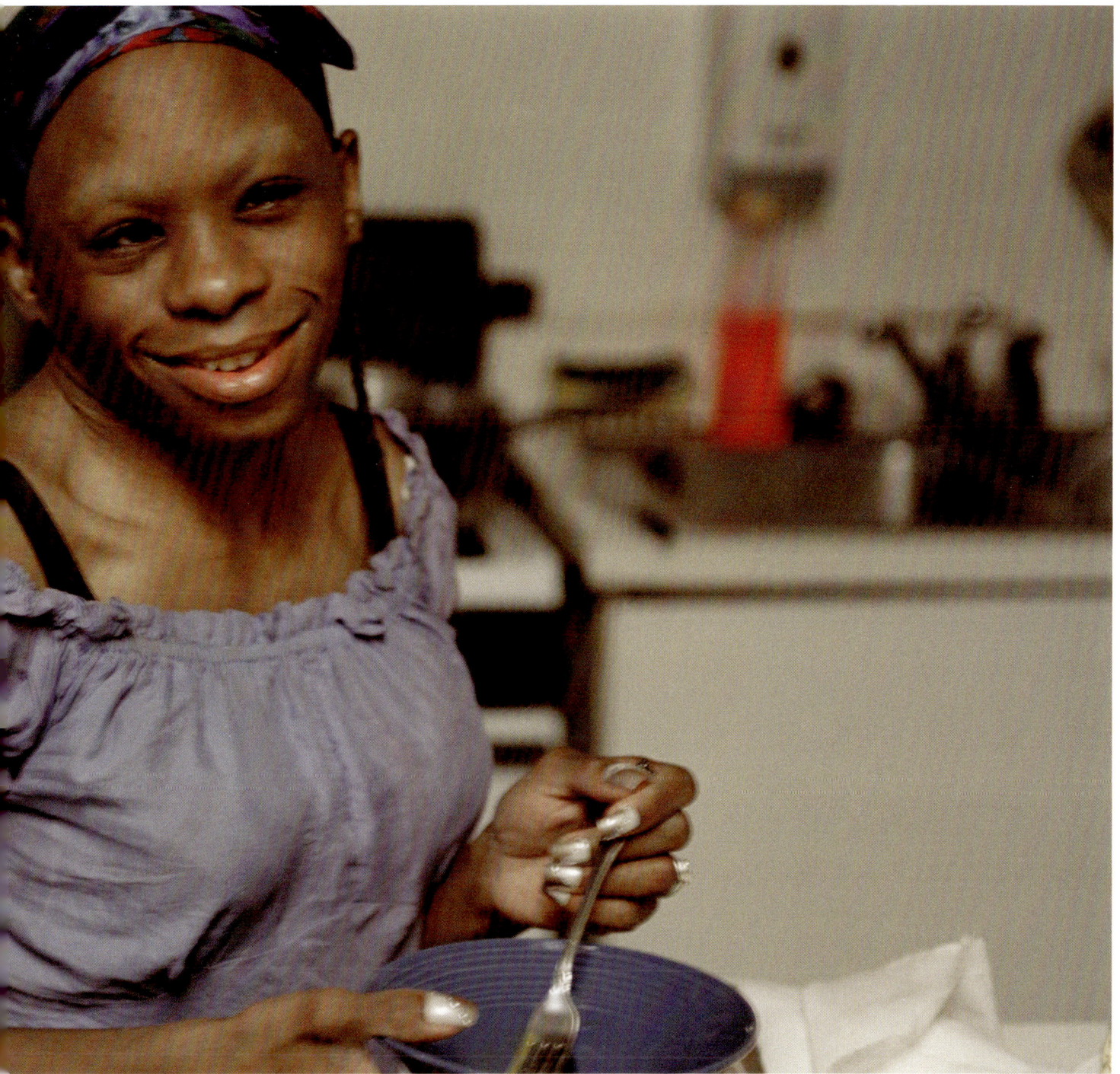

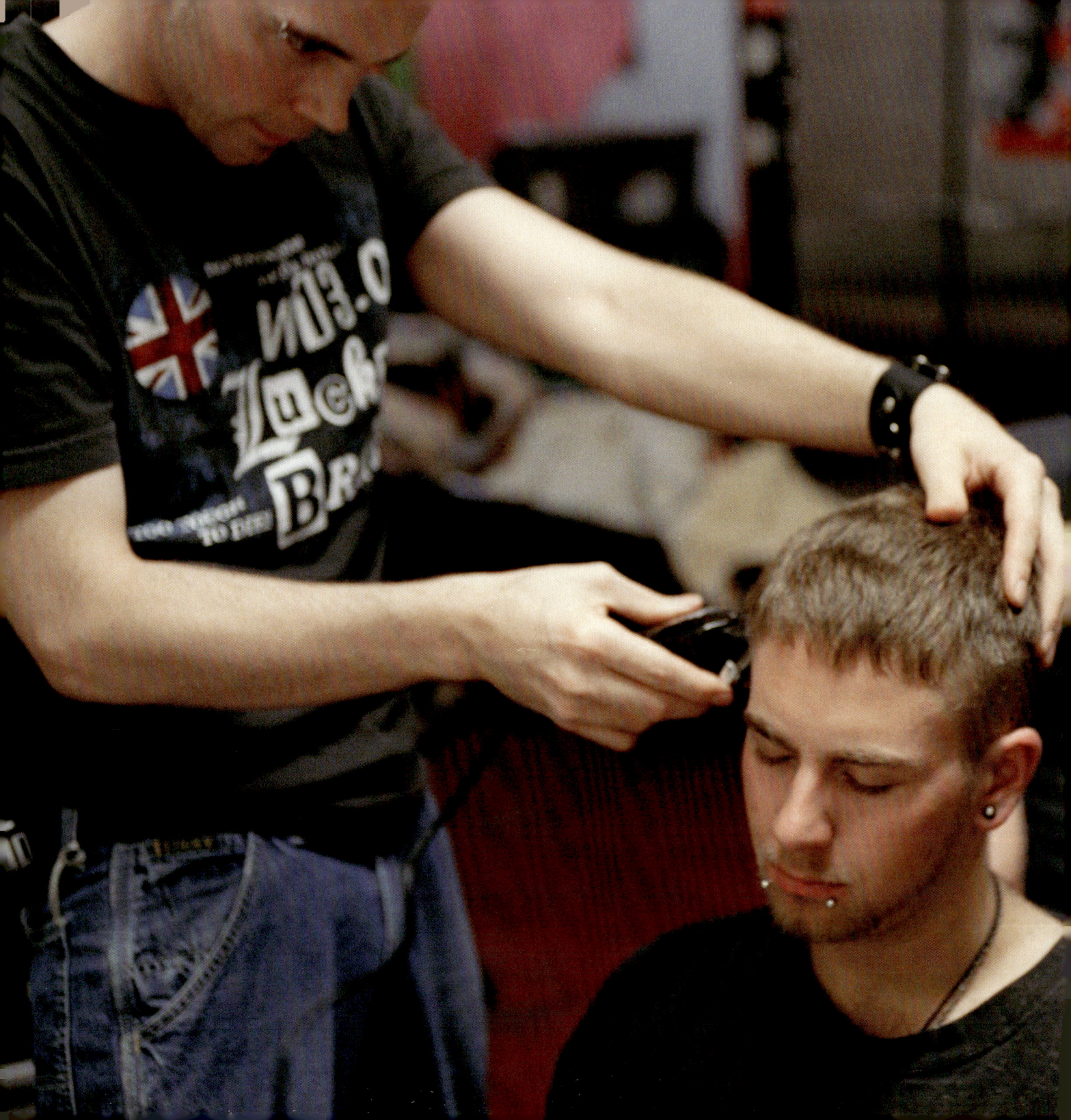

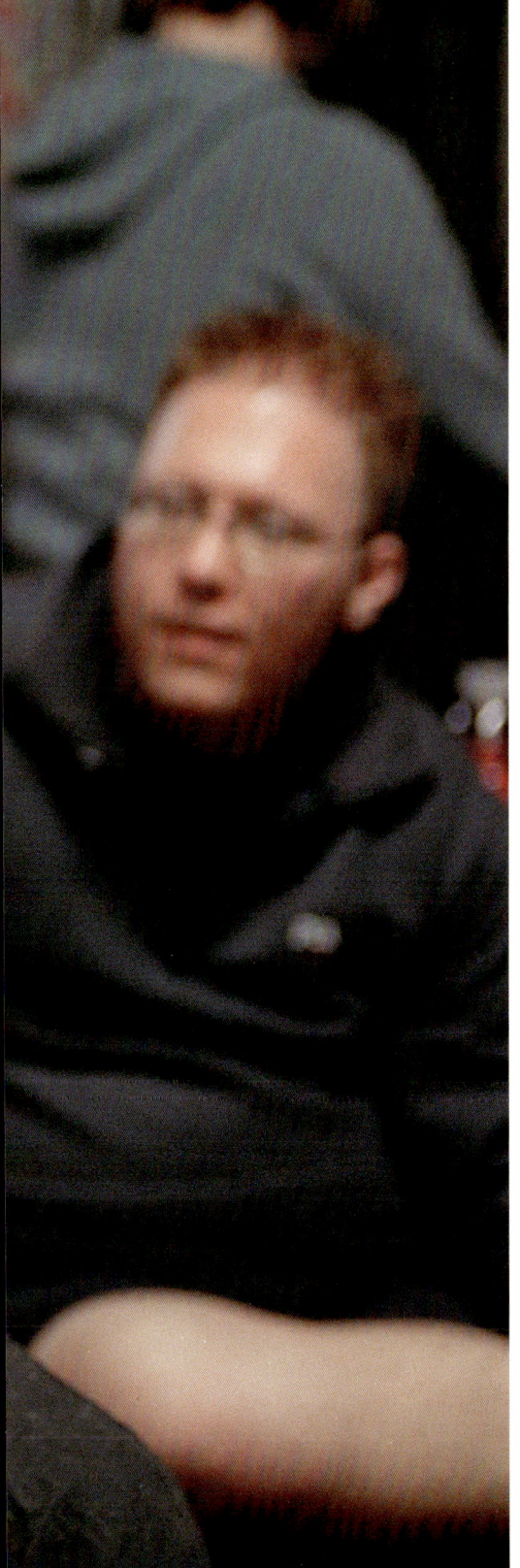

And then I met these two really great people, named Tanino and Lucky. Me and Mark, we named them Mom and Dad of Sylvia's, 'cause that's basically what they were.

After I realized I could call this place home, that's what it really felt like. When I first got here, I wasn't really looking to get attached or anything, because, I'm going to admit it, I have abandonment issues. I don't like when people come in my life and then leave. When I actually did get attached to Mom and Dad, then I got attached to my sister Charlene and Mark and Ron. Eternity

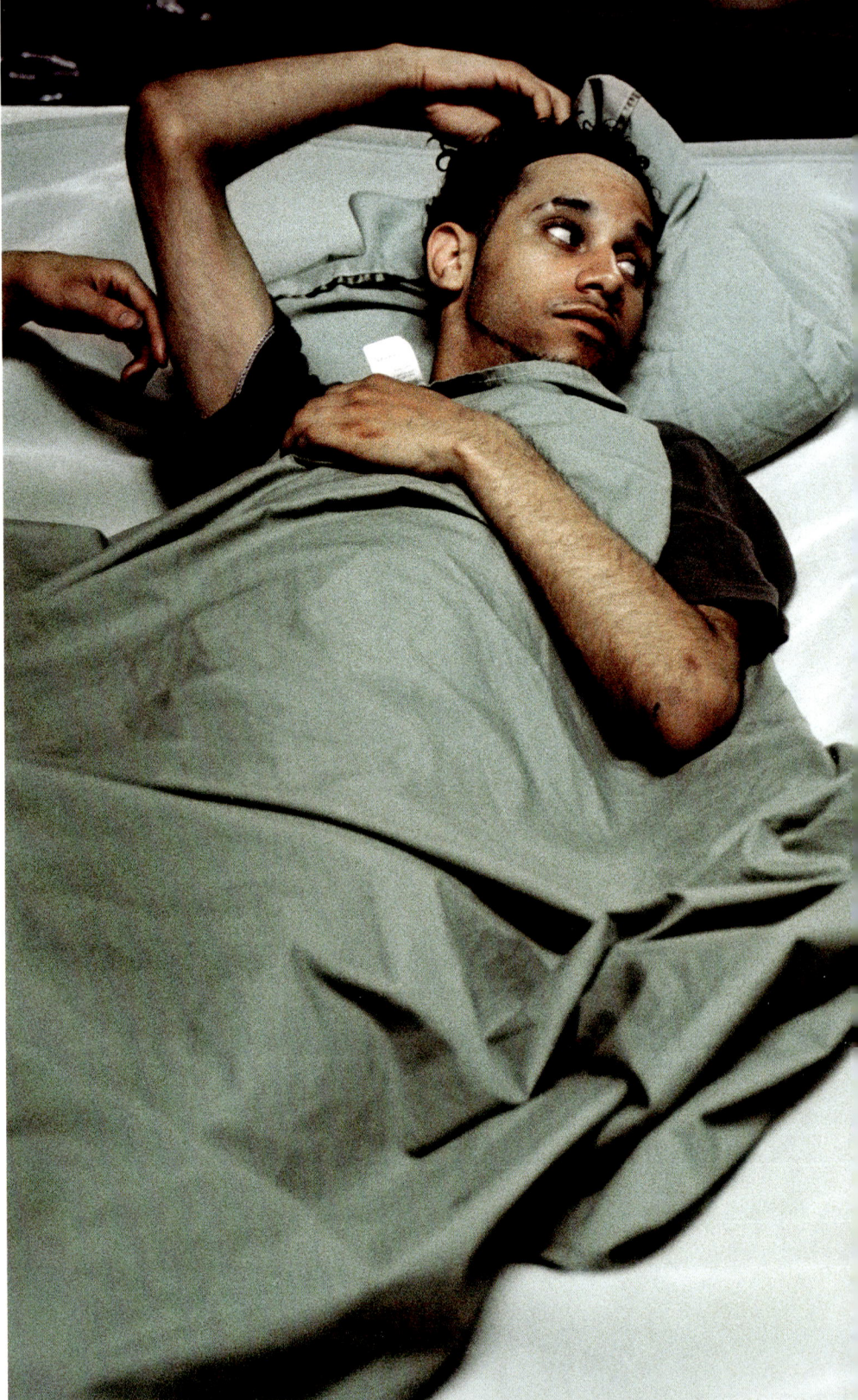

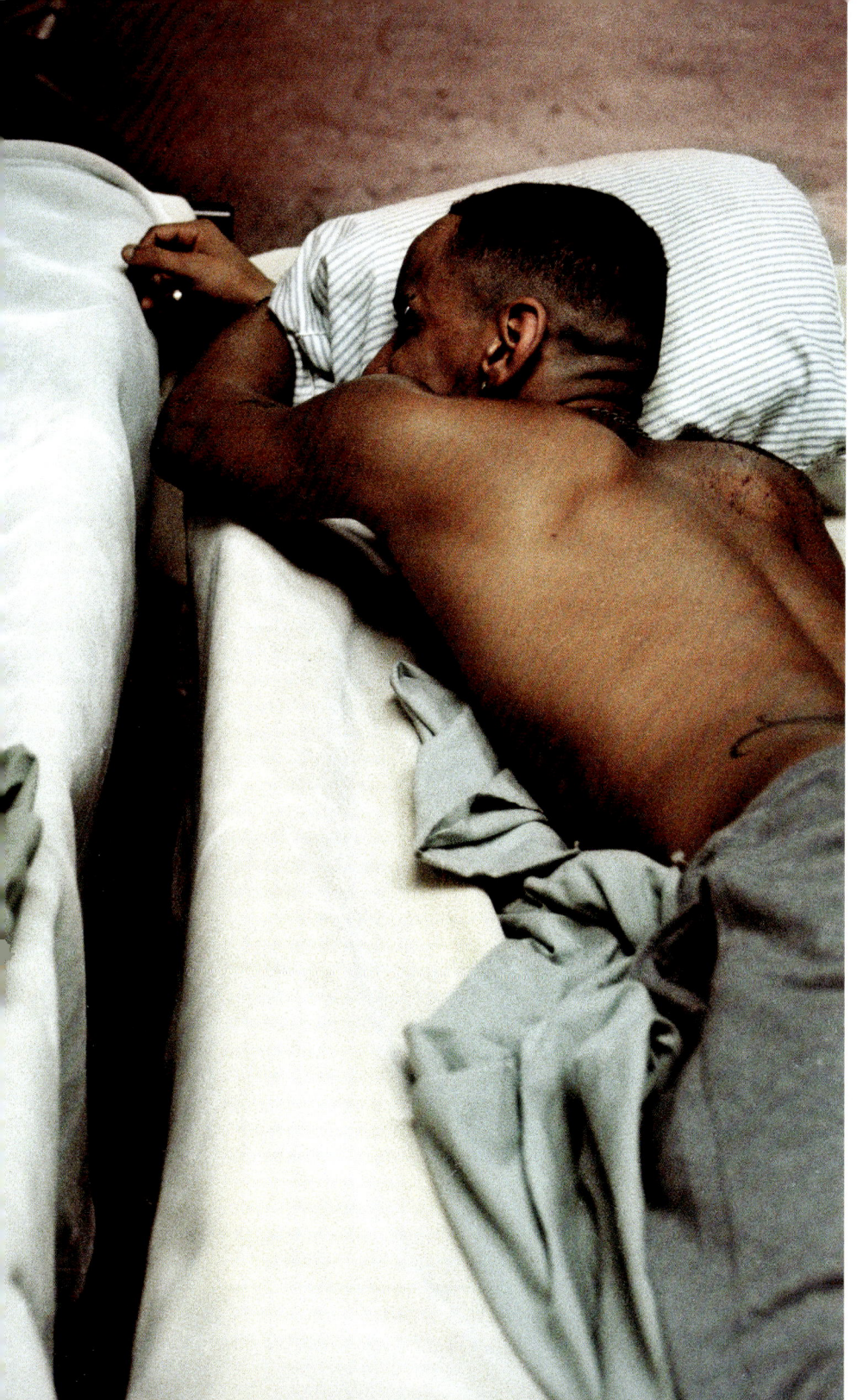

As Sylvia's Place braced for its first summer without air conditioning, two lesbian couples continued a feud that came to a frightening climax on a late night in June. Several youth arrived at the shelter early to warn the counselor that night that both couples were threatening an all-out brawl if they saw each other. Tanino and the residents made every attempt to keep each couple away from the other, but one off-the-cuff comment sparked a fight that became dangerously aggressive in a matter of seconds. The couples were corralled outside the shelter doors, where the fistfight escalated, fuelled by rage and frustration. Other residents gathered outside to watch, adding to the chaos of the scene. Tanino attempted to stand between two of the girls, but was tossed aside. The police were called immediately but did not arrive for almost 20 minutes. By that time, all four girls had been hurt. One couple fled the scene just as the police arrived. After the police gathered scraps of information, they left the shelter in search of the couple to place them under arrest. One girl waited for an ambulance to dress her wounds. Tanino, left to deal with the aftermath, corralled the other residents back into Sylvia's Place. With their help, he quietly set up the shelter for the night. Despite the overwhelming events of the previous hour, the residents found support and comfort in each other.

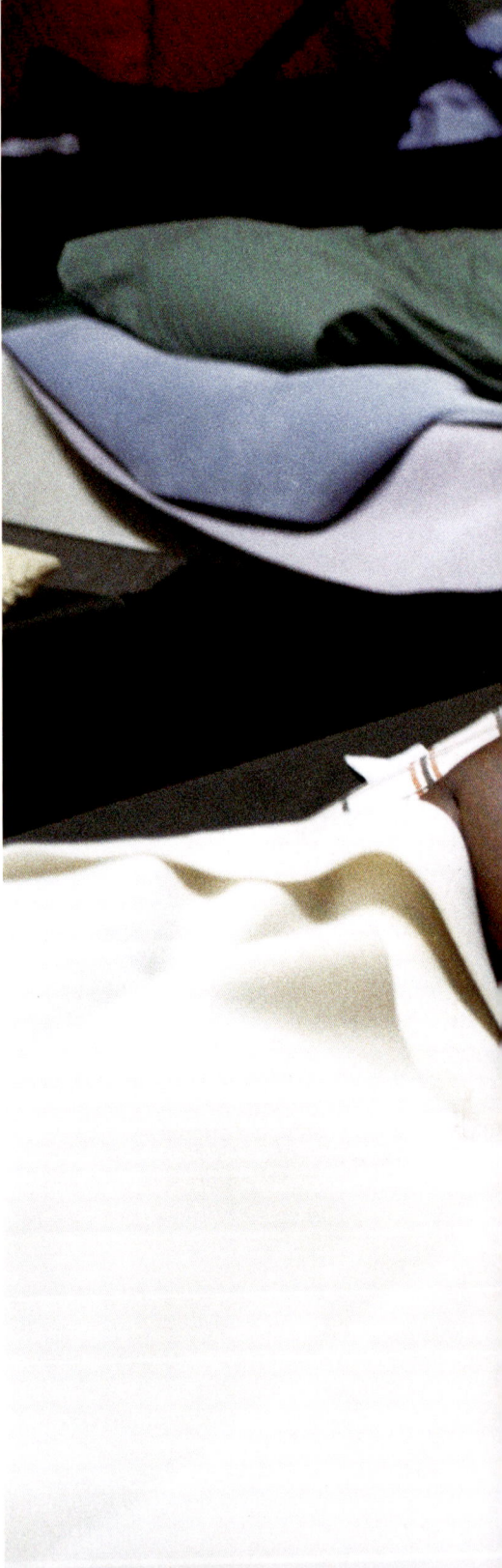

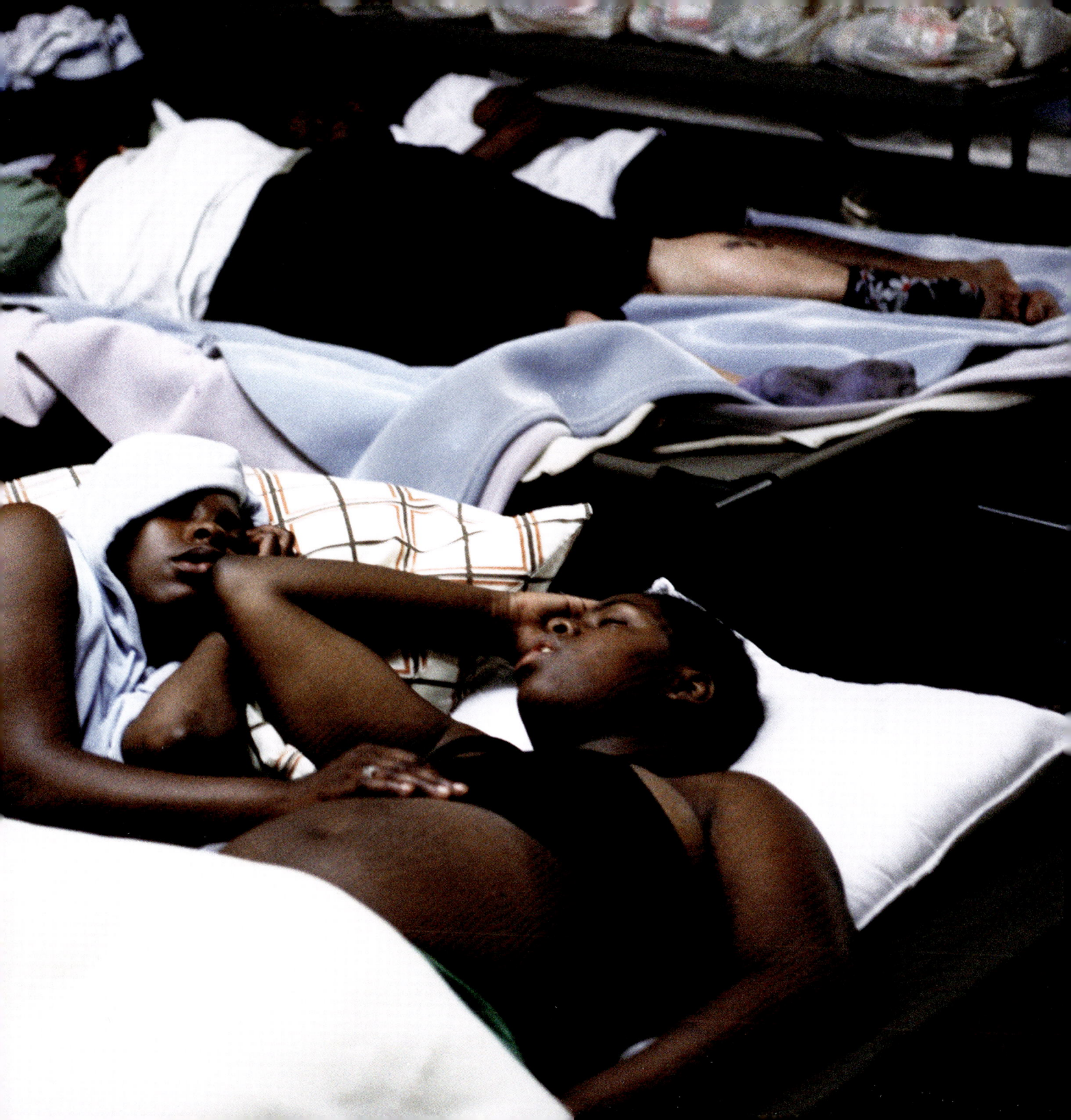

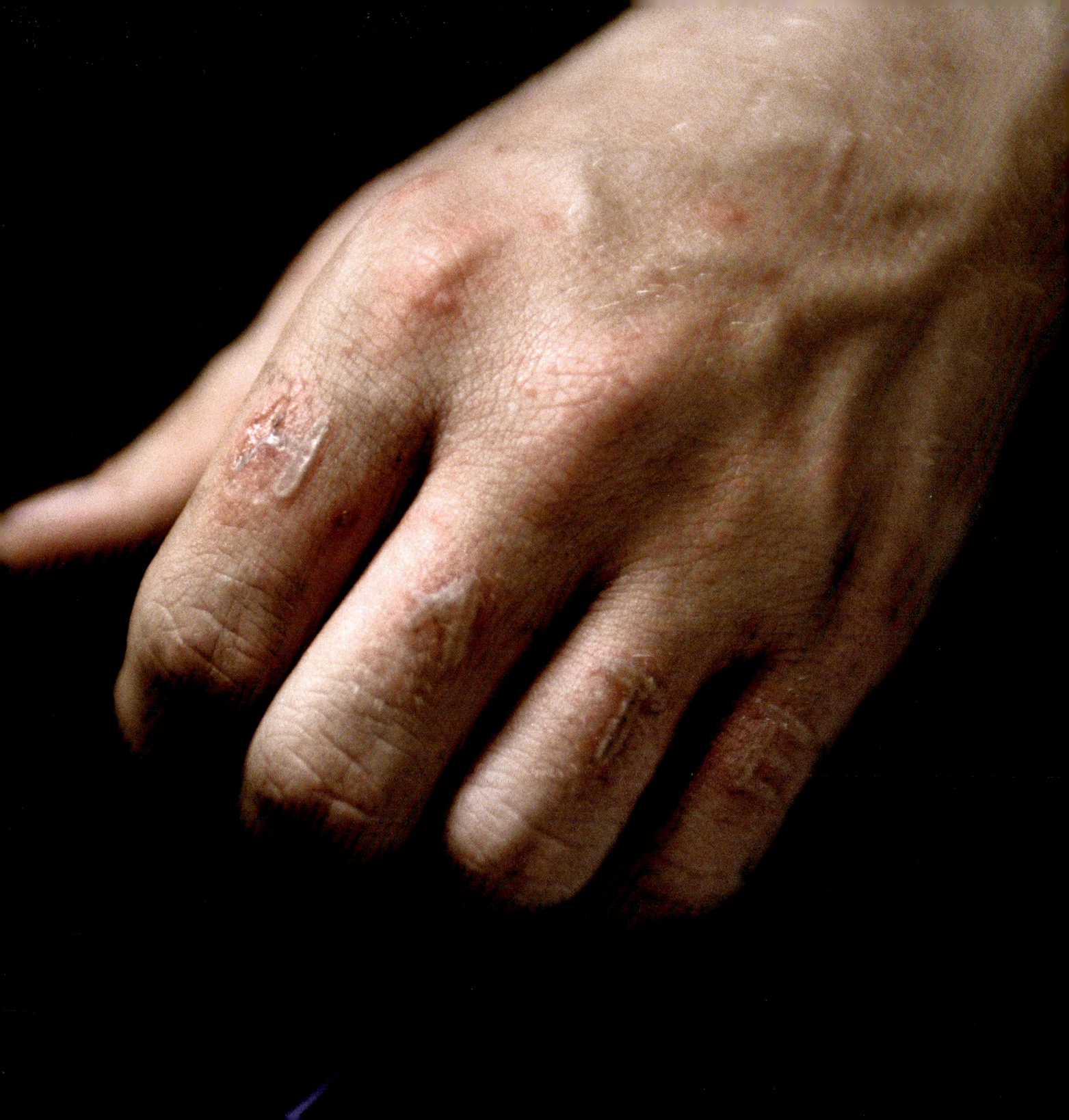

Sometimes, the lives of the young people who stay at the shelter or live on the streets can become so overwhelming that suicide seems the only way out. Countless clients have contemplated suicide while staying at Sylvia's, but fewer have attempted. In most cases, the staff can see the signs and steer them towards help. Sometimes, it isn't until the final cry for help that the staff have to step in and save a life. A suicide attempt might also be an unconscious act, taking the form of a drug or alcohol overdose. In either case, there are no guarantees. Occasionally, the attempt, conscious or not, will be successful. Sylvia's has lost two former clients, but saved countless others. There's no way to know how many other lives will hang in the balance within the shelter's walls.

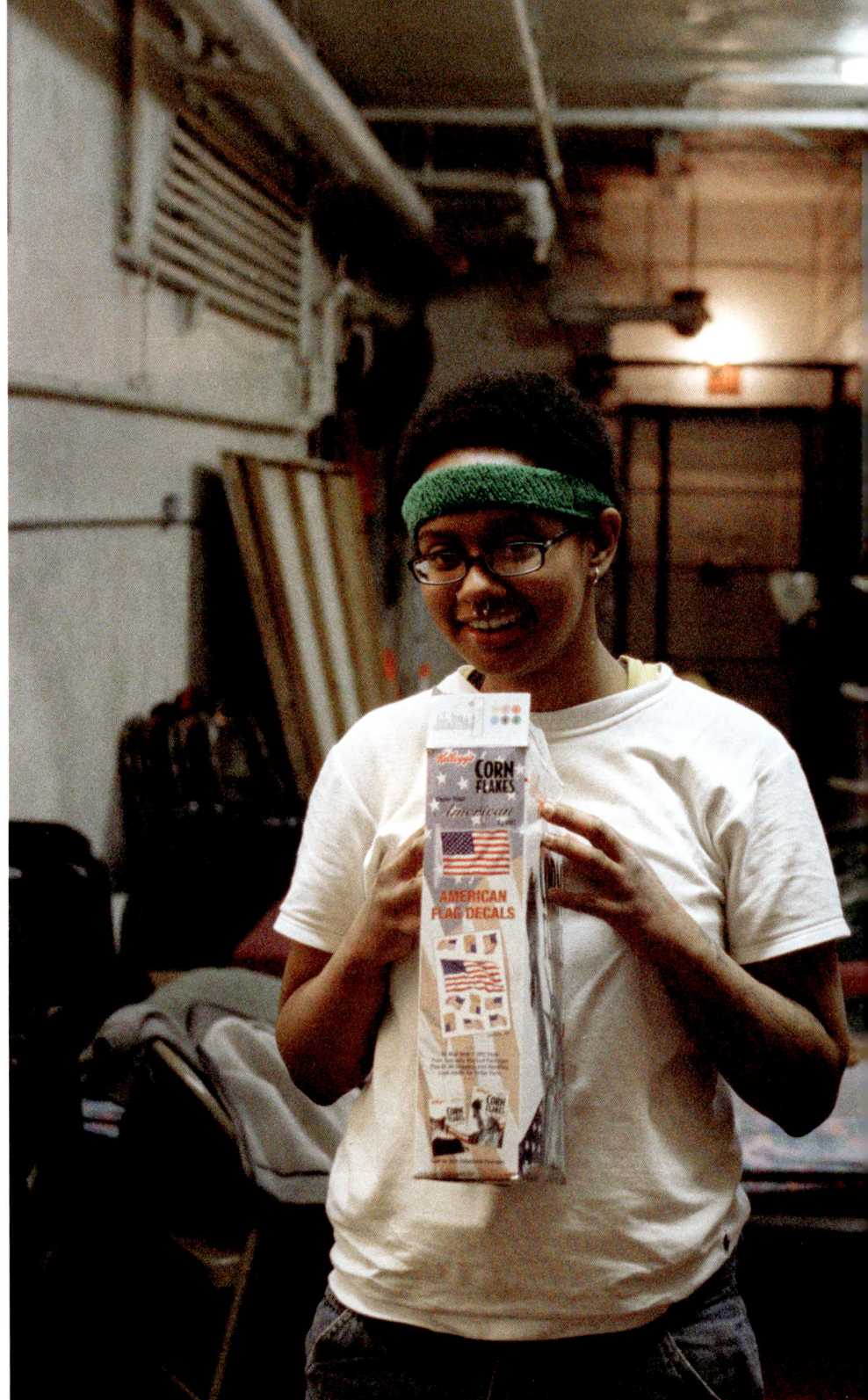

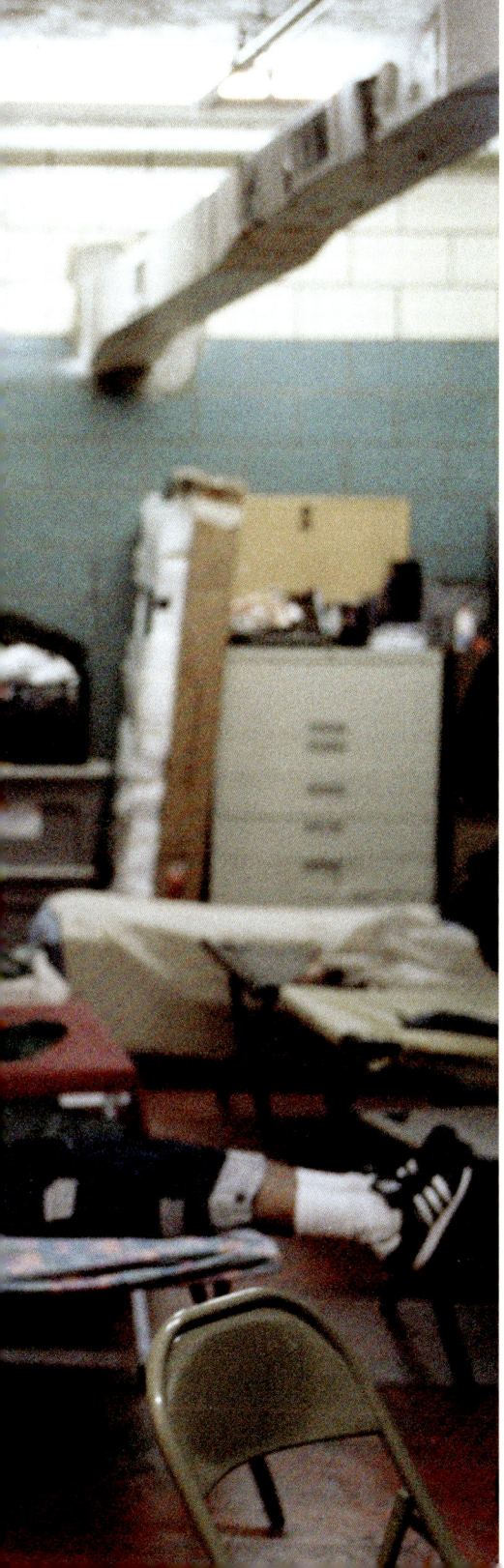

# Fact

Each year approximately 5,000 homeless and runaway youth die from assault, illness and suicide.

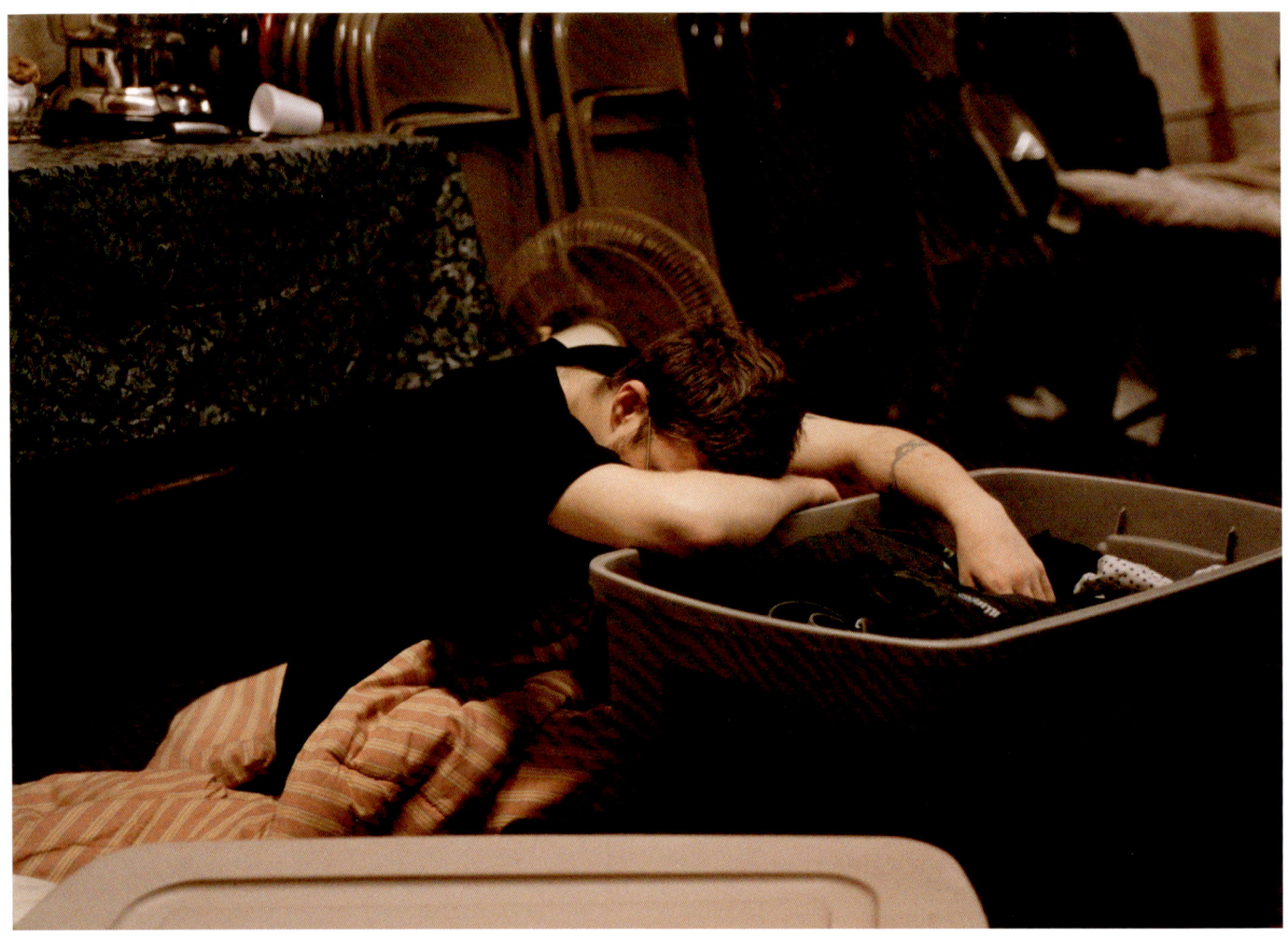

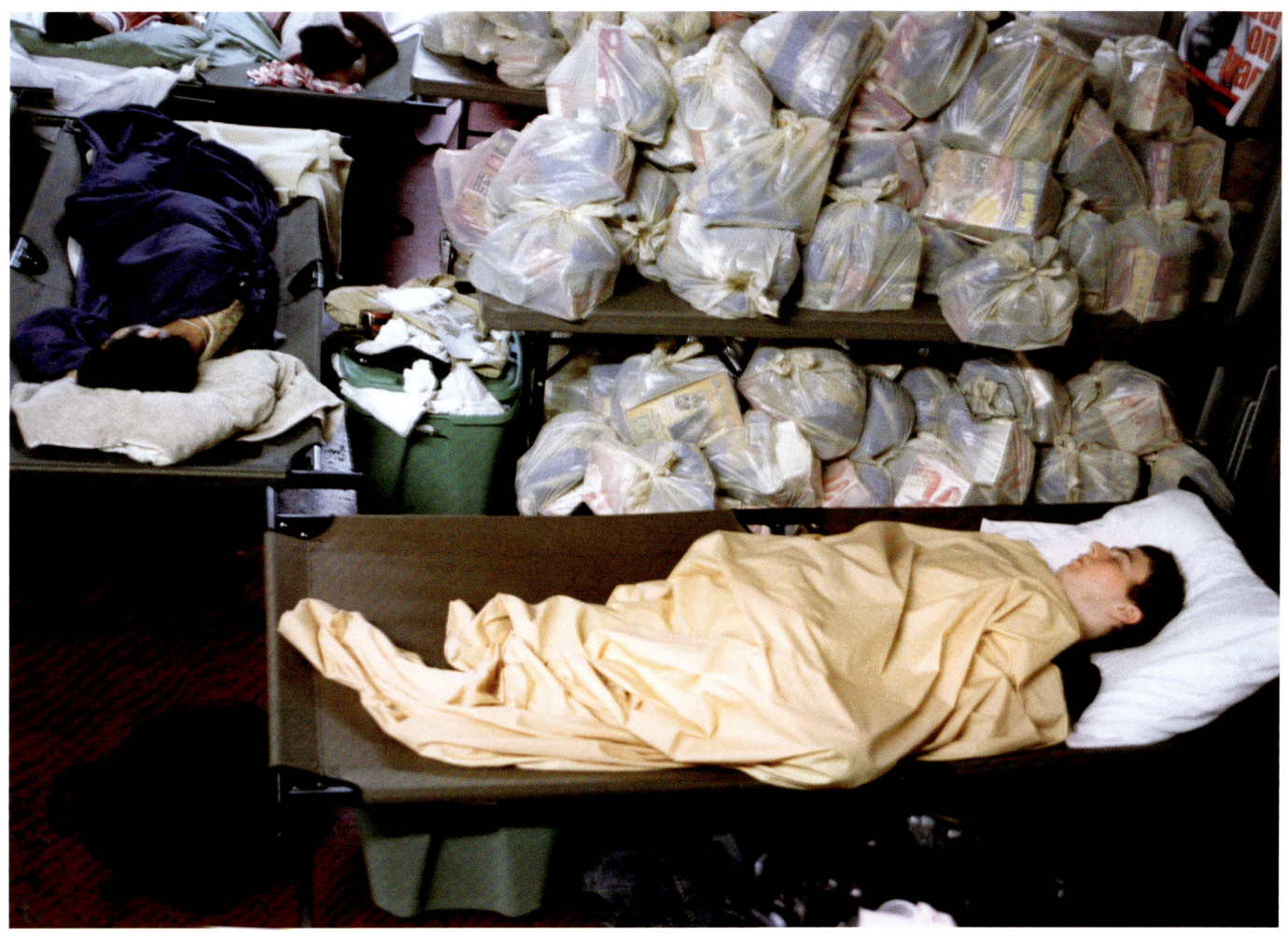

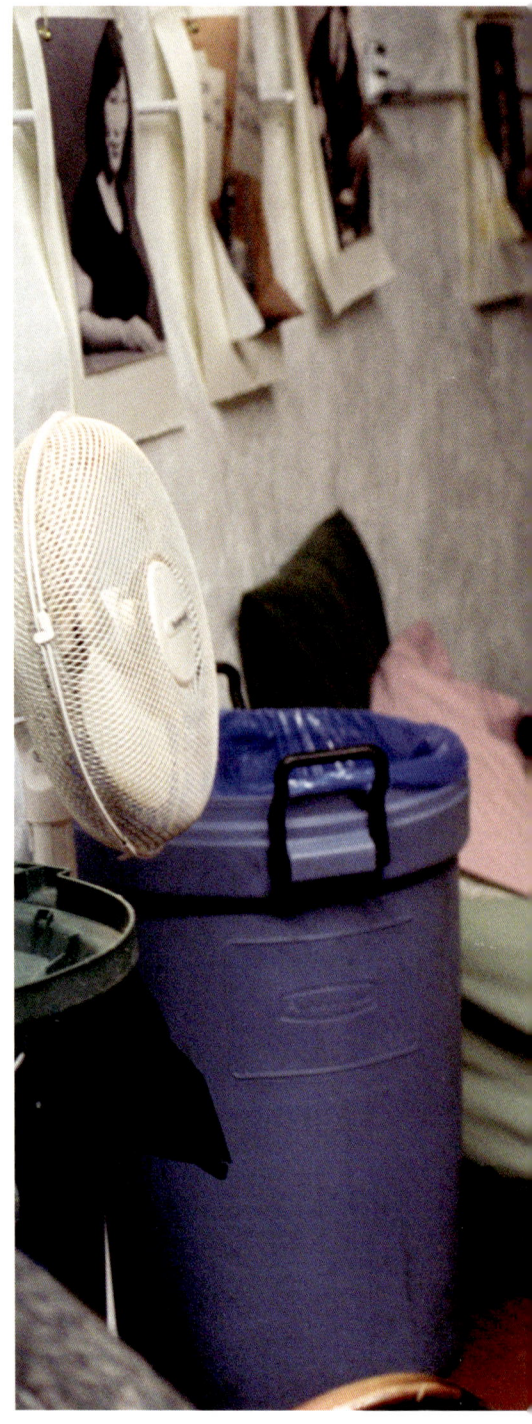

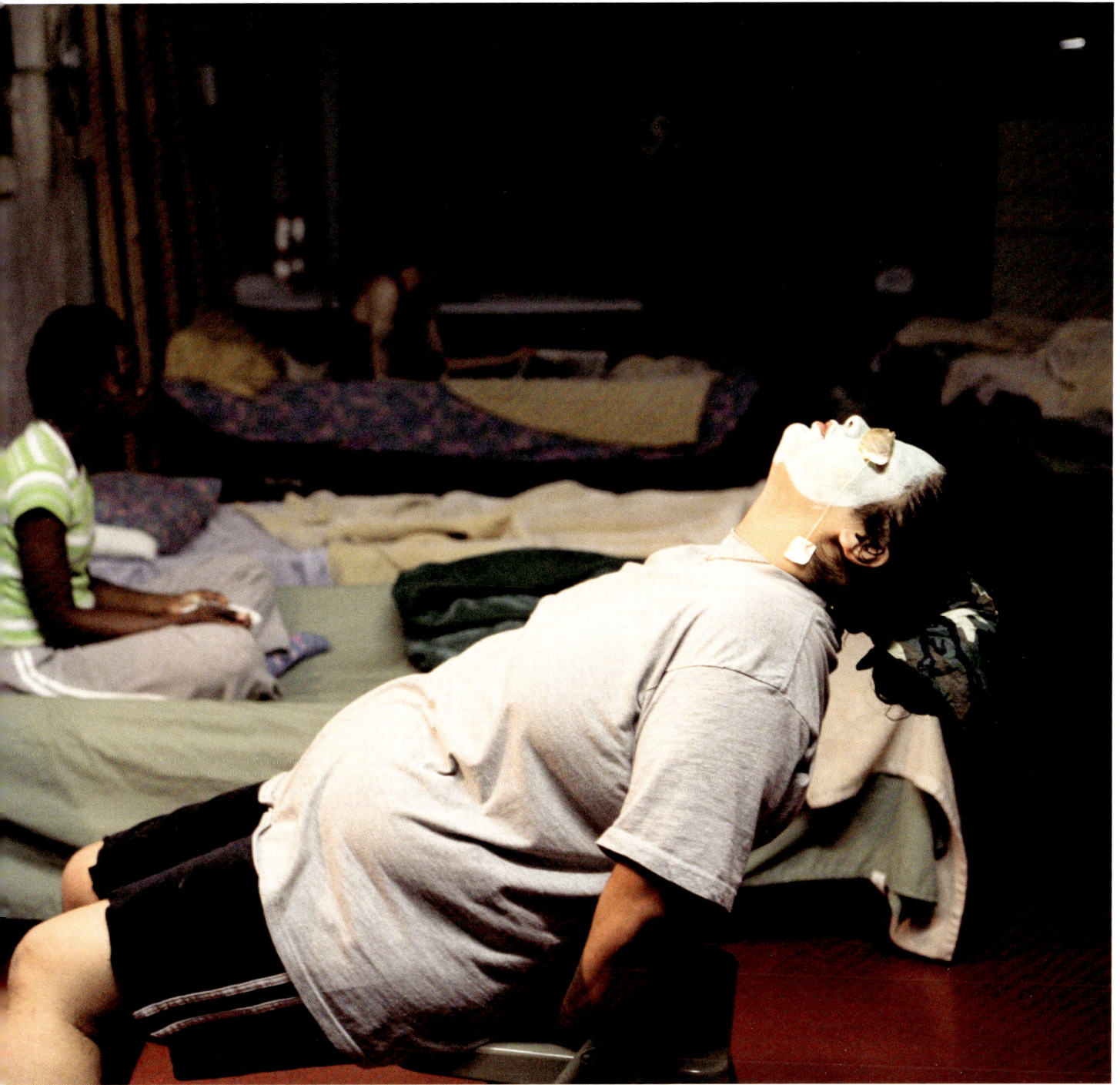

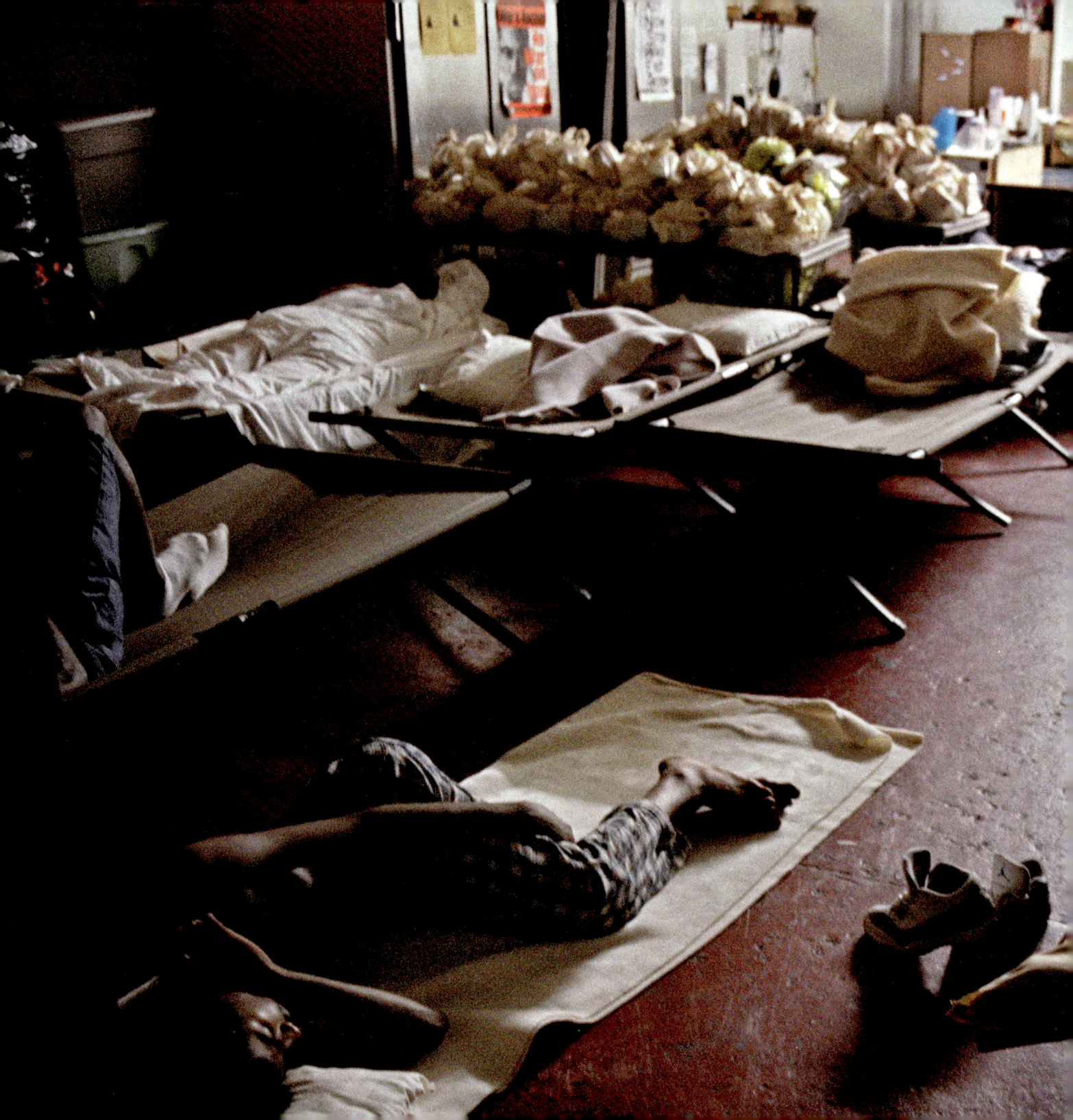

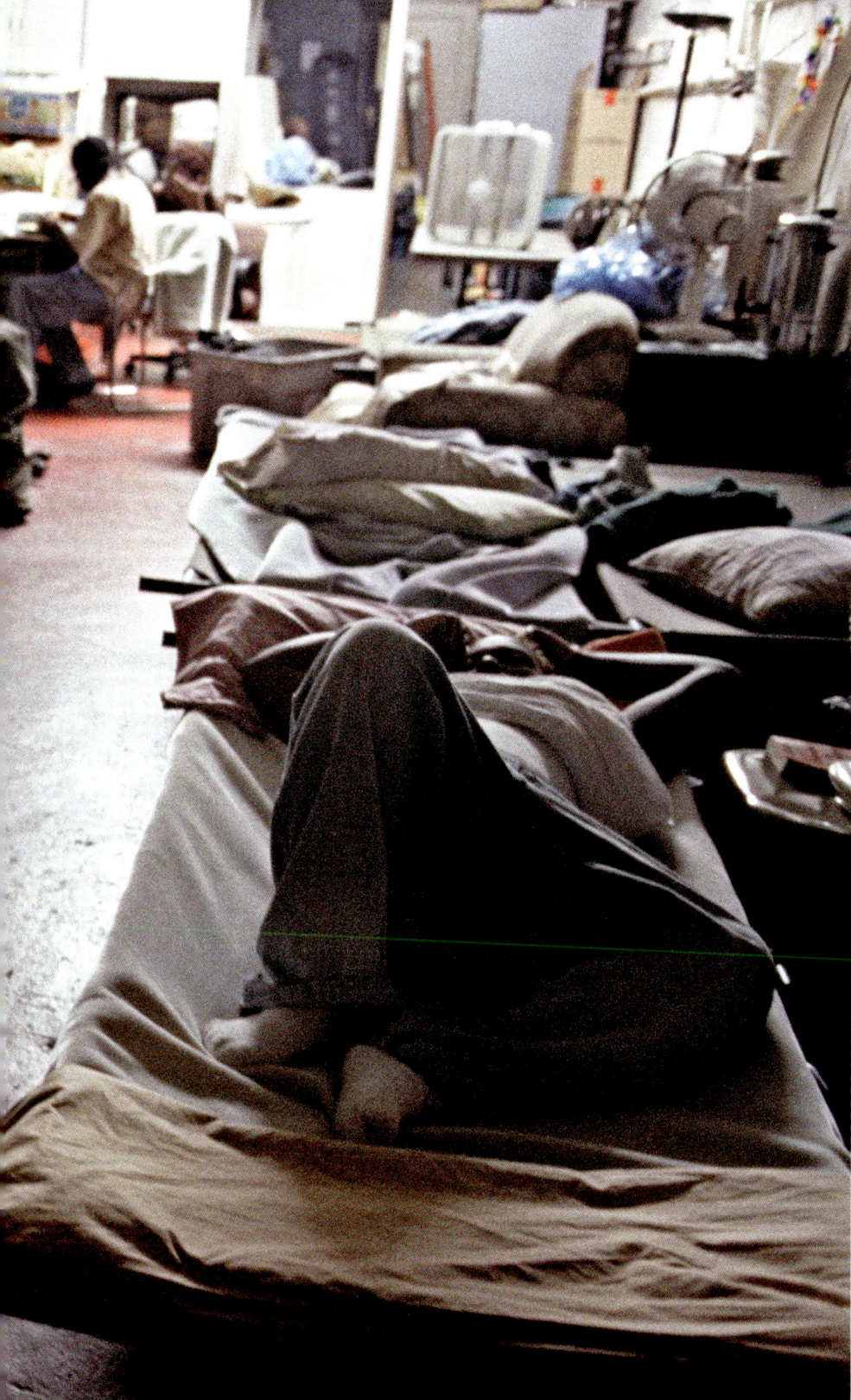

Having to wake up was the bad part about Sylvia's. Waking up and there's snow outside to your ankles and neck. That was the bad part about Sylvia's: trying to figure out where to go at 7:45 in the morning, it's snowing and you don't have metrocards. Charlene

# Blackout

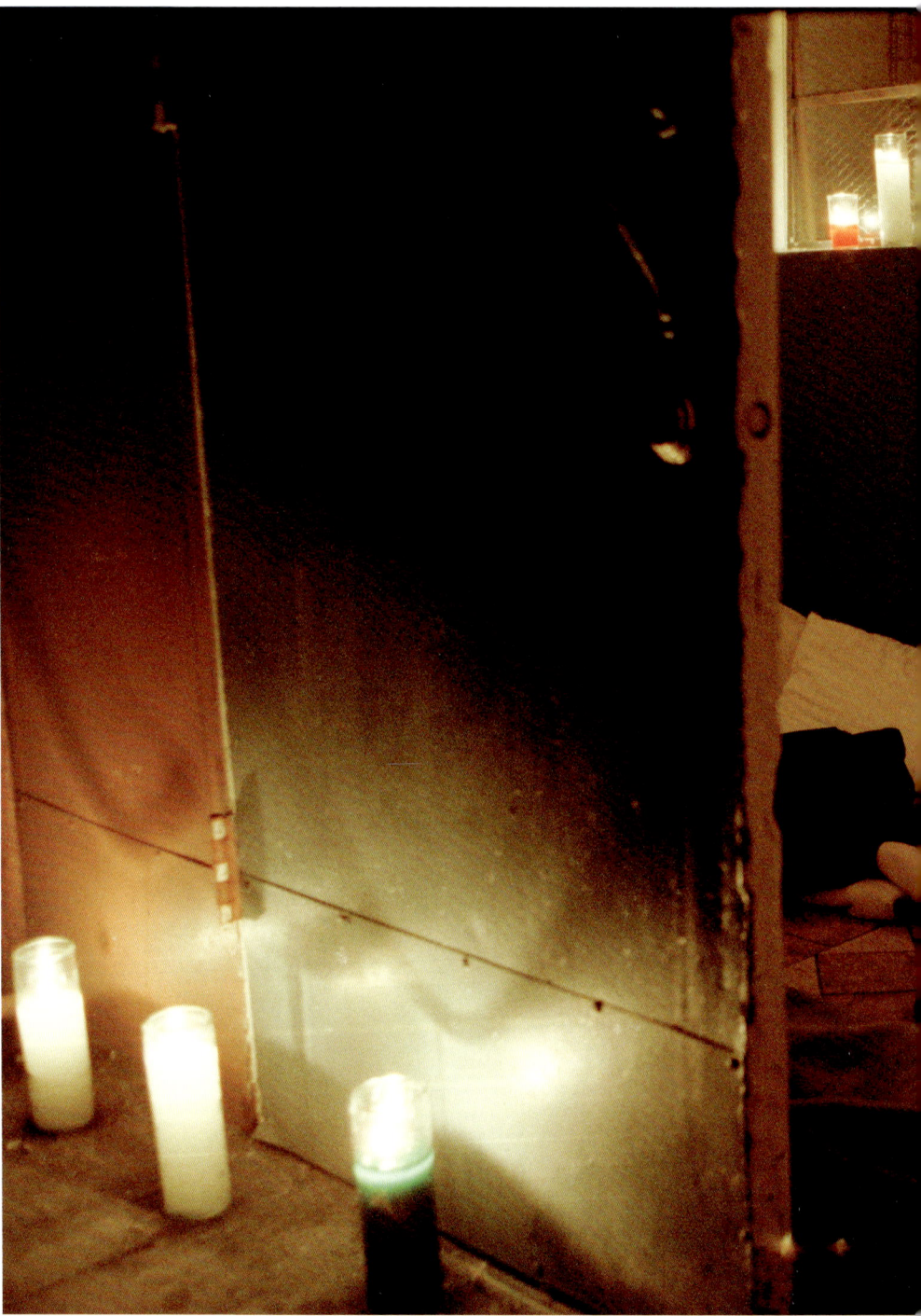

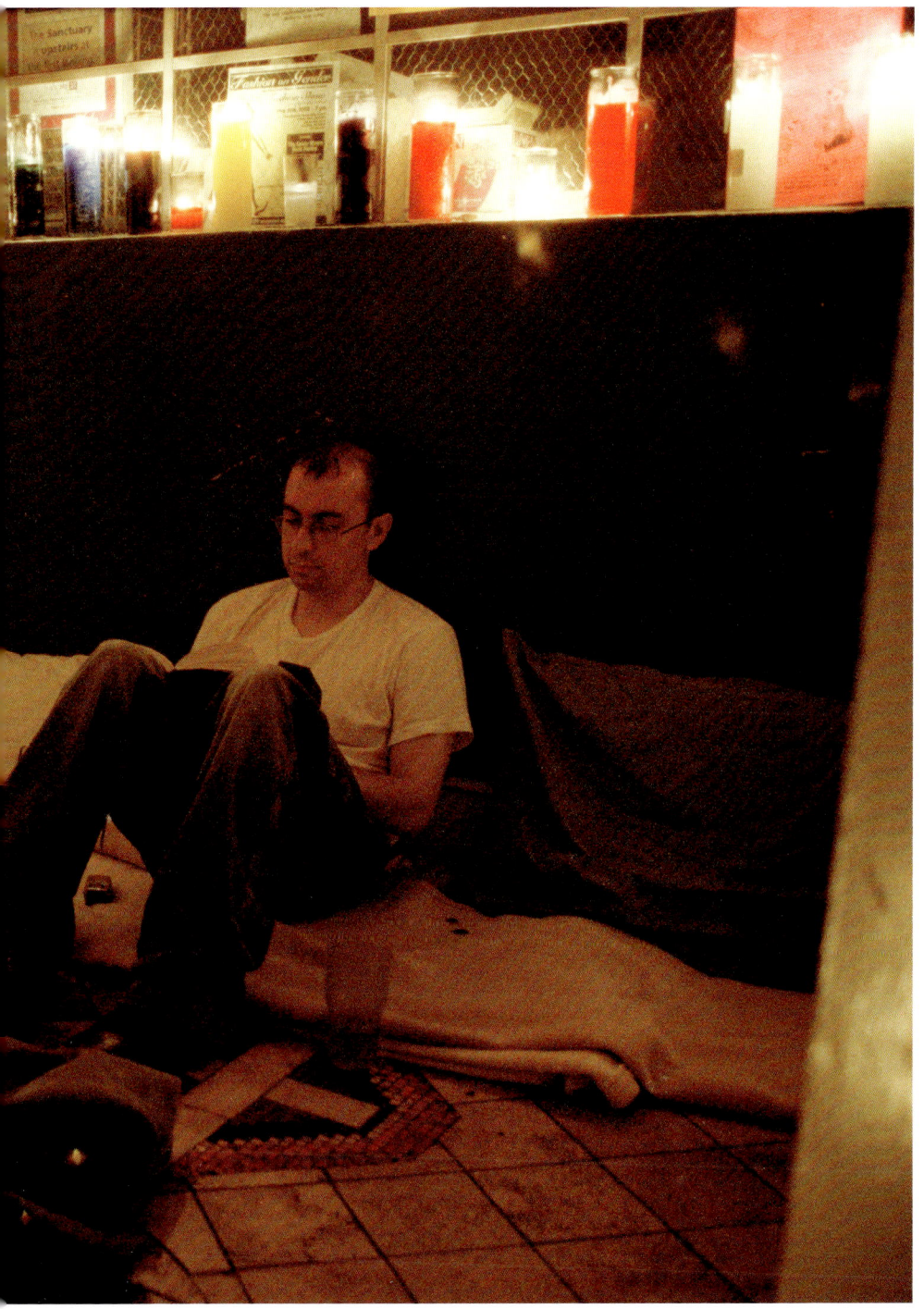

At 4:10 pm on August 14, 2003 New York City shut down as a massive power outage plagued areas in the northeast. As New Yorkers flooded the streets and sidewalks of the city to find a way back to their homes, the residents of Sylvia's Place struggled to reach the shelter doors before the blackness blanketed the streets.

When the youth found their way home, rows of candles lit the entrance to the shelter. Awaiting their arrival, counselors had prepared macaroni and cheese on the gas stove and set out pillows and blankets for the youth. There was no way to navigate around the pitch-black space beyond the black gate at the shelter's entrance, so the counselors held everyone in the front lobby until they could prepare the inside with enough candles to light a path. Temperatures were very high that night. The combination of extreme heat and darkness put everyone on edge. Two residents threatened a counselor, going so far as to bring two police officers to the shelter to cause a scene. The stress of the evening had become too much for them, just as it had cradled the other residents on the darkest night in Sylvia's short history, shielding them from a city temporarily void of light.

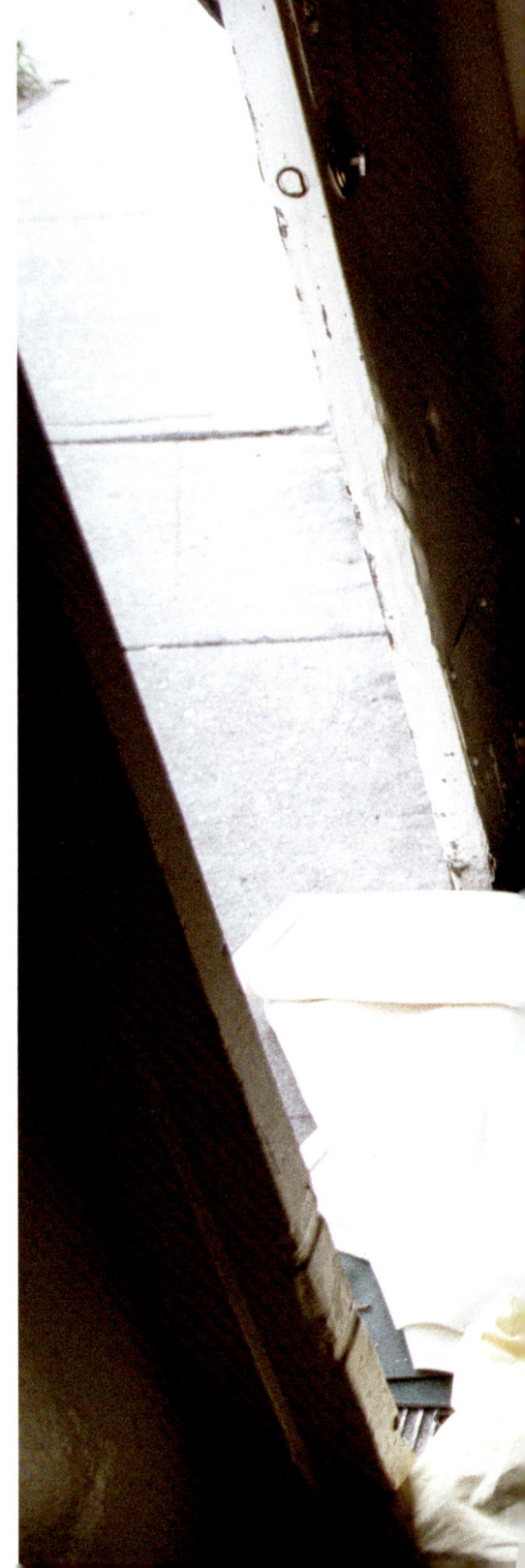

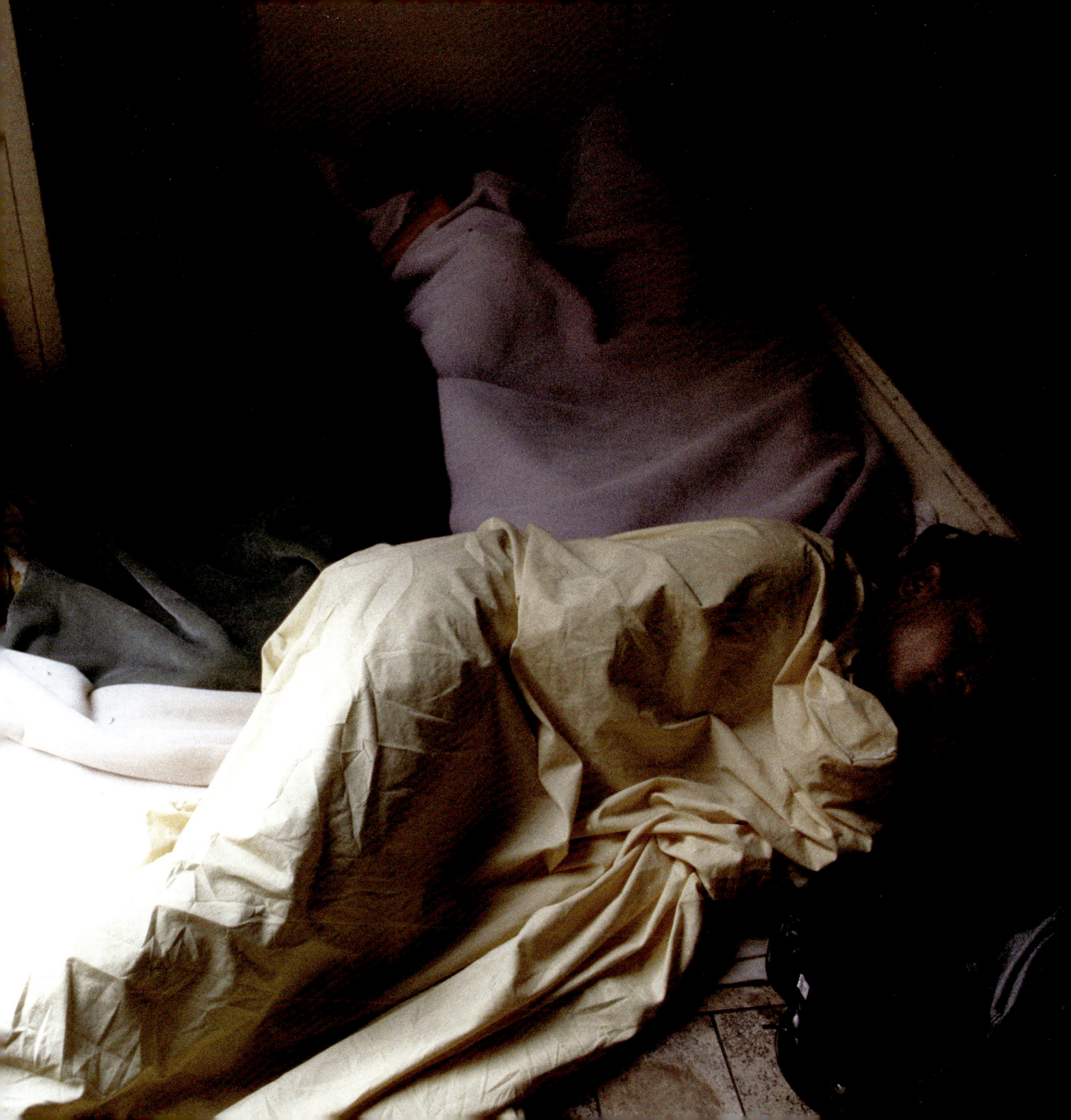

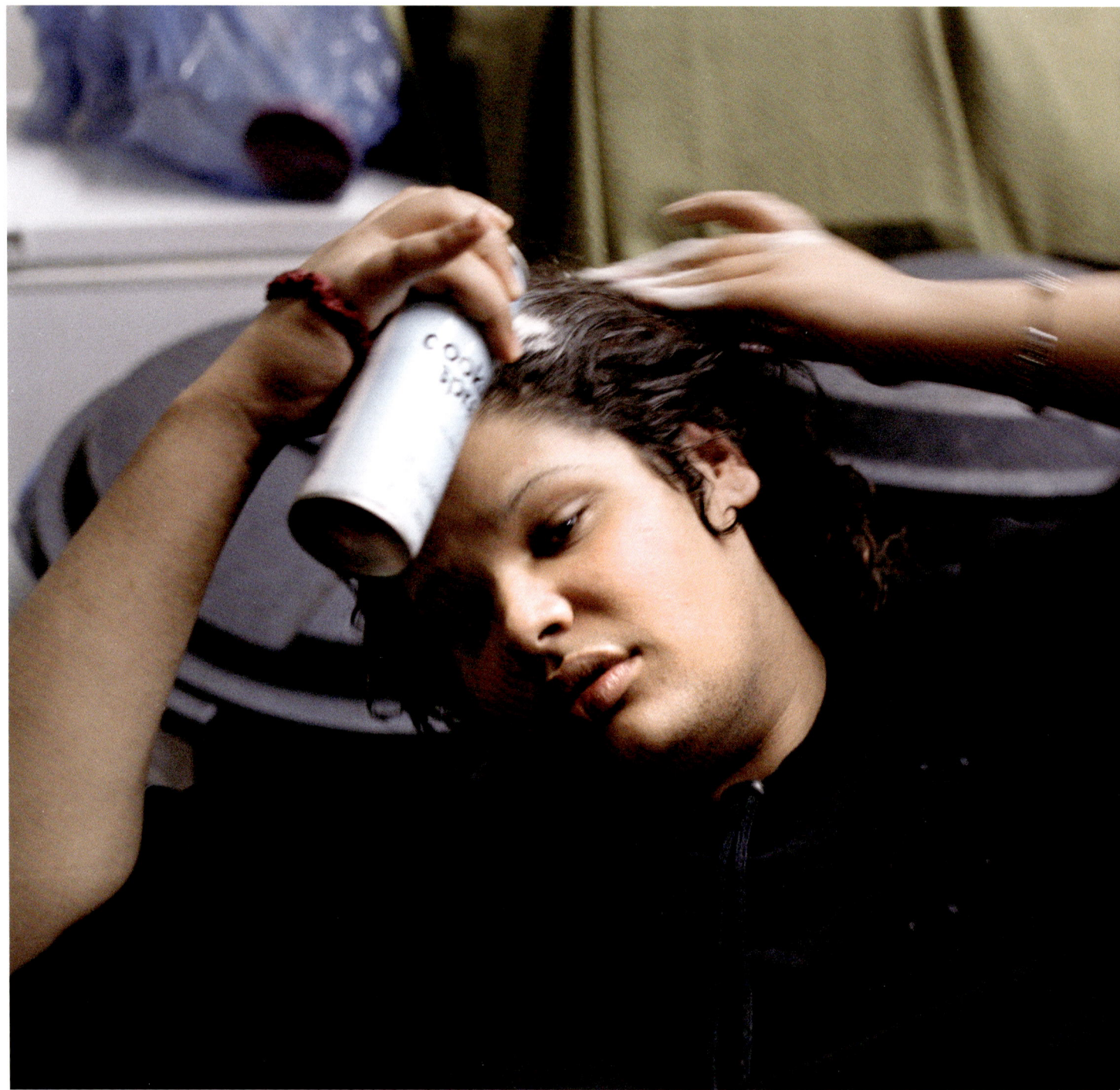

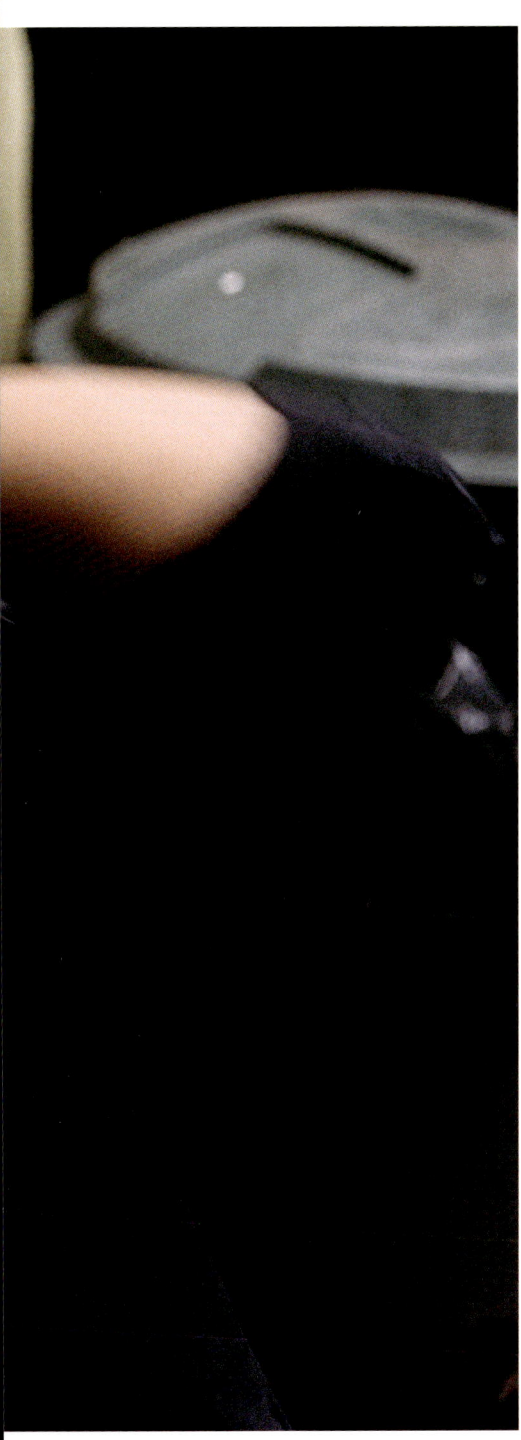

# Fact

A study found that 78% of LGBTQ youth in NYC were removed or ran away from foster care placements because the placements were either un-welcoming or hostile toward their sexual orientation or gender identity.

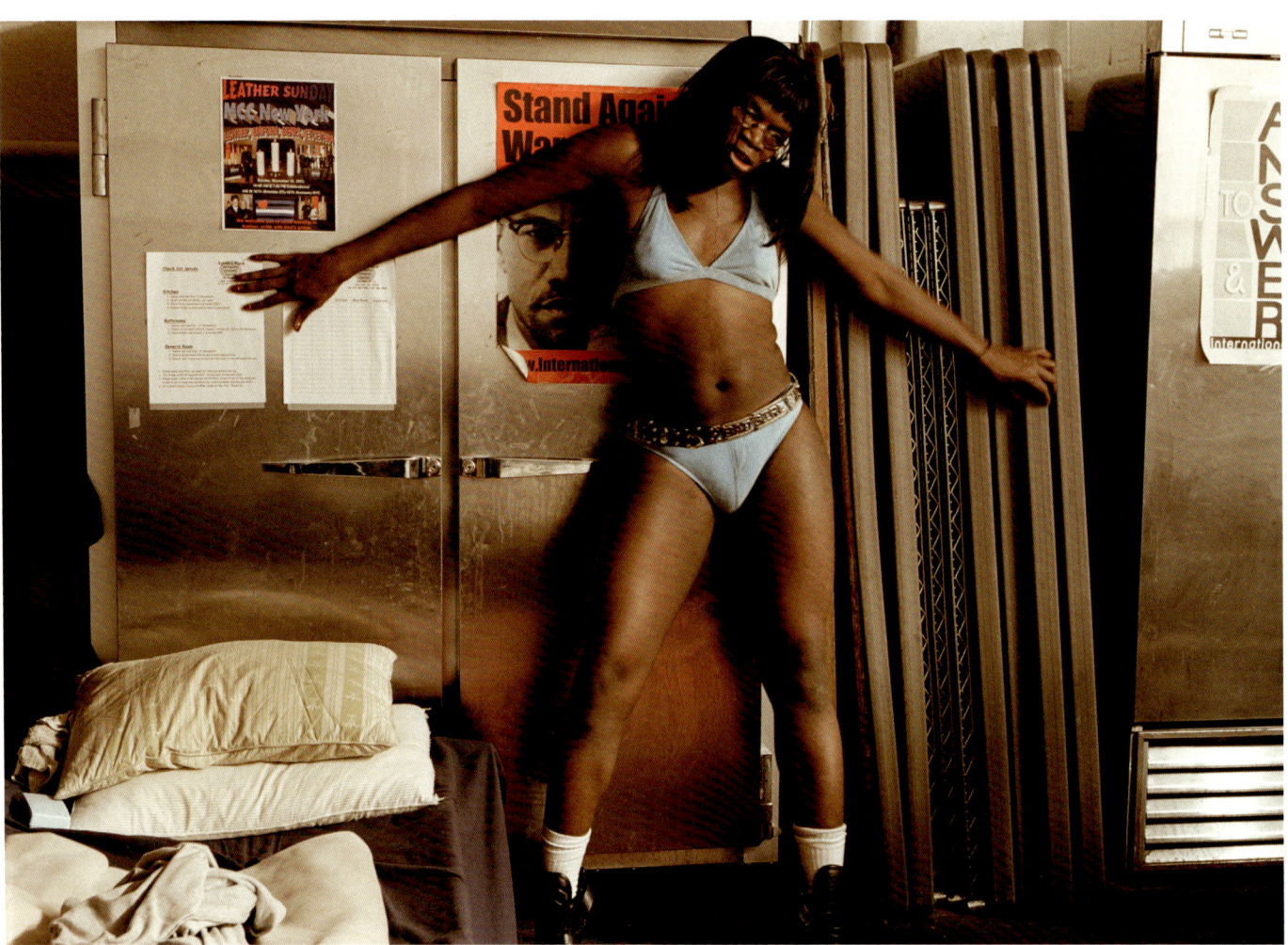

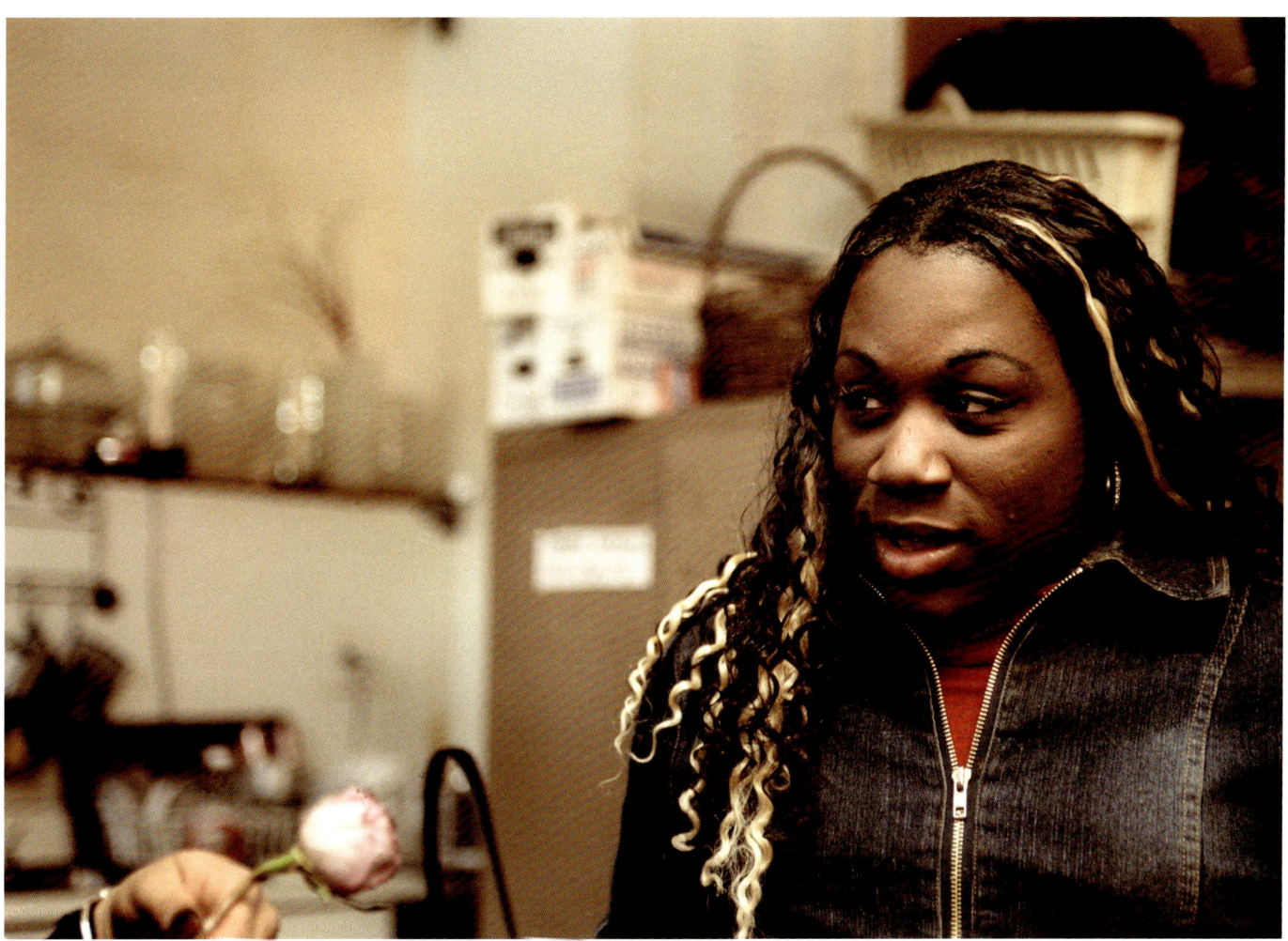

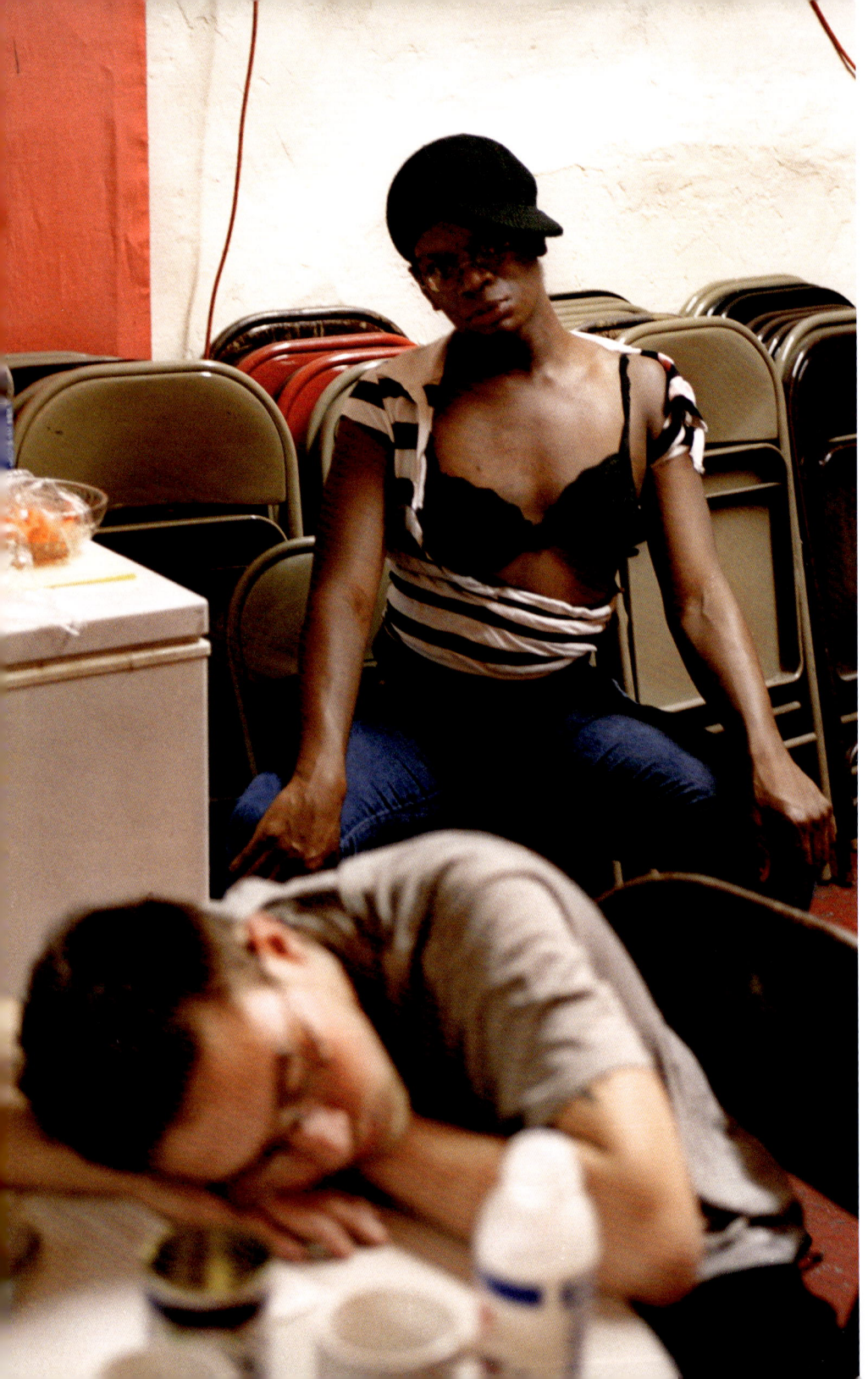

You feel like nobody wants you. Nobody cares, nobody wants you. Nobody's respectful. It's a lot to deal with.

Actually I've been doing drugs for a long time. I've been doing drugs for 12, no, 11 years now. When I first started doing drugs, I could control it. But then I started using drugs as an escape. Everyday I had to smoke something or pop something. It was an every day thing for me. I would wake up in the morning and have four 40's, then I'd have hard liquor. I was drinking and popping and partying. I've done heroin, I've done ecstasy, I've done acid, I've done them all. But drinking was my main drug of choice. It got to a point where I realized that no matter where you go, no matter what you do, people are not going to like you. And I came to the realization that people are just assholes. They don't care about you.

They're just one-minded people. Everybody's out for themselves. When I learned that, I became a real mega-bitch.

There was a point when it was just too much. When I saw one of my boyfriends and he was up on the roof and wanted to commit suicide, that was an all-time low. He didn't commit suicide, but I realized I'm not getting anywhere. I'm running around, smelling like all kinds of liquor, all kinds of this, all kinds of that. I just didn't like where I was.

I felt like I was never going to go nowhere. I was trapped being homeless. Everybody has their problems and their moments. I was having my moment. I just wanted to get rid of everything. I wanted to let it all go. I was going to slit my wrists. But, you know, God was there for me.

Charlene

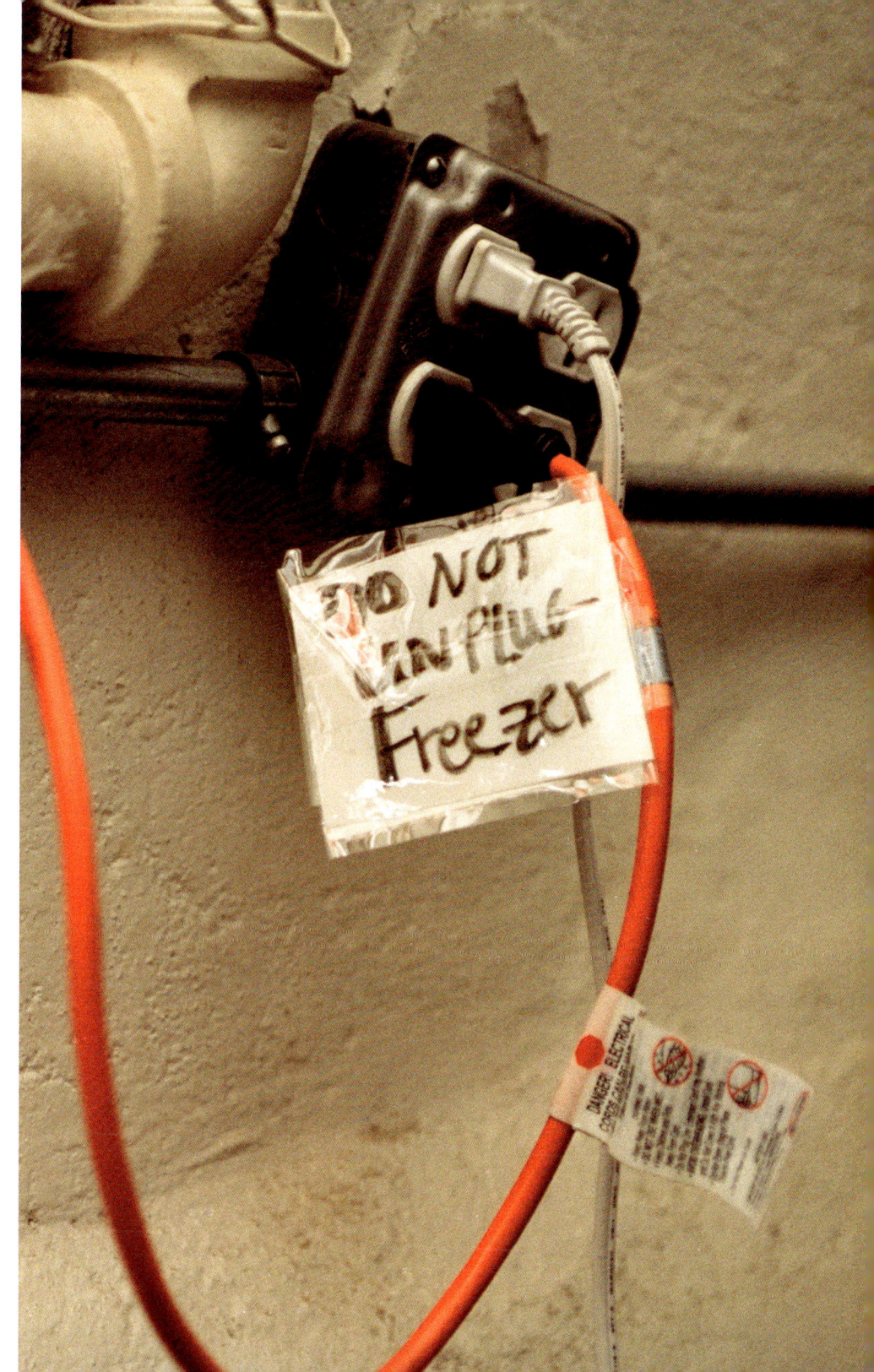

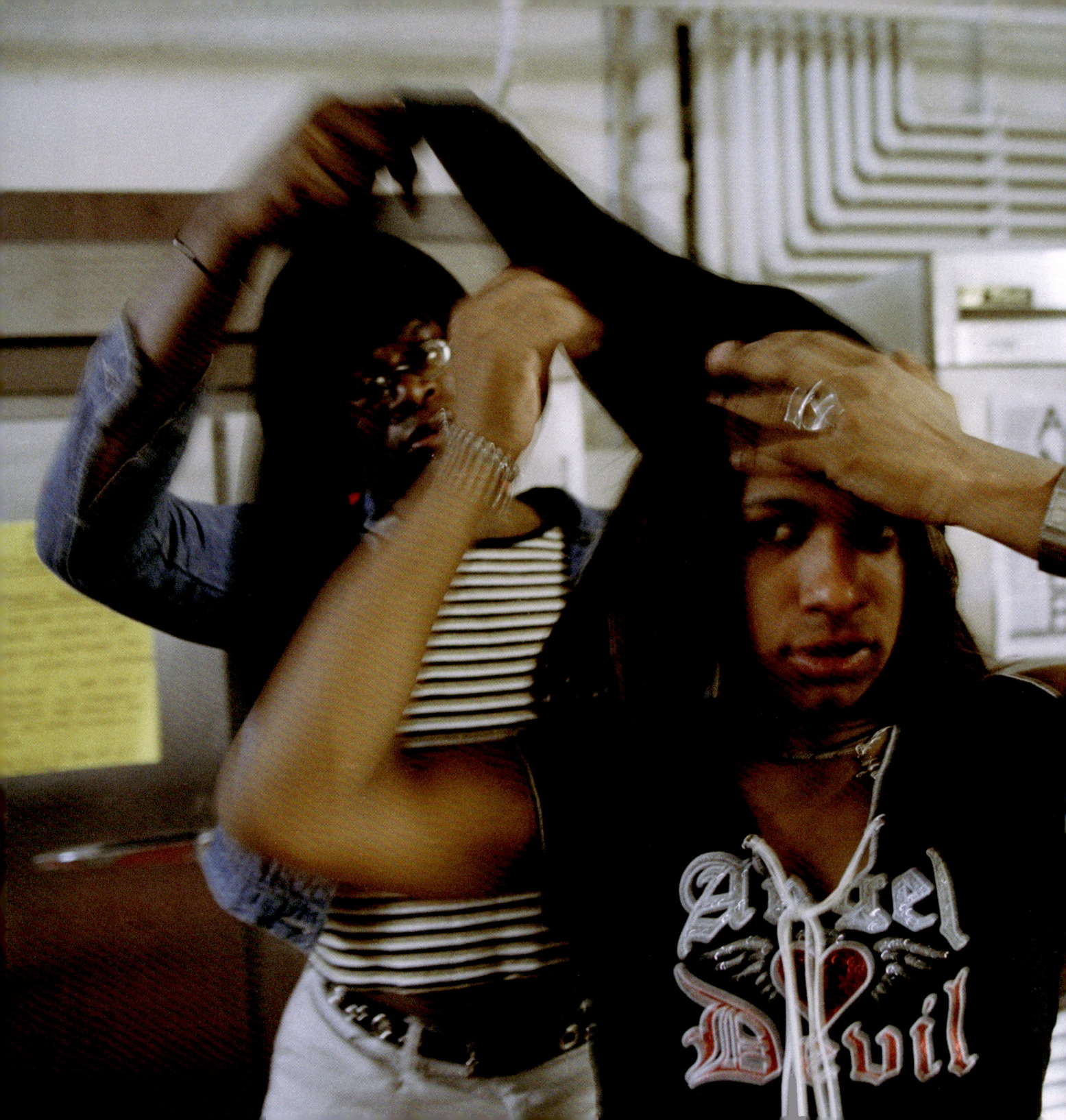

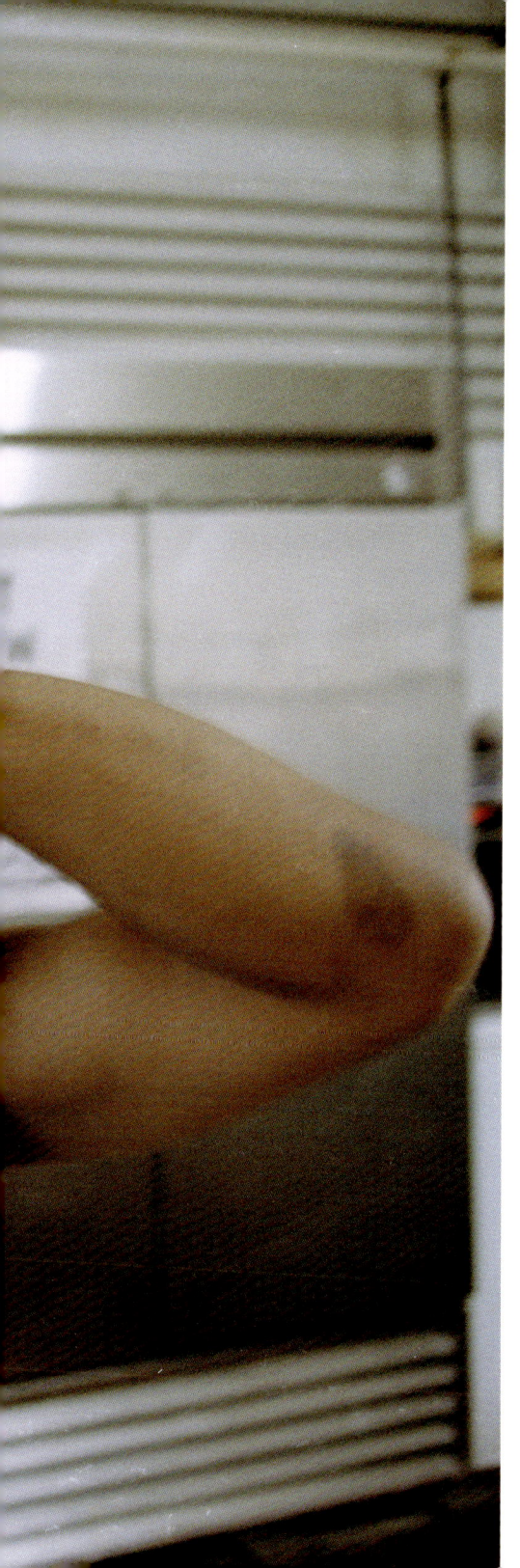

# Fact

About 1/3 of transgender people earn $10,000 per year or less. 29% have no employment.

For Charlene, surviving on the streets included being in and out of jail. Each time it was either for shoplifting or prostitution. She's been in jail as many as 15 times. It didn't really bother her though. For Charlene, this was part of the life.

*There were times when, if I didn't have no money, I would do a little shoplifting. I'm not proud of that, but you gotta do what you gotta do. There was times I would take deodorant, lip gloss, underwear, clothes, stuff like that. There was this one time I tried to take a CD player, but that didn't go so well. I got caught, I went to jail and then I got back out the next day. And then I was trying to steal CDs and shit that I did not need. I'd always get caught.*

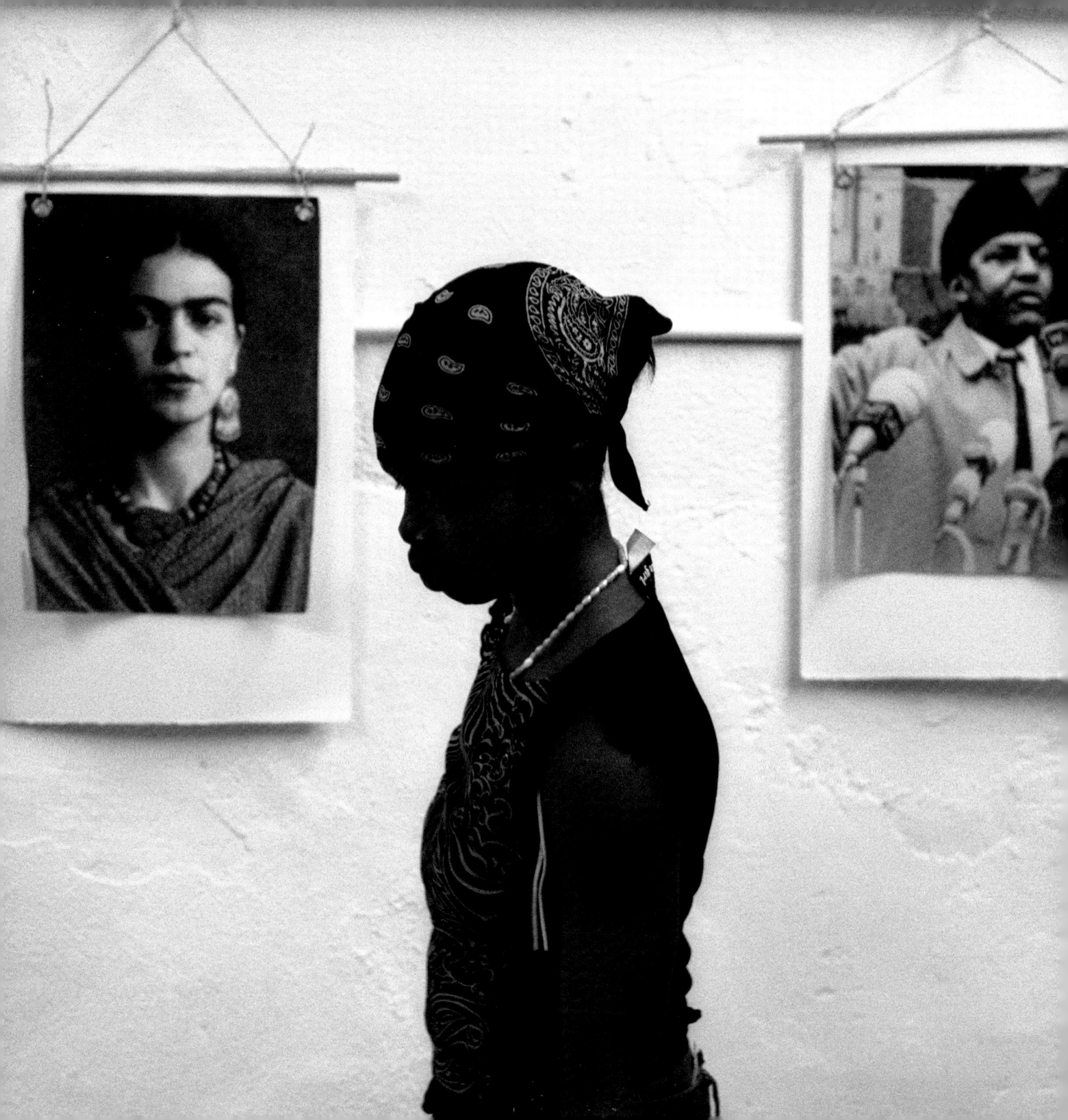

# Toilet Water

With a group of residents waiting to get into the space, Lucky arrived to open the shelter doors. The sounds of leaking water greeted him upon opening the first door and when he stepped into the foyer, water was raining down on him from the ceiling. The sounds of falling water were stronger from behind the fire door leading into the main shelter space. Opening the fire door revealed a scene of water pouring from the ceiling, flooding the floor beneath it. Lucky called Rev. Pat, and then the plumber, with the bad news. The water was brown and dirty, and the residents had to walk through it to get into the space. Waiting for help, Lucky put down baking pans to collect the filthy water. The plumber arrived followed by Rev. Pat, and they discovered that the brown rainstorm originated from a stopped up toilet on the third floor, flooding the sanctuary on the second floor, and finally filling the shelter. The toilet was fixed, and then Lucky, Rev. Pat and the plumber found mops and cleaned up the space for the next several hours. The residents reluctantly looked on from a distance, slightly disgusted that toilet water was raining in their shelter.

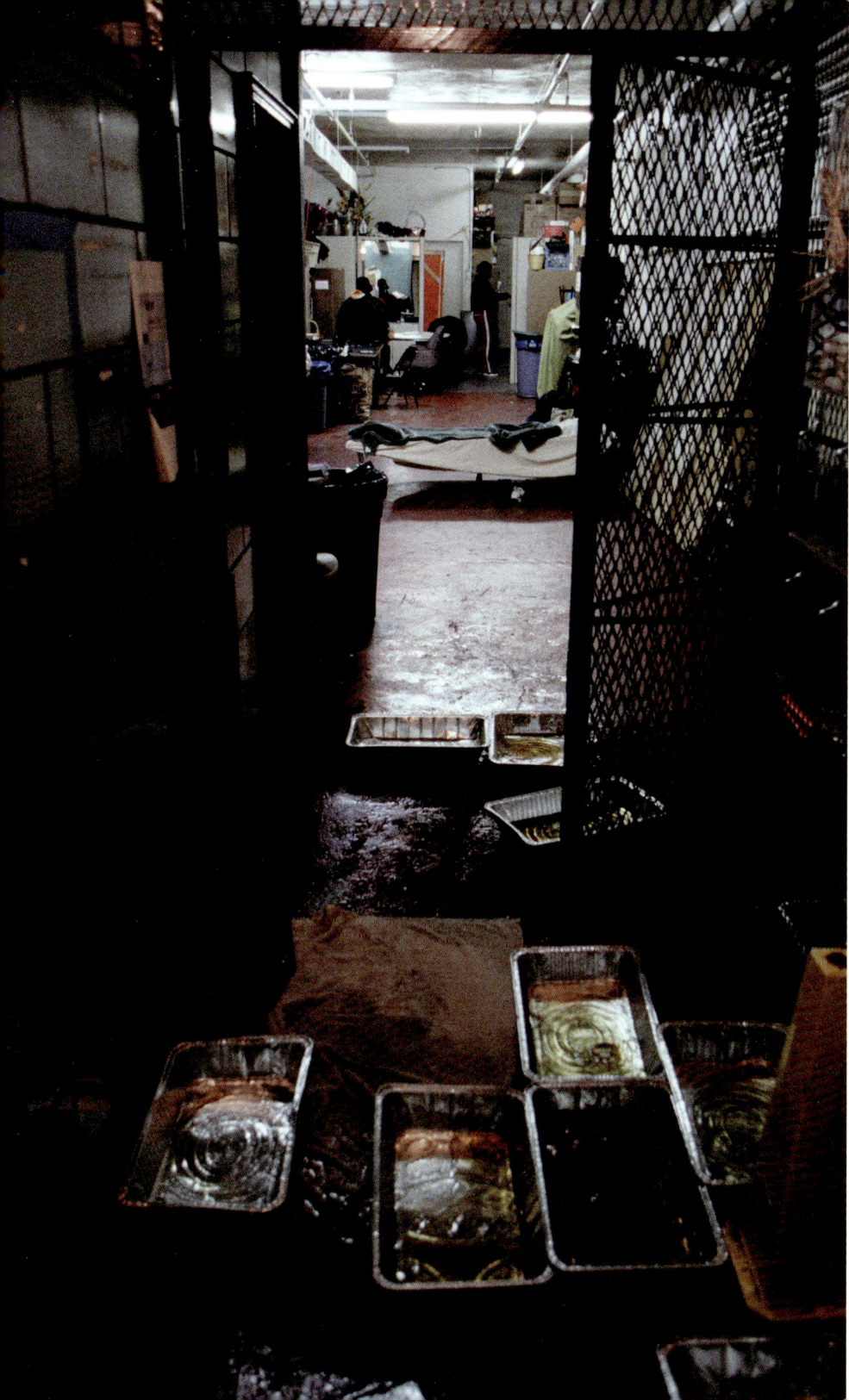

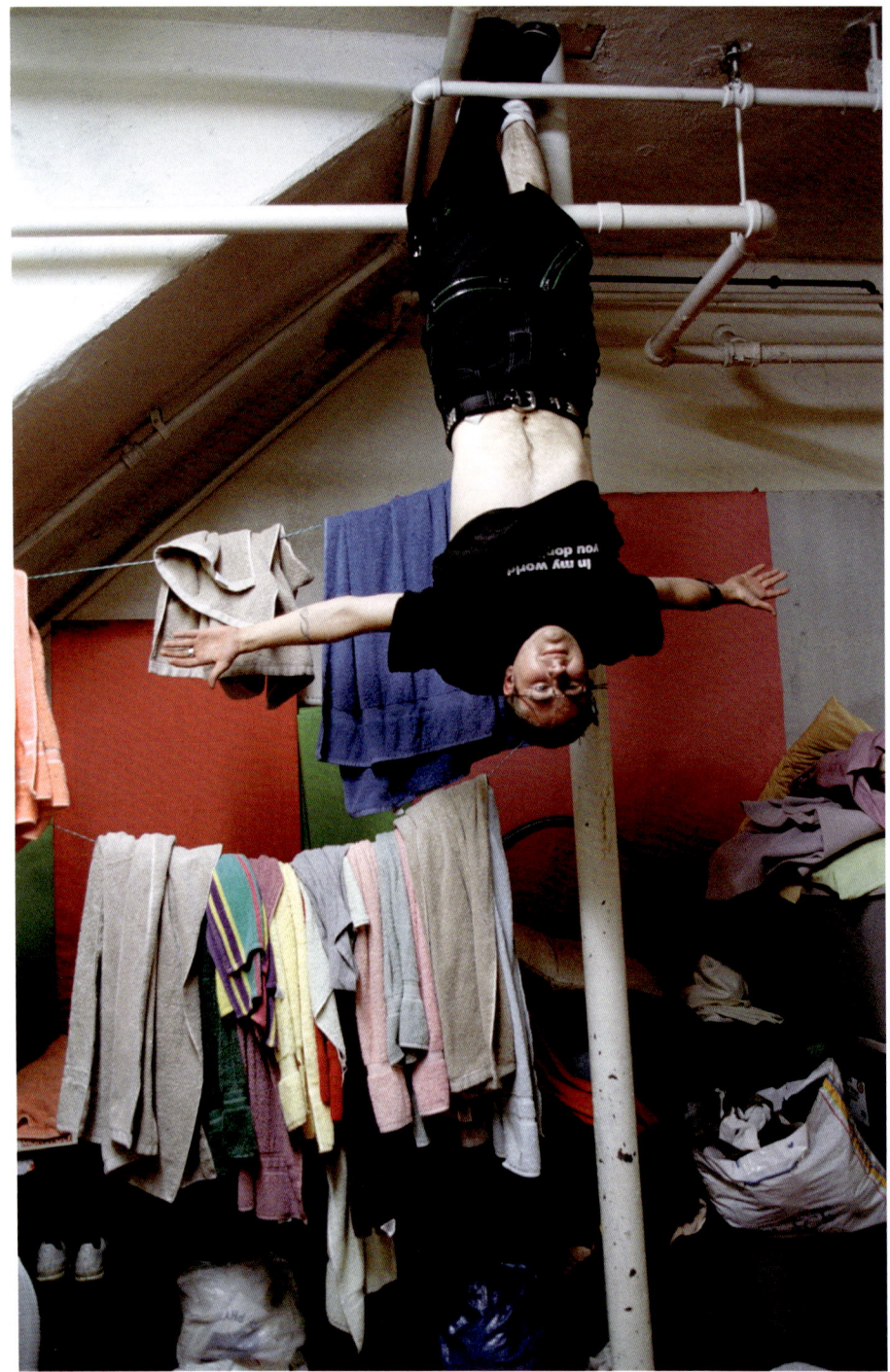

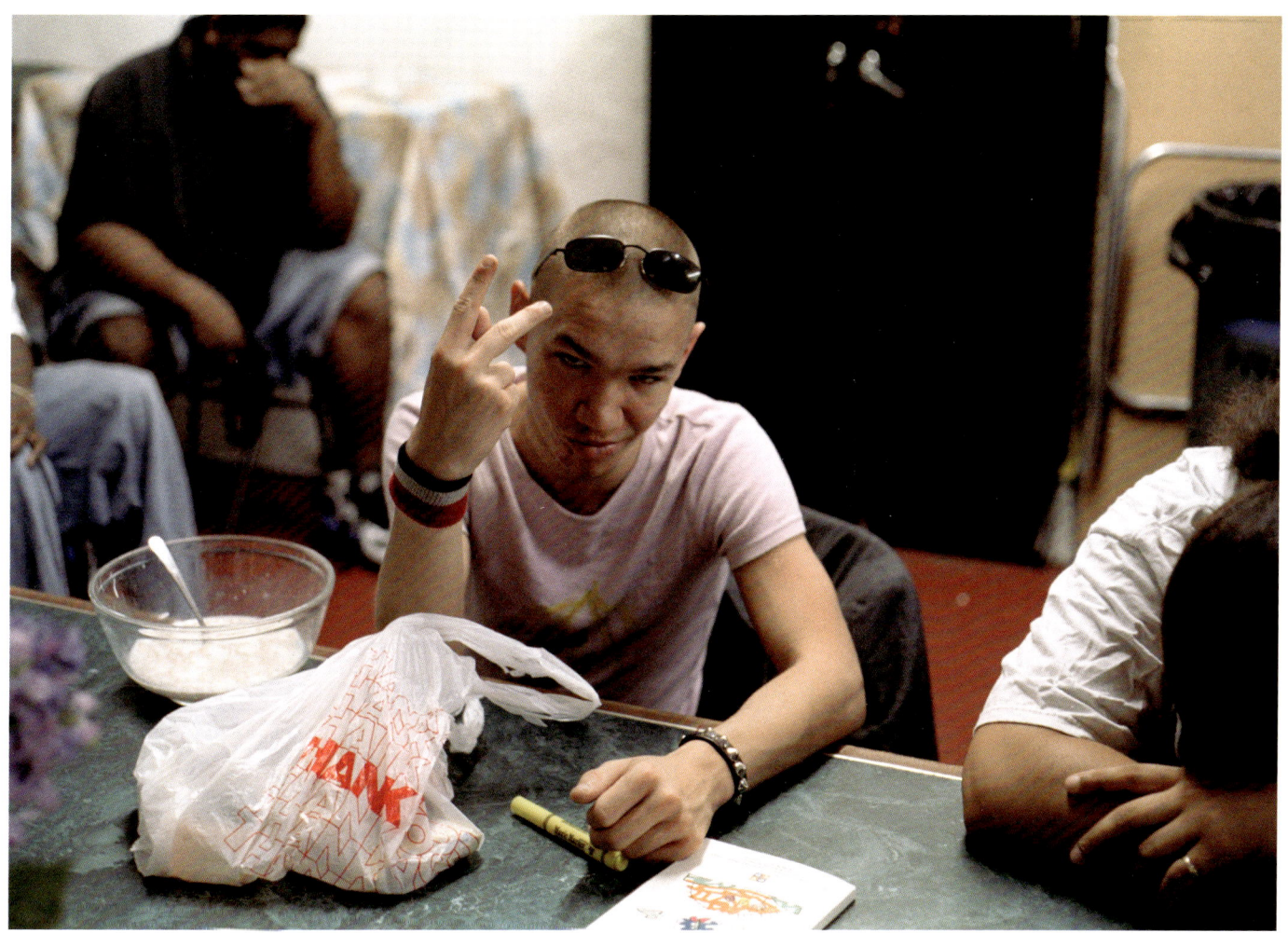

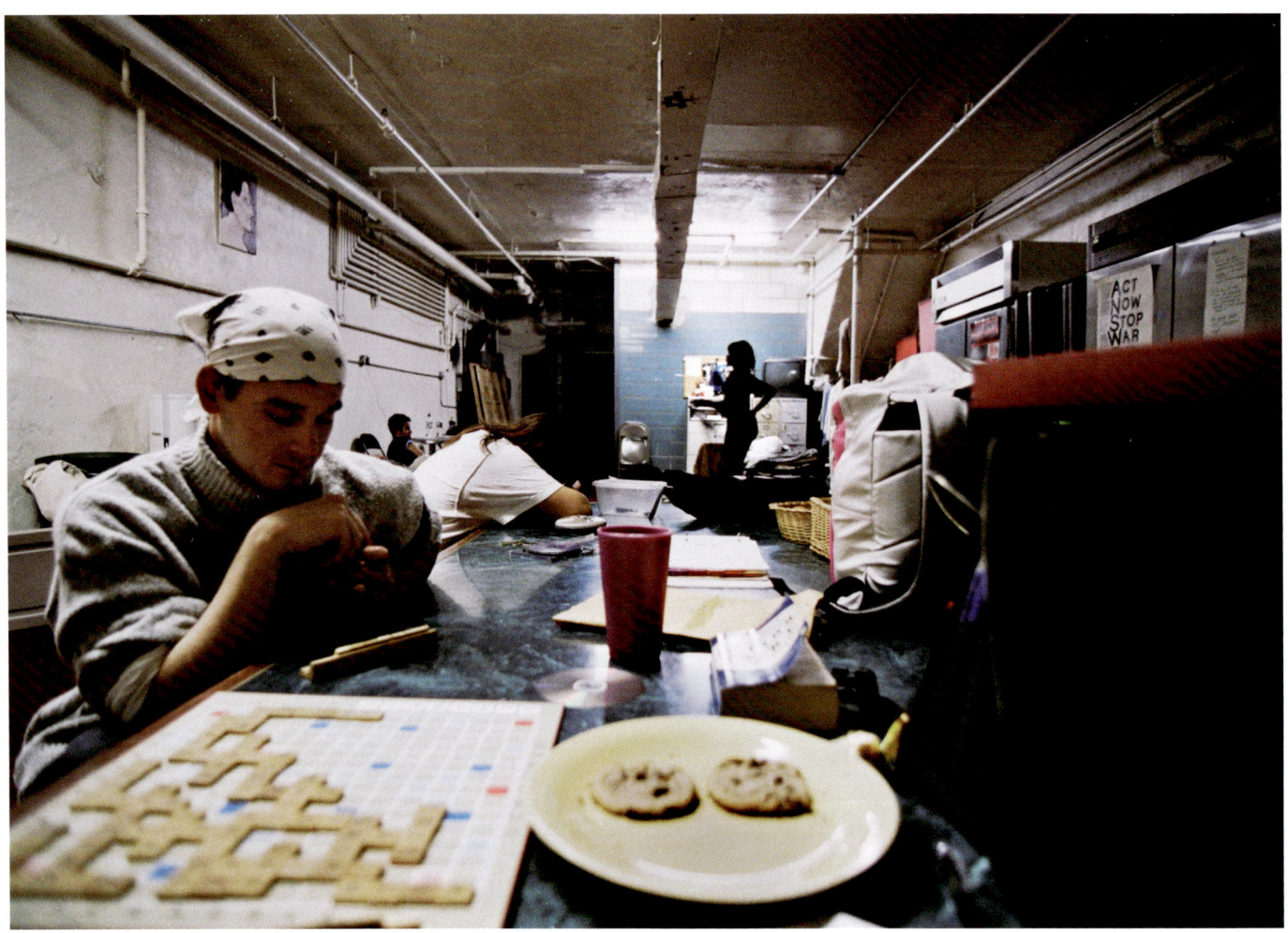

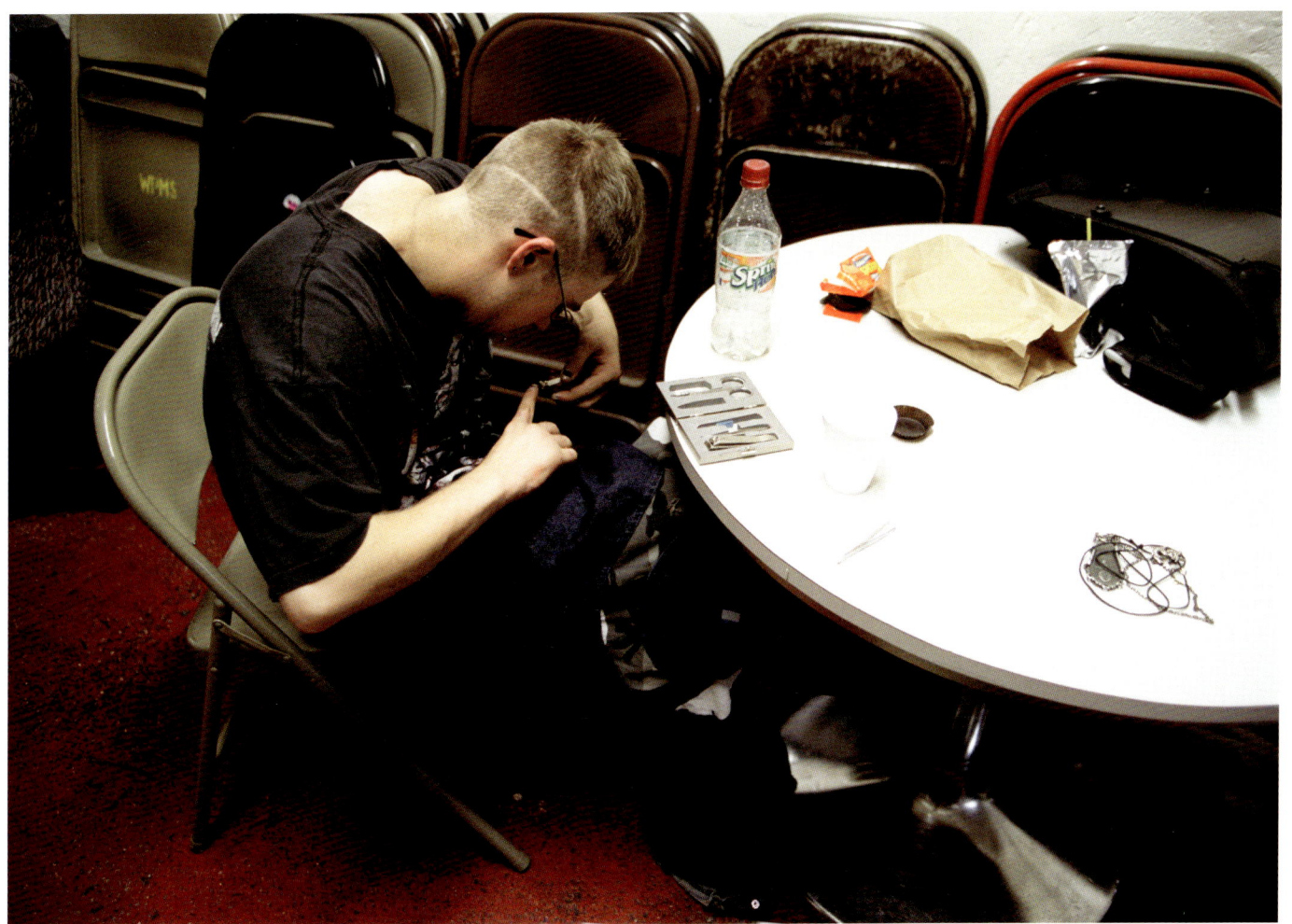

# Fact

Half of all LGBTQ youth report that their parents rejected them.

Over 1/4 of LGBTQ youth are forced to leave home because of conflict over their sexual orientation.

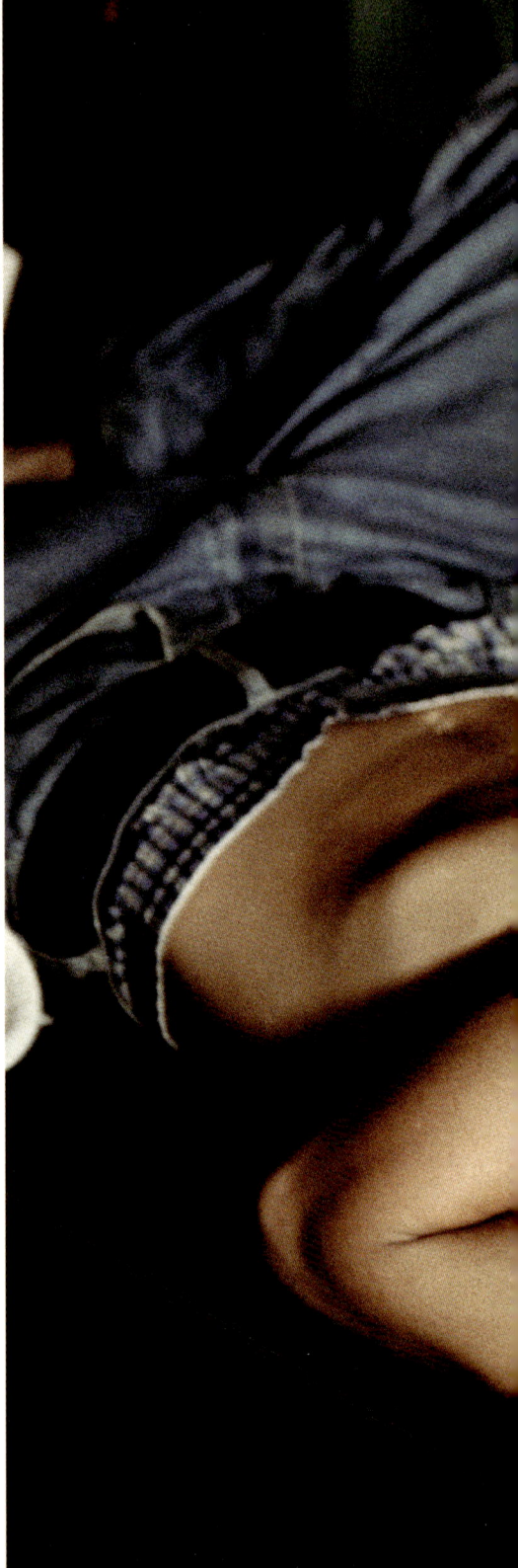

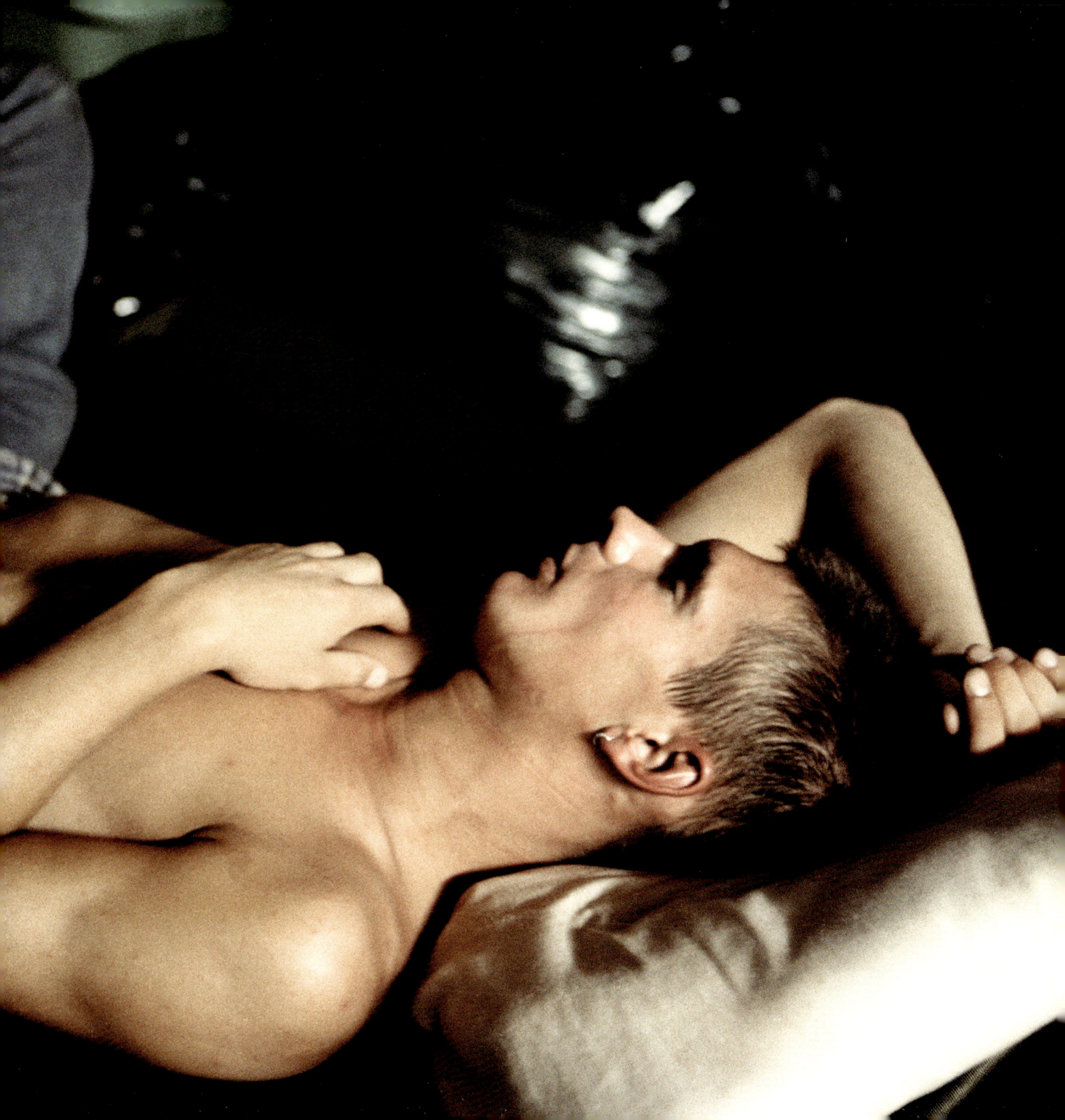

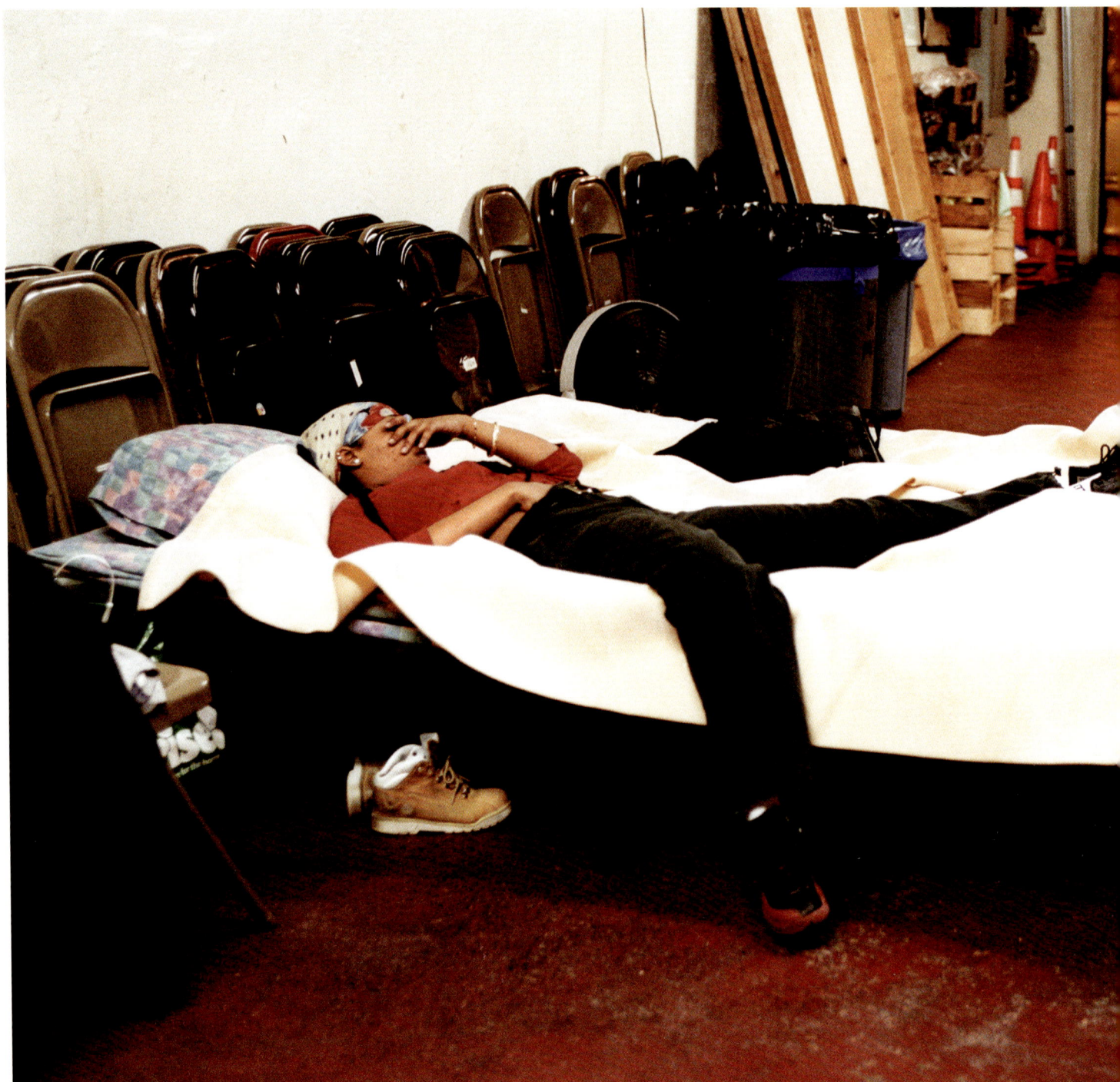

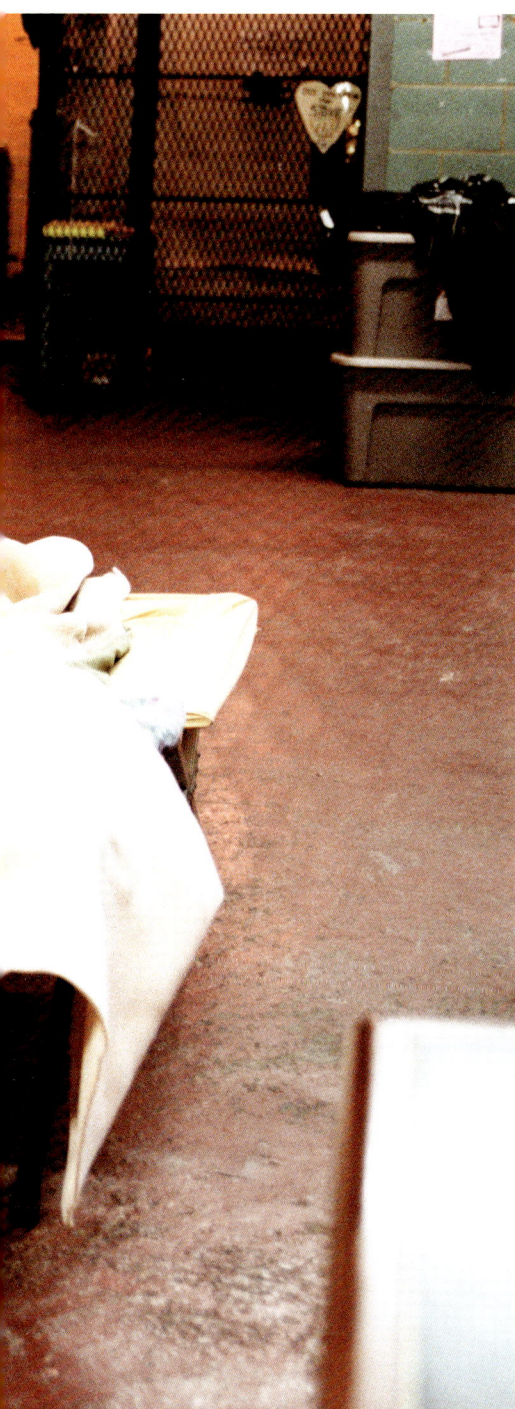

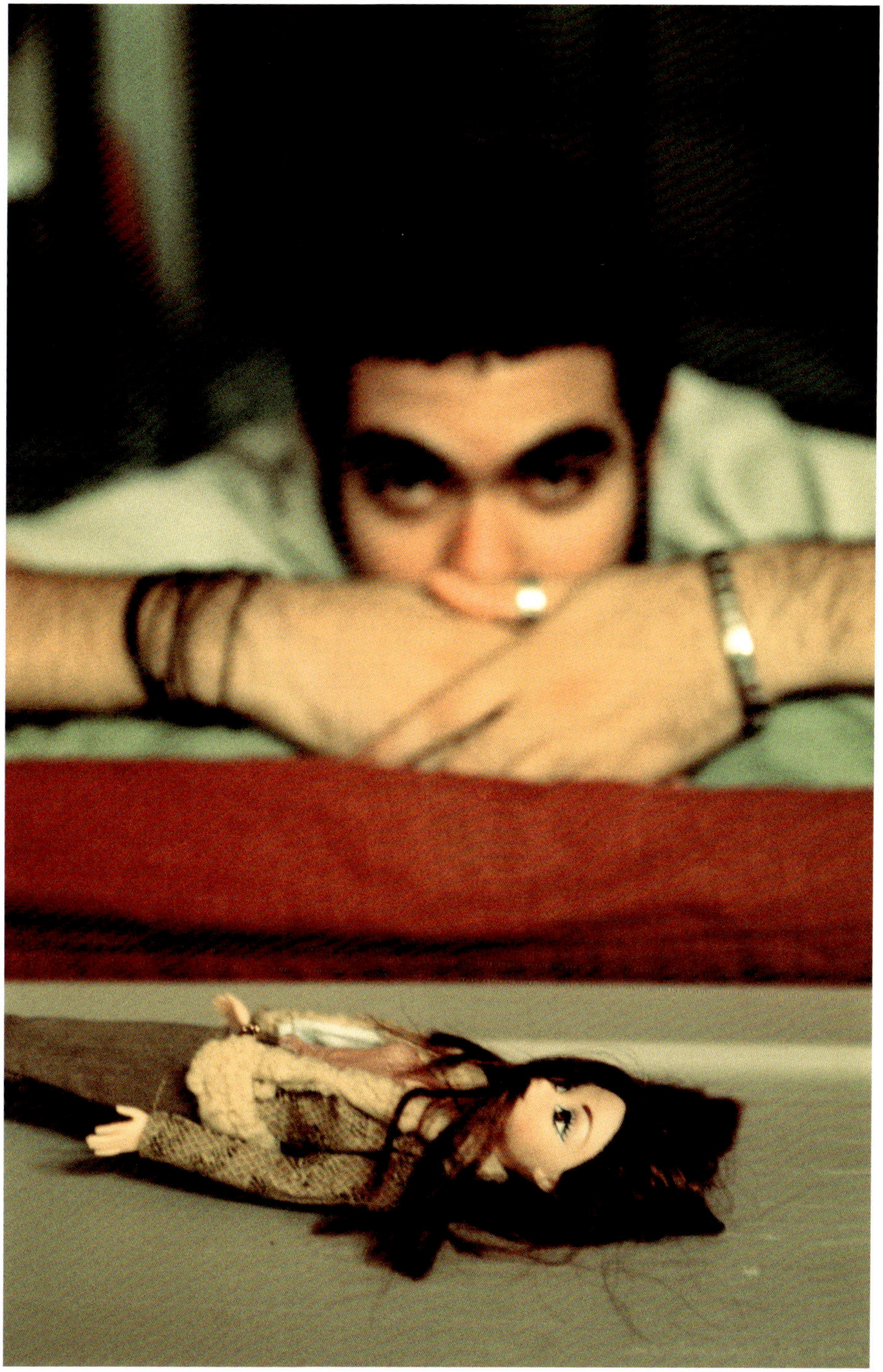

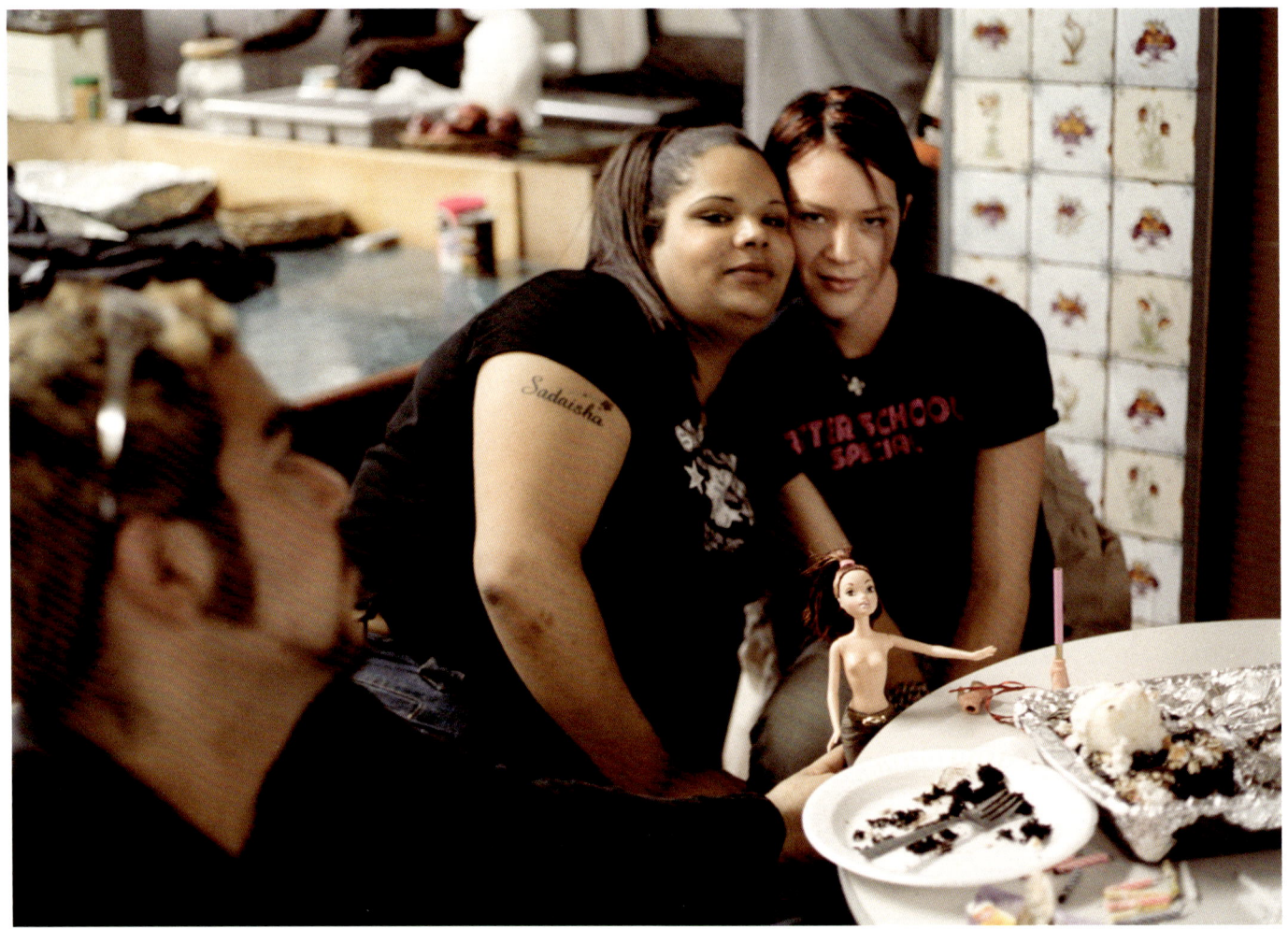

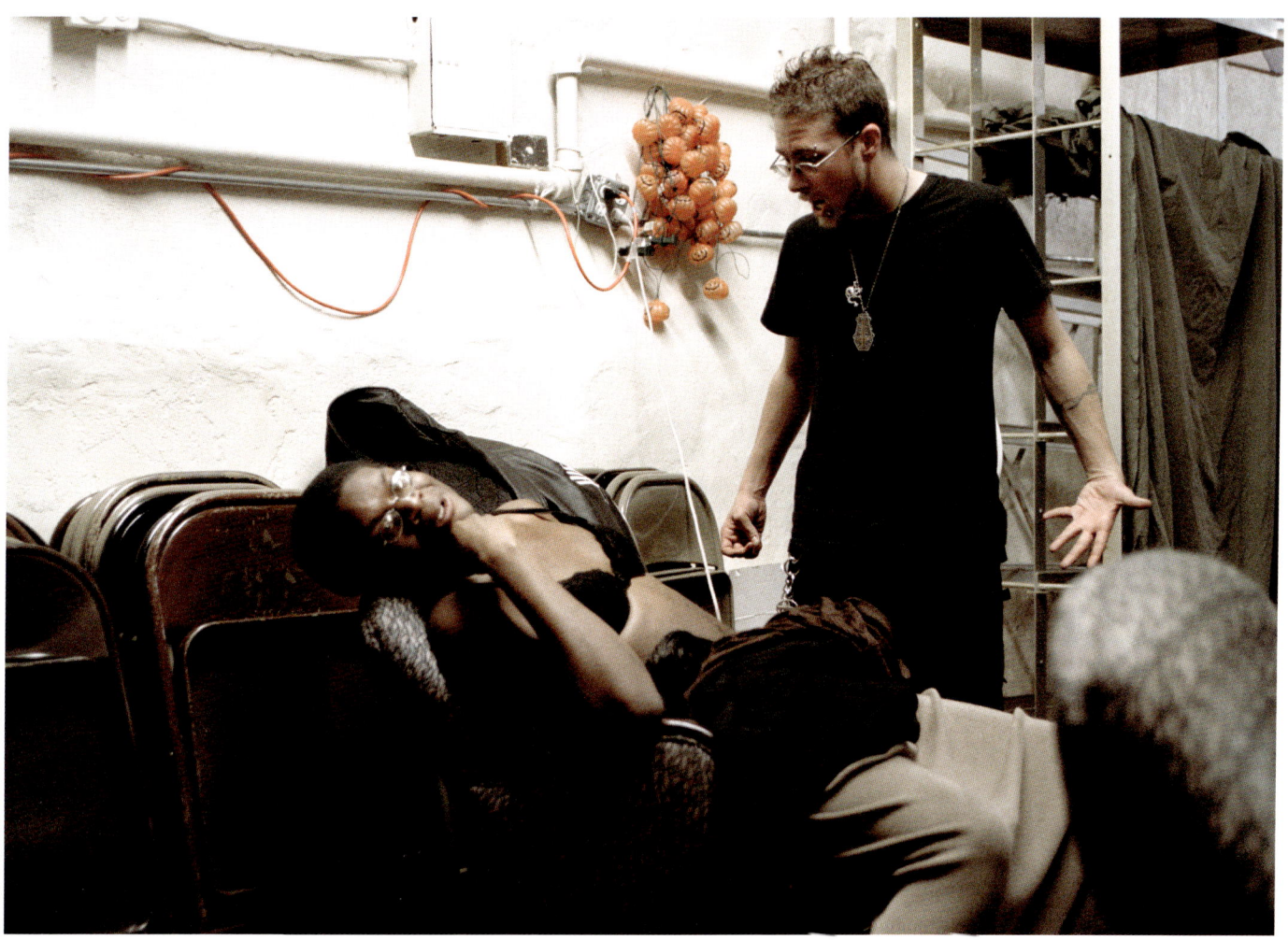

# Thanks giving

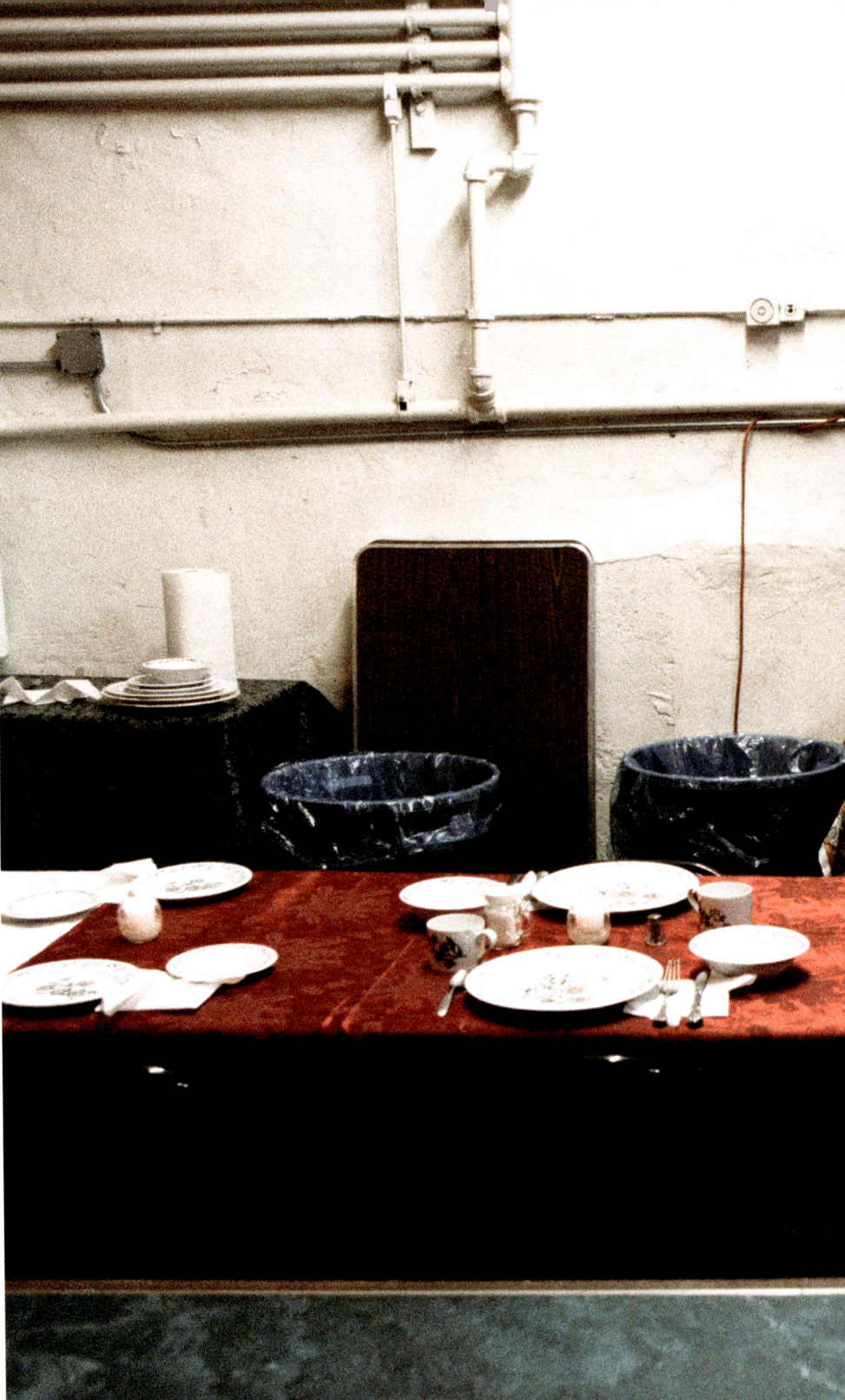

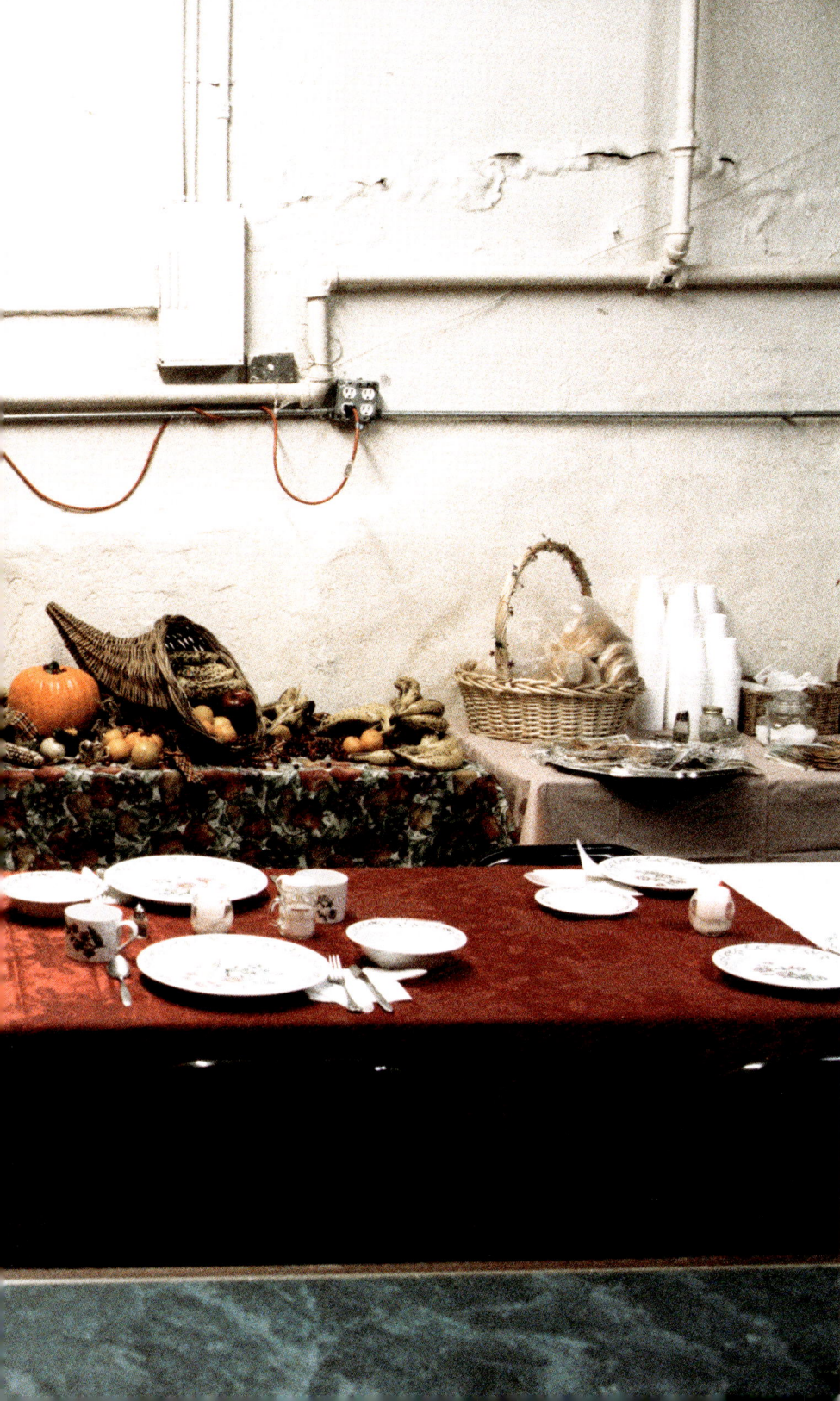

It came unexpectedly, driven by a desire to make the first major holiday at Sylvia's Place a warm and homely experience for the residents. Food was offered from members of the church and volunteers, but much of it had been left out and was dry by the time they arrived to set up the Thanksgiving table. Fortunately, Tanino had brought some food from a house party he had been to earlier in the day, and it was still fresh and tasty. There was no way to know who would be there to share the feast. Some residents found family members to celebrate the day with. Others found friends or other programs to join for the day. But, even if one were to show up, they wanted them to have a real Thanksgiving, the table decorated, the food plated, the mood of a family meal. One by one, a handful of residents showed up to find the shelter transformed into a cozy dining space. Staff and residents joined hands for a Thanksgiving prayer and ate together as an unconventional, but genuine family.

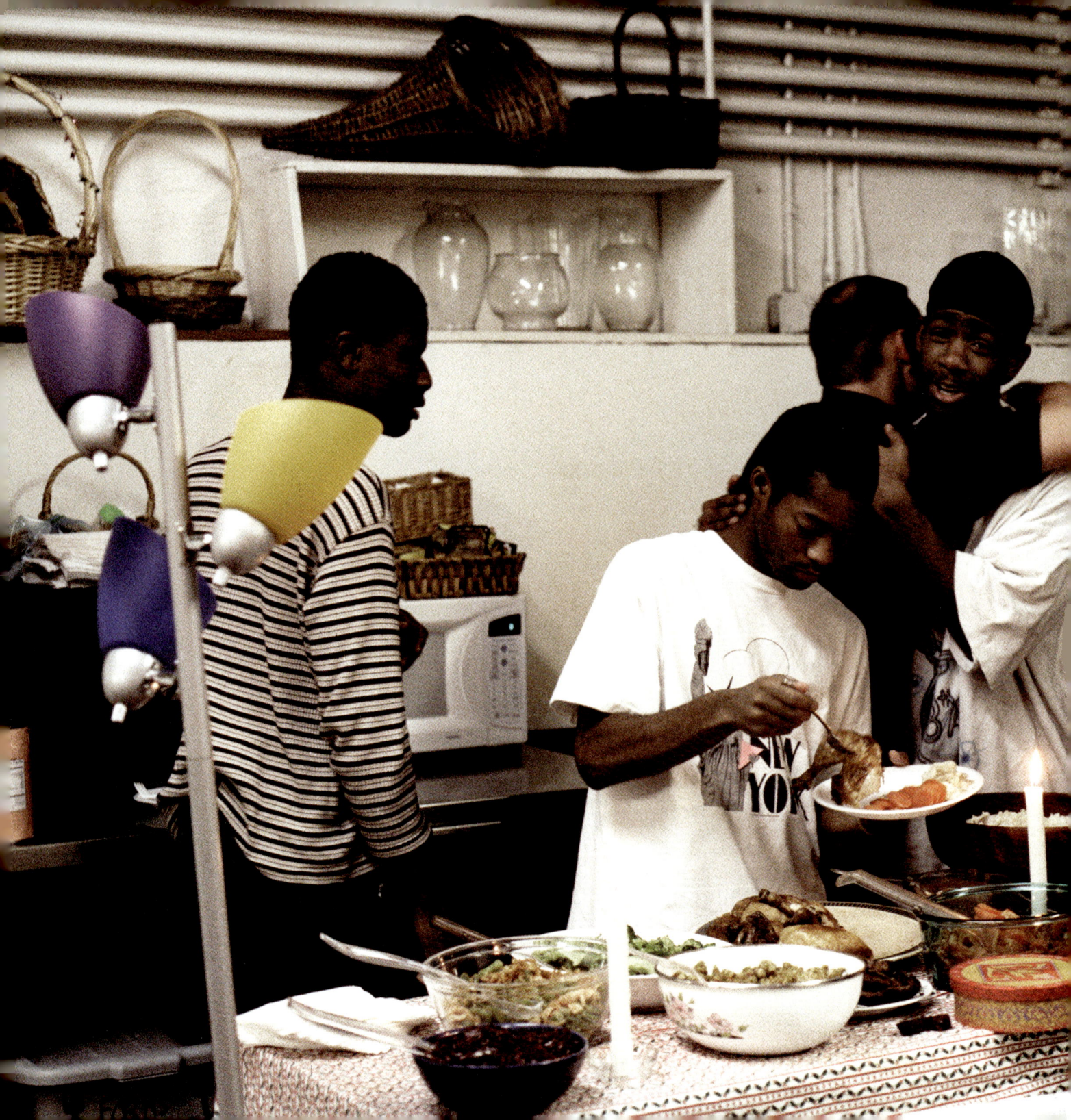

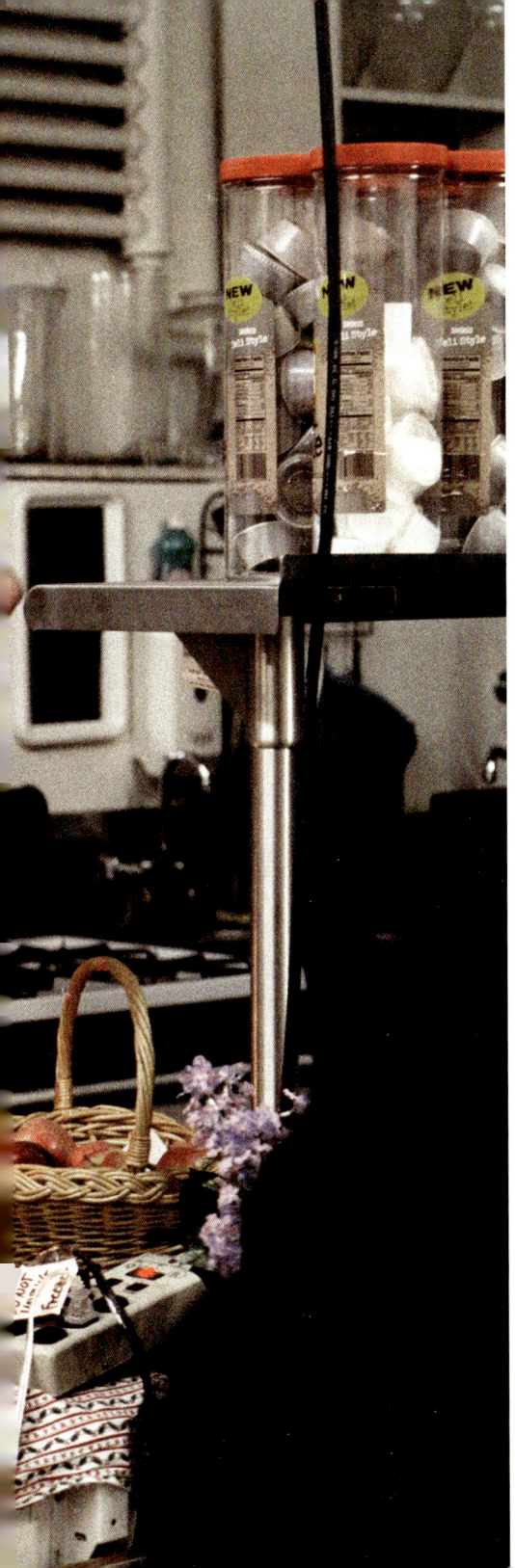

# Volunteers

The staff at Sylvia's Place work long, hard hours and somehow there is always more work to be done. Without the help of the dozens of volunteers the shelter has welcomed since it opened, it may not have survived. From the church congregation, the gay community, and sometimes from surprising connections, volunteers have come out of the woodwork to help out. They've been there to cook dinners, brighten the holidays with food and presents, drop off useful donations, mentor residents, supervise field trips, offer an extra set of hands on busy nights, and takes on countless other seemingly small tasks that make a big difference. Volunteers can be the salvation of the staff and a resident's connection to a way out. Sylvia's couldn't exist without them.

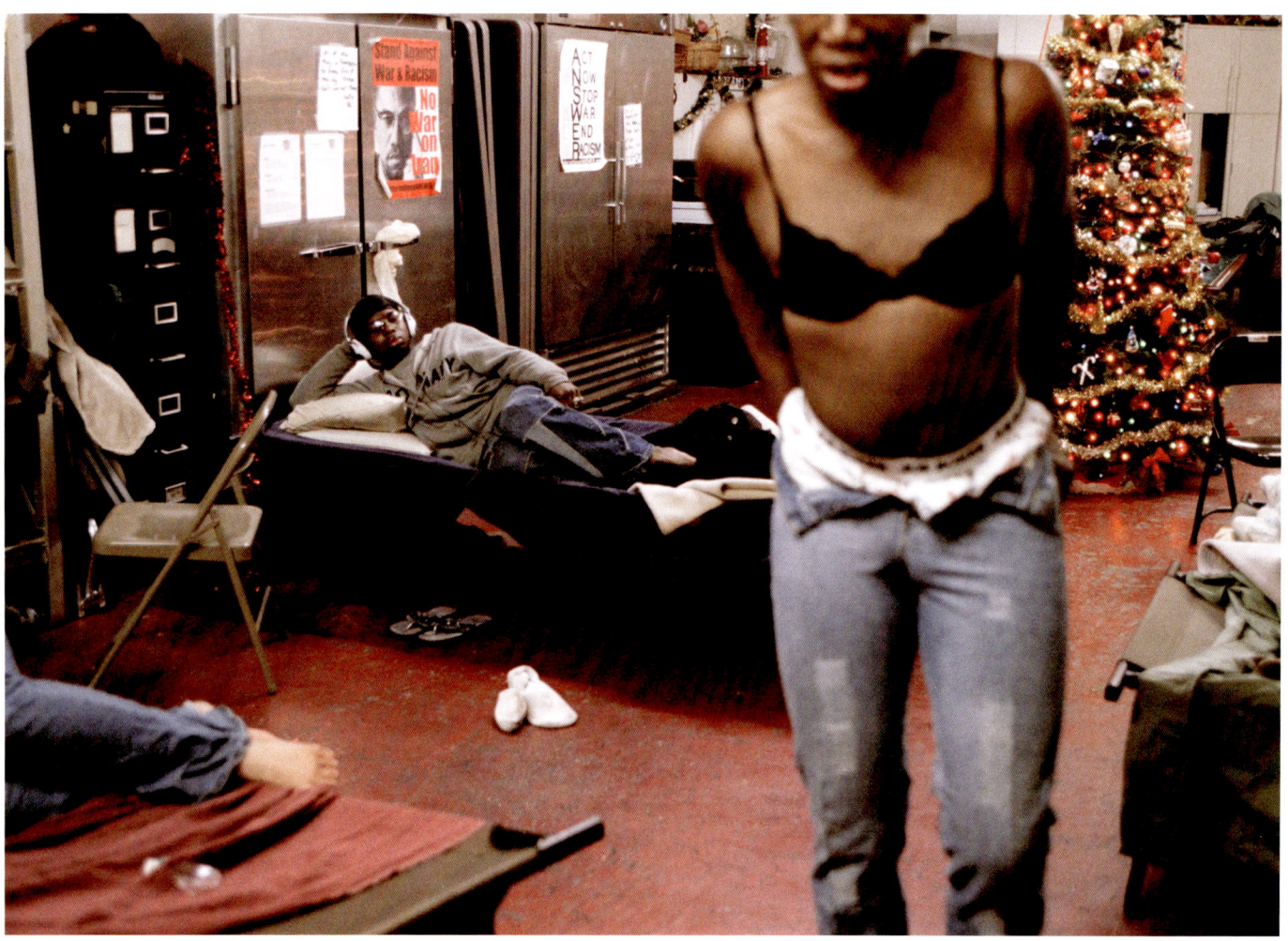

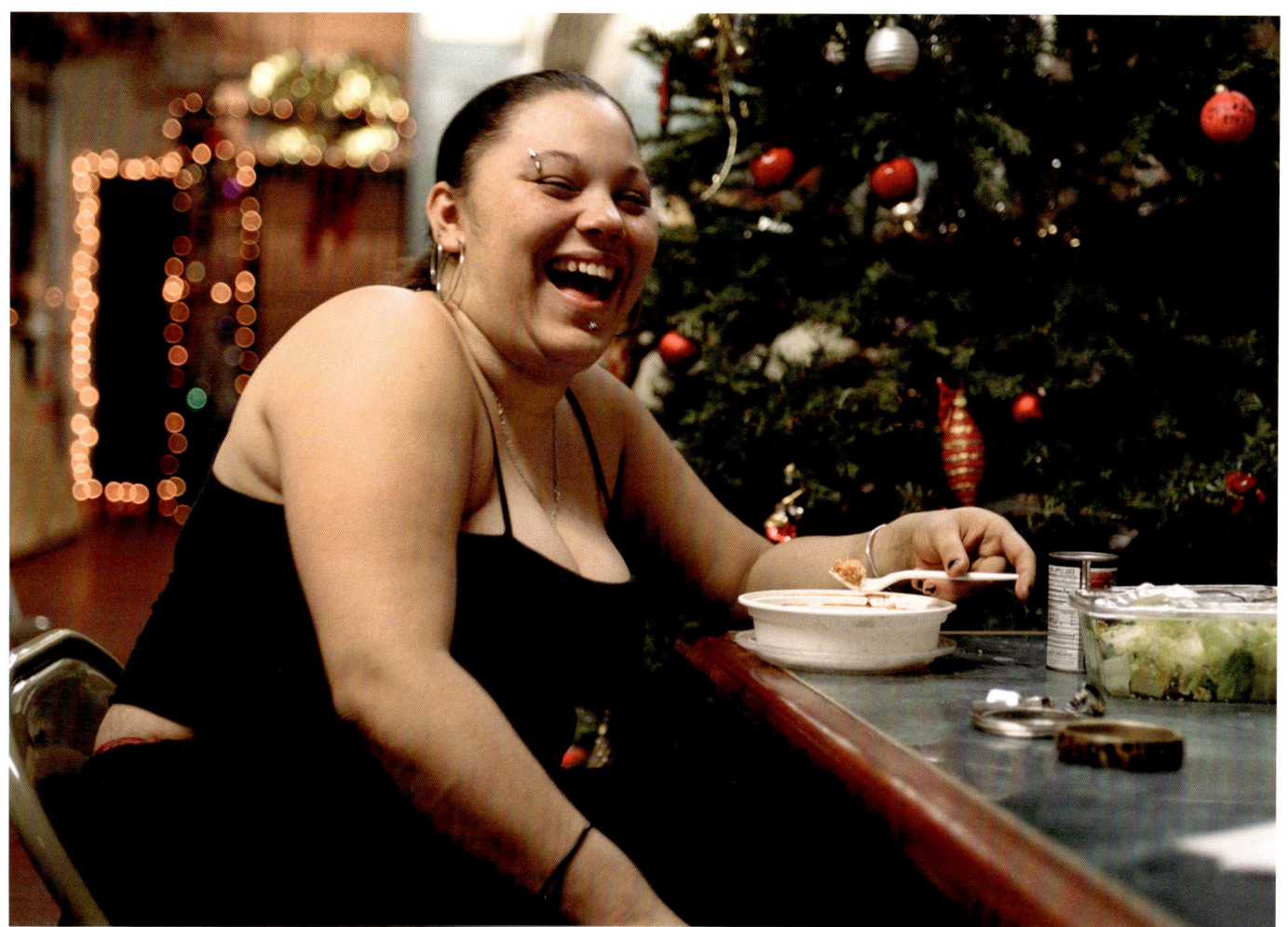

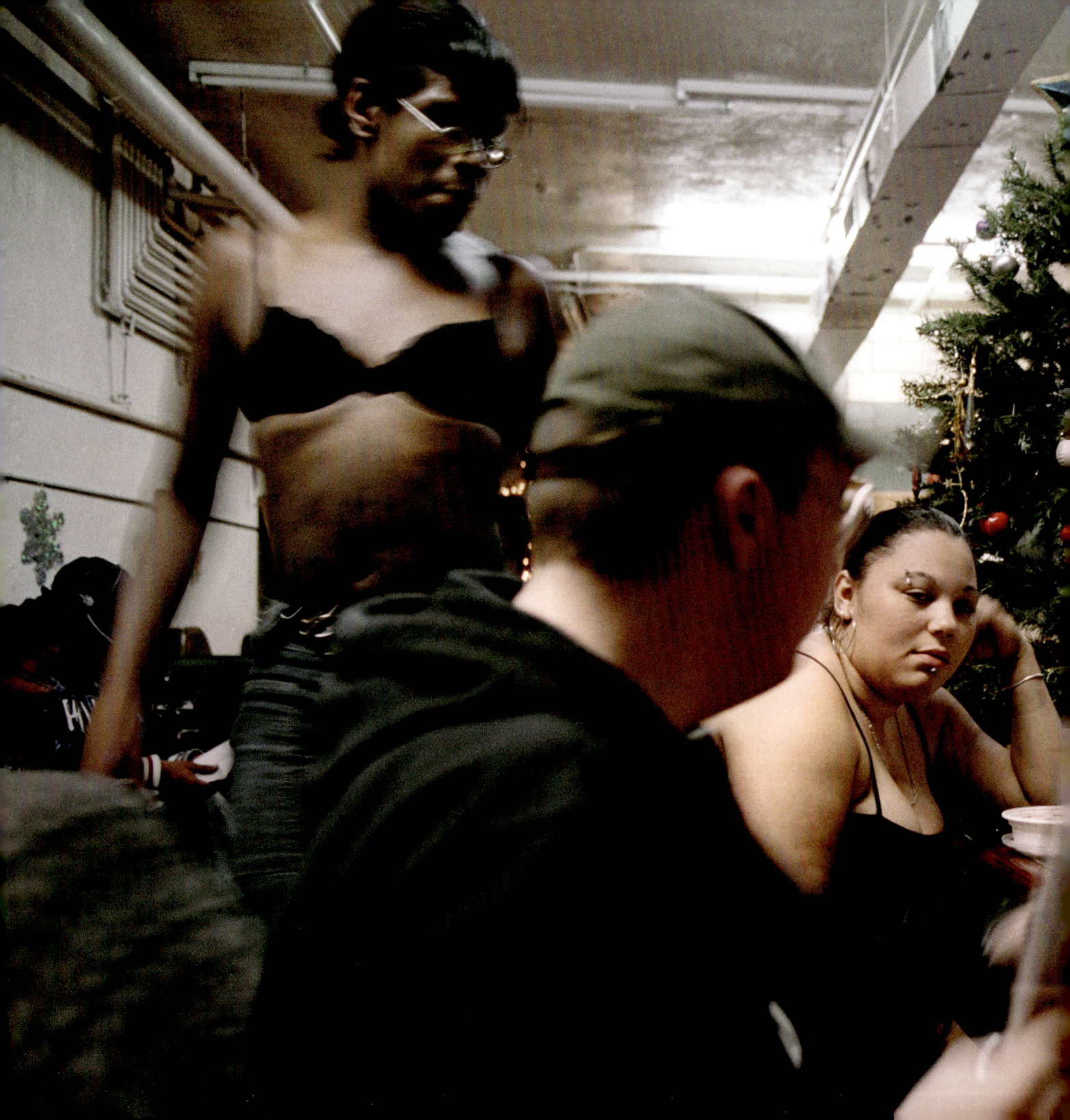

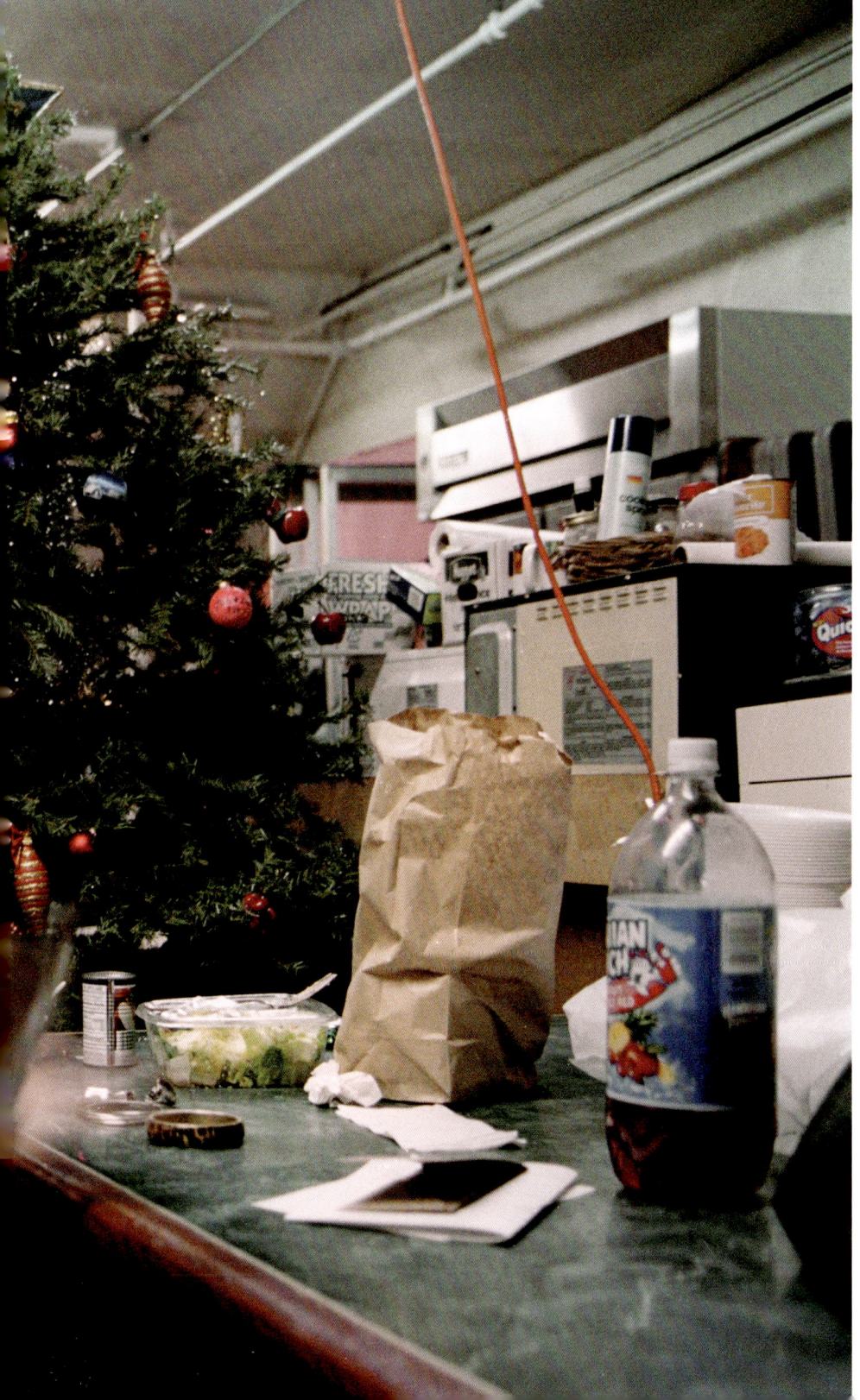

It wasn't until I was 13 that I fell in love with the first girl. She was so gorgeous. She was a seventh grader and I was a sixth grader, and I wasn't talking so I really couldn't say anything to her. But even if I did, you know that whole rule in Junior High. You know, seventh graders don't go out with sixth graders. When I finally did open up my mouth and did start talking again, I would smile and I'd say "Hi". But she never really thought nothing of me or whatever, until years later.

I got with her when I was 18. So, my mom kind of had this thing where I had to choose between being with her and living in the house. So, I chose to be with her, and not to live in the house. During that whole summer... it was fun. We lived at her aunt's. If not, we found this furnished apartment. Well, not apartment, but a furnished house... it was on top of

the hill, right next to, so convenient, monster #3 and my sister. But, they didn't know we were staying there. But, it had running water, carpet, they had beds in there.
It was awesome. It was like we had our own little house, rent free and everything. We could come and go as we please. It was abandoned, but it looked like the owners had moved out, but we were there for like three months. It was pretty cool.

Me and her split up and she moved. I didn't want to be there by myself.

This guy had handed me a condom and it had the address in it and I was like, "What the hell is this?" And he was like, "You just look like you might want to talk to someone." I was like, "Do I look like a people person? Why are you handing me a condom? I don't even fornicate like that." Seeing as I got tired of bumping from place to place,
I said, "I'll go here and see what this is about."

When you're younger you hear people tell stories about shelters, like that they rob you and they do this and that to you in there. So, I didn't want to be one of those people that said, "Yeah, they robbed me." I didn't want it to be like that. I got here, and it was actually pretty cool. Eternity

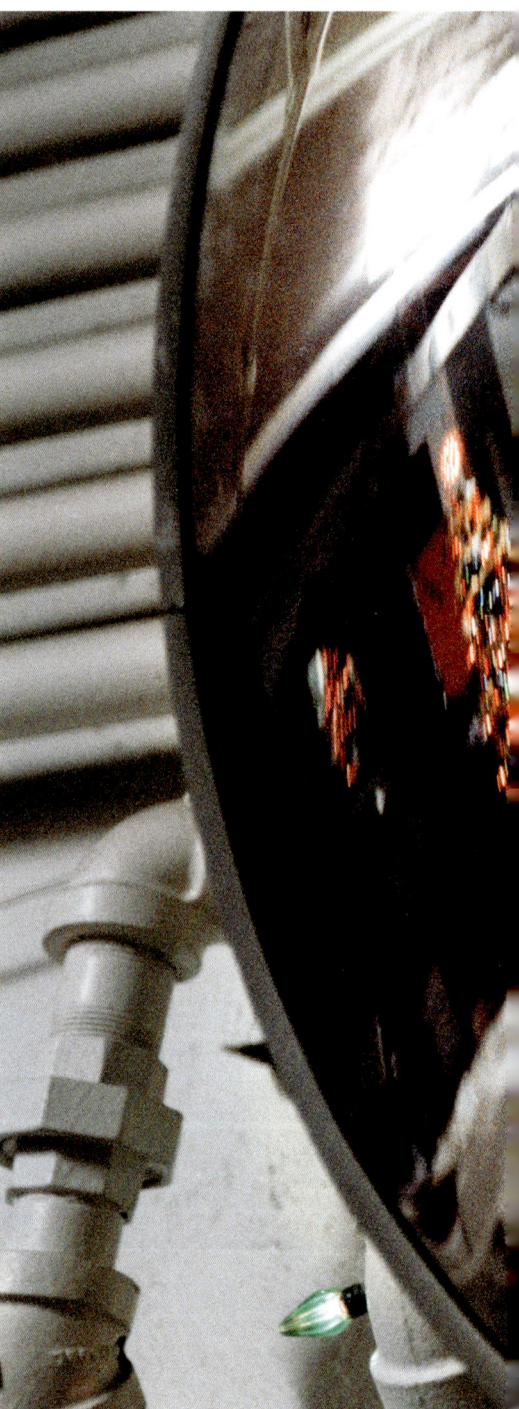

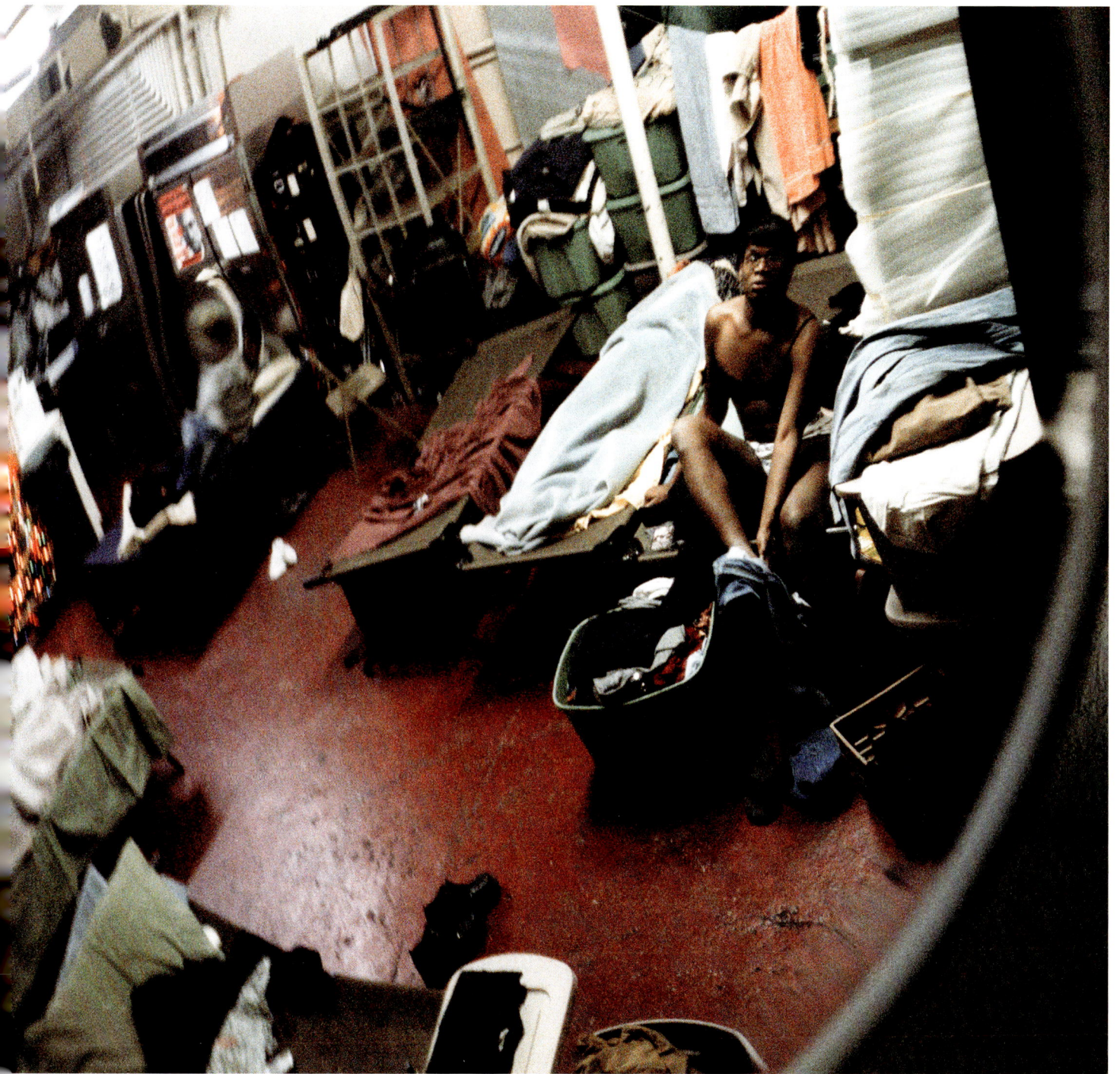

# Christmas

The Christmas holidays were a time of mixed emotion within the walls of Sylvia's Place. Some residents enjoyed the hustle and bustle of the season, while others were reminded of happier times or childhoods they never had. In the weeks leading up to the holidays, they took charge of turning the concrete box of a shelter into a room that reminded them of what Christmas ought to be. By using the decorations the church had stored in boxes, they found a way to disguise the shelter. As the temperature continued to drop outside, they came in earlier to set up a tree and decorate it with lights and ornaments and they hung cutouts of Santa and Frosty on the walls. When Christmas had finally arrived, they were surprised to find that the staff had pooled together their own money and collected more so that each resident had some presents to call their own. For some, it was a pale comparison of what Christmases had been in the past, but for others it was perhaps the only one that ever mattered.

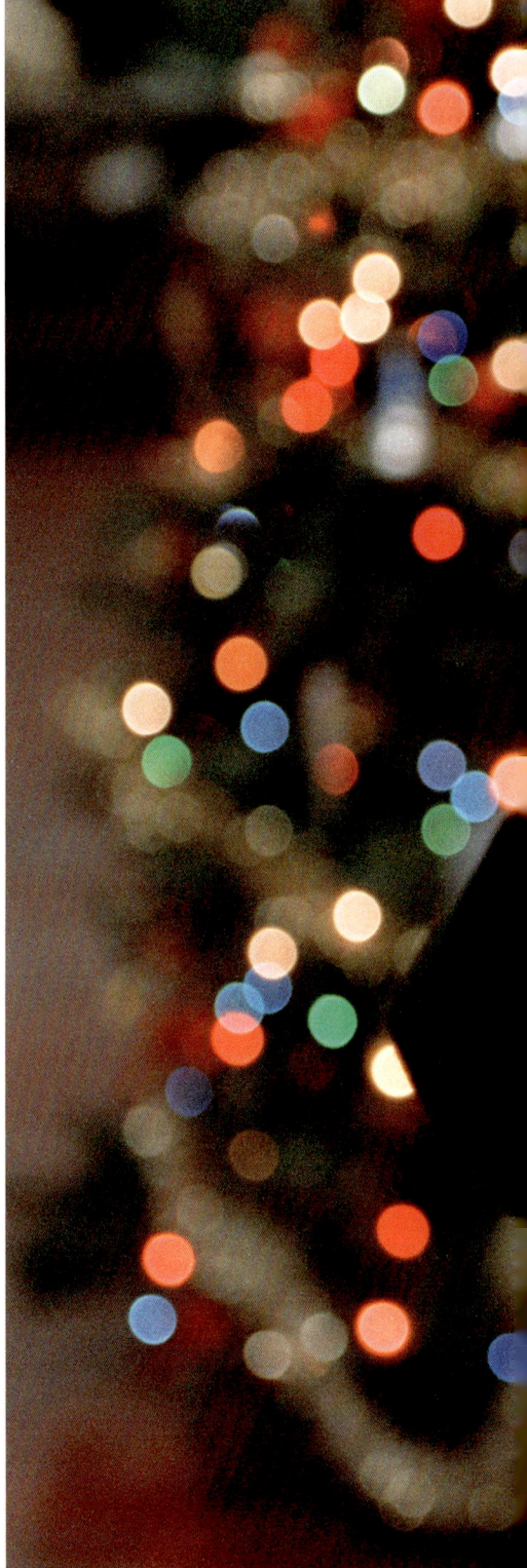

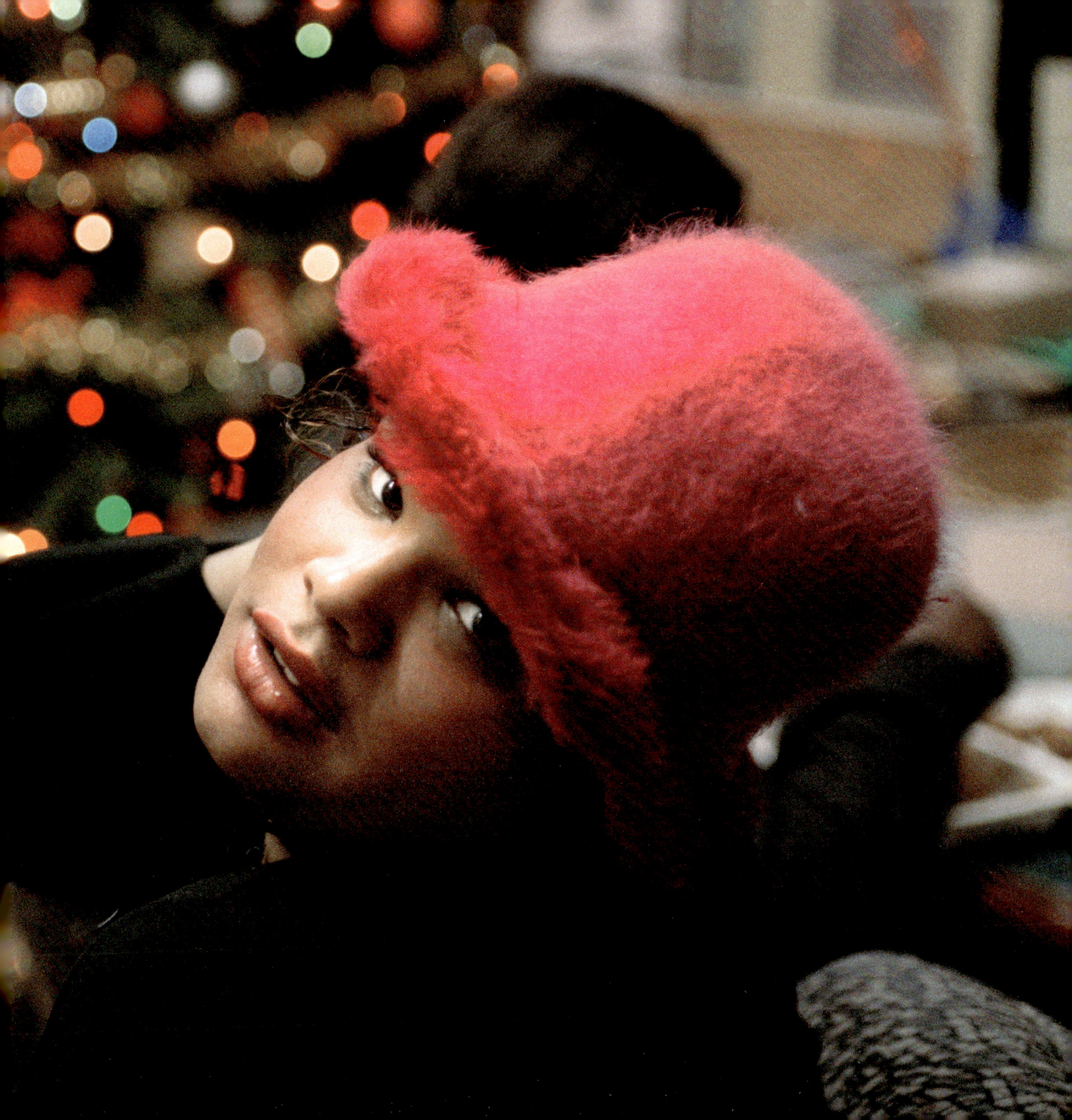

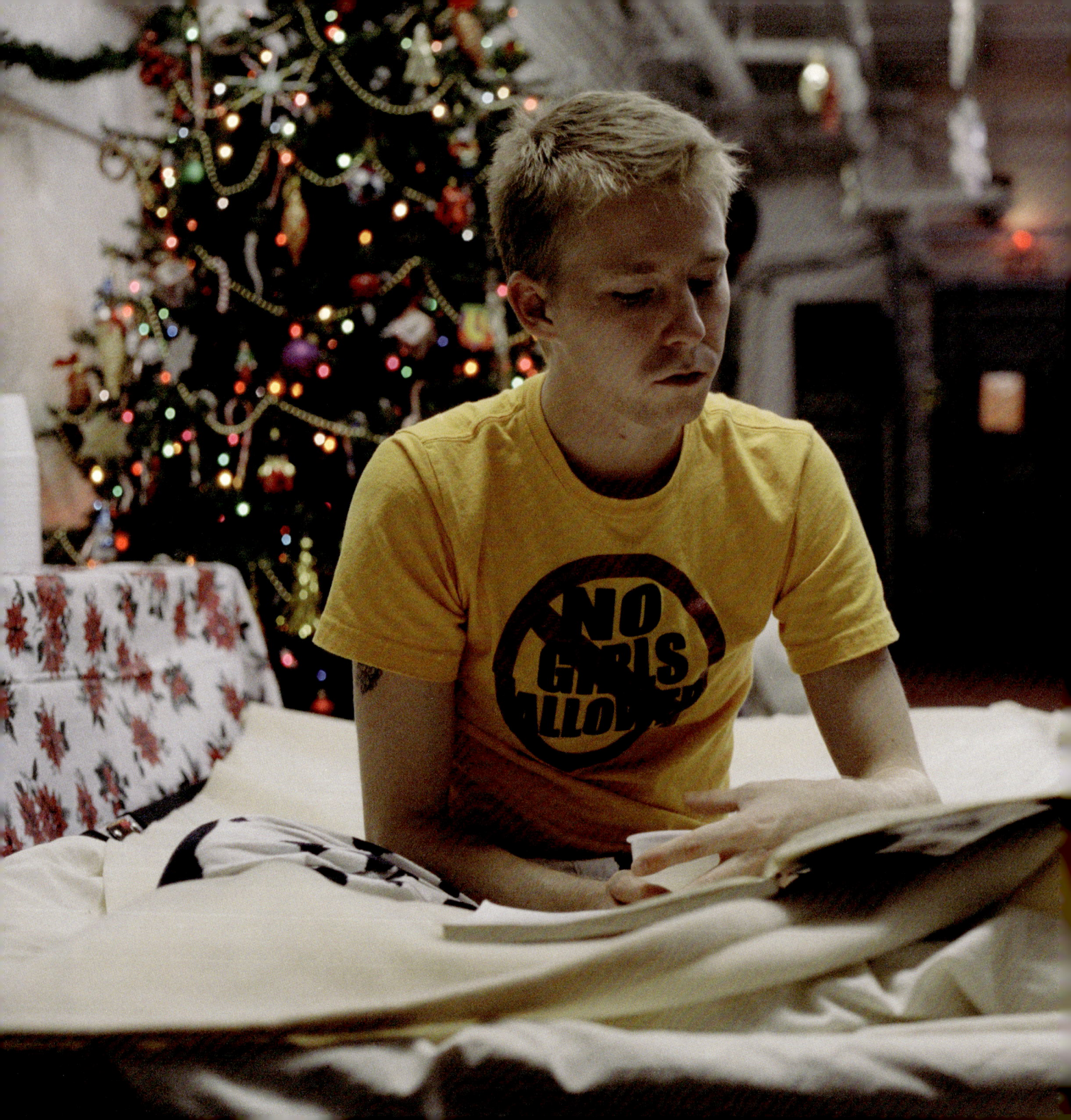

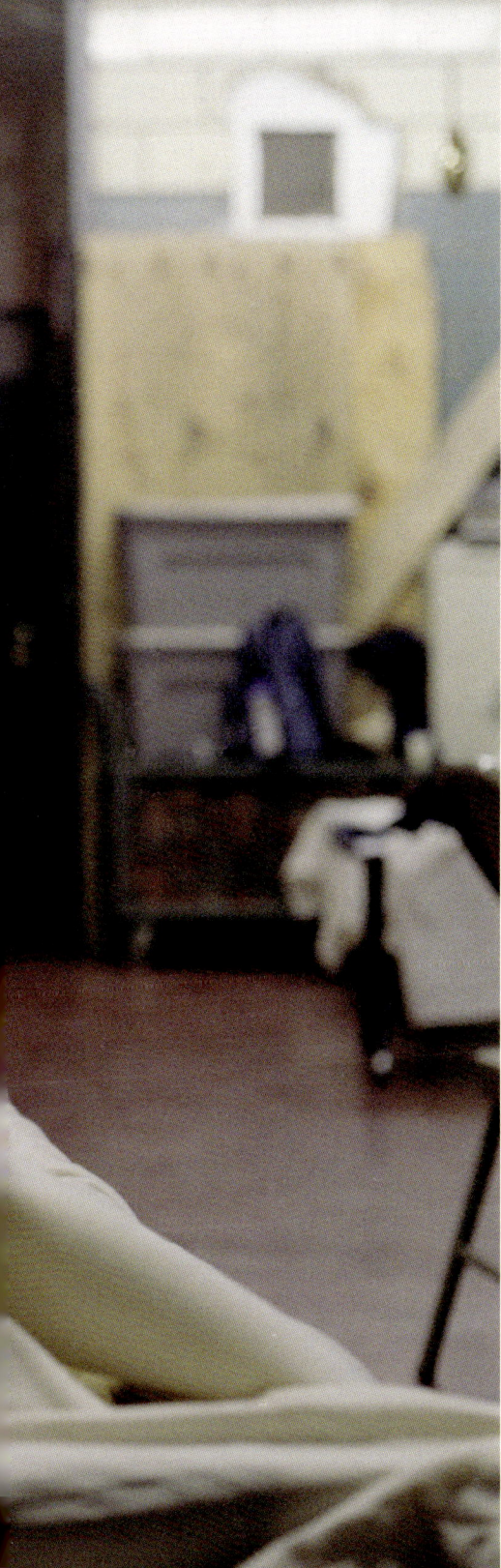

# Benji

Of the hundreds of Sylvia's Place residents who have touched the lives of the staff, few have had the emotional resonance of Benji. With a charming demeanor and a genuine heart, his fall into the depths of turmoil and chaos was as heartbreaking as his recovery was miraculous. His story is often painful, but always real.

*I didn't realize how much I enjoyed sleeping. Sometimes I'm busy and I can only get 6 hours of sleep and I think, wow, when I was on drugs that was so much. Now, it's so little. It's really rewarding when you wake up and know that you have a place to stay. Especially when you've been in and out of shelters.*

*The first time I came up here, I was staying with my dad. And he kicked me out when he found out I was gay. And, you know, he's a bastard. I didn't know he was quite that much of a bastard. You know, he said I could stay with him in New York before I came here. When I got here, he found out I was gay. He told me he didn't want me influencing my stepbrother and stepsister, so he kicked me out. And I didn't know anybody here. I didn't know anybody. I was sleeping at the Pier. Just a couple nights. Off and on, I was finding guys online and sleeping at their house and all that. I didn't really have anywhere to go though. I couldn't go back to Indiana.*

Benji became a slave to his addiction. He would frequently disappear for days, weeks, or even months at a time. However, he had yet to hit rock bottom.

*The very first person I met online, when I came to New York, was a dealer of tina. I had some money, so I bought some, and started selling it, because I knew people made a lot of money selling tina. And that's what I was going to do.*

*I was trying to figure out how to incorporate being able to do drugs and being able to have a stable life. I would get little jobs here and there and the only job that I found that I could actually make money was selling drugs. So, I always kept coming back to that, or escorting. I figured I just needed to figure out a way to do it, and do it right.*

*Drugs were really all that I had. The only thing I looked forward to doing was drugs. It was the only thing I could actually feel. I liked what it did to my body. I liked it that I was so skinny that it'd look like I had a six-pack. I had absolutely no body fat whatsoever. I'd go days, I'd go six days sometimes without eating.*

*And it got to the point where, when I was staying at Sylvia's, I was dealing tina a lot of the time, because I had no other way to get money. I didn't want to sleep with guys for money anymore. I felt that it was the lesser of two evils.*

*For a while I was really trying to get out of it. Somehow, I just always seemed to get back in to it. For four years I was doing it constantly.*

*Adam was this guy, a lawyer that I met online. He was really cute and really charming. And he found out where I was staying and invited me to stay at his house. We had done drugs together recreationally, but I didn't know how bad it was with him, until I moved in. I mean, he did it all the time. And at the time I was fine with it because I had a place to stay. And it started getting worse and worse. I started eating less. Things just went to hell in a hand basket from there.*

*I was doing a lot of crystal. Then he started being very controlling, and then by that time I was so addicted that I just had to put up with it. We were doing it constantly. It was like a 24 hour, 7 days a week thing. And this went on for over a year. We barely slept. He would get mad at me for sleeping. It got to the point where I just wanted to quit, and I just didn't want to be with him anymore, but I didn't know how to make that transition. I didn't have anywhere to go.*

*Adam gave me HIV. He told me he was negative. I honestly didn't care, because I believed him. And even if he was, I figured we were going to be together forever. I was having unprotected sex, from being so uninhibited on the drugs. Now, I would never have that kind of sex.*

*He got very abusive. First it was verbally, then it was emotionally, then at the very end, the last couple of weeks, he started pushing me around.*

With the help of Sylvia's Place, Benji found his way to rehab more than once. He resisted. Benji still had not hit his rock bottom.

*I was just getting frustrated because, I don't know. It wasn't that I wanted to be doing drugs, it's just that I didn't know the structure of rehab. I didn't know that every hour that you were awake you were going to be in some stupid group. And I didn't want to sit there and list off all these things. I just wanted them to tell me what I needed to do and not do drugs anymore. That's not easy. I just became frustrated. But I also thought that I could maybe juggle my life while still doing drugs sometimes. But it never worked. It never did.*

*I had been partying with this other cute guy I had met online. He used to be a singer and I knew who he was. I'm not star-struck, but it's kind of cool to be able to hang out and do things that I like with this guy. We had partied once for like a week. Finally I passed out and when I woke up two days later, I was in his bathroom. I had these cuts; I was bleeding. I had these cuts all over my body and I was covered in glass and I was butt naked. And when I woke up, I had all this money. I had a lot of money. And there was like 10 or 12 guys sprawled out, passed out all over the house. I had no idea who they were. It was really scary. I couldn't have told you my name when I woke up. I didn't know where to go. I didn't remember people's names. I had that money, but I didn't know where to go.*

*It turns out I had been slammed. When I had passed out they had slammed me with crystal meth, you know, injected it into my body. They did all kinds of things to me.*

*That was kind of like the biggest eye-opener. That's when I really, really, really started trying. Not that I hadn't tried before. But I really, really tried. Ever since then, it's been a process.*

*I haven't done any drugs. No tina, no K, no G, no nothing. And I think it was going back to Indiana and talking to my mom. I finally talked to her about everything. She freaked out at first. Then she started crying. She pleaded with me not to lead such a sketchy existence. She's not going to be around forever. I'm not going to be around forever. And she just doesn't want me to go before her. And it's not only that. She knows that my health is compromised. She's kind of opened my eyes a lot. I think a lot of my family relationships is what I was lacking. I'm not saying that's the cause of it, but I didn't have any other relationships besides the people I was doing drugs with, any type of relationship where I felt a connection. And I think I was looking for it in a lot of places.*

For Benji, the process will be ongoing. To many residents who have come and gone, Benji is known as the Mayor of Sylvia's. The title may be superficial, but the feeling behind it is one of reverence.

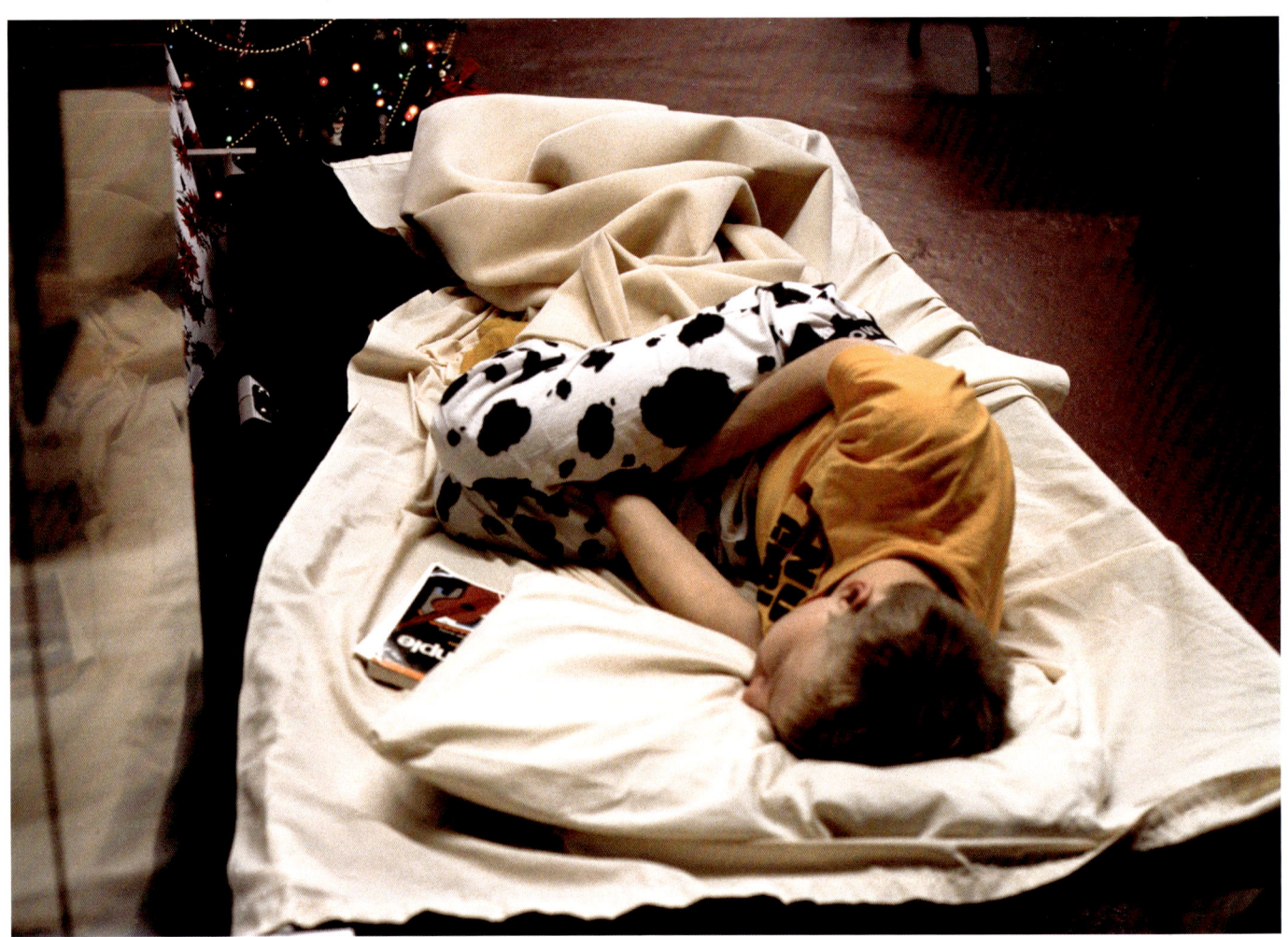

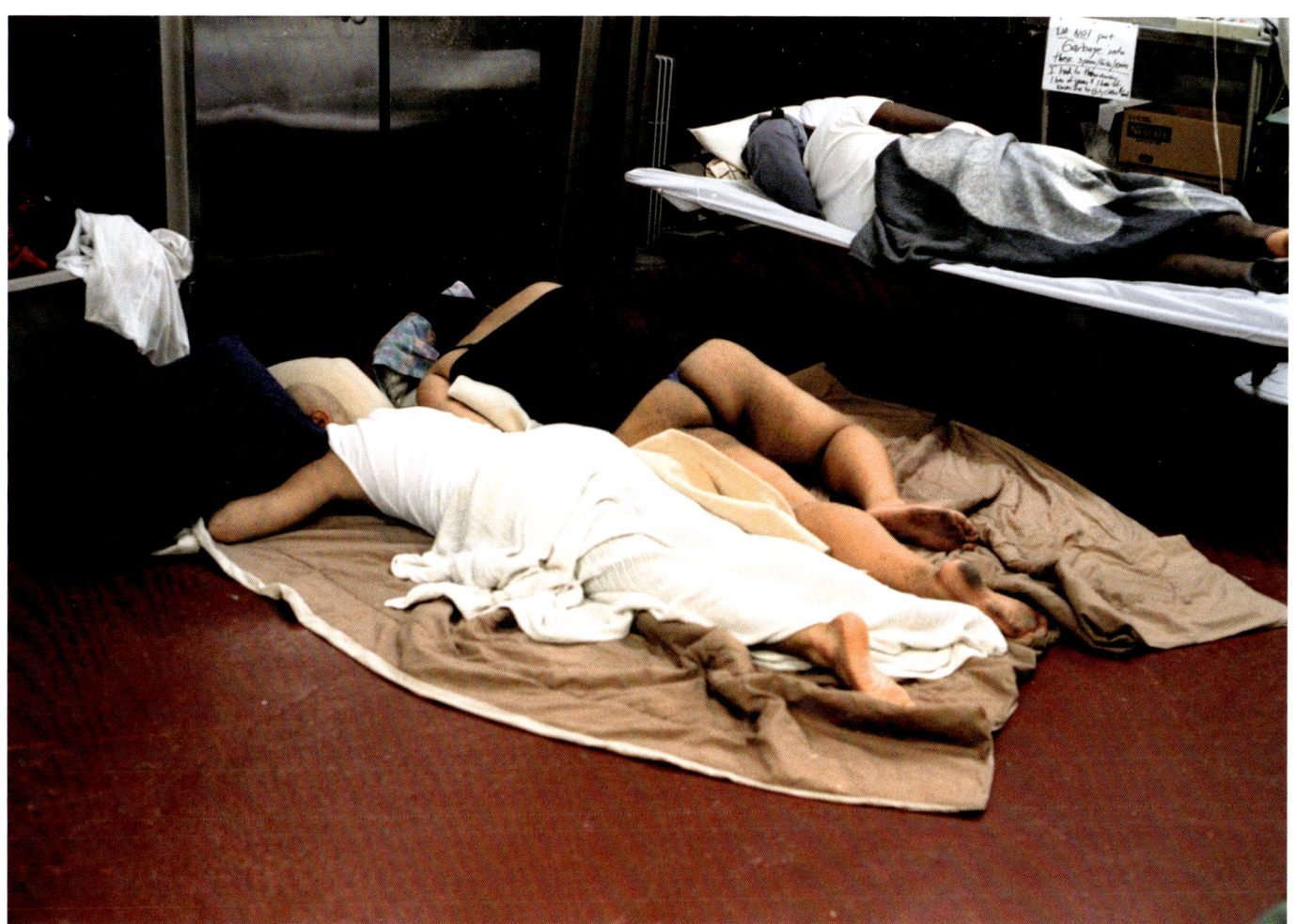

123 Shelter

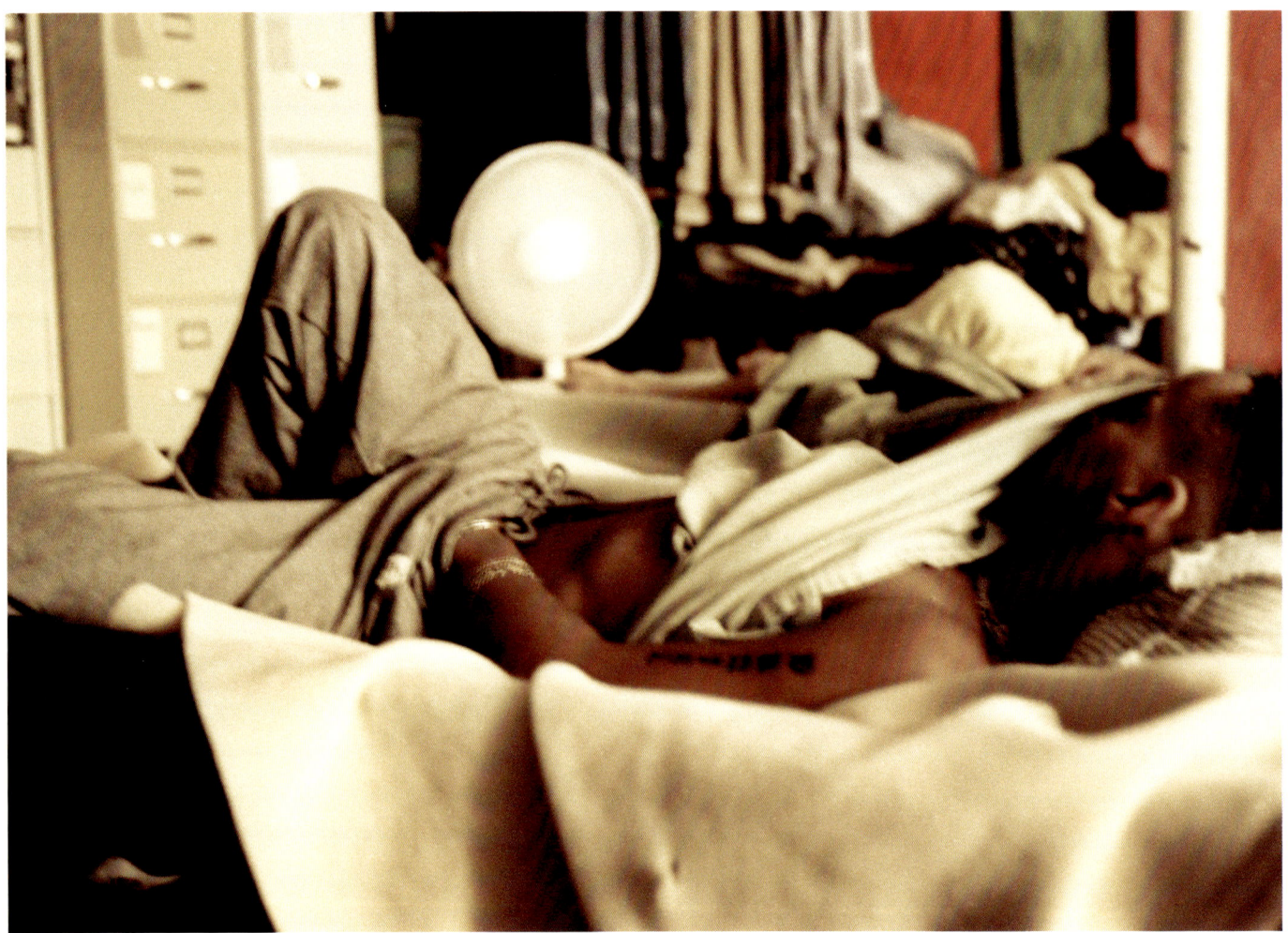

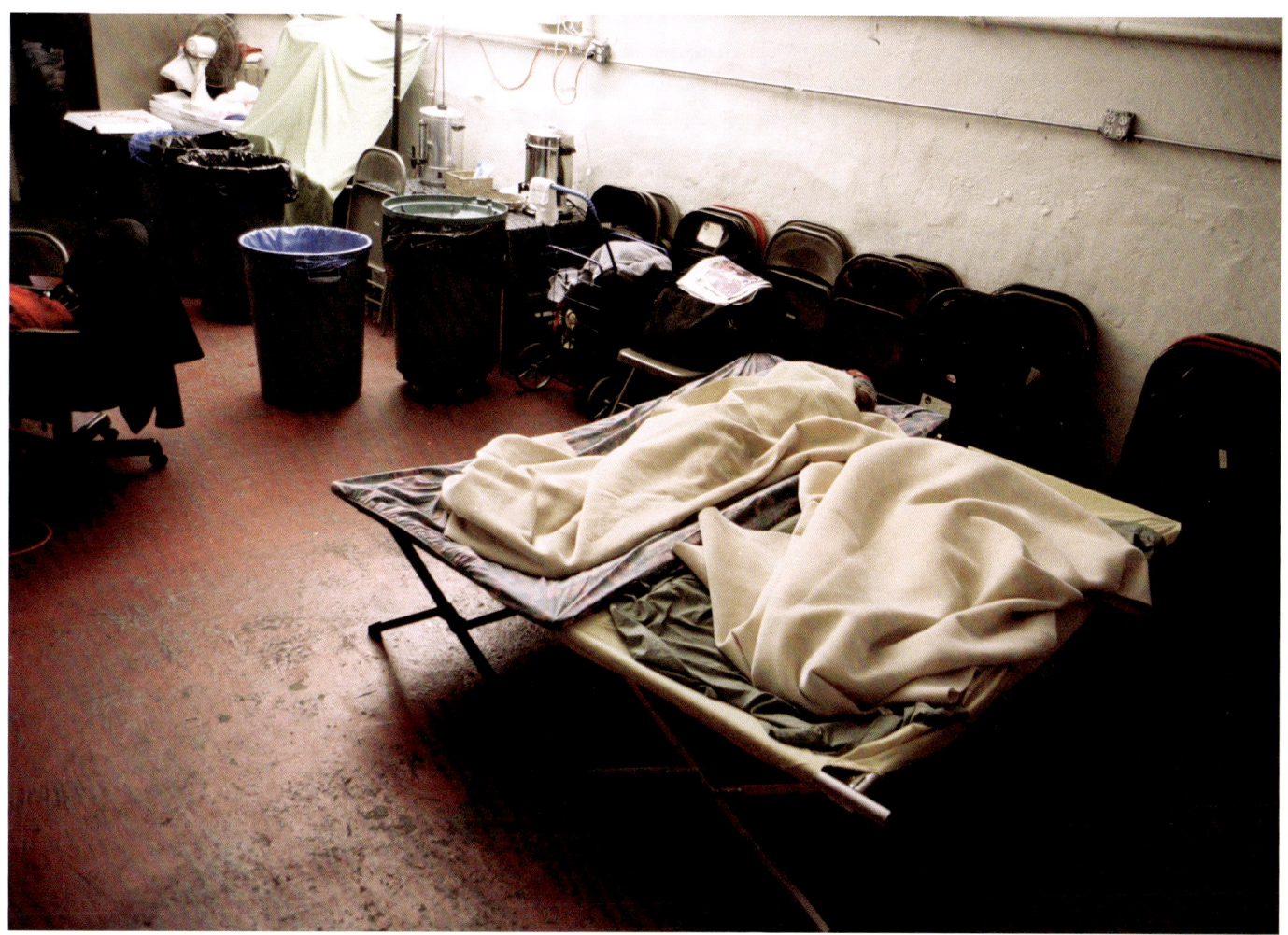

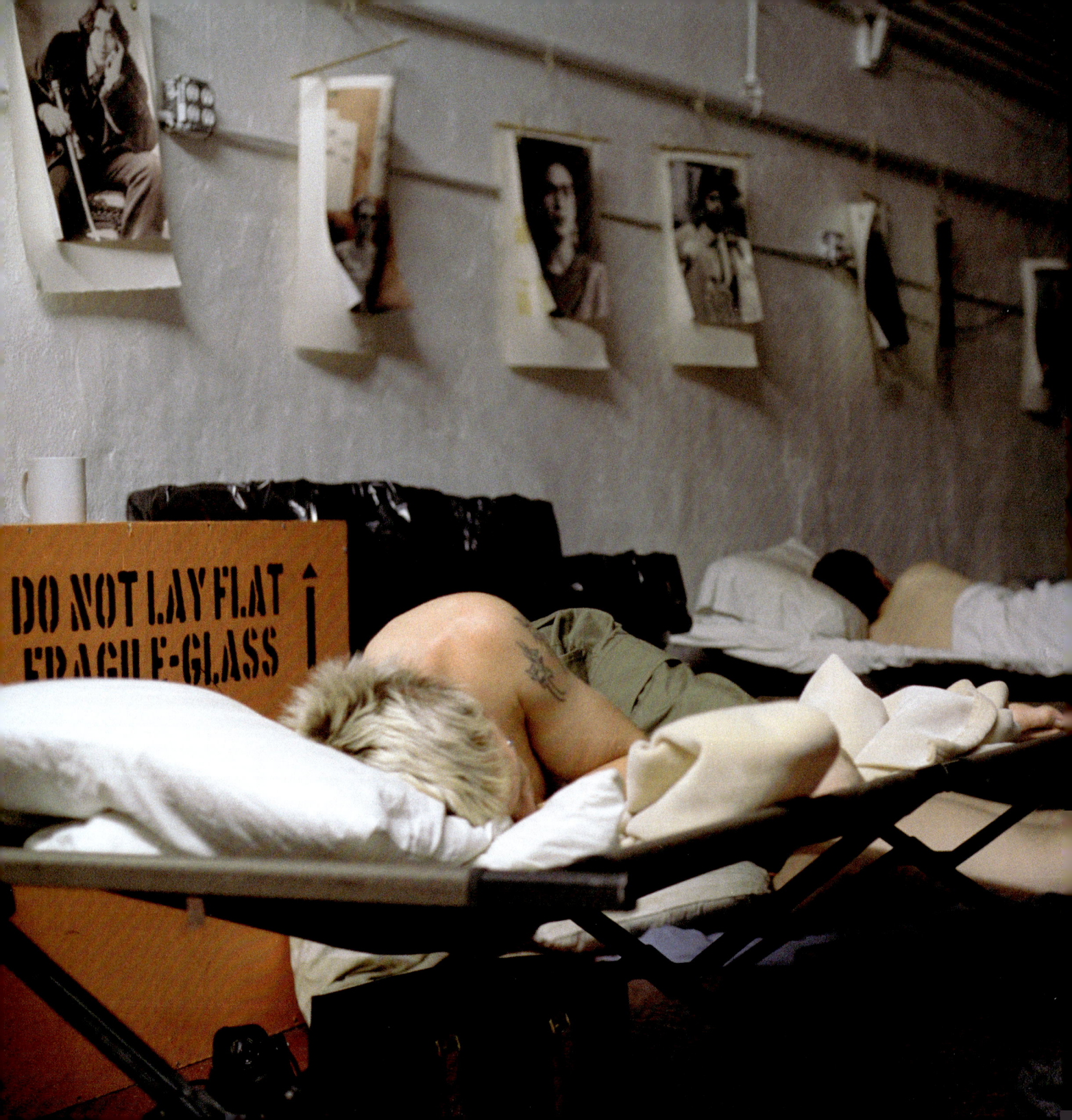

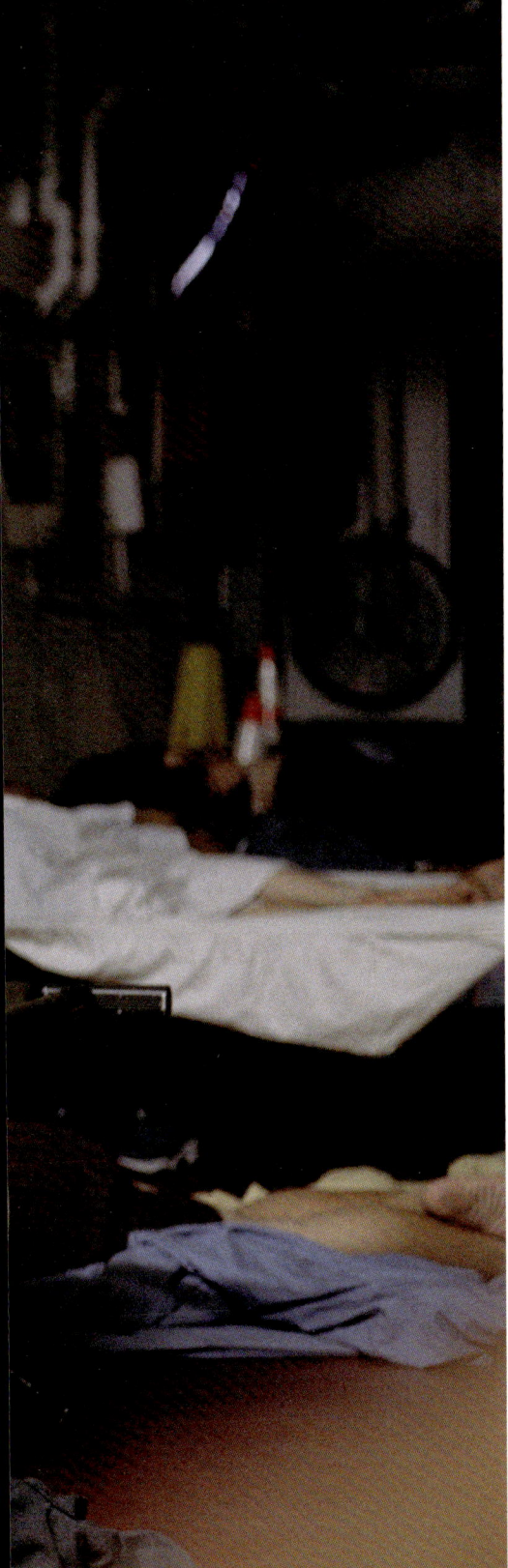

My good dreams are nightmares to other people. My good dreams was when I was killing him. Since the whole not sleeping thing, it started taking a toll on me 'cause I started not wanting to eat, not wanting to do anything.

Eternity

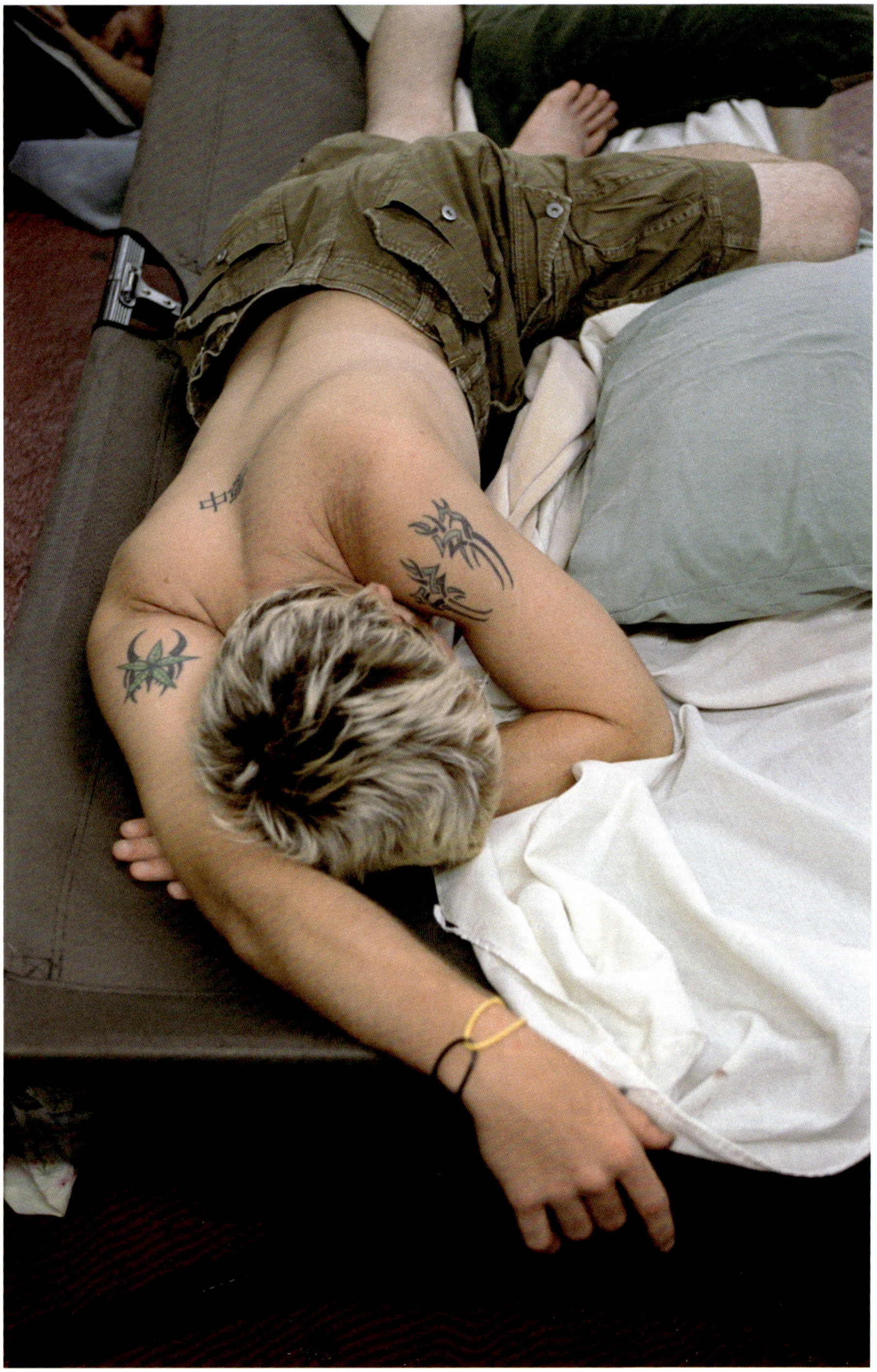

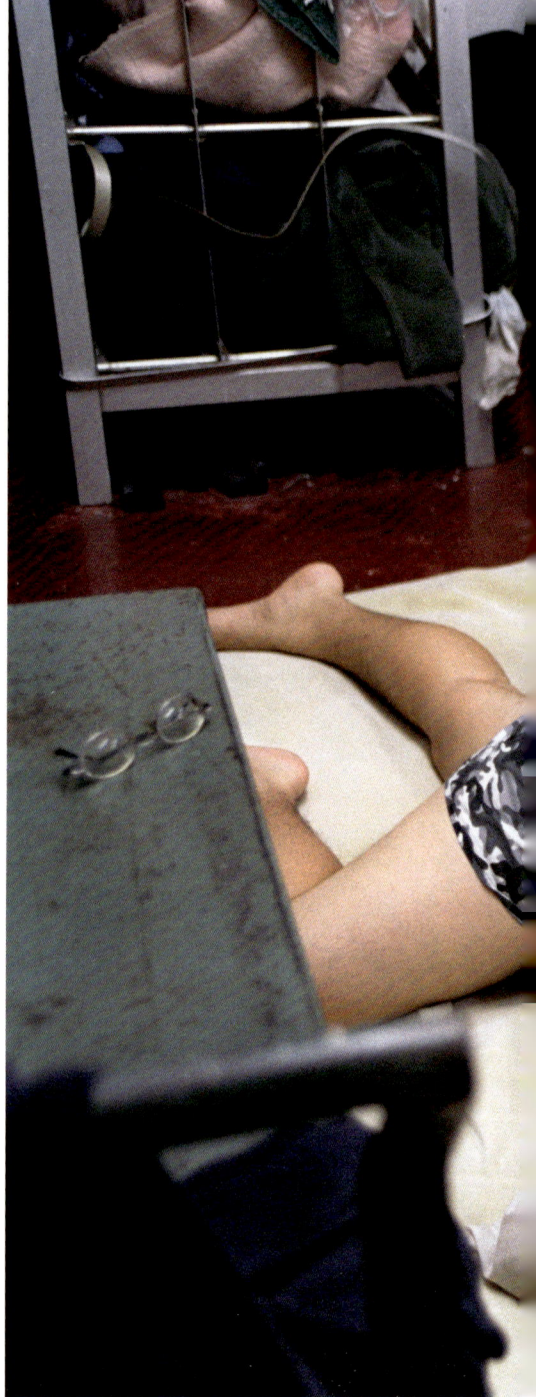

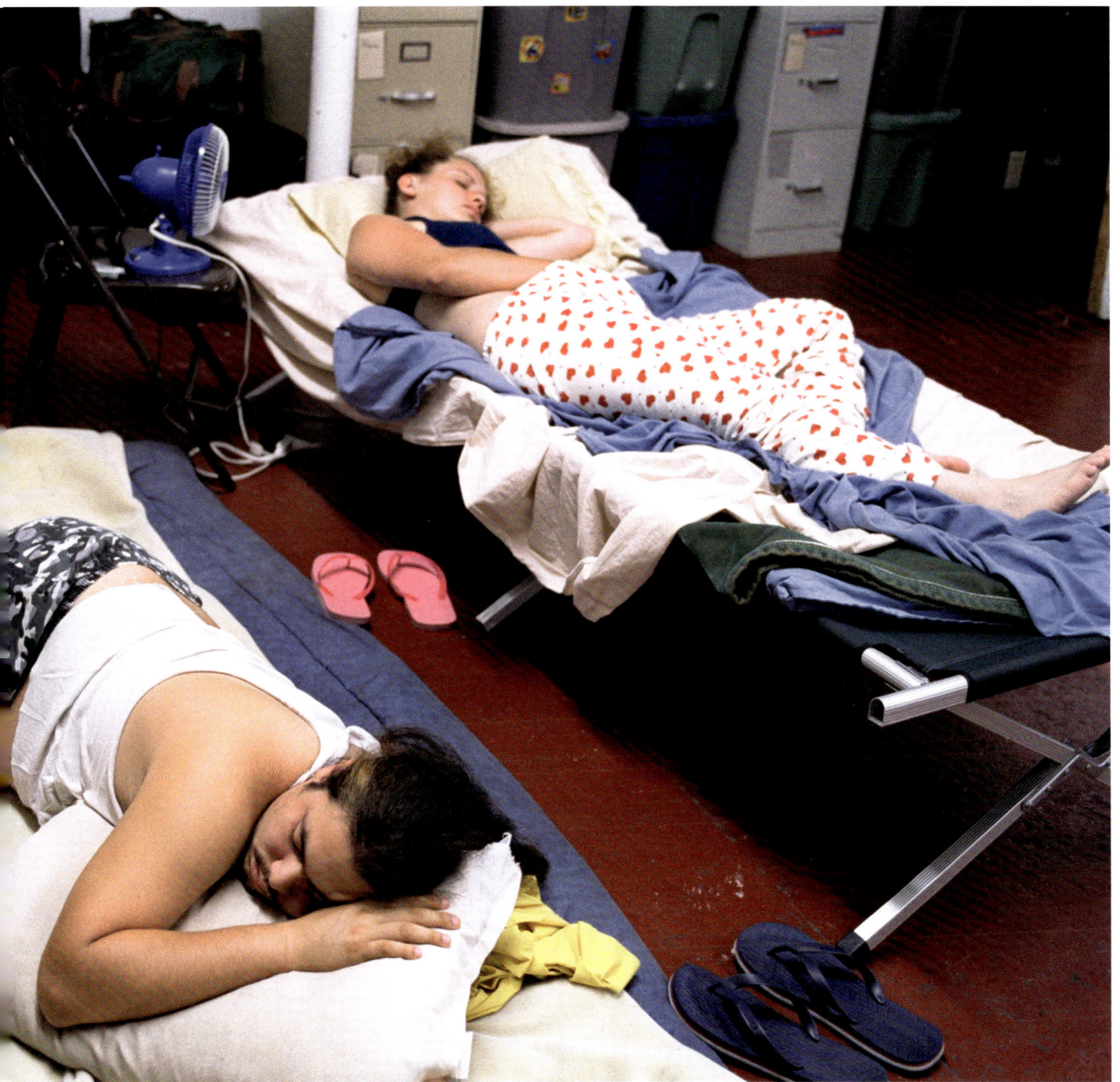

129 Shelter

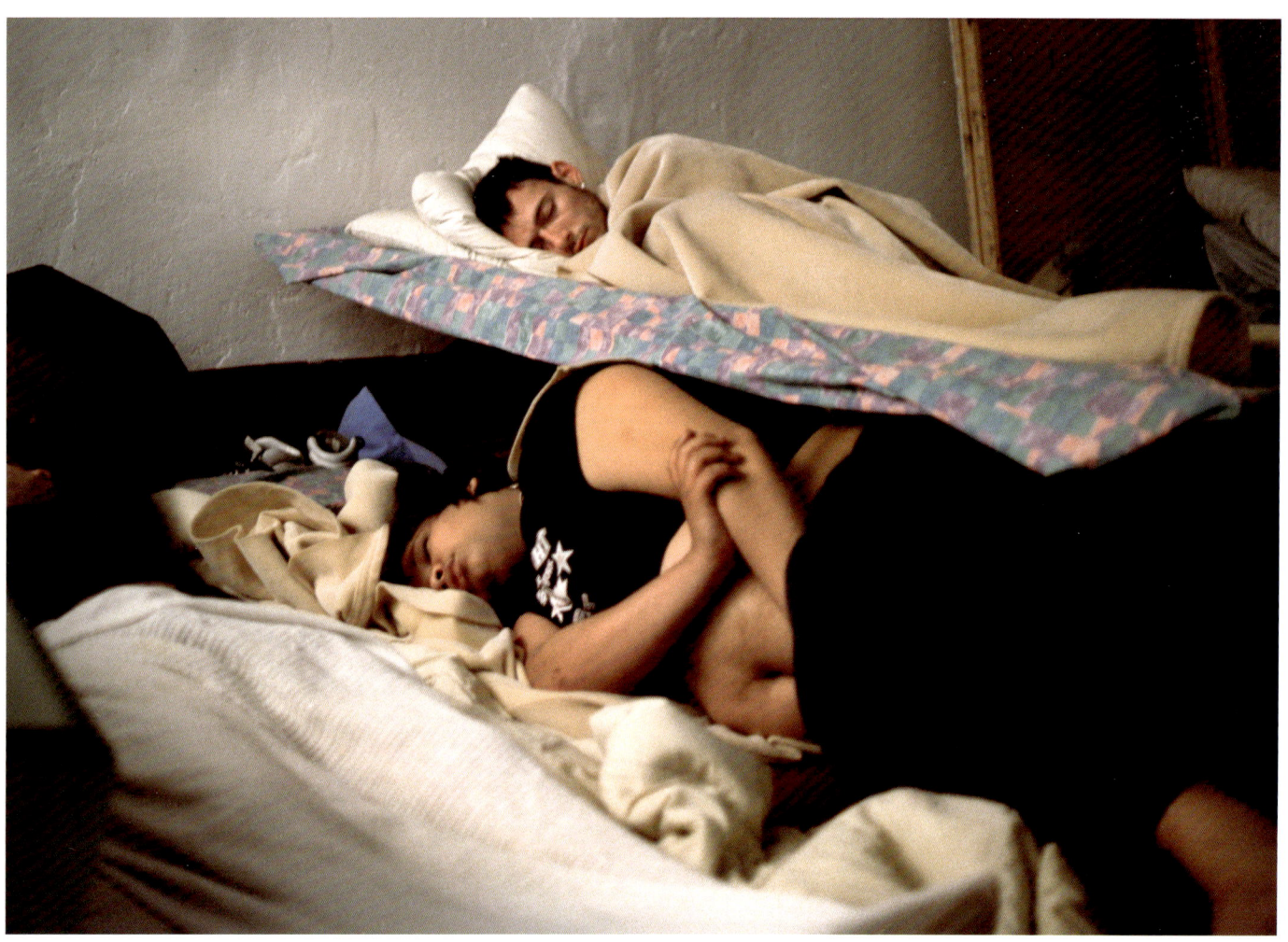

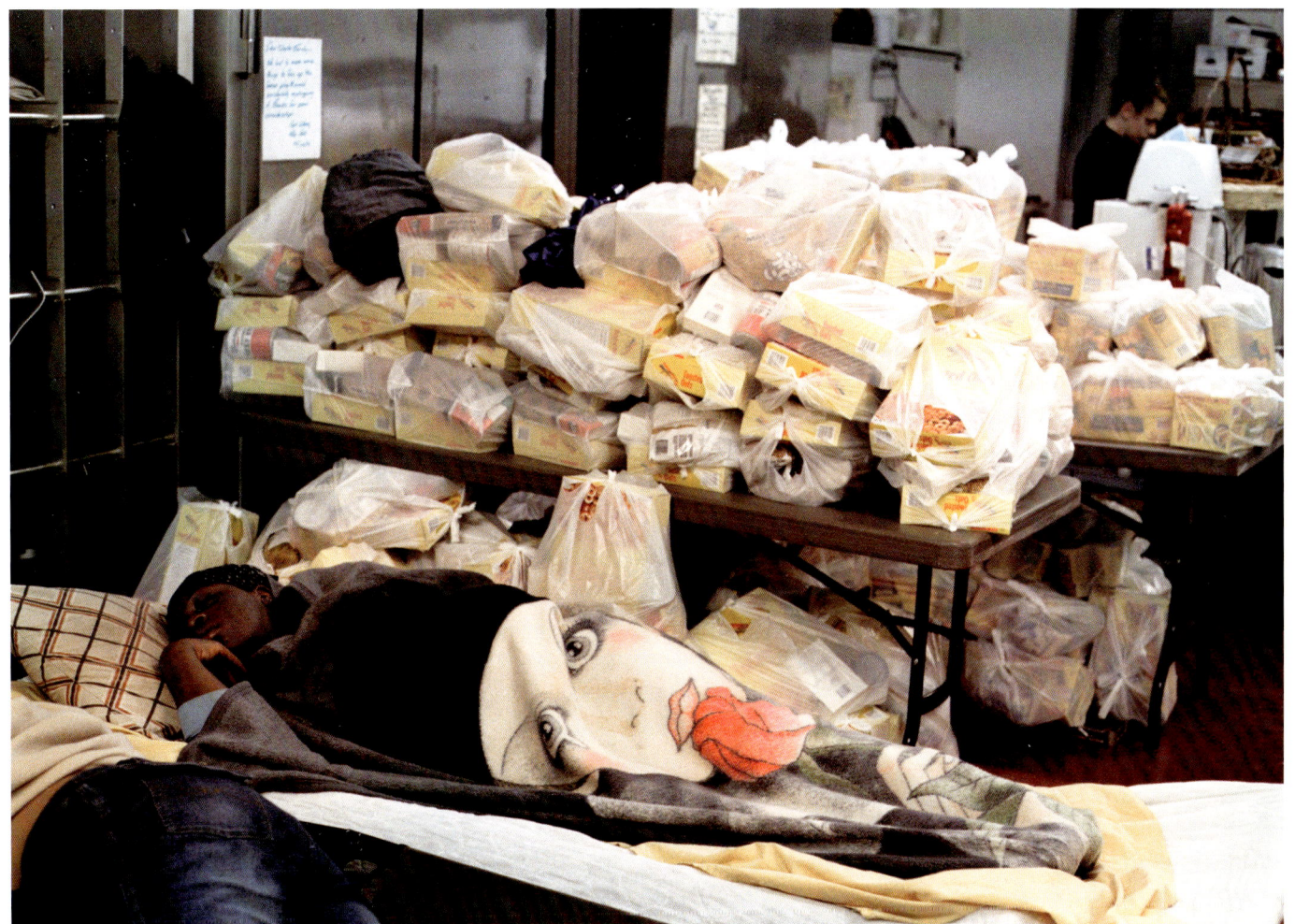

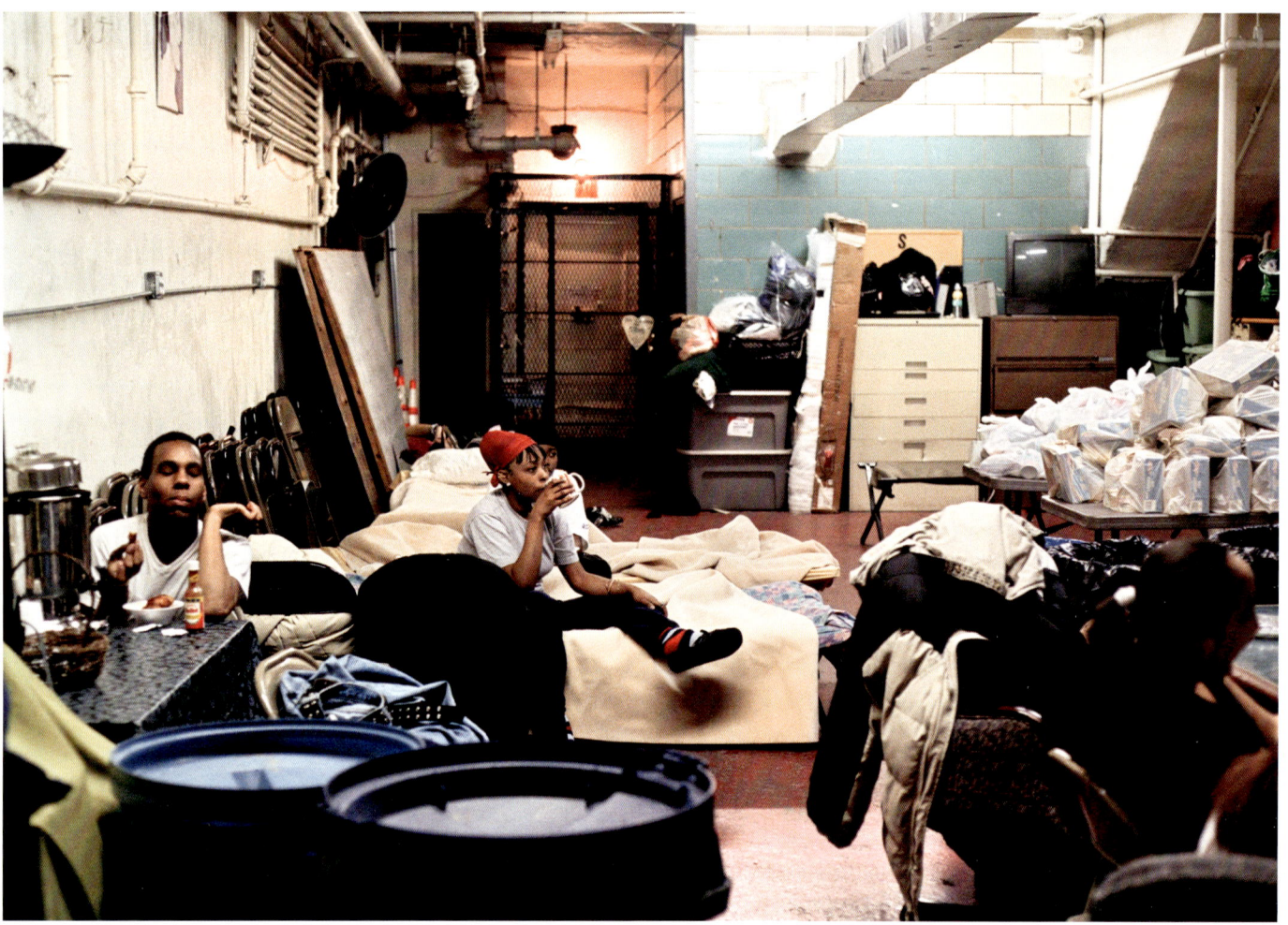

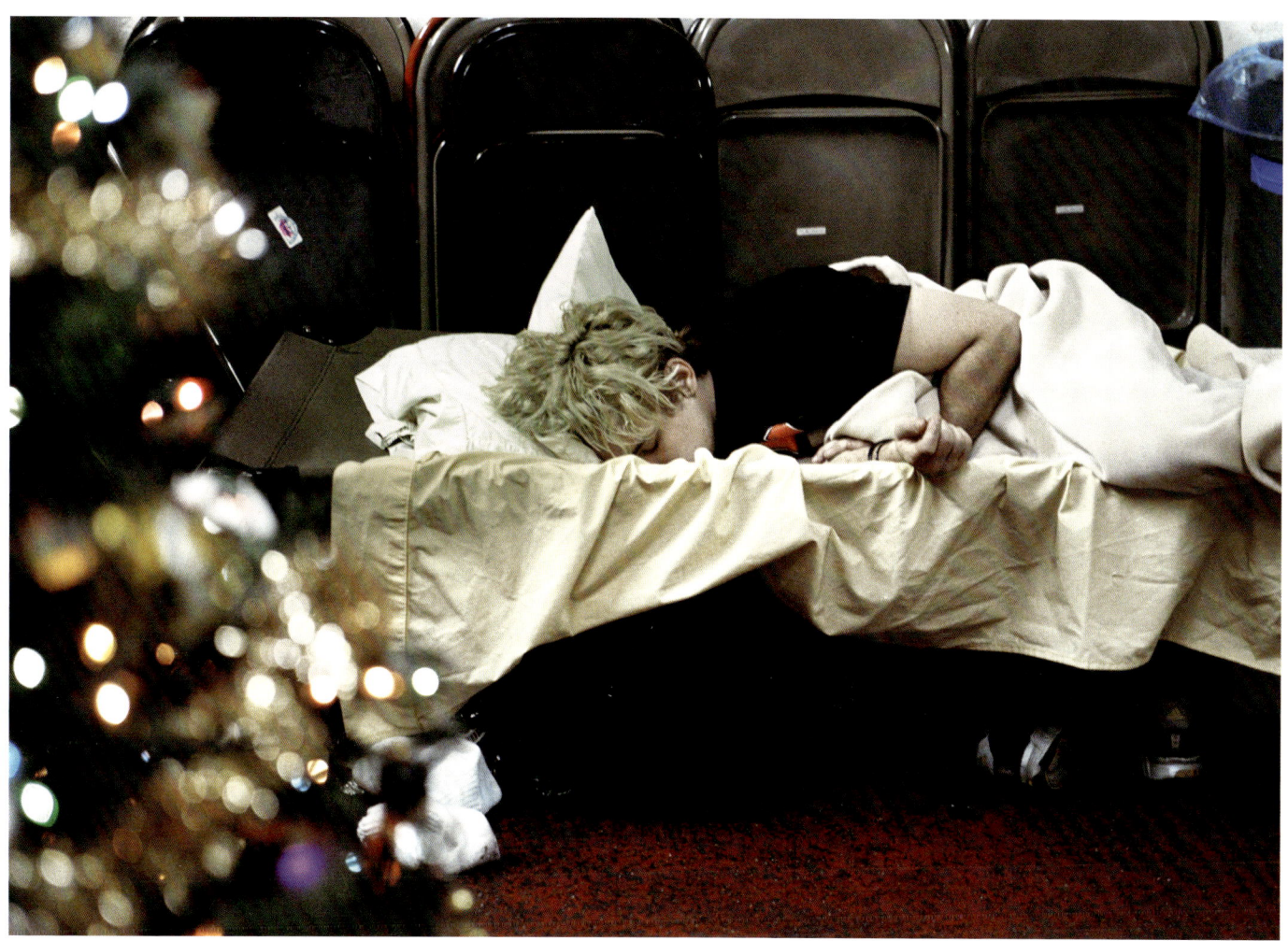

# Fact

Over the course of one year, between 2003 and 2004, 193 calls were made to a single shelter requesting beds for different LGBTQ Youth.

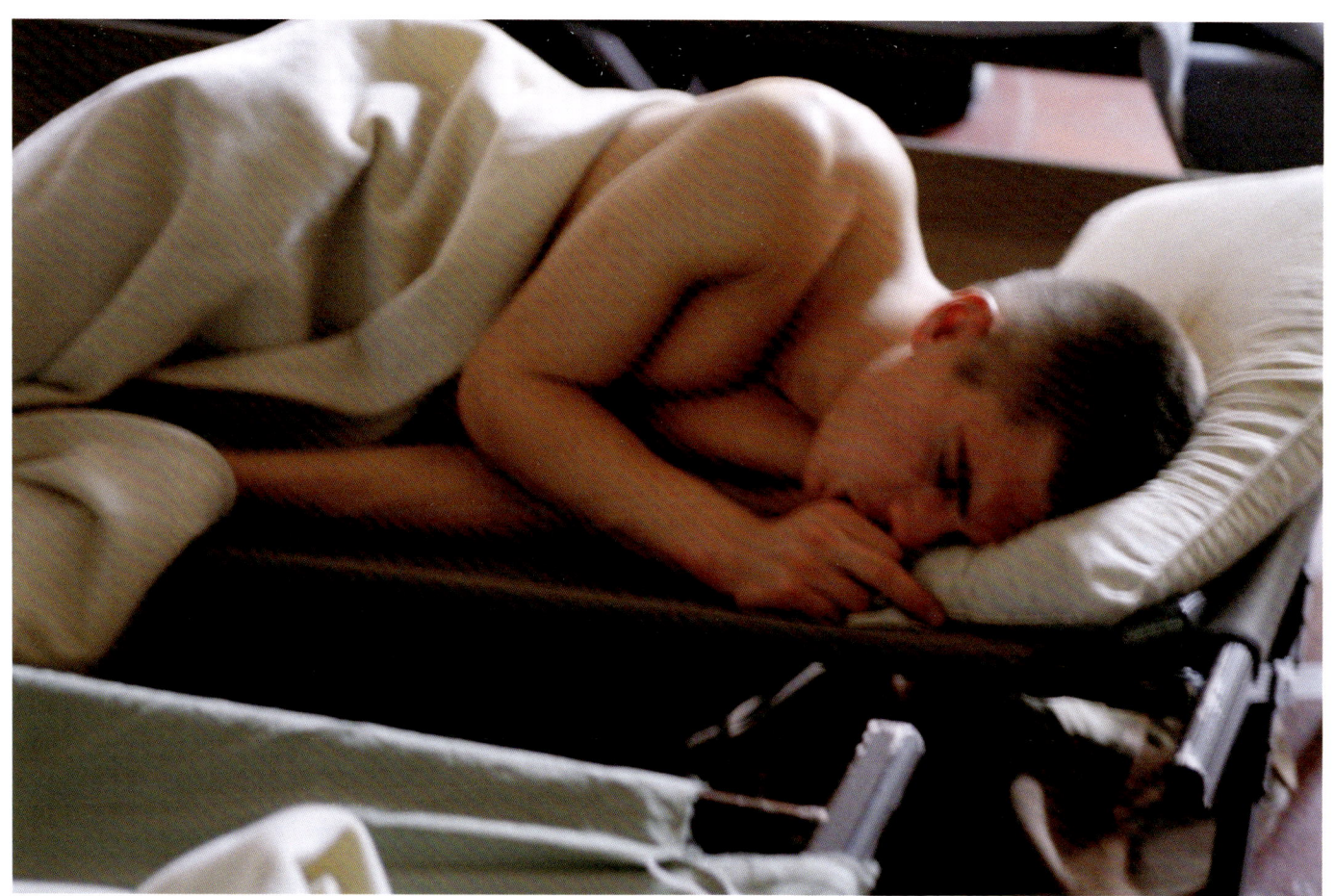

135 Shelter

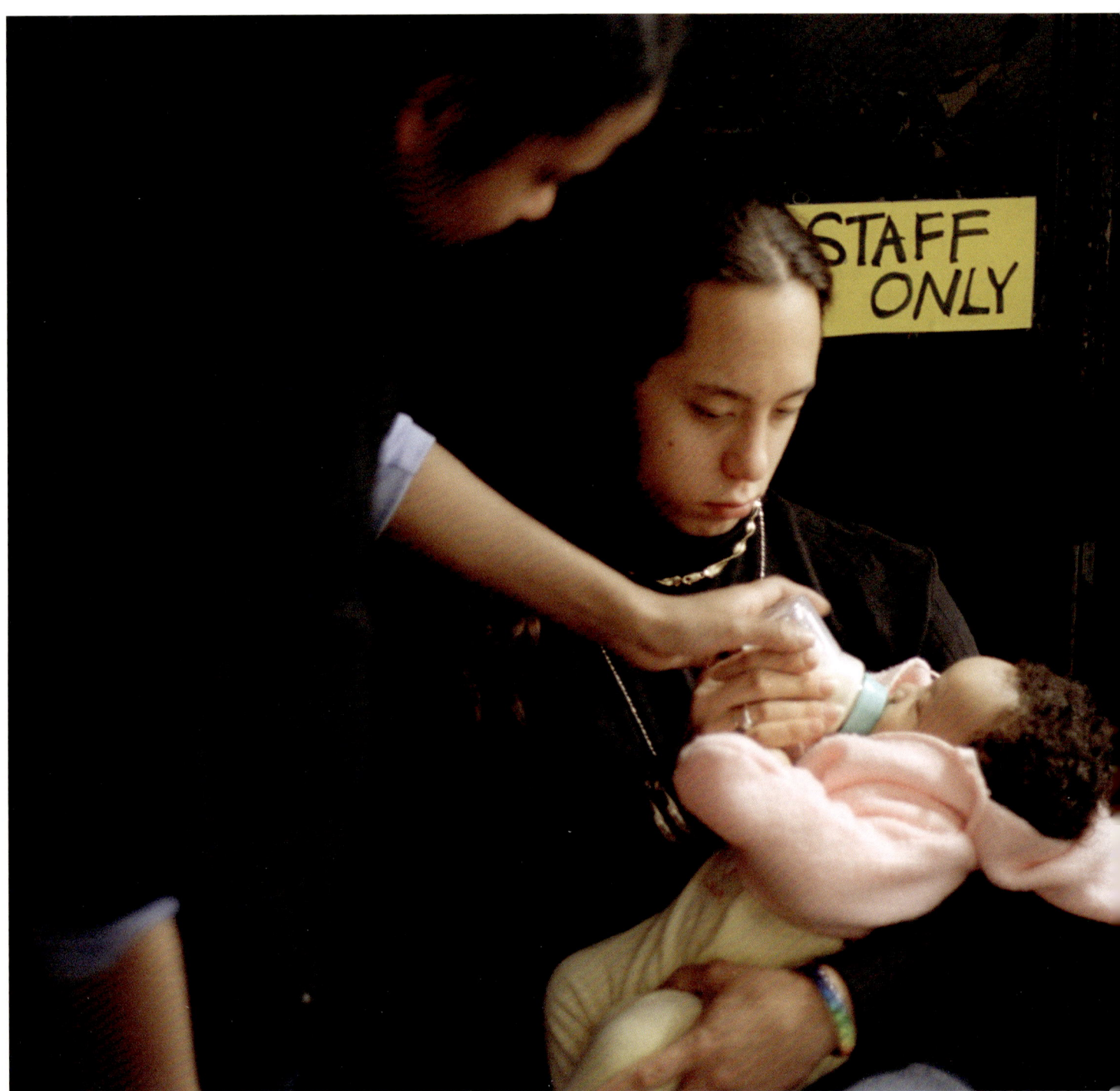

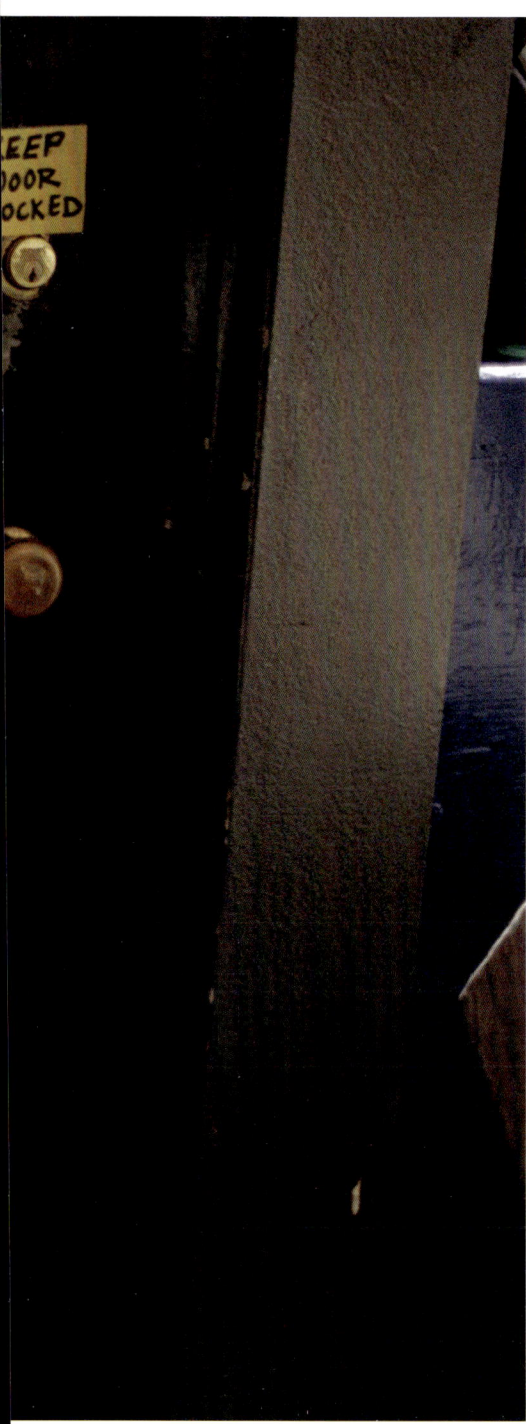

# New Years Eve

On the night of December 31st, 2003, residents of Sylvia's Place slowly shuffled into the black gate and set up their beds as if it were any other night. Some of them had been there longer than they had hoped they would be, while others were just barely becoming familiar with its surroundings. A new year was about to dawn, and for some this brought a painful reminder of the struggles they continued to deal with year after year. Underneath the frustration, however, there remained a glimmer of hope and promise. Gathering in front of a small TV, the clients raised their styrofoam cups filled with juice or soda, and counted down the new year with the thousands of people watching the ball drop just a few blocks away in Times Square. After a few celebratory hugs, most of the residents curled up in their cots, or spread out on the floor, and fell asleep waiting for morning to come. Eternity, like she had done so many nights before, lay awake the whole night avoiding the nightmares that most surely awaited.

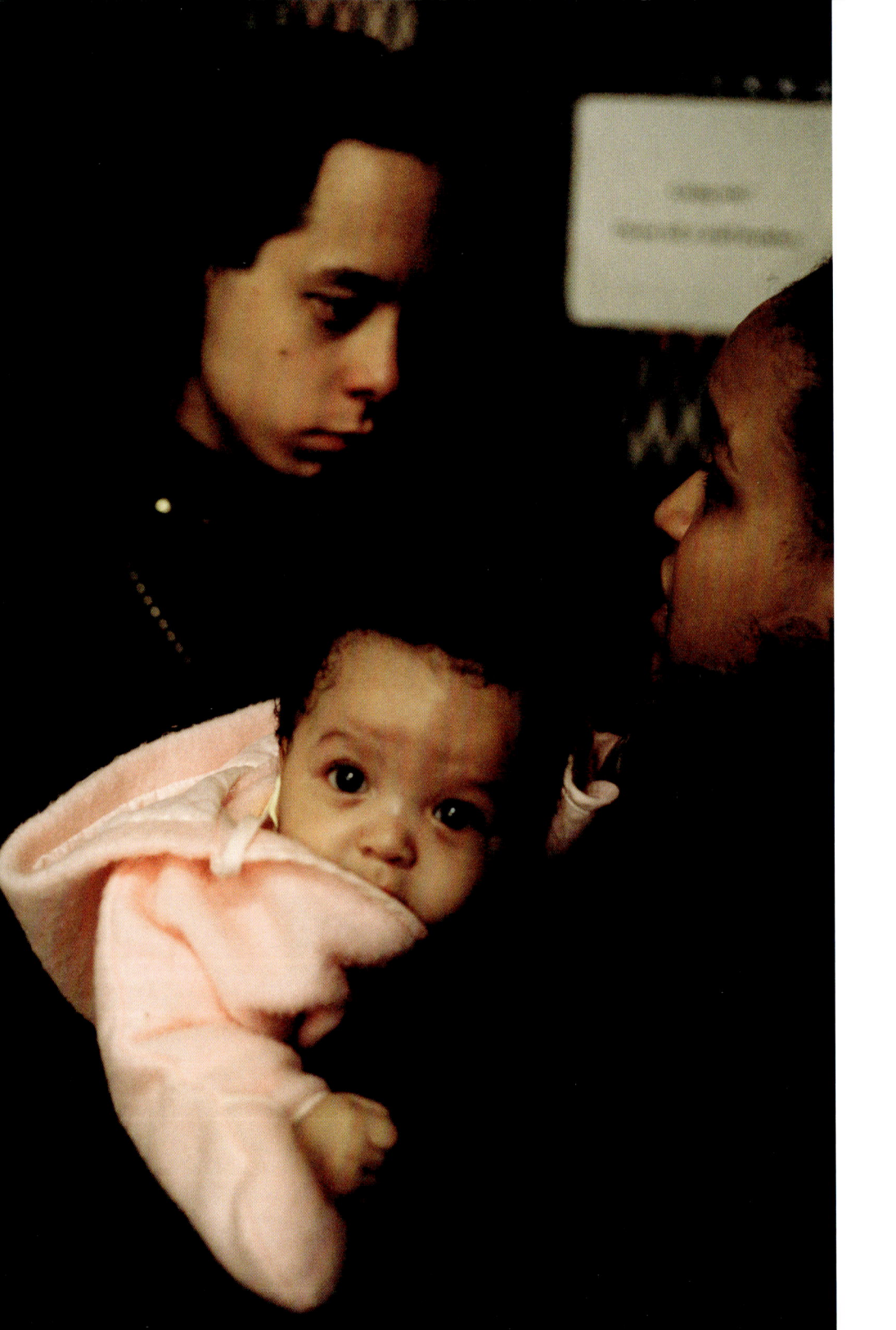

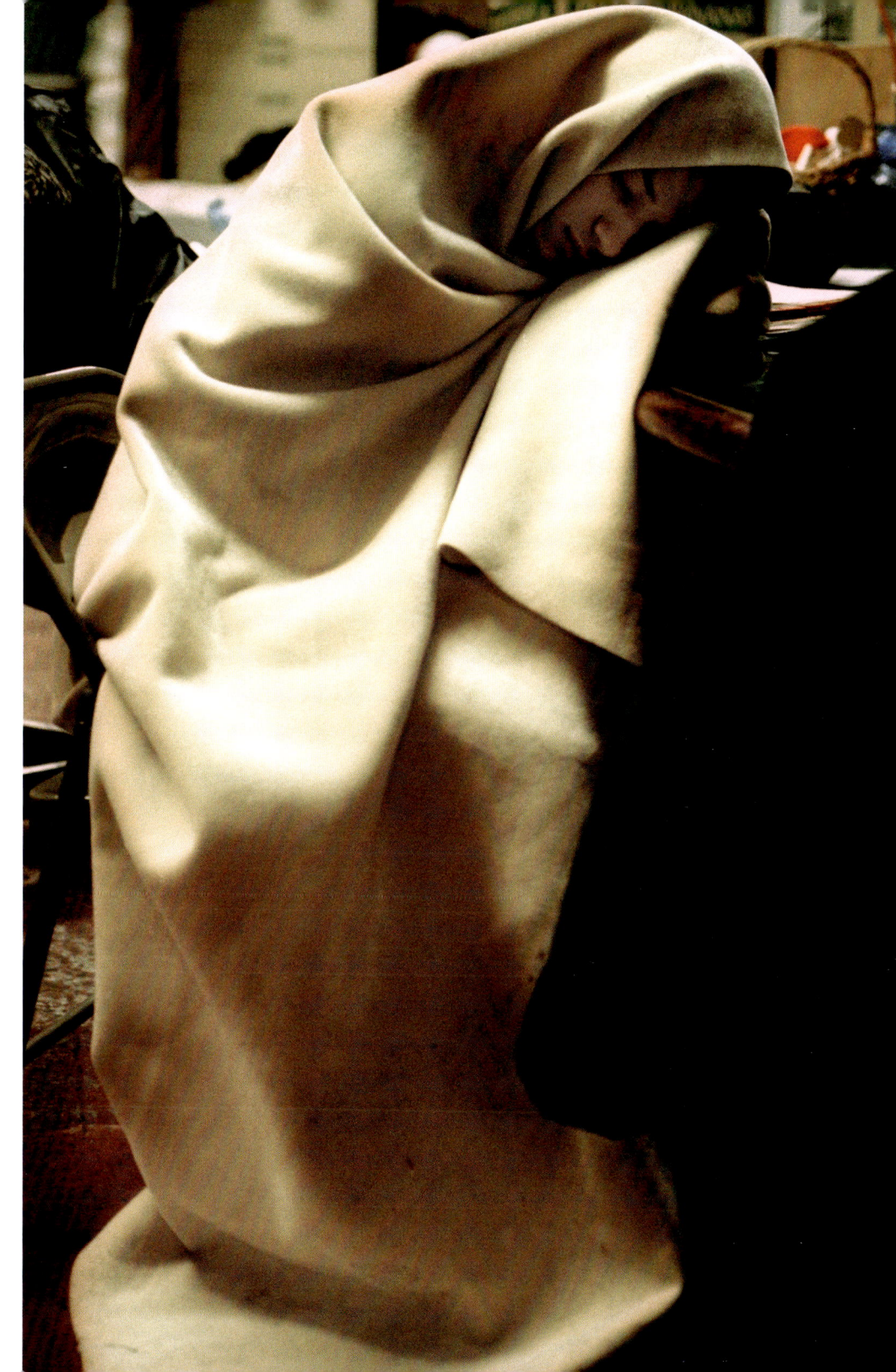

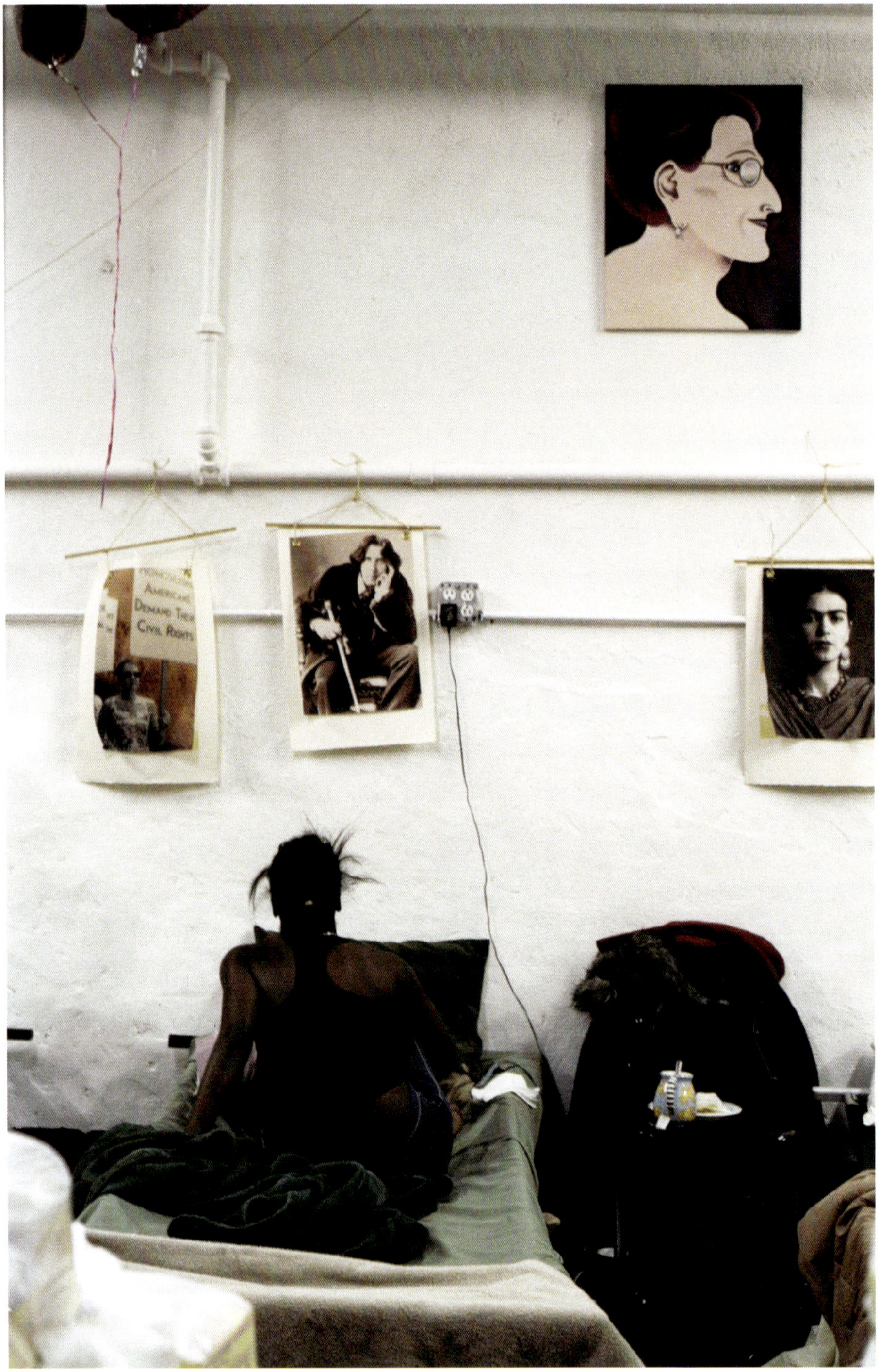

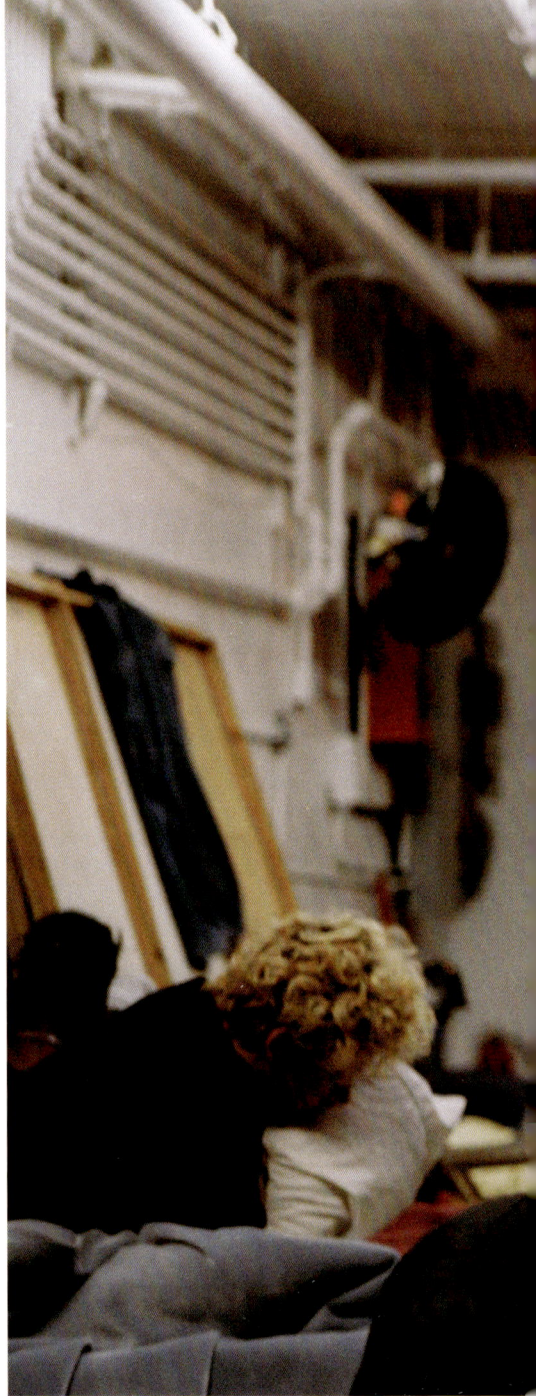

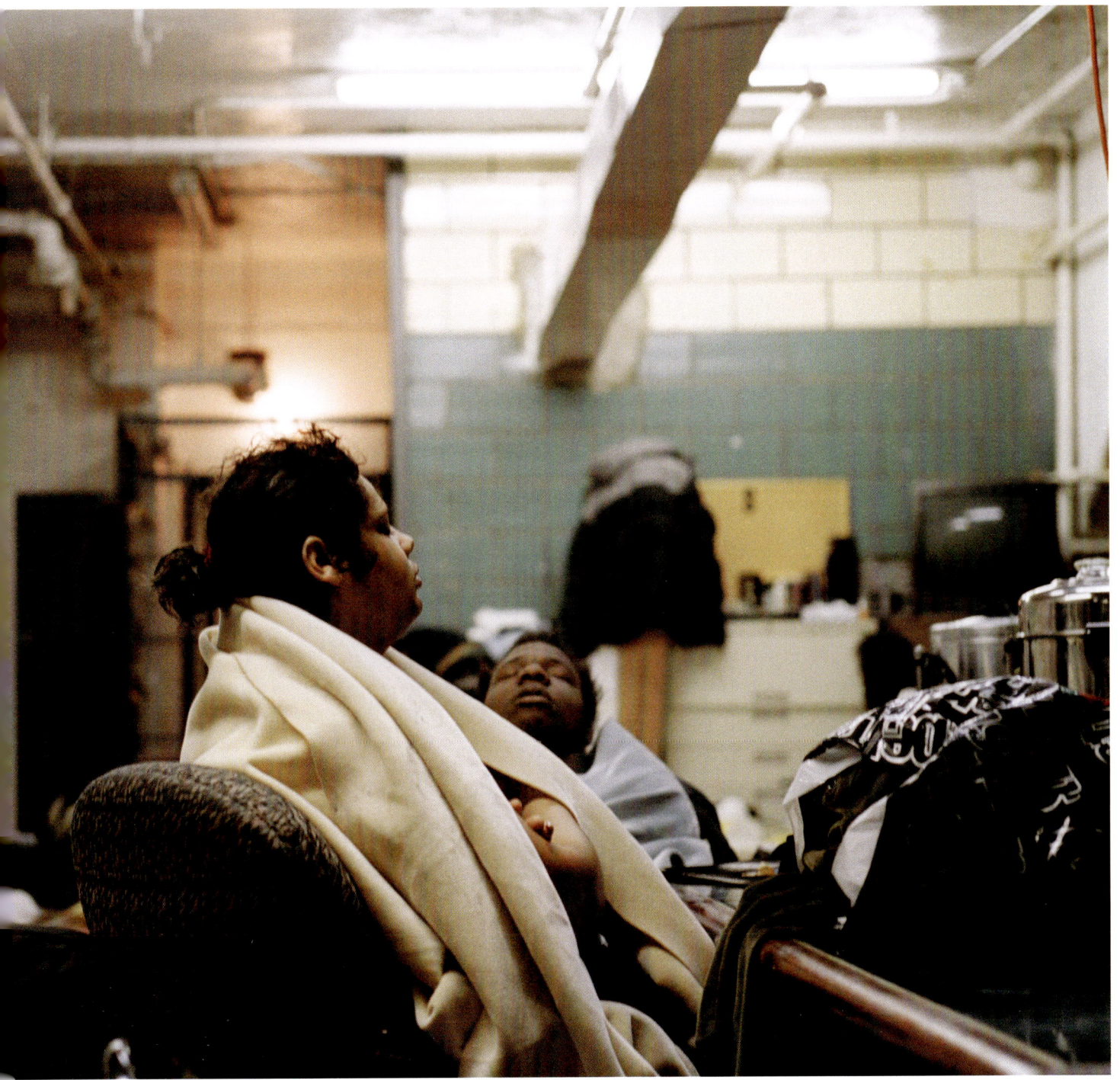

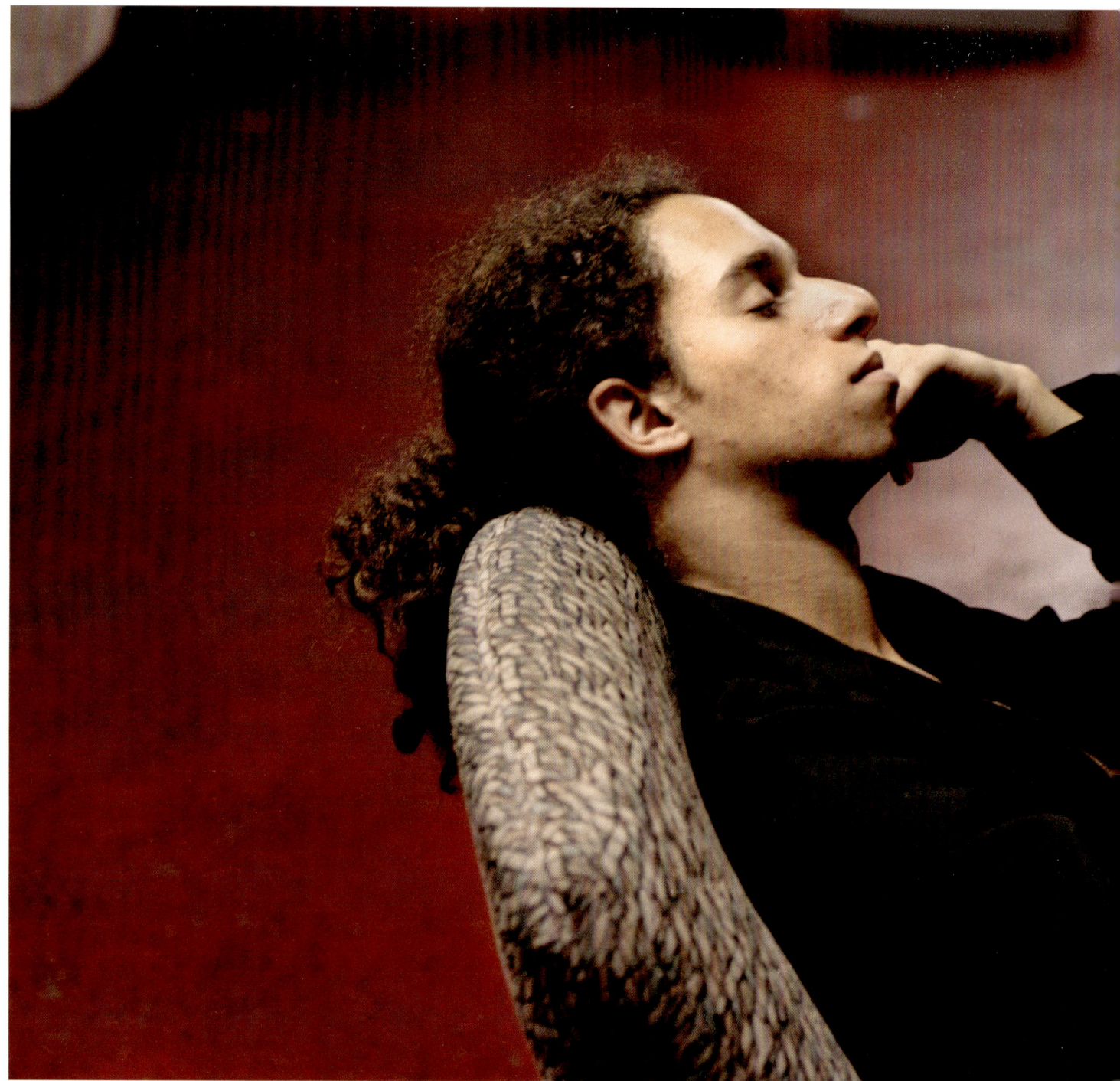

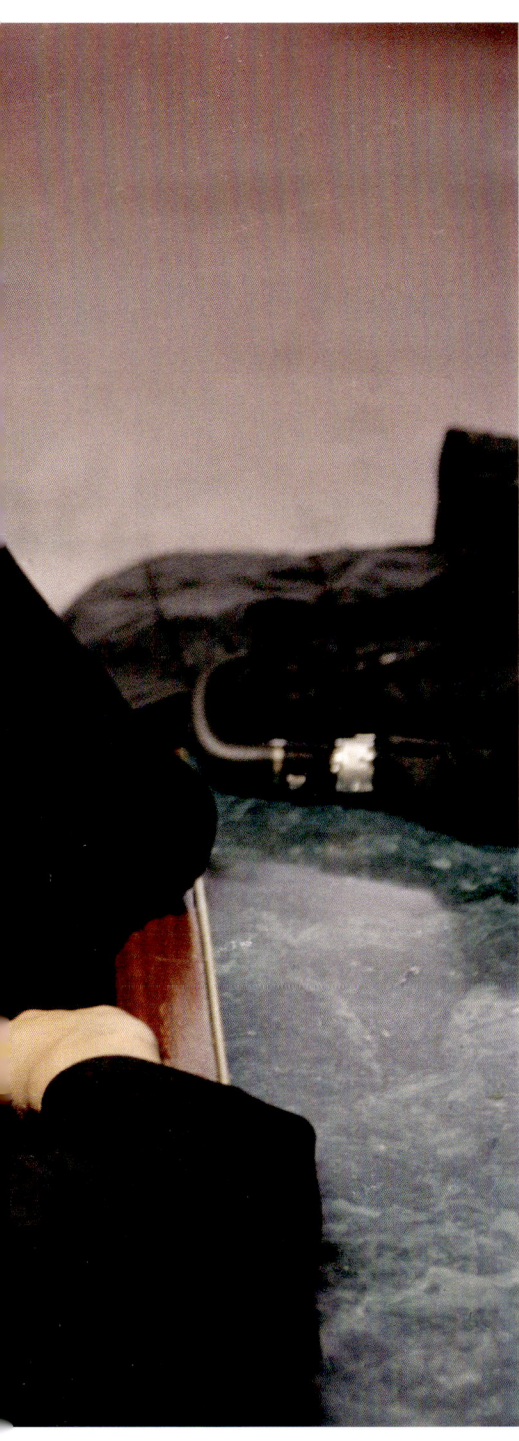

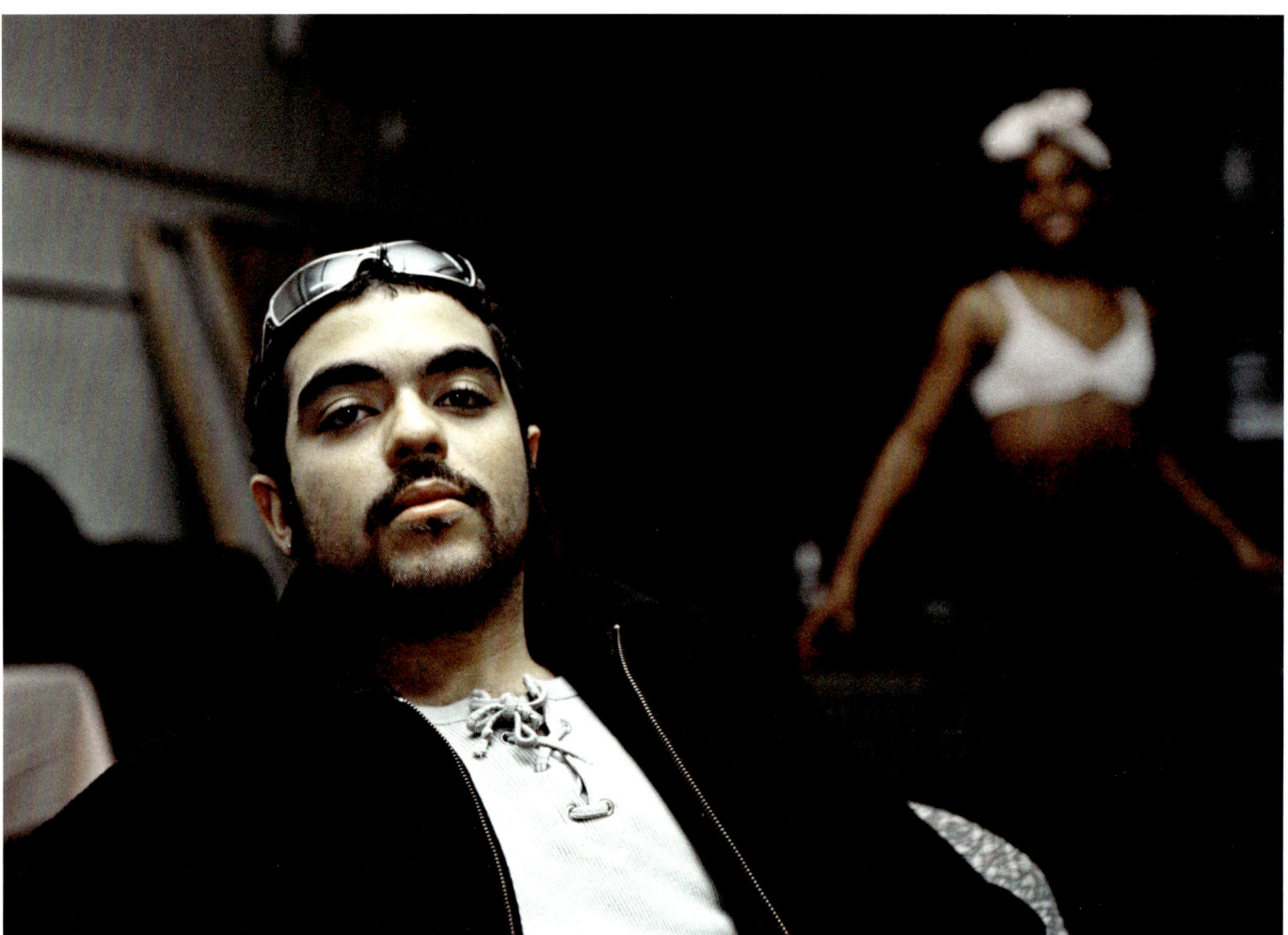

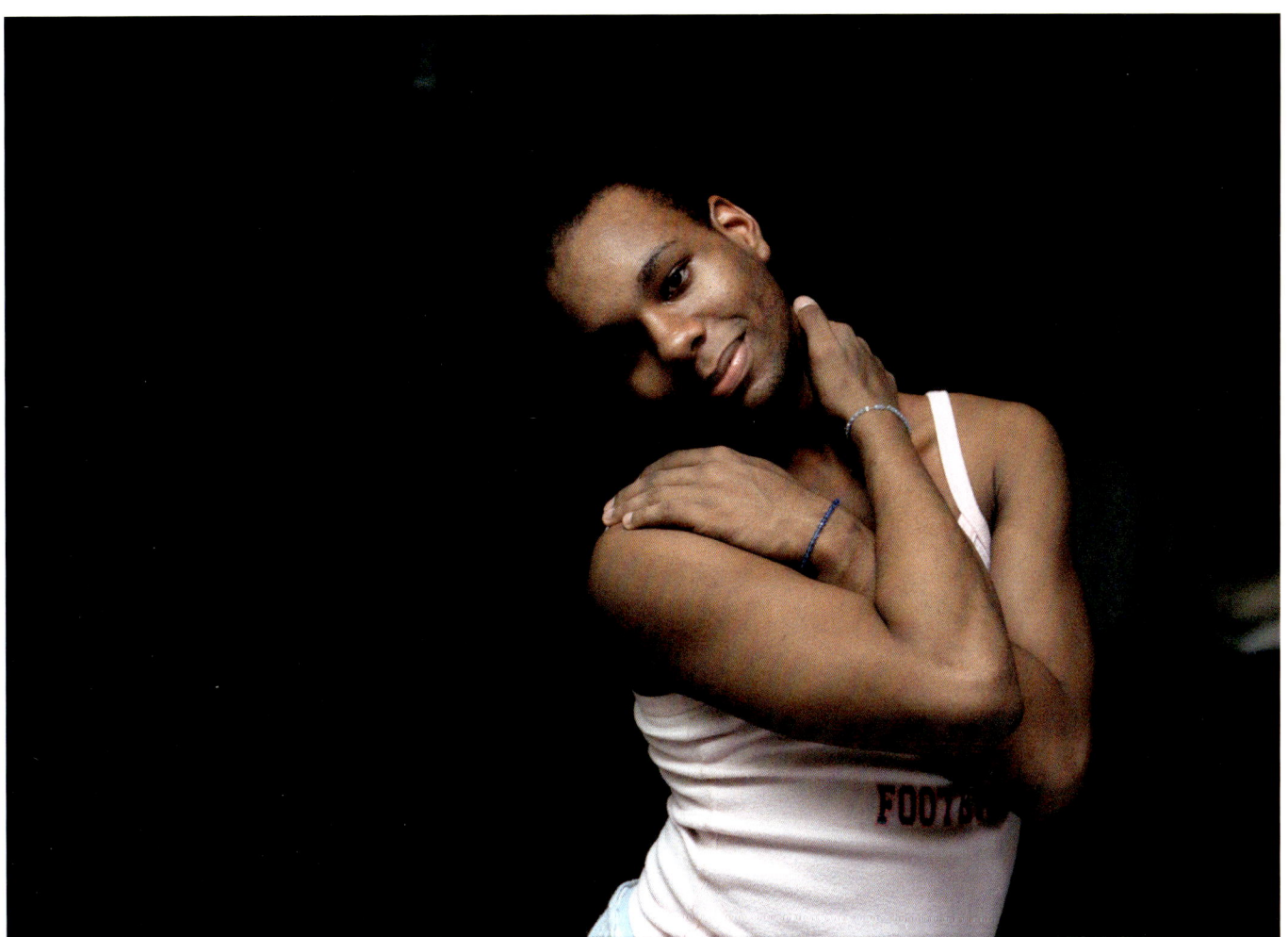

# Hate Crime

*I call my friend at about 7:30 at night. I tell him that I have a business proposition for him. I'm going to give him all of my drugs, a lot of drugs. I'm going to stop selling it. I'm moving out of this business. I'm gonna take this cash and I'm going and fixing my life. So, he tells me to meet him out in Central Park at about 9:30. 9:45 hits and he comes walking up the hill and sees two guys walking up to another guy that was sitting there with his girlfriend. They did not know it was me.*

Malice was sitting under a tree in Central Park when it happens. He has almost no memory of it. He only knows what people have told him.

*One guy just comes out of nowhere. Started beating me with the truck, the metal truck of the skateboard. He hit me so many times and so hard, the last time he hit me he swung it at me and goes to pull it back and it slipped out of his fingers 'cause it was stuck to my head. He grabbed it and dragged me for about ten feet, stepped on my stomach and ripped it out. When he pulled it out, that whole scar on my head was crushed and gone. The whole left quarter of my skull was shattered to little pieces. I don't have full memories of it, but because it happened so long ago, I'm starting to get them back.*

*As soon as I said I was not gonna do this no more. As soon as I was planning on changing my life…*

For over a month, Malice was in a coma. He was touch and go for most of that time. Most of his friends assumed him dead. The staff at Sylvia's Place received updates from his father at the hospital. No one knew if he would wake up.

Thankfully, he did.

*After the accident, I came out of the rehab center and everything, and I get off the bus at the Canal street station and I go walking up. I'm passing by the cube area, around 8th St. and St. Mark's. Somebody sees me. Out of nowhere, I didn't expect to see anyone, I didn't even remember I had friends.*

*So out of nowhere I hear, "What the fuck? Malice!"*

*I seen three people. They came running in my direction, they look at me, and two of them drop straight to the floor and pass out. I was like, what happened?*

*The guy looks at me and says, "Malice, you're not alive, you're a ghost, aren't you?"*

*I poked him in his lip.*

*"Malice, everybody thought you were dead. We held a wake for you at Union Square. We had your picture, candles, incense, everybody crying their eyes out, they thought you died."*

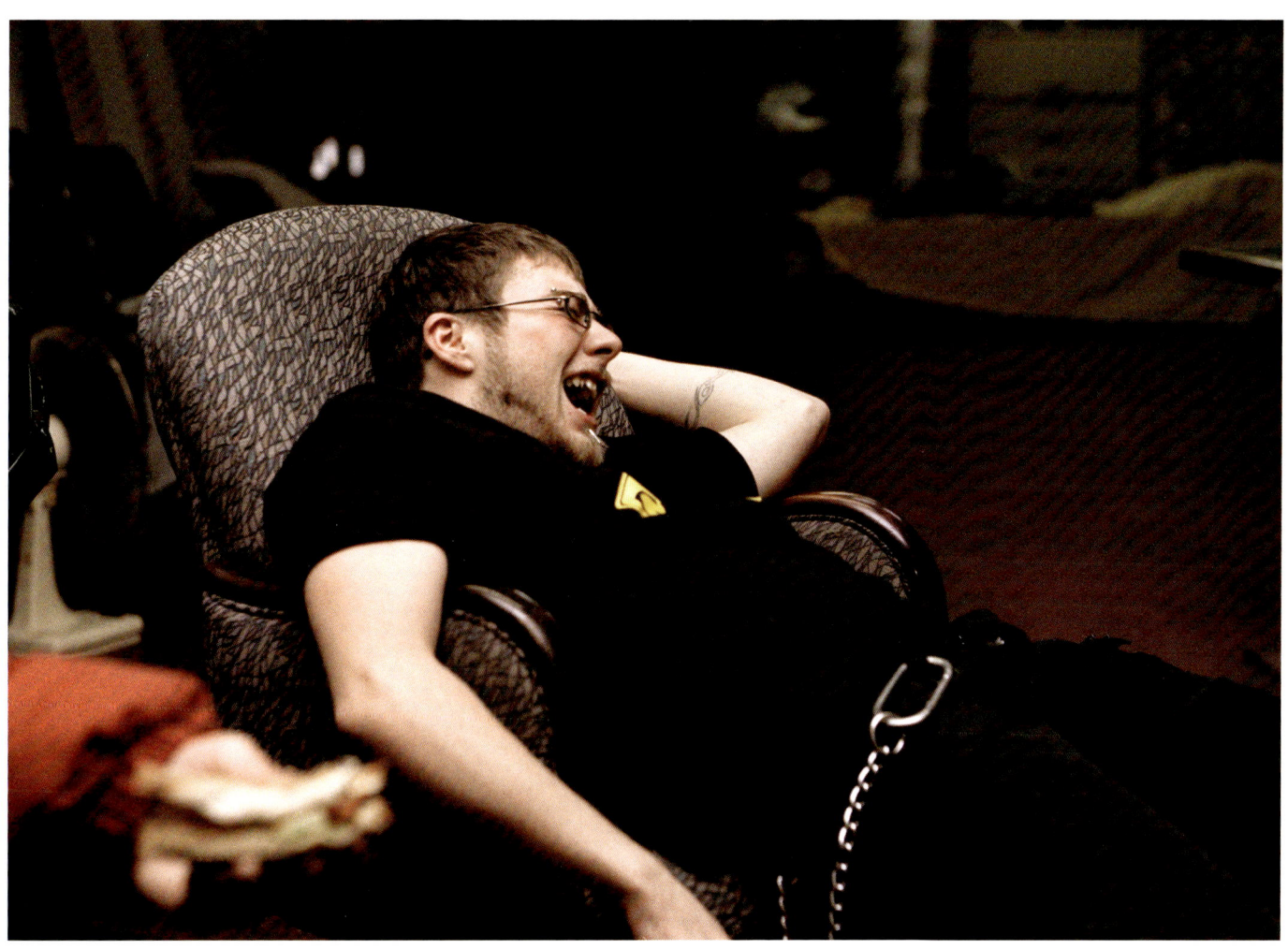

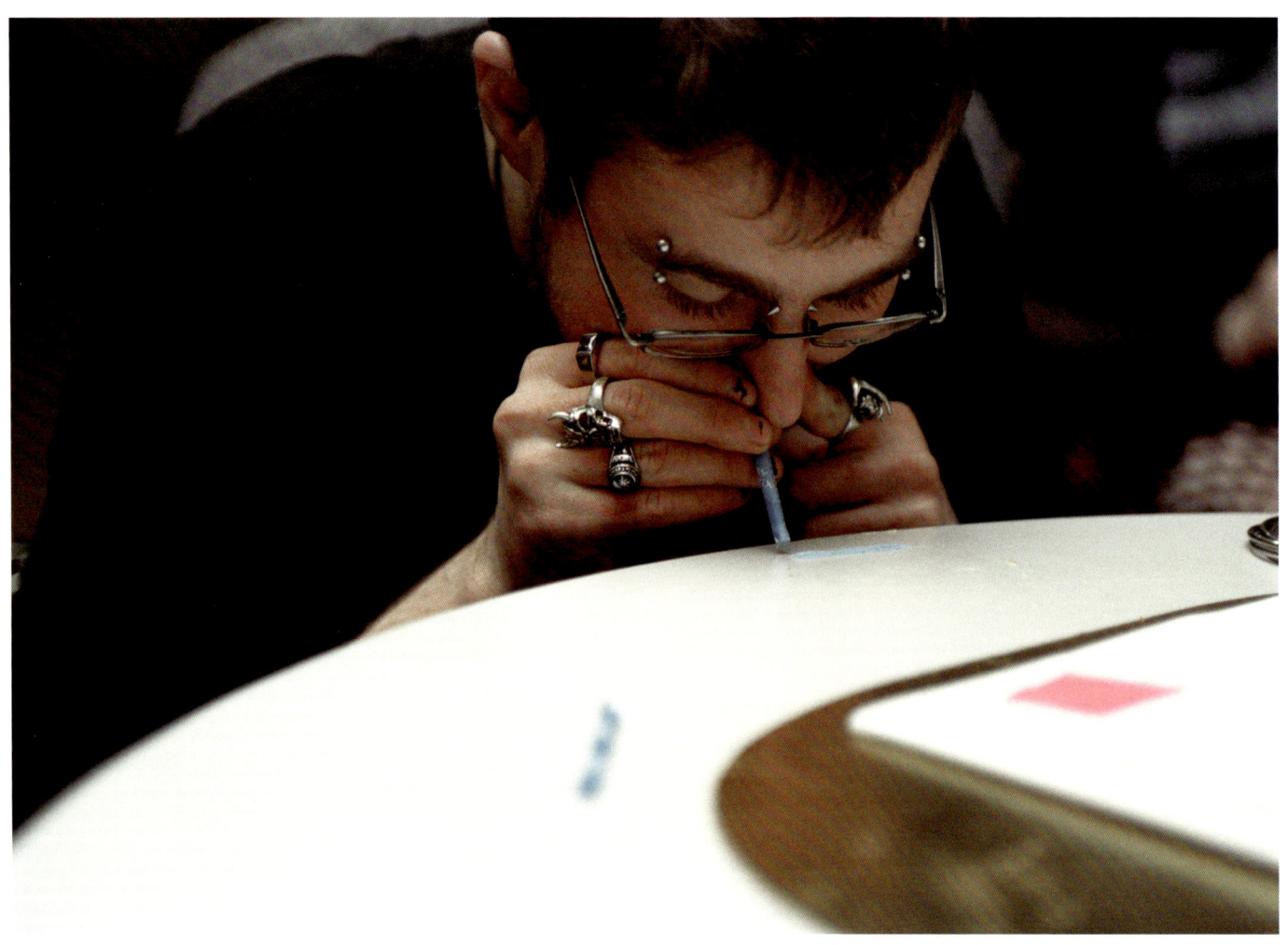

The attack changed Malice's life forever. The surgery's left him with permanent brain injuries and socially he was never quite the same. His memory was mostly gone and didn't know where to go. He couldn't even remember the name of the shelter he'd spent so much time at the year before.

*I had no memories because the left quarter of my brain was damaged. I was on the streets. I mean, I had a couple of friends that I could spend a couple days at their house but that's it.*

Eventually, he had a chance encounter that led him back to Sylvia's Place nearly four months after he left rehab. It was the first time Sylvia's Place staff had seen Malice since the accident. Immediately, staff began getting him connected with the social services that he clearly deserved. In a familiar environment, Malice started slowly getting his memories back and eventually, got back in contact with his mother.

*When I made it back here to Sylvia's I started getting in contact with my mother and talking to her. And she said she wanted me to come back and live with her. So, I thought, cool, why not? So, I went to Florida to live with my mother. It was going good for about two, three weeks. And then I found out that her and her boyfriend were smoking crack. That hurts. There are two drugs in this world that I can't stand: crack and heroin. In my eyes, they are the worst drugs in*

*this world. And when I found out my mother smoked crack, I started feeling down right there.*

*I got a job working at a gas station. Pumping gas early in the morning. Going back in the afternoon, sweeping, mopping, stocking stuff up and everything, just setting up everything. I get my first paycheck. $85.*

*I go home, I had a huge smile on my face, my mother comes up to me:*
*"Give me your money!"*

*I said, "What?"*

*"That's not yours, it's mine."*

*"No it's not, I worked for it."*

*"I don't care, give me half of it. You're living with me, I want half of it."*

*"And what's that for?"*

*"It's for my crack. Give it to me right now!"*

*You're gonna take your son's work money for crack? That's not nice. That's why I left Florida. I came straight back to Sylvia's the day I got off the plane.*

# Fact

Queer youth are 7 times more likely to be the victim of crime than their heterosexual counterparts.

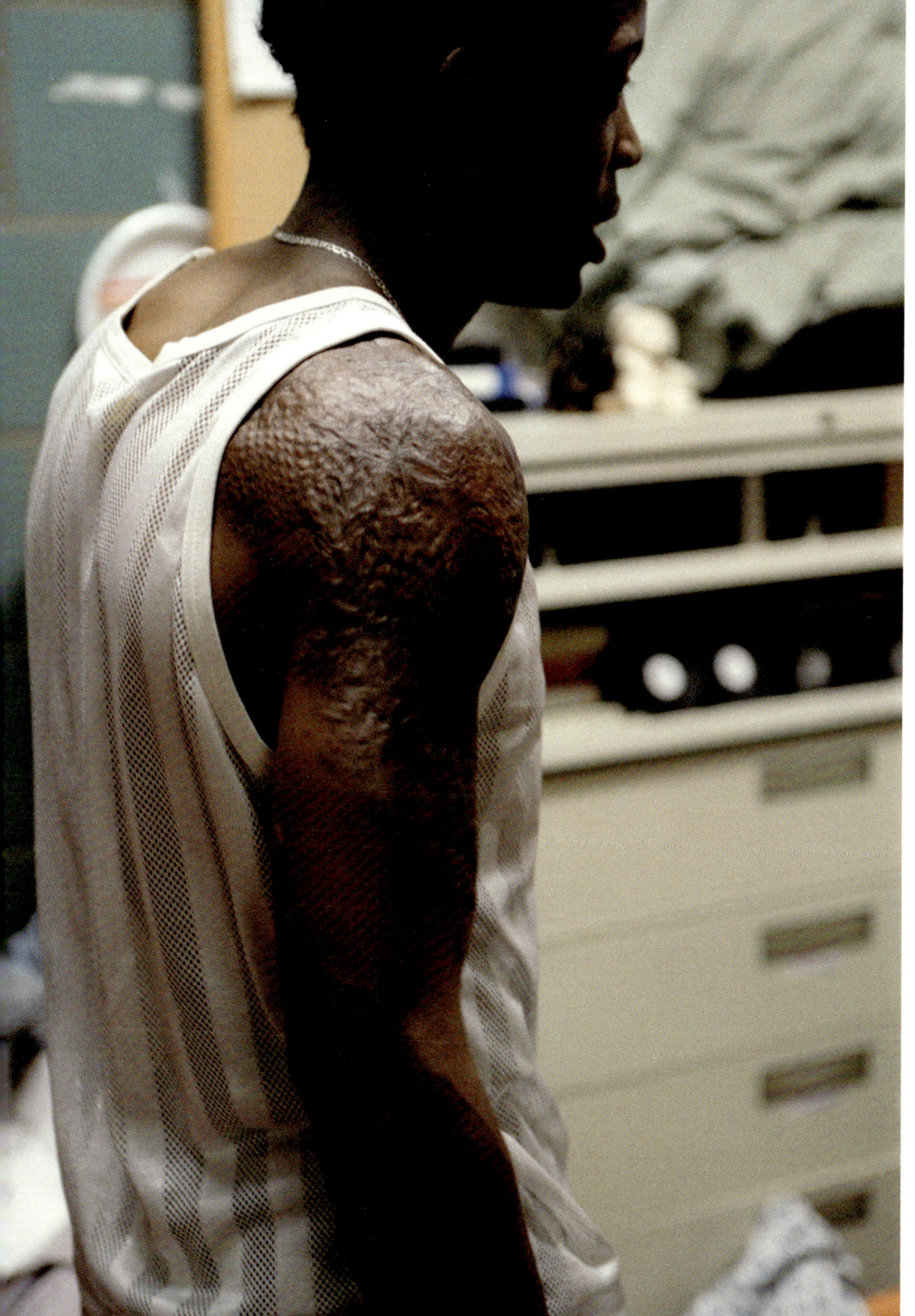

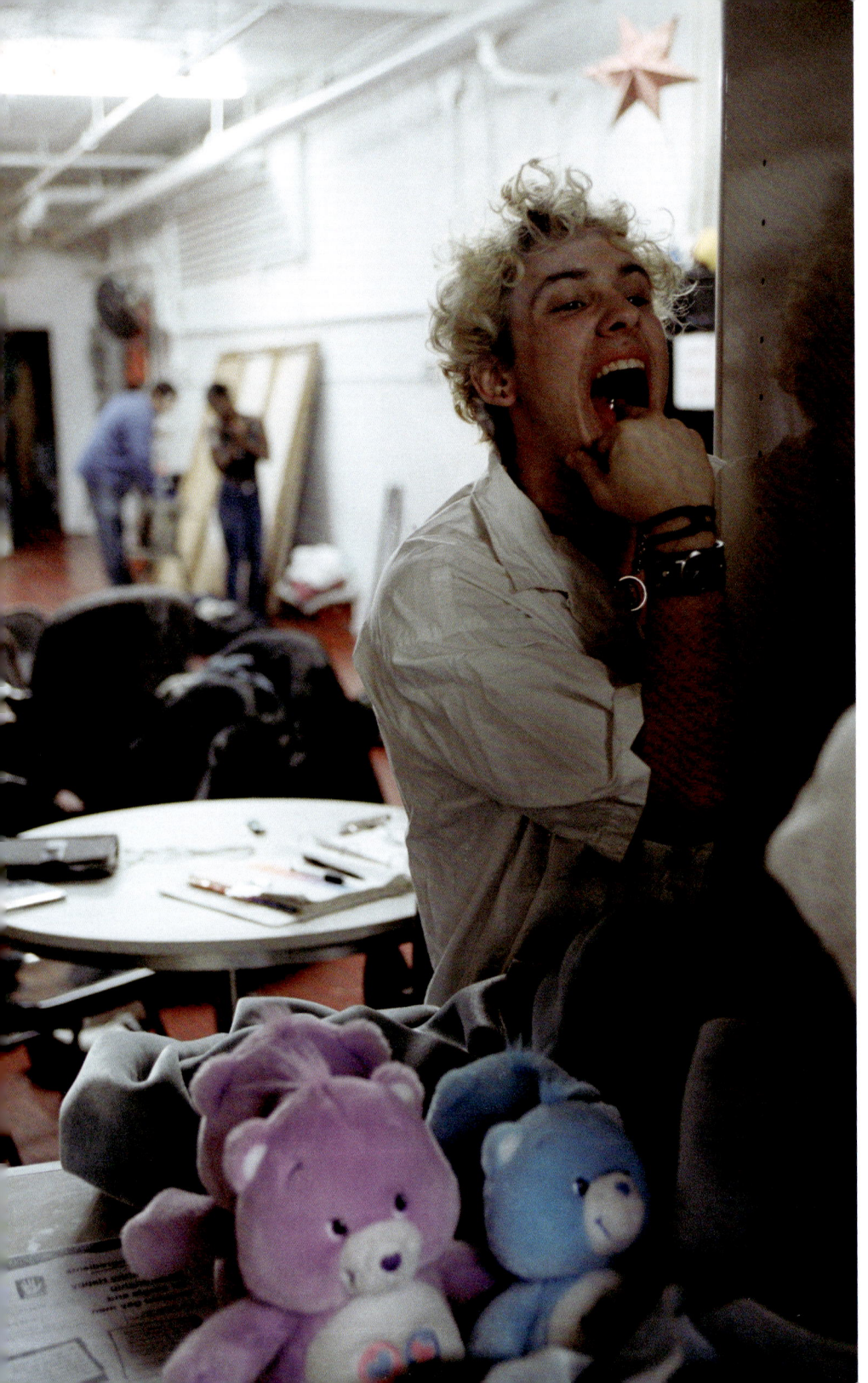

Within the walls of Sylvia's Place, many residents have found relationships in the most unlikely of people. Connections like these have made bitter pills a little easier to swallow, or added scars to an already damaged heart. Some of these relationships have had more success than others, but all of them served their purpose. For Eternity, relationships she had at Sylvia's Place had varying degrees of impact. None of them lasted.

*There's this one guy that stole my heart and his name was Idrees. He was great. He meant the world to me. He still does in a way. He's a bastard but I still love him.*

*There was this other boy here, by the name of Will. He was an asshole. I can't say that I actually love him anymore. All the love that I had for him is just ice cold now. He kissed this girl, while I was sleeping next to him. That relationship lasted about a month. We got married on Halloween and we called it quits on Thanksgiving.*

I love my children because they actually talk to me and most people find that weird or strange, because I can hear them talking to me. It sounds kind of funny. My children talk to me, but they're stuffed animals. I just know that they love me...I know my Care Bears love me. Eternity

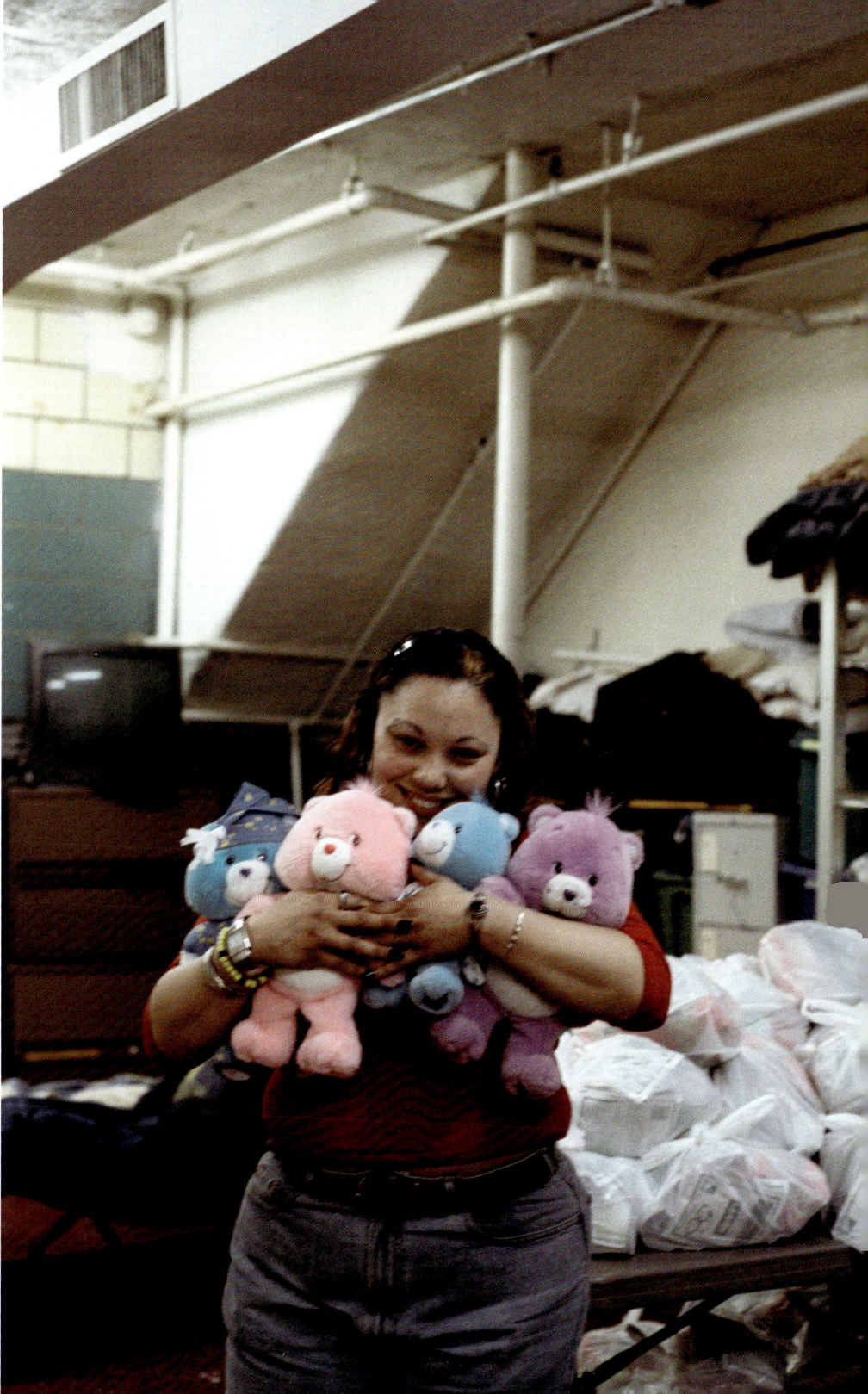

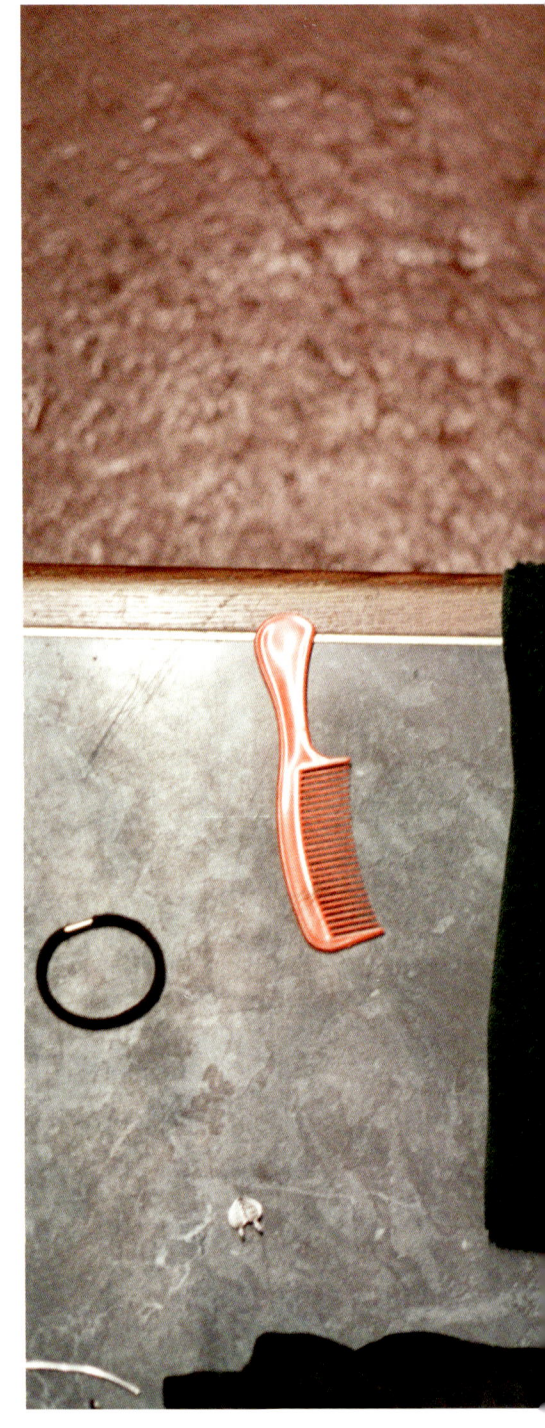

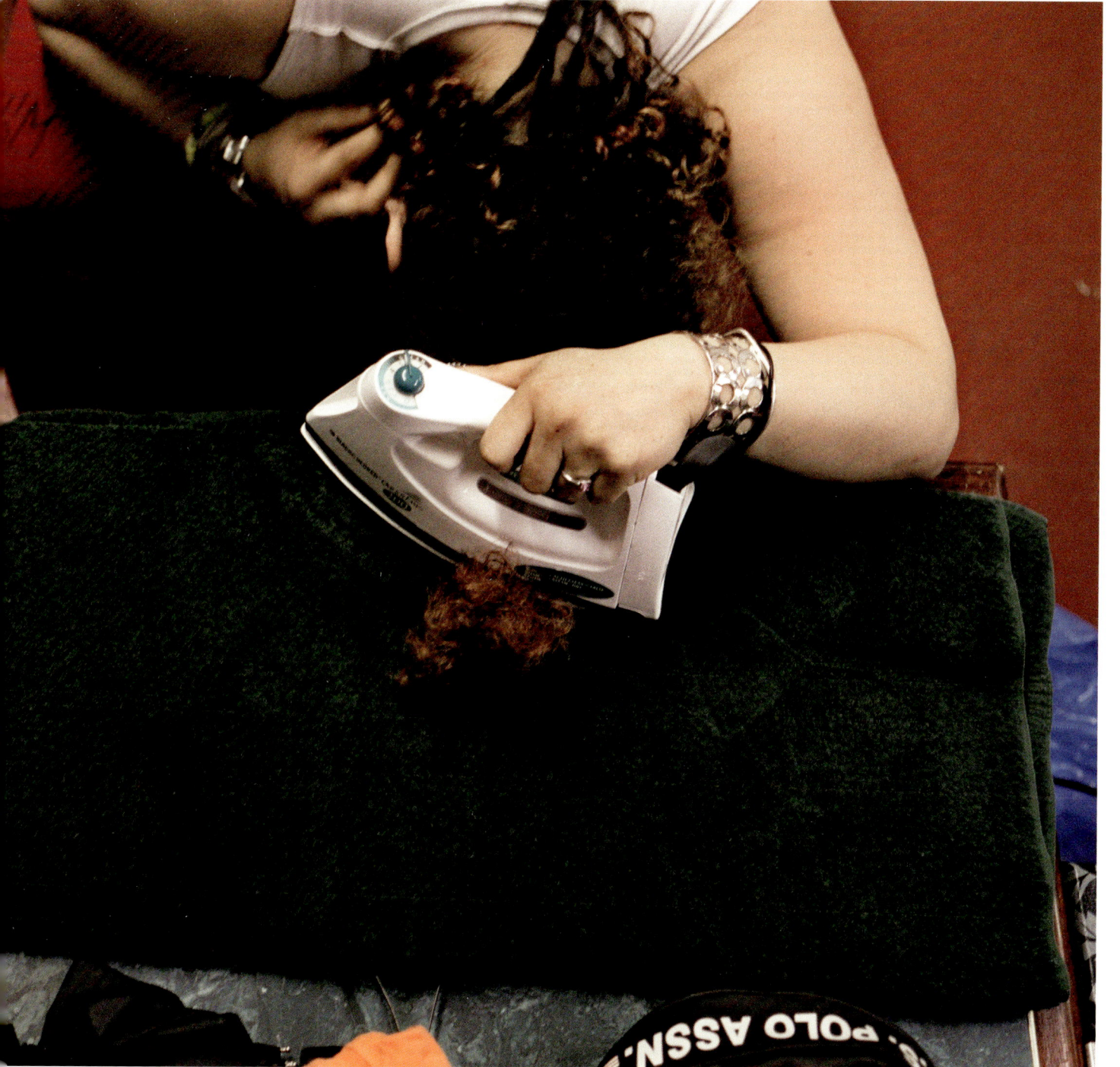

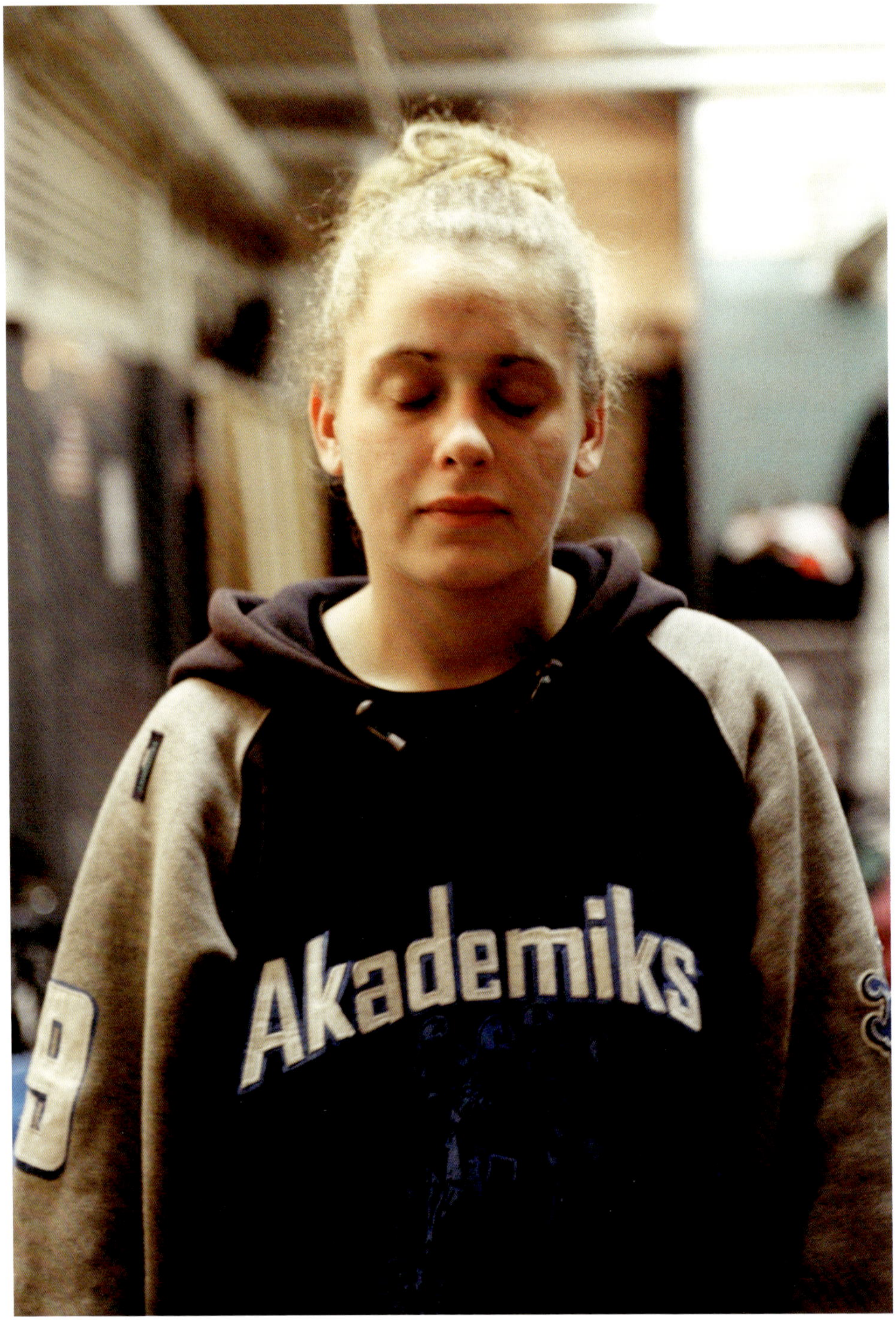

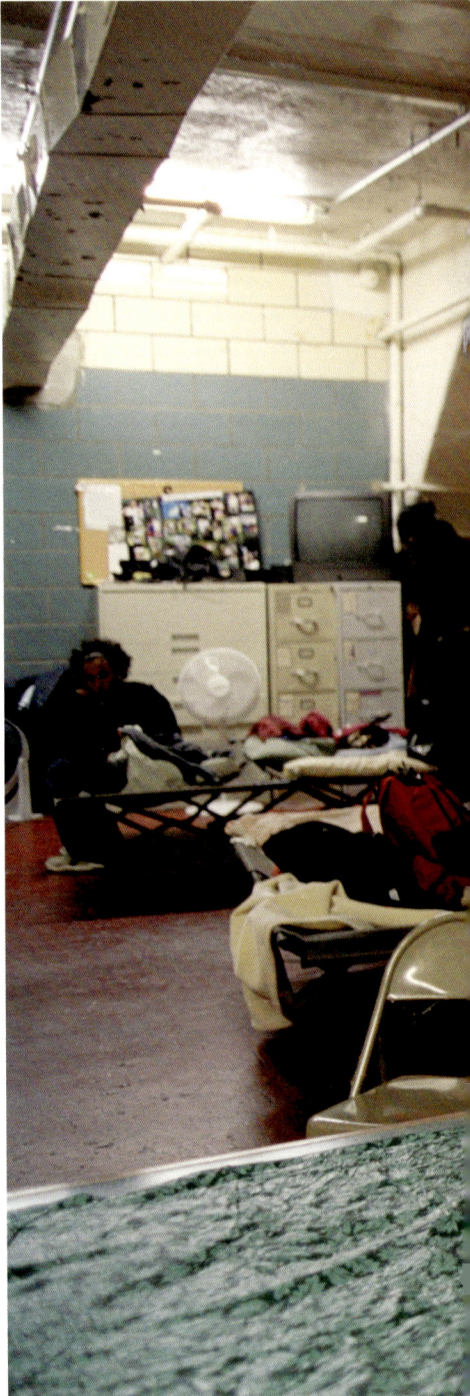

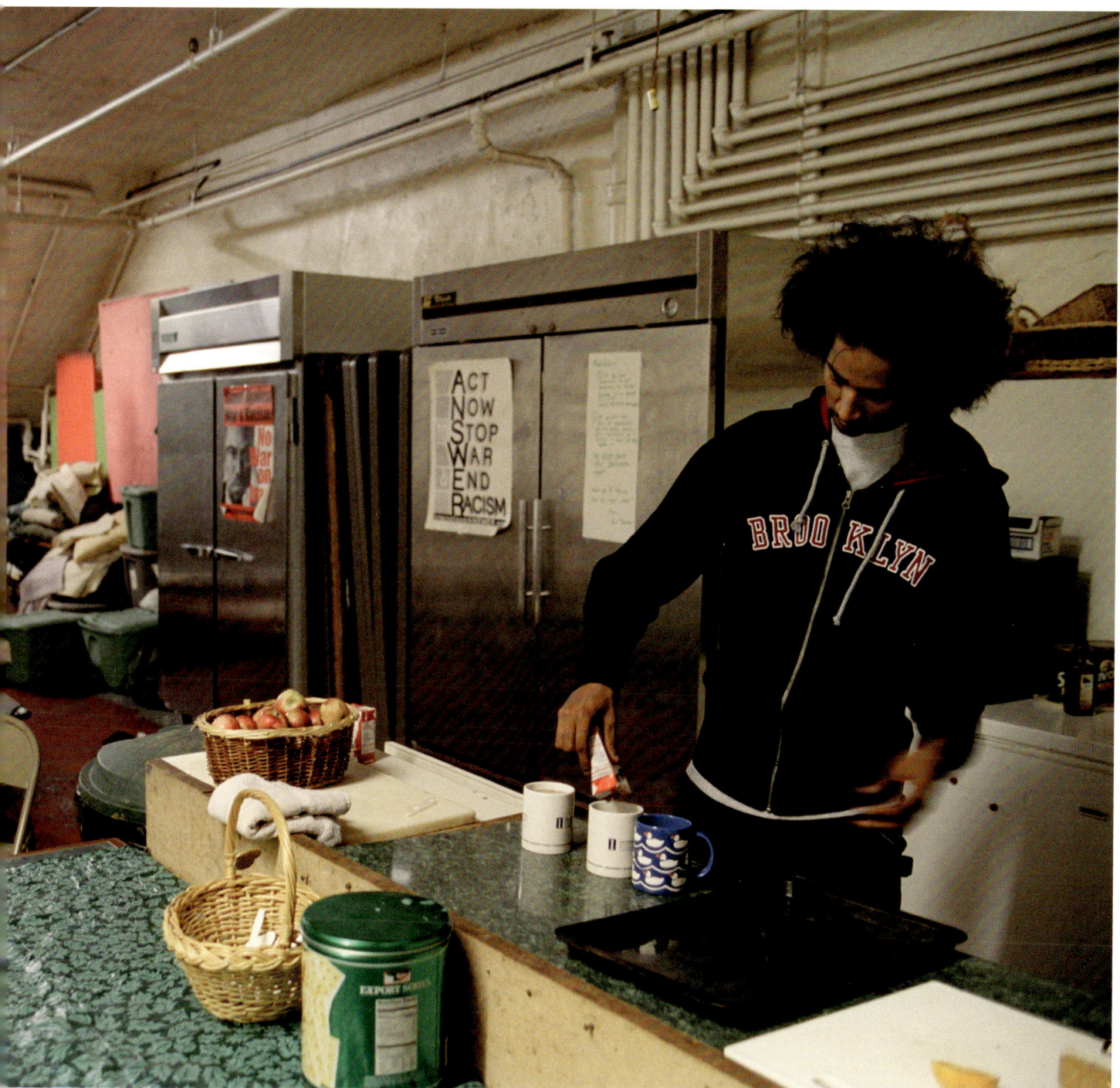

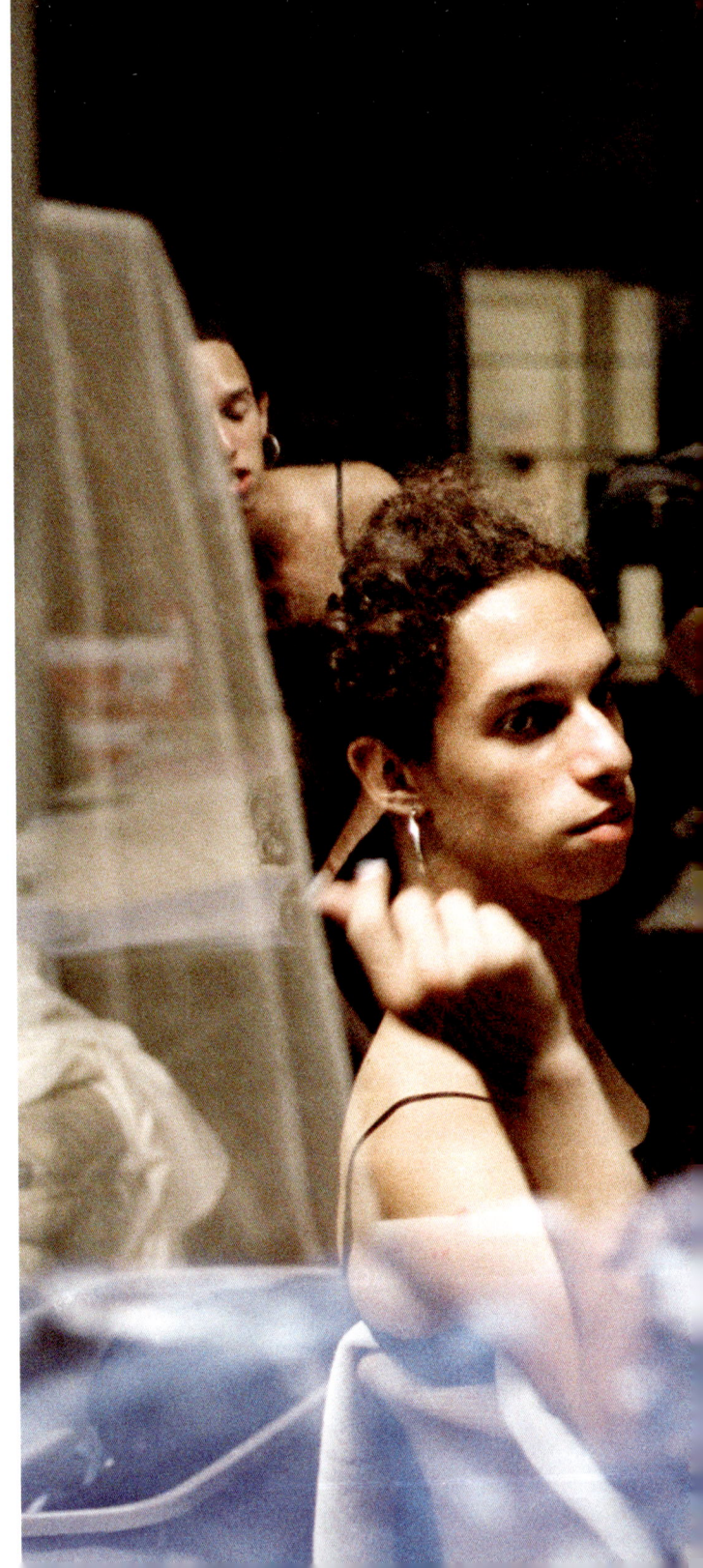

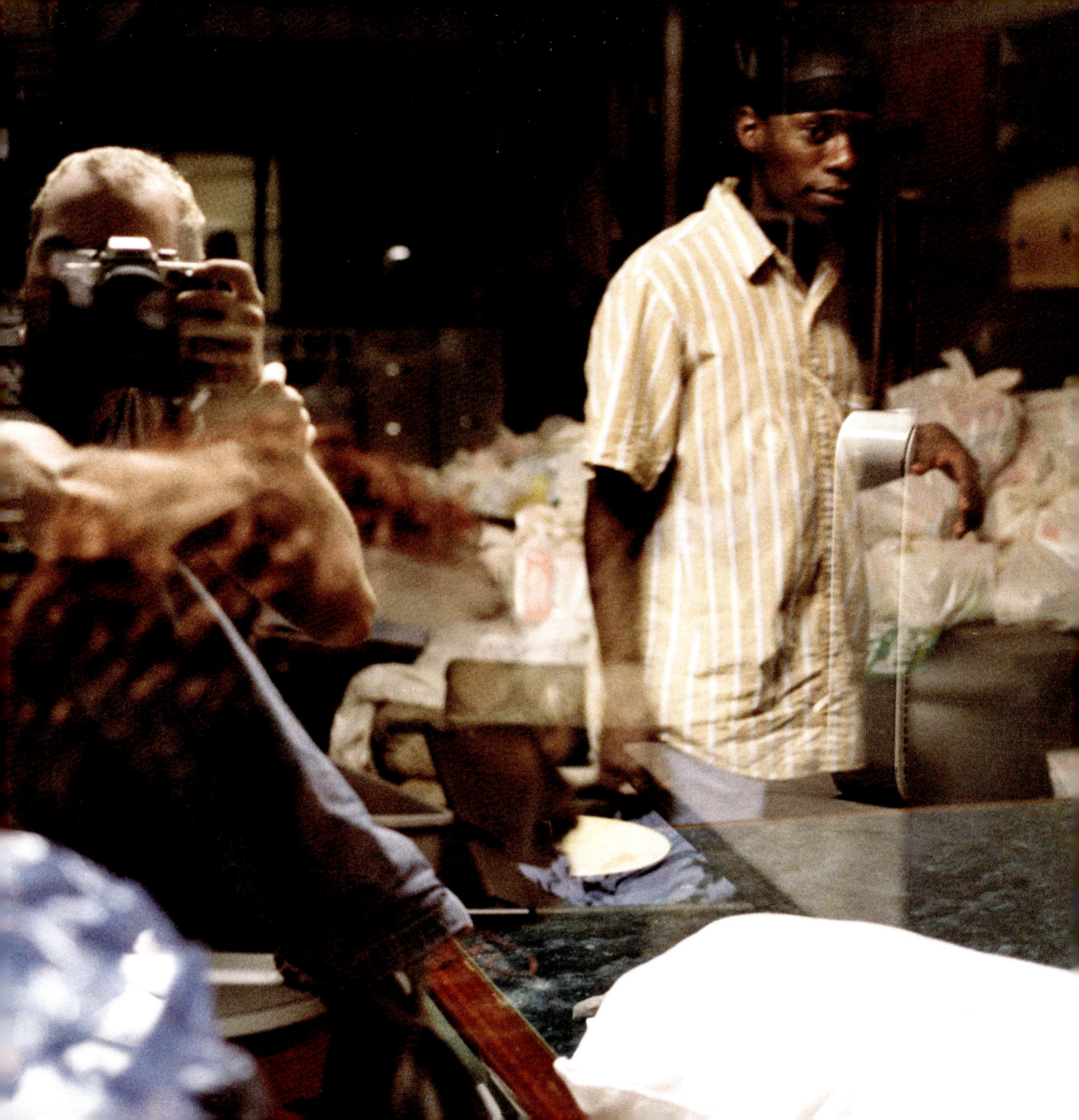

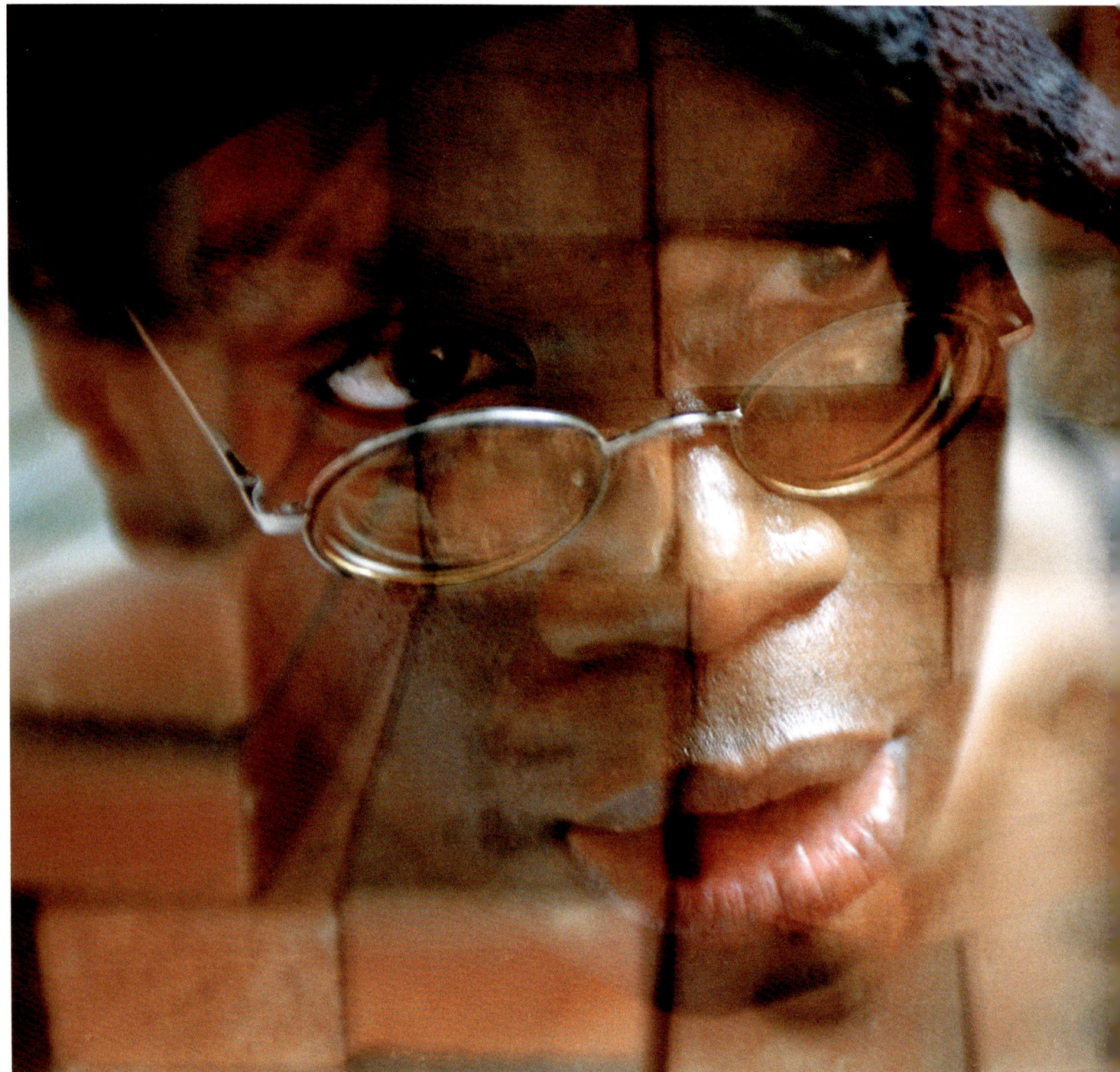

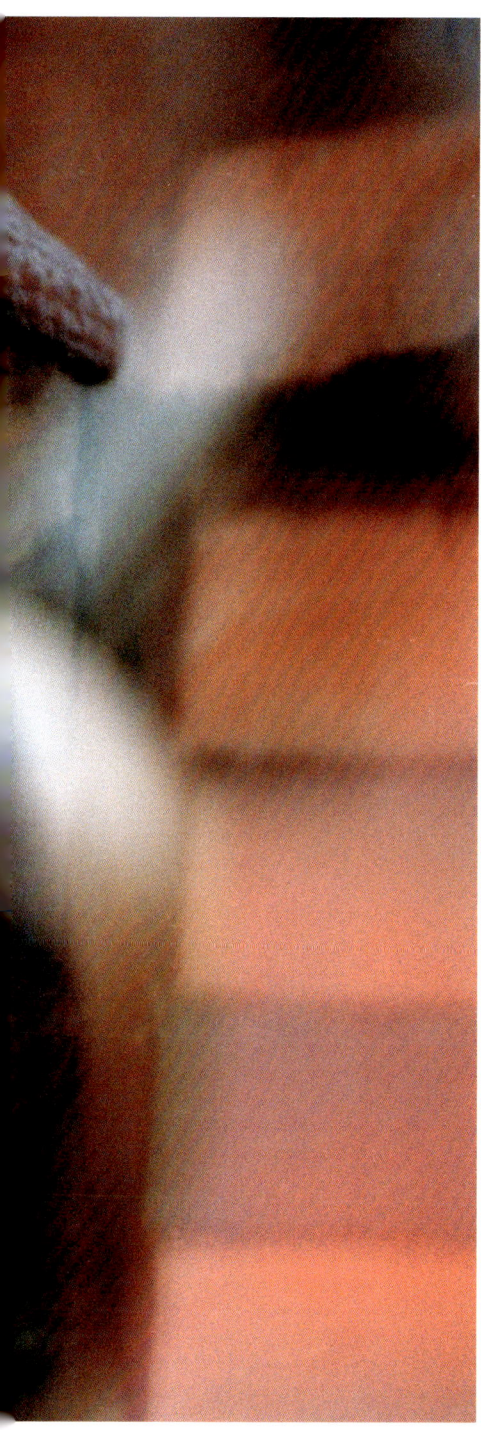

While Sylvia's provided Charlene with a safe and welcoming environment, it was never something she grew to love. Being in a shelter still meant being homeless, and no amount of friendship and support would change that fact.

*Everybody has bad days. You try to talk to people and people don't want to be talked to and the kind hearted person that I am, I would talk to people anyway and I'd get my head bit off, and my arms and legs. It's like two personalities. There was a lot of divas in that room.*

*After I was there a little while, I was like, okay I'm here. I want to move on now. Then it was like, I'm still here. I'm still here. I'm still here. Still here, still here. It started getting nerve-wracking after a while, because I started to feel like I would be homeless for the rest of my life if I would stay here.*

After almost a year at Sylvia's, Charlene found her way into another program, which eventually led her to a place of her own. After years of homelessness, this was a welcome, if unfamiliar, new direction for her life that didn't come without temptations.

*I have my own place in downtown Brooklyn. Sometimes I still feel like it's not mine. I feel like I'm house-sitting for someone or that I am staying at someone's house. At first it was hell on earth, 'cause I started thinking about my drugs and stuff like that. And then I thought about it, and I decided I'm not going to do that. I couldn't go back there. I worked so hard to get here; I went through hell to get here.*

Her time at Sylvia's Place had its high and low points, but Charlene accounts for her time there as a period of change and awakening.

*It made me learn not to take things for granted. It makes you appreciate life. God, I never thought I'd say those words.*

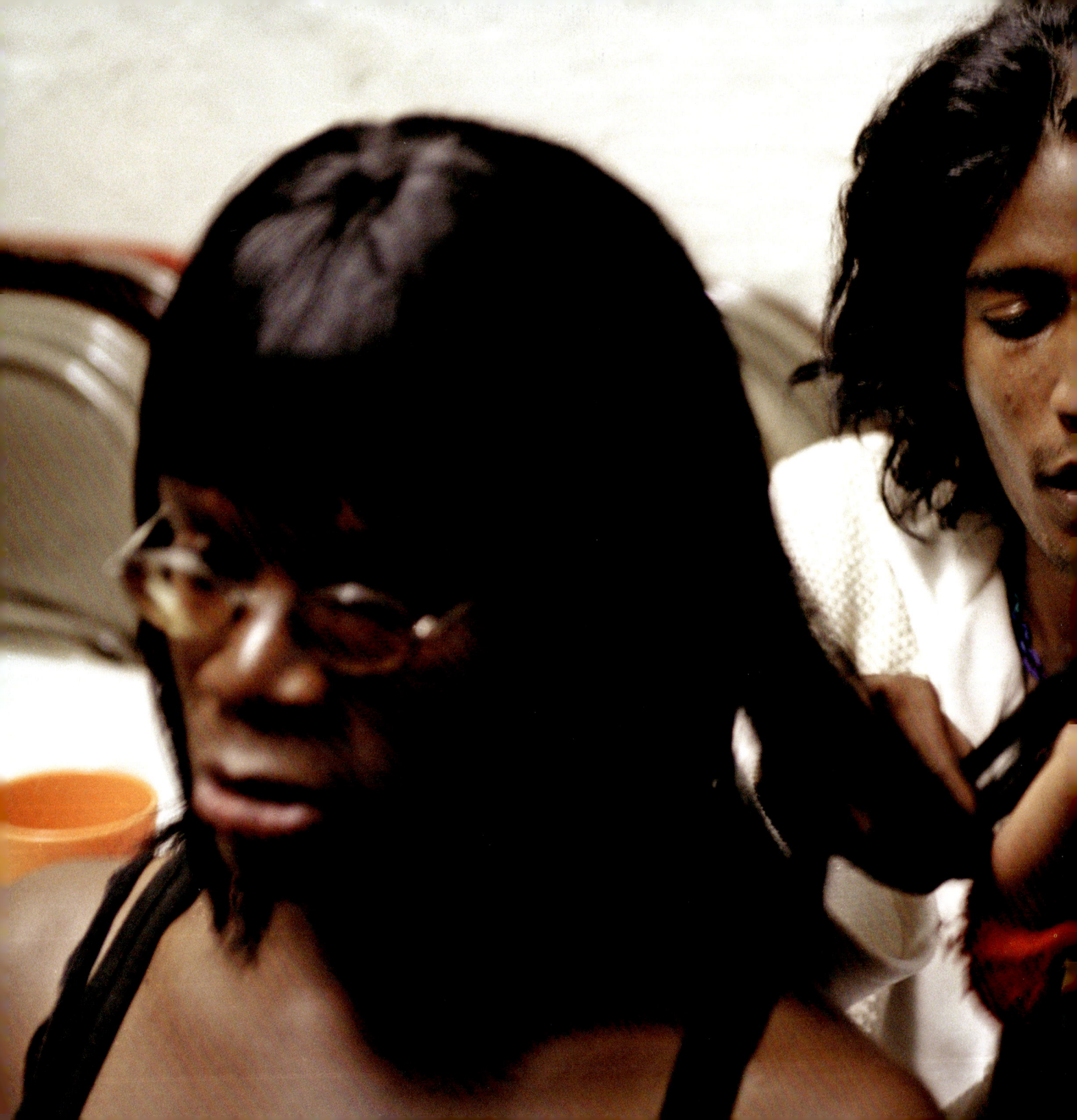

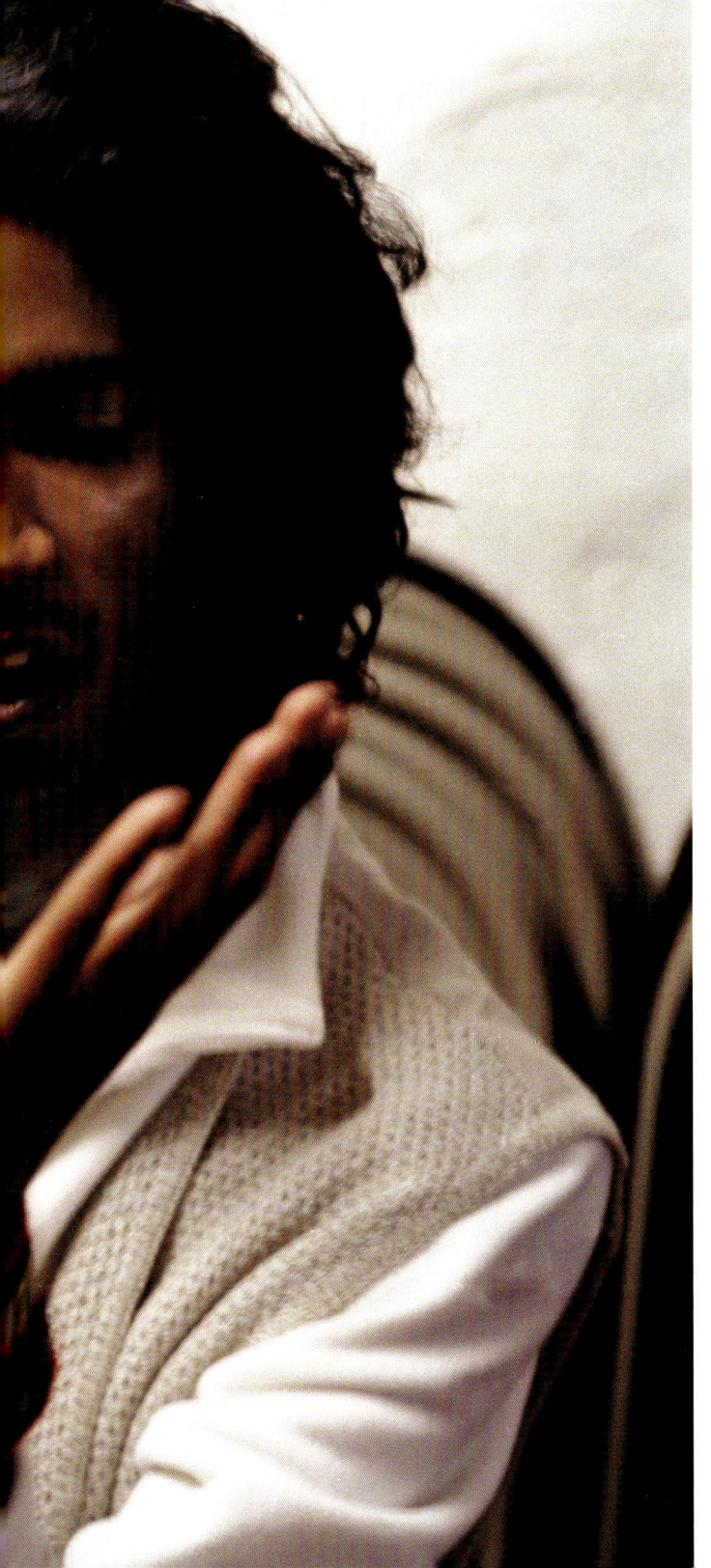

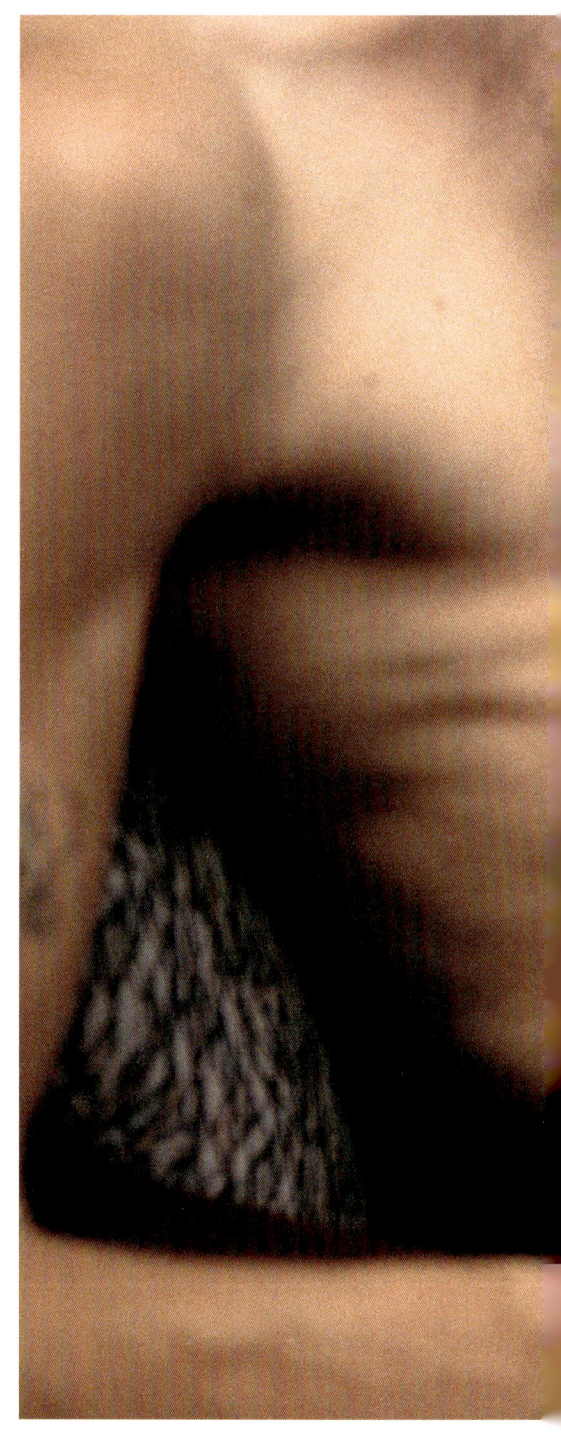

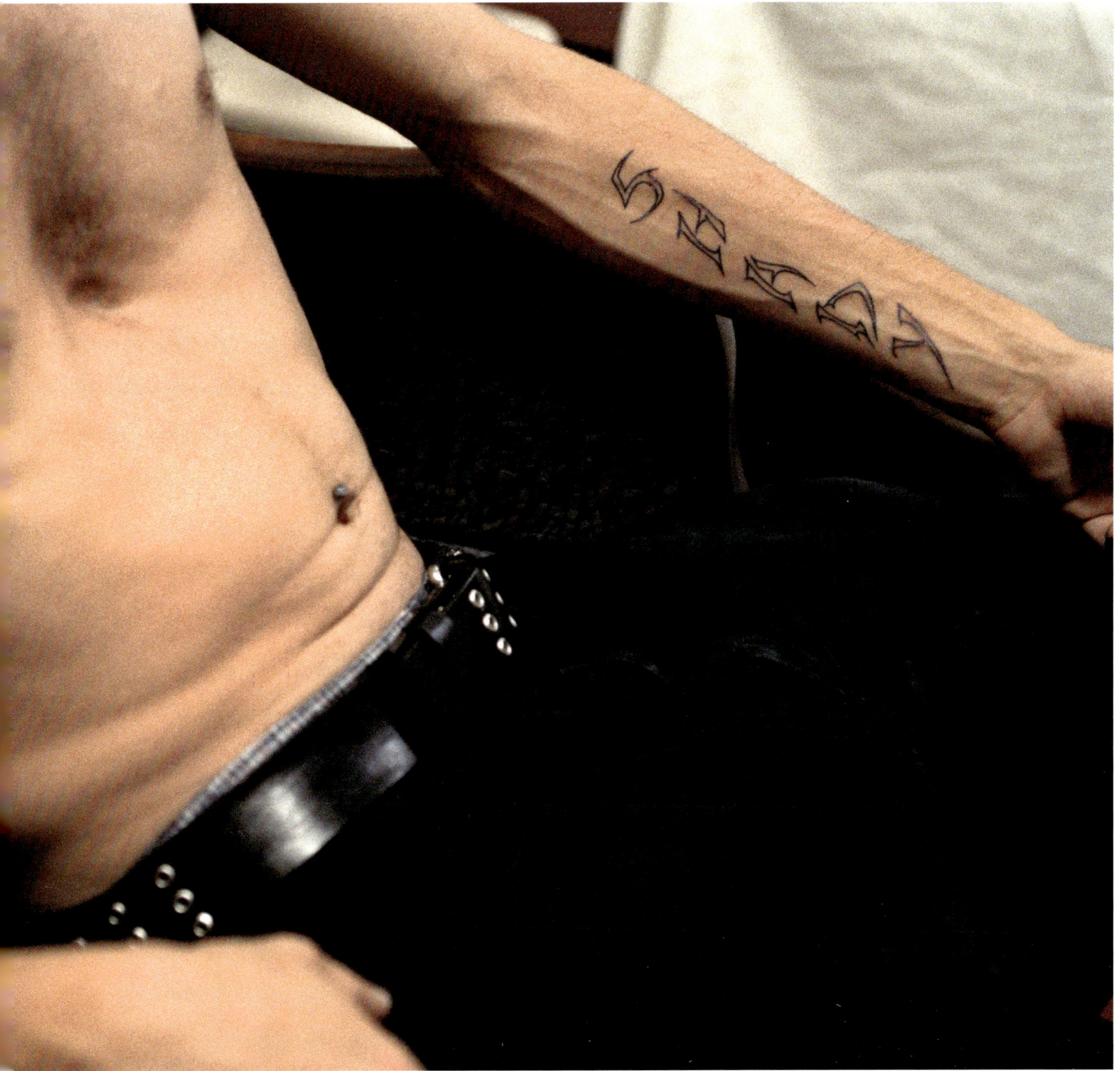

165 Shelter

*I don't like needles. That sounds so funny, because I have so many piercings. You would think that someone who has 17 piercings would be used needles already. No, I'm not. Especially if they're taking blood away from me. I mean, c'mon, how do you know I don't need that blood.*

Eternity wasn't always called by that name. The name that she listed on her intake form was the one that her mother gave her at birth, but those close to her know never to use it. Her birth name is a symbol of years of pain and suffering. To Eternity the old name is a symbol of weakness and tragedy.

*I changed my name. Not that I got tired of my old name, but I have this thing where I'm not that person anymore. Now I have a new face and a new name. My face to me is my piercings. I figure if I cover up my old face, people will see my new face. And this is the person that I am. I am not that little whiny person. I'm not that pathetic person. I'm not a loser anymore.*

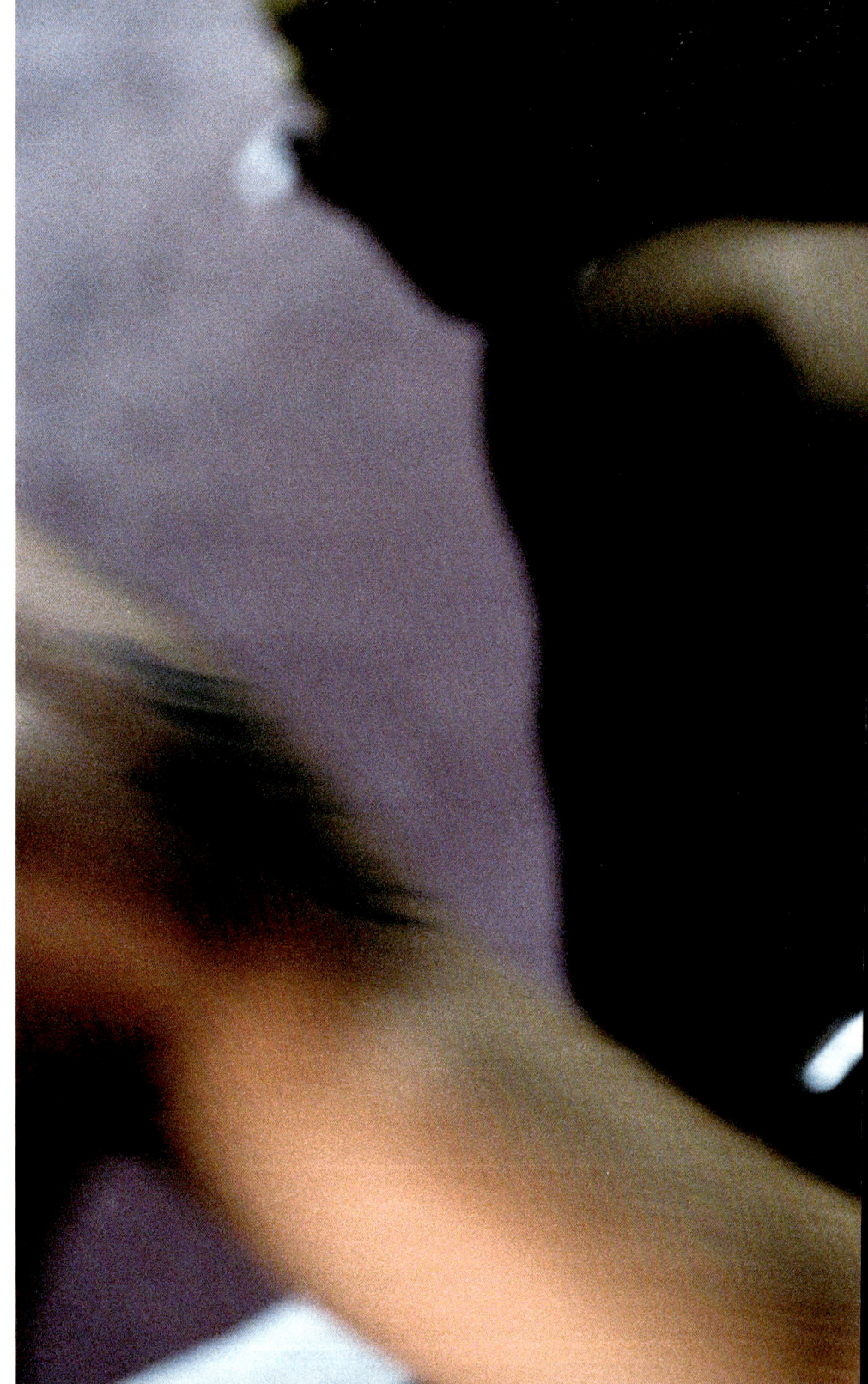

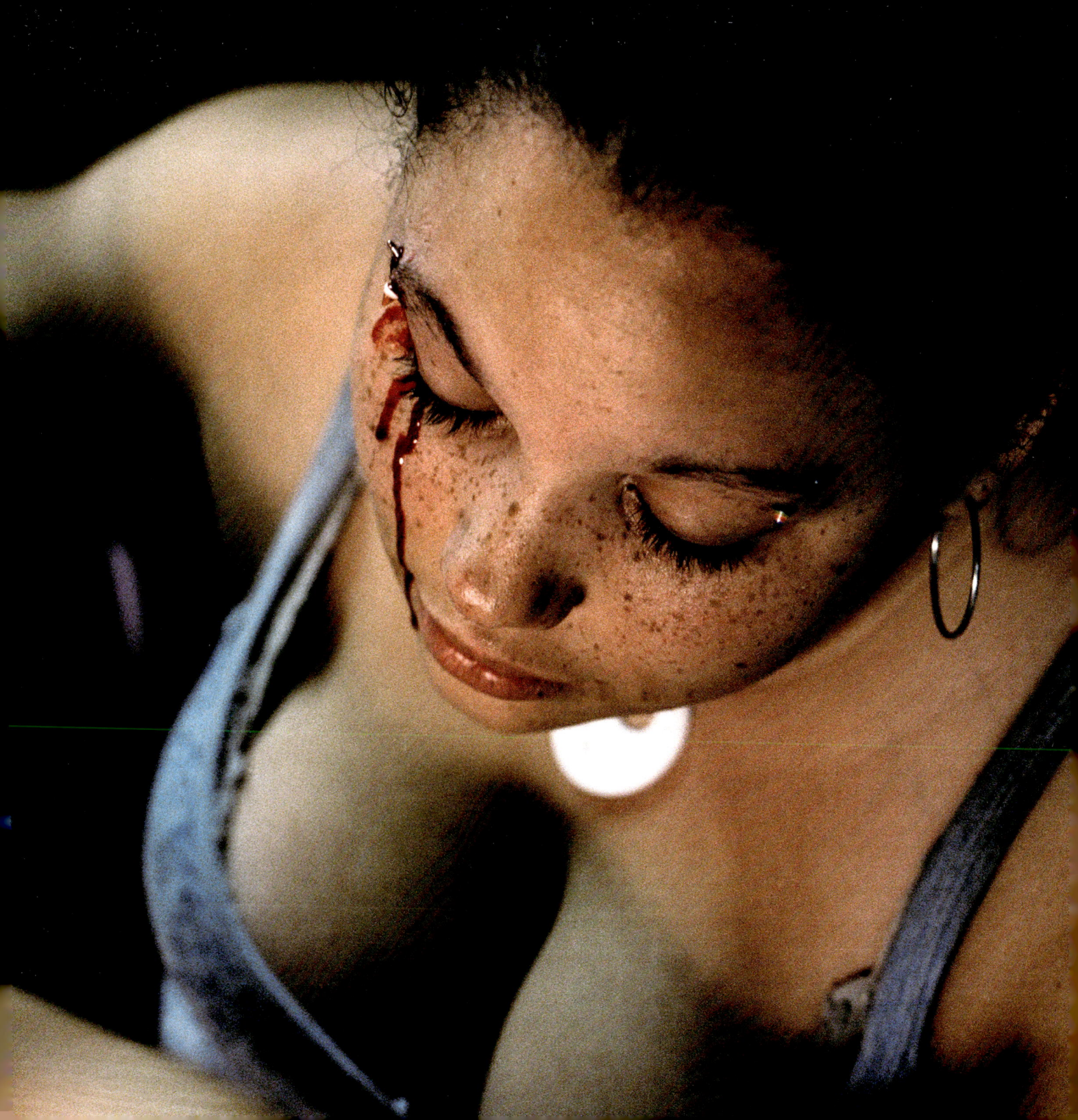

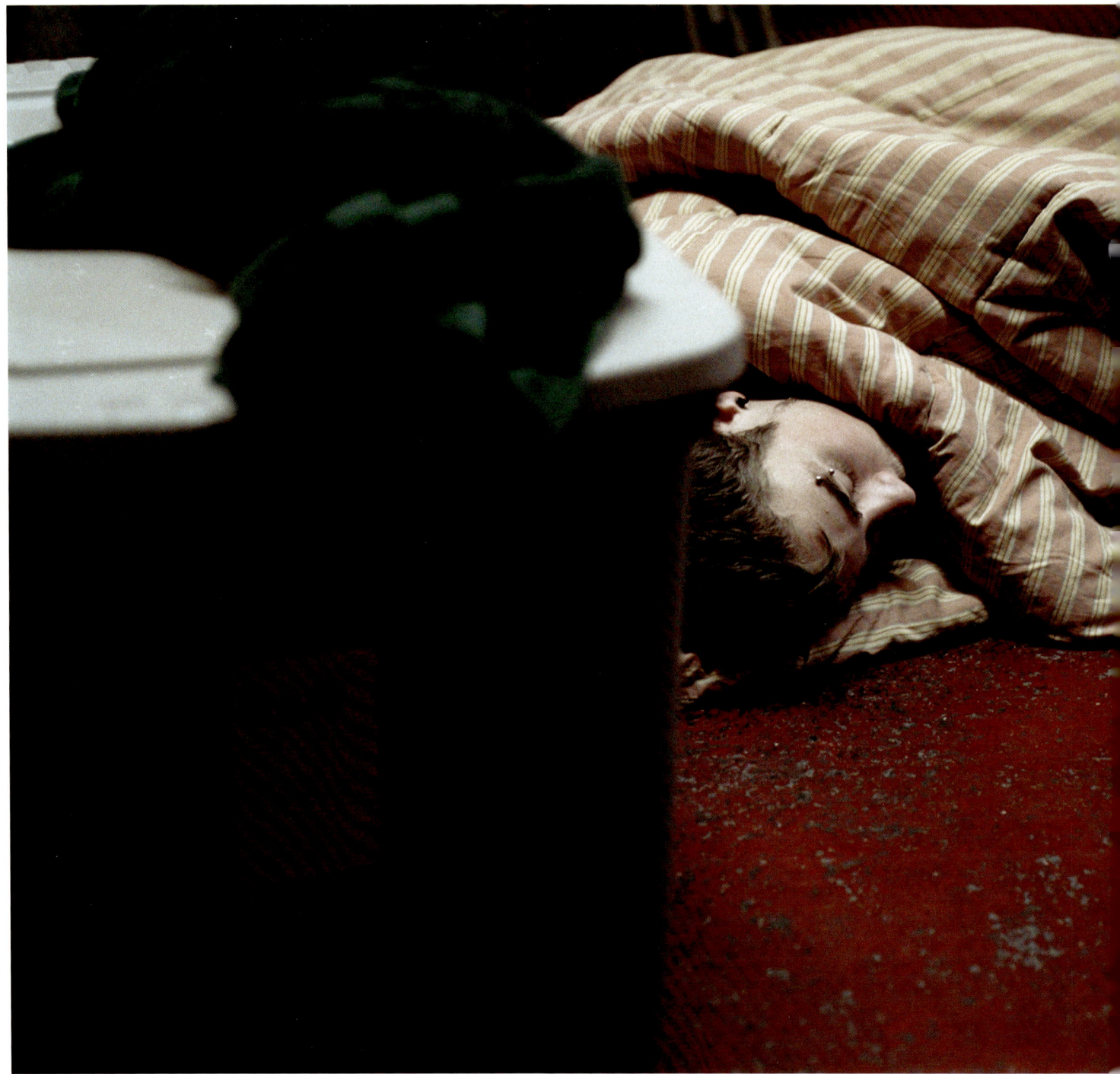

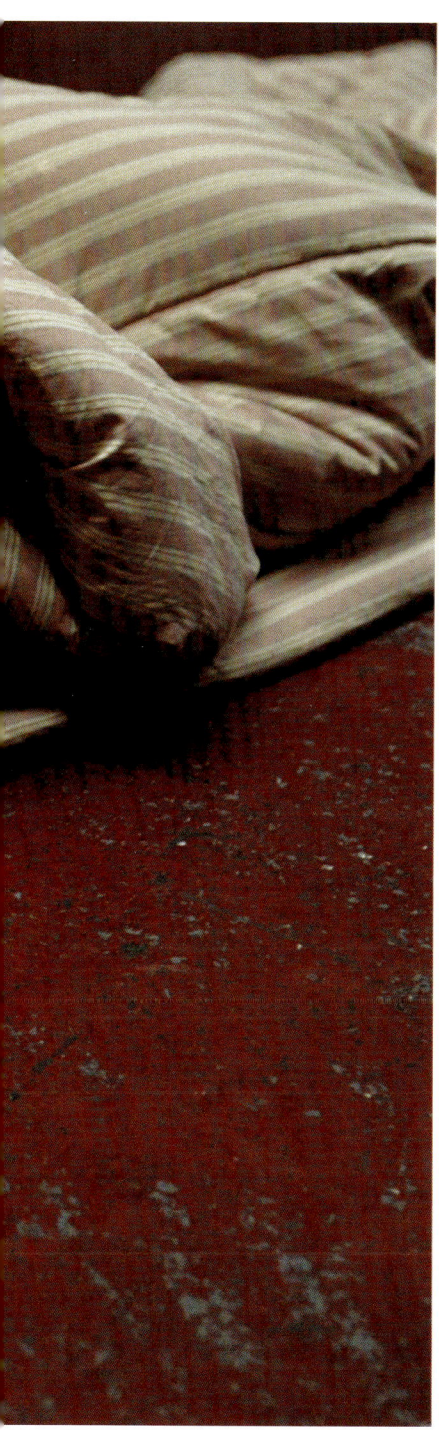

# Fact

100% of New York City's LGBTQ youth in ACS group homes reported that they were verbally harassed while staying there and 70% reported that they were victims of physical violence because of their sexual orientation.

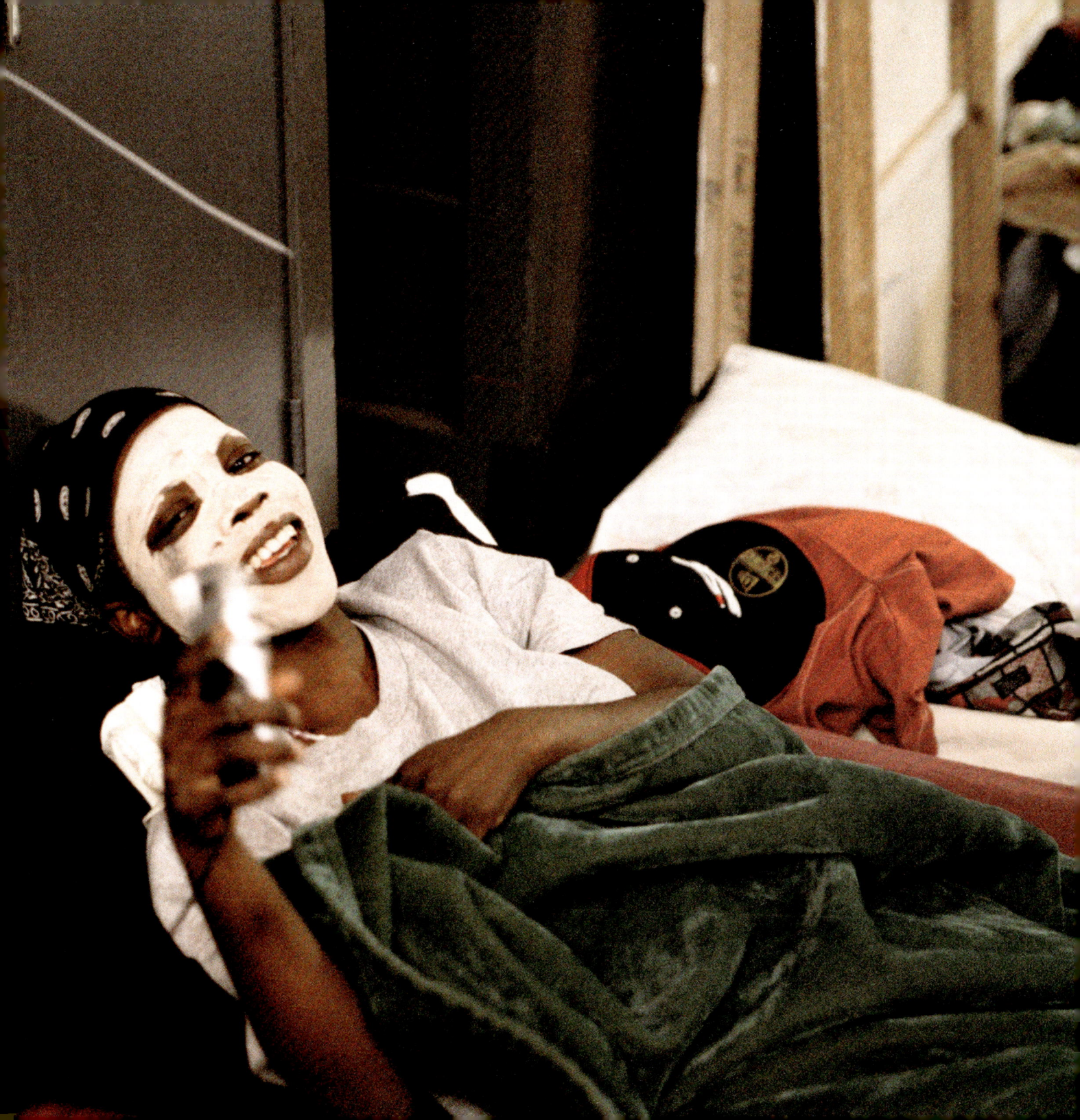

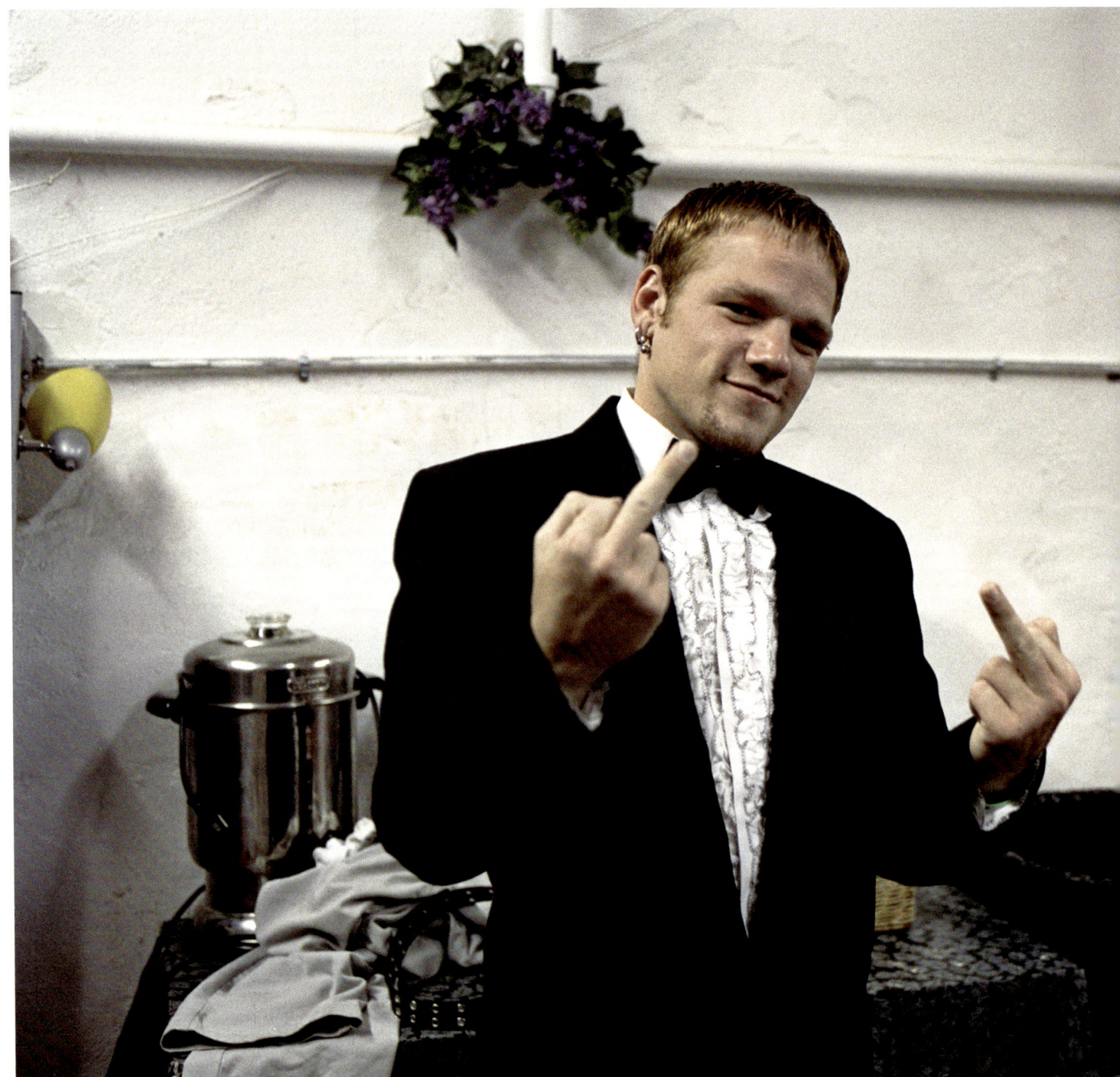

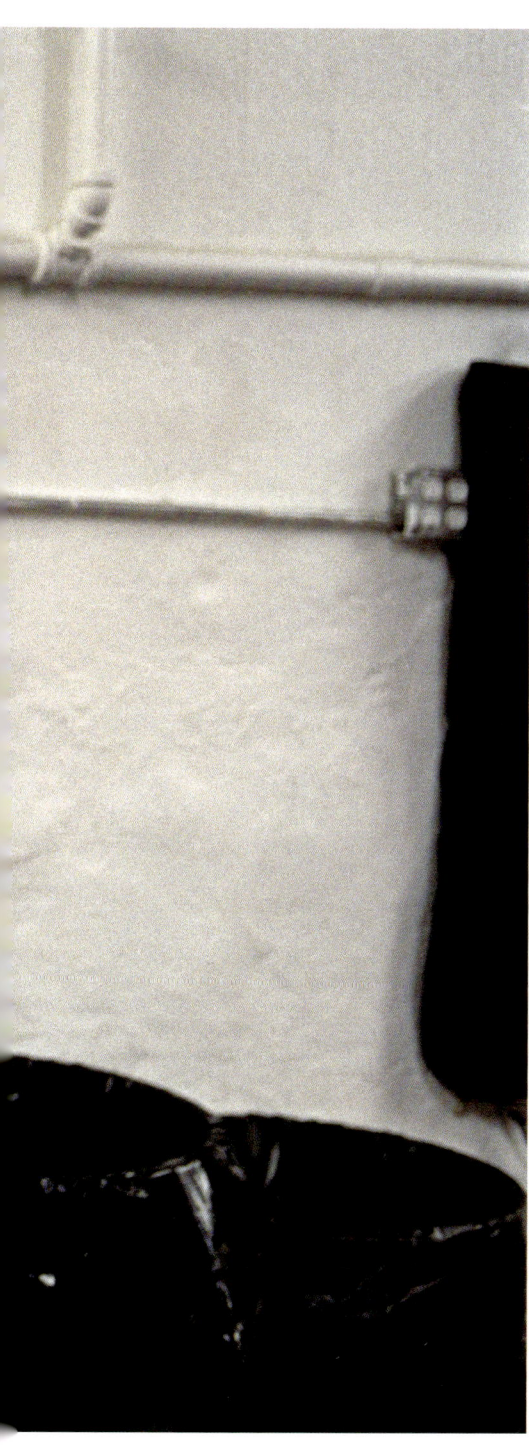

# Benefit Gala

In the fall of the shelter's second year, Metropolitan Community Church of New York held a gala fundraising event that, among other things, would help fund the growing costs of Sylvia's Place. The glamorous event was held at the famous Copacabana nightclub just a few blocks away from the church, and asked its attendees to donate generously to the charity projects of MCCNY. Rev. Pat asked that residents of the shelter come to represent the program, and Lucky wanted to be sure that they attended in style. He gathered his old tuxedos so that Jeff and Shady would be suited up for the event. On the day of the gala, Lucky met Jessica on the street where she normally panhandled and took her shopping. She found a beautiful red dress that ensured her night would be one to remember. Jeff, Shady, Jessica, and Misty met at the shelter early so they all had time to shower and dress. Stripping out of their daily clothes and into elegant dinner wear, they all prepared for a fun, elegant night in their honor.

# Kate

By August of 2004, many of the residents at Sylvia's Place had found a case manager, advocate, and friend in Kate Barnhart. Kate had been working at another LGBTQ youth agency, when a shift in staff had left her without a job. It came at a time when the population at Sylvia's was growing, and the counselors were finding it difficult to keep up. Rev. Pat brought Kate on as a new member of the overnight staff to the cheers of the residents and staff alike. When Rev. Michael, who had been overseeing the shelter, moved out of state to take on his own congregation, Kate took over as the new director of Sylvia's Place. Having already worked with many of the residents before and with so much case management experience, Kate helped to transform Sylvia's Place. The older residents already trusted Kate, and her ability to connect with new additions was undeniable. The shelter became a program able to deal with every part of being homeless. As the staff continued to grow, Sylvia's became better equipped to help its residents transition from an emergency shelter into long term housing.

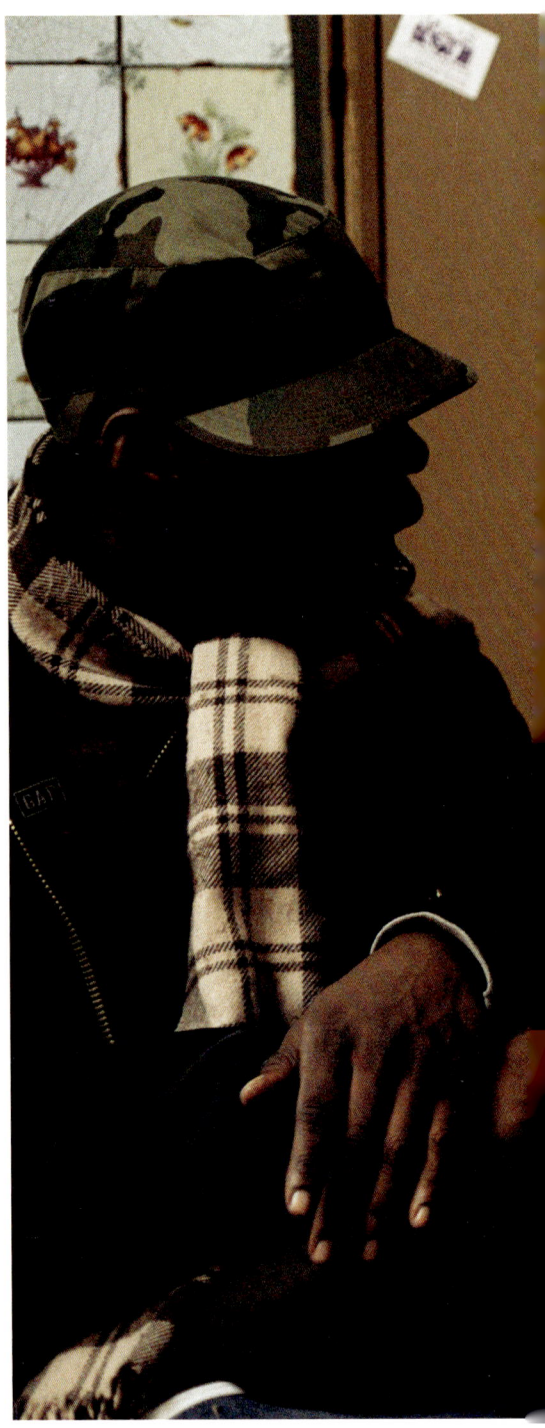

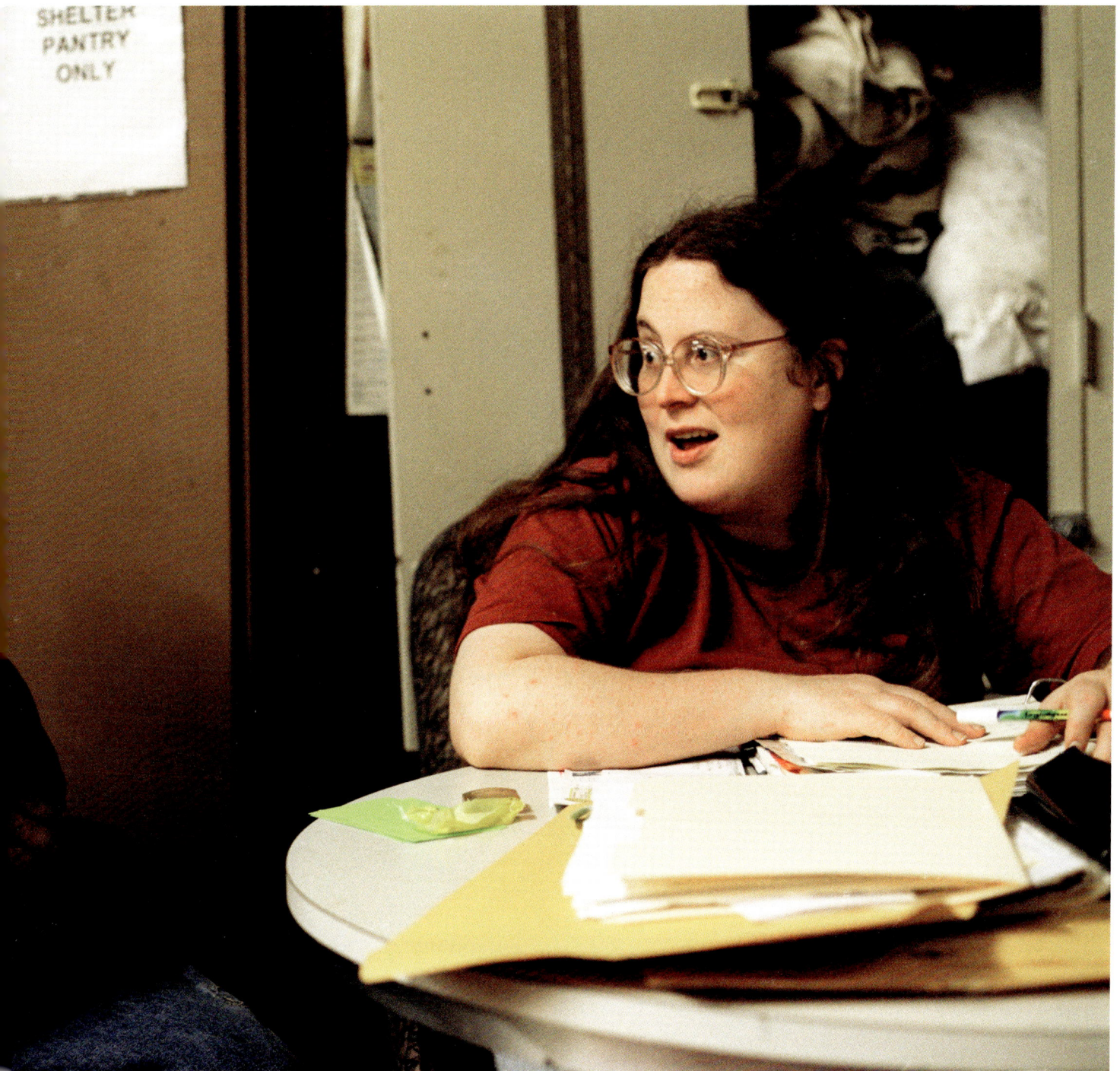

SHELTER
PANTRY
ONLY

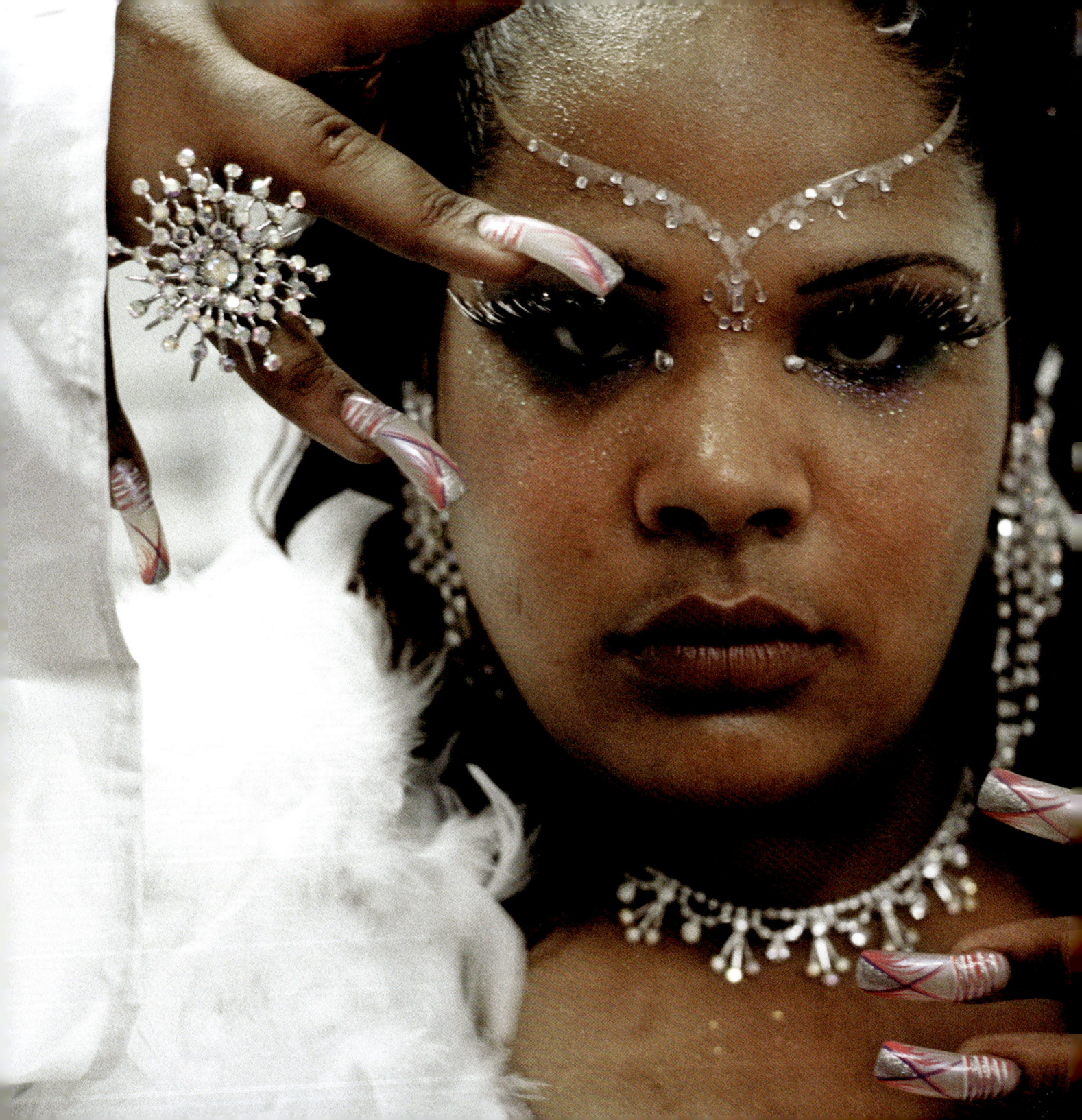

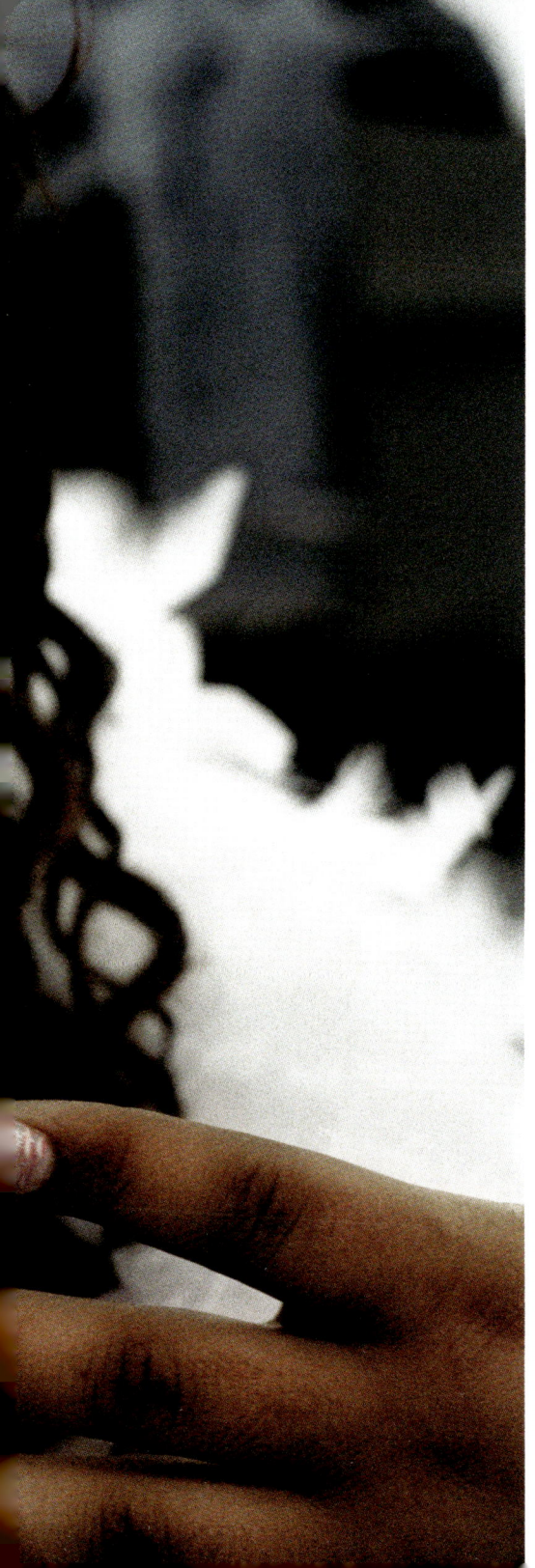

# Fact

Over 50% of national youth servicing organizations report that they have no services or resources in place to educate youth on sexual orientation or to support gay and lesbian youth.

# Fashion on Gender

In the spring of the shelter's third year, Metropolitan Community Church of New York hosted Fashion on Gender, a fashion show event. The program was the project of Deaconess Moshay Moses of MCCNY, who envisioned a fashion show in conjunction with her transgender support group, Genderpeople. Part of the proceeds from the event went to benefit Sylvia's Place at a time when funding was very uncertain and its future was unclear. Many of the shelter's residents sprang into life and volunteered to help out with the event, participating as models and in one case, as a guest designer. Among the highlights of the event was a professional photo shoot designed to create publicity photos for advertisements and local publications. With Lucky Michaels at the helm, many residents arrived on a Saturday to create their own unique looks, from the scraps found in the donation bins, to be represented in the gritty fashion shoot. Being treated like fashion models, they burst with energy as they posed and were primed for the camera. The final image appeared in magazines and newspapers all over the city, and was the focal image of promotional postcards distributed for the event. Feeling like celebrities, the residents poured their souls into the fashion show and walked for an audience filled beyond capacity.

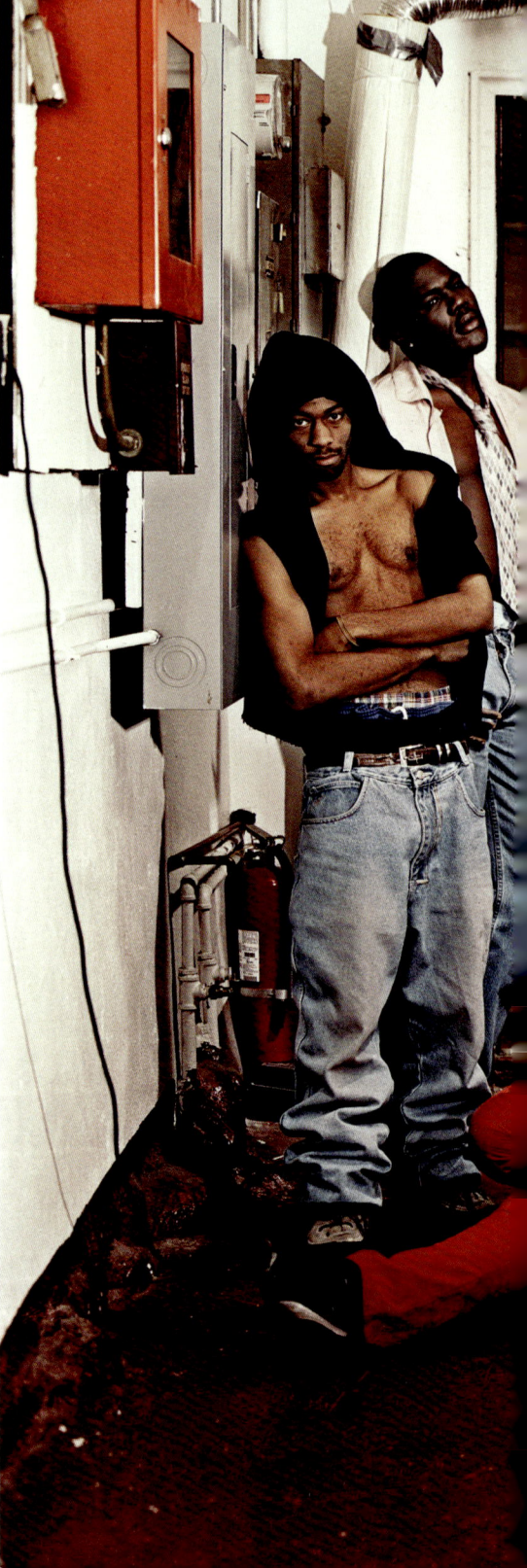

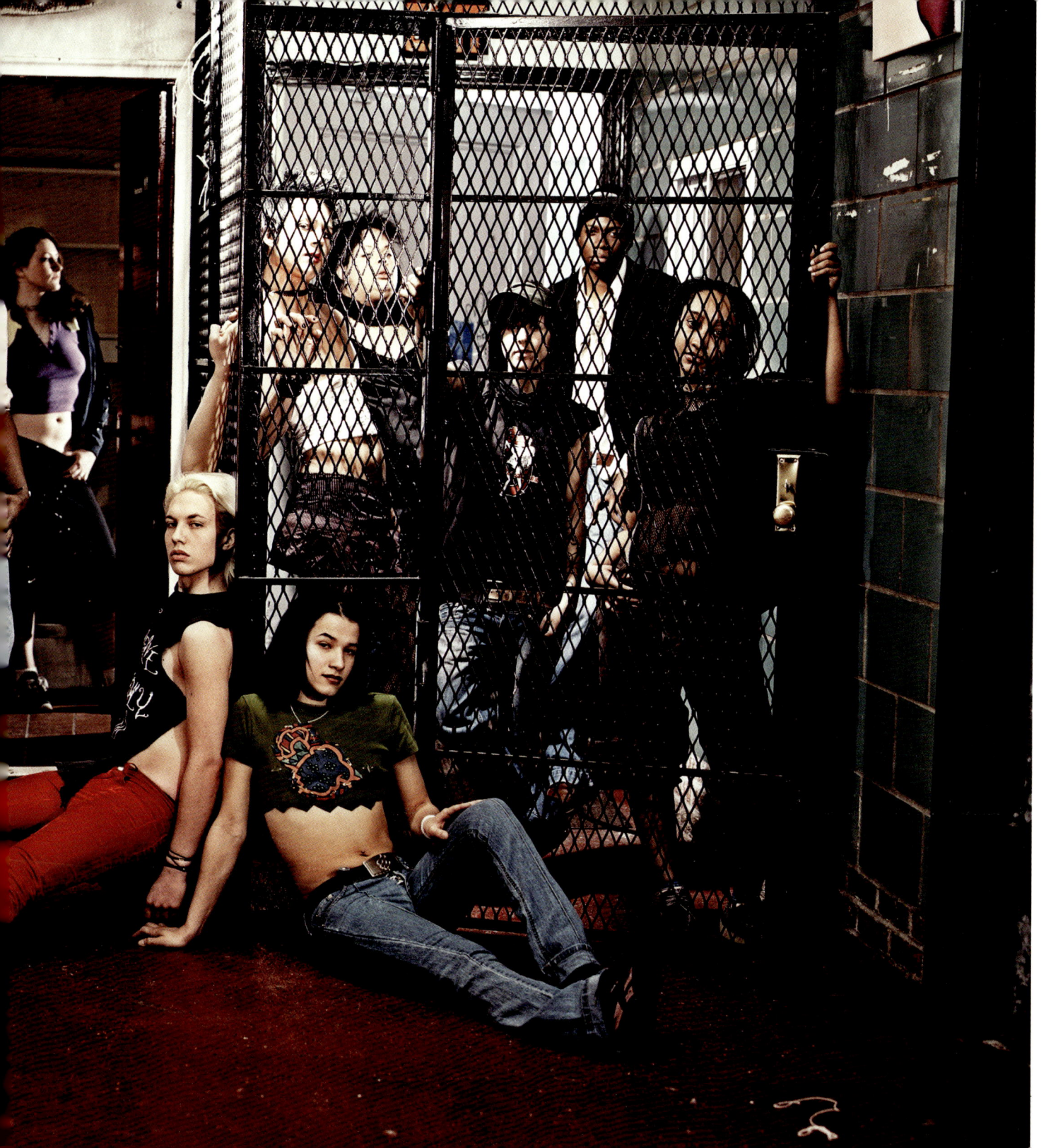

I came out to my friends in high school first. Then I came out to my mother after my father died. But I think they had always known. They had to know. How can you raise someone for that many years and not at least know something? I was always a shopper; I loved to shop. I always loved to match my clothes. I always wanted the high name brand clothes. Charlene

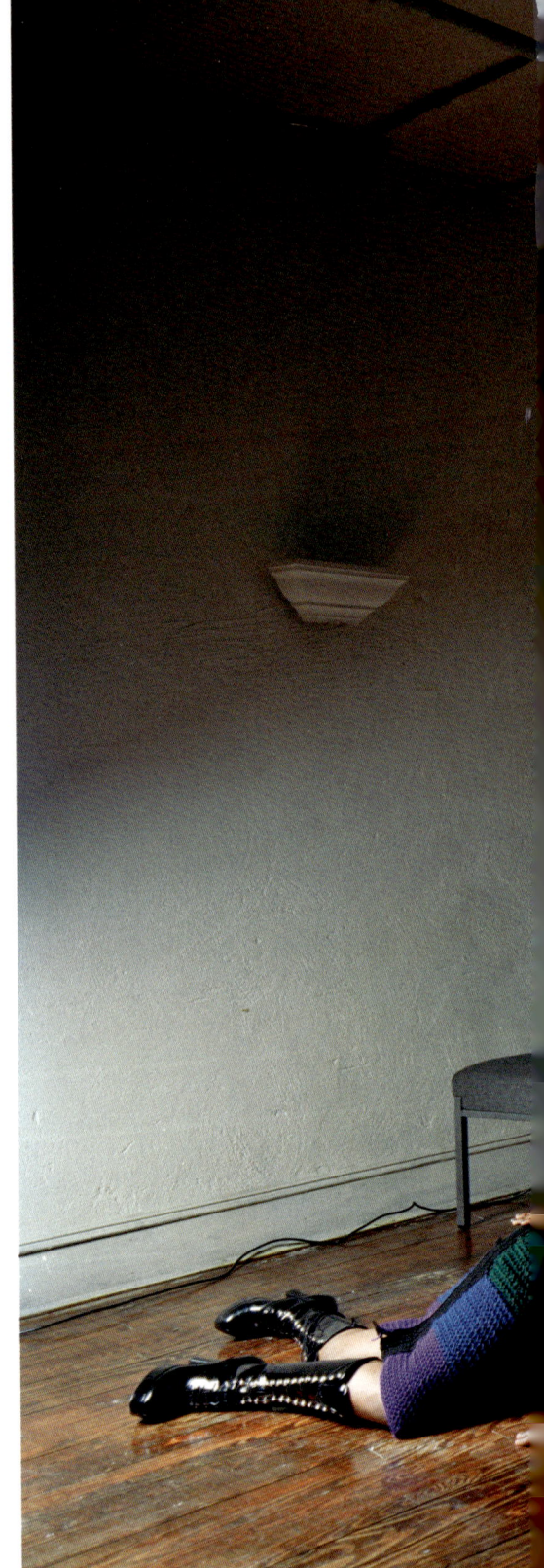

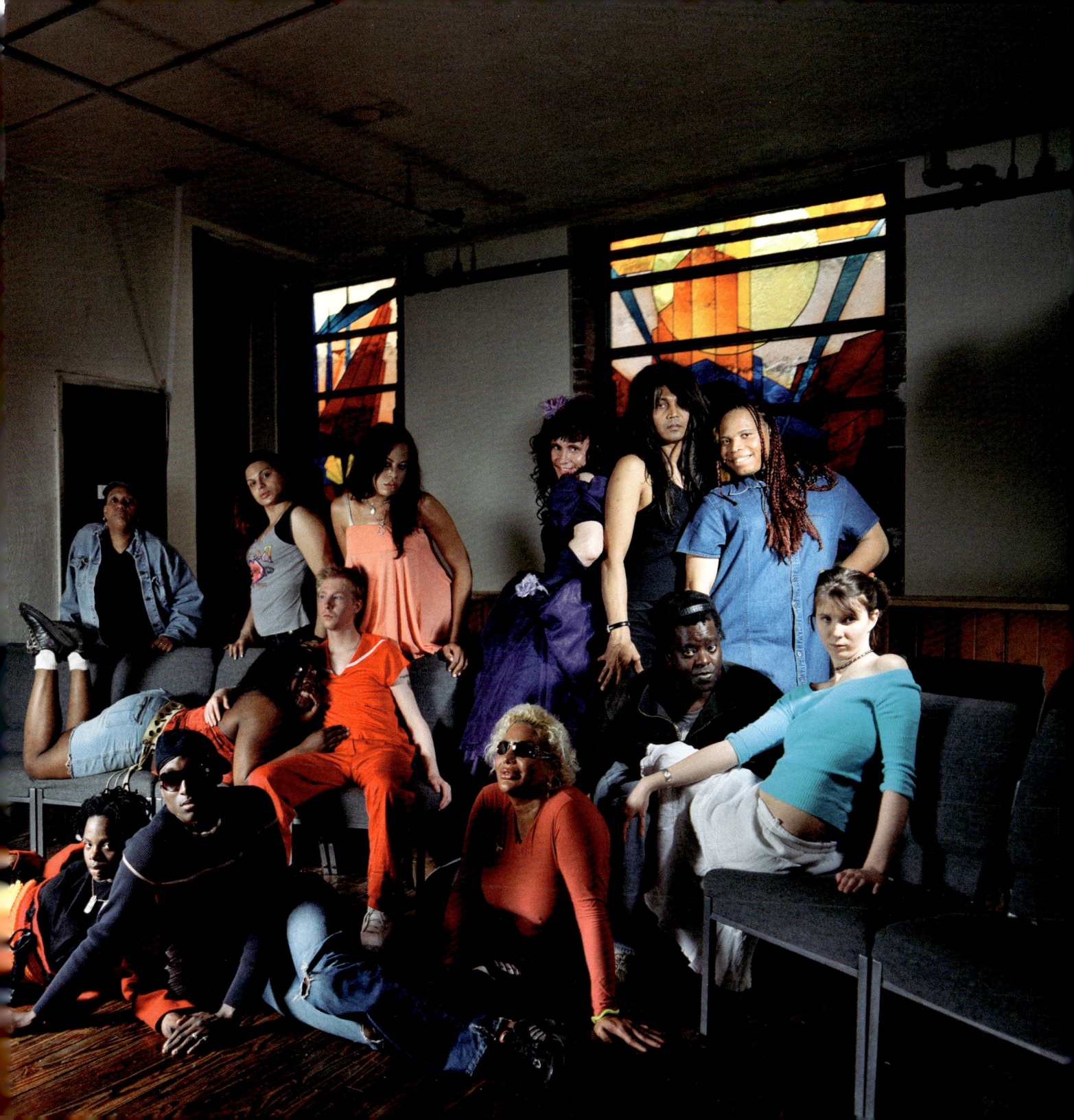

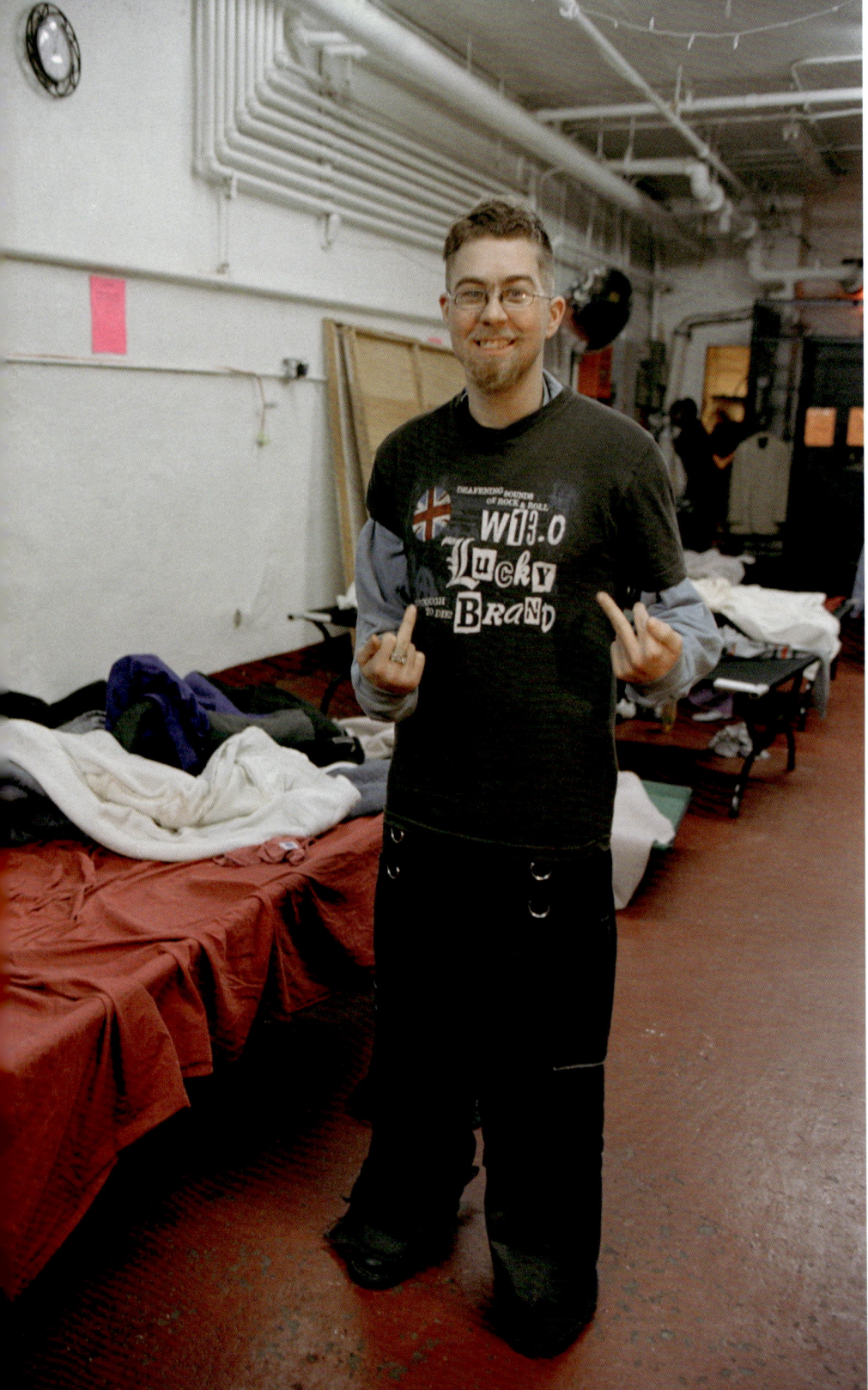

Once again, Malice returned to Sylvia's Place after coming back from his disappointing stay at his mother's place in Florida. His situation was only getting worse, and it was taking a toll. Malice wanted his own place. Malice started wondering if anything would ever work out for him.

The staff at Sylvia's and other agencies fought together to get Malice social security benefits for his injuries. His case demanded that he have a payee to distribute his benefits. He stayed with the only place he could trust. Rev. Pat became his payee, setting up a weekly allowance to make sure he had enough to eat during the week. The rest of his money was being saved to help him afford a place of his own, but after several failed attempts at staying in a rented room, his hope began to fade again.

*Life sucks. I need a place to call my own. A place where I can be outside with my friends and I'll just be there and I'll be like, "I'm tired, I'm going home." I'm gonna take my shower, eat my dinner, and go to bed. I want my own house. I can't take much more of this, I mean it. I can't keep this shit up. I mean it. It's been going on two and a half years.*

Malice is still waiting for something to go right. After a series of escalating outbursts, staying at Sylvia's Place was no longer an option due to the growing responsibility to keep our space safe for all within. He is back out on the streets, getting his weekly allowance, and trying to find a place to live. He is back where he started before showing up at the black gate of Sylvia's years ago.

*If I don't get a house, I really don't know what the fuck I'm gonna do. I'm really ready to flip the fuck out.*

*You know what I'm seriously thinking about doing? Walking and not stopping. Just going for a walk and not stopping. Just disappear from everybody. Vanish from the face of this earth. Just disappear.*

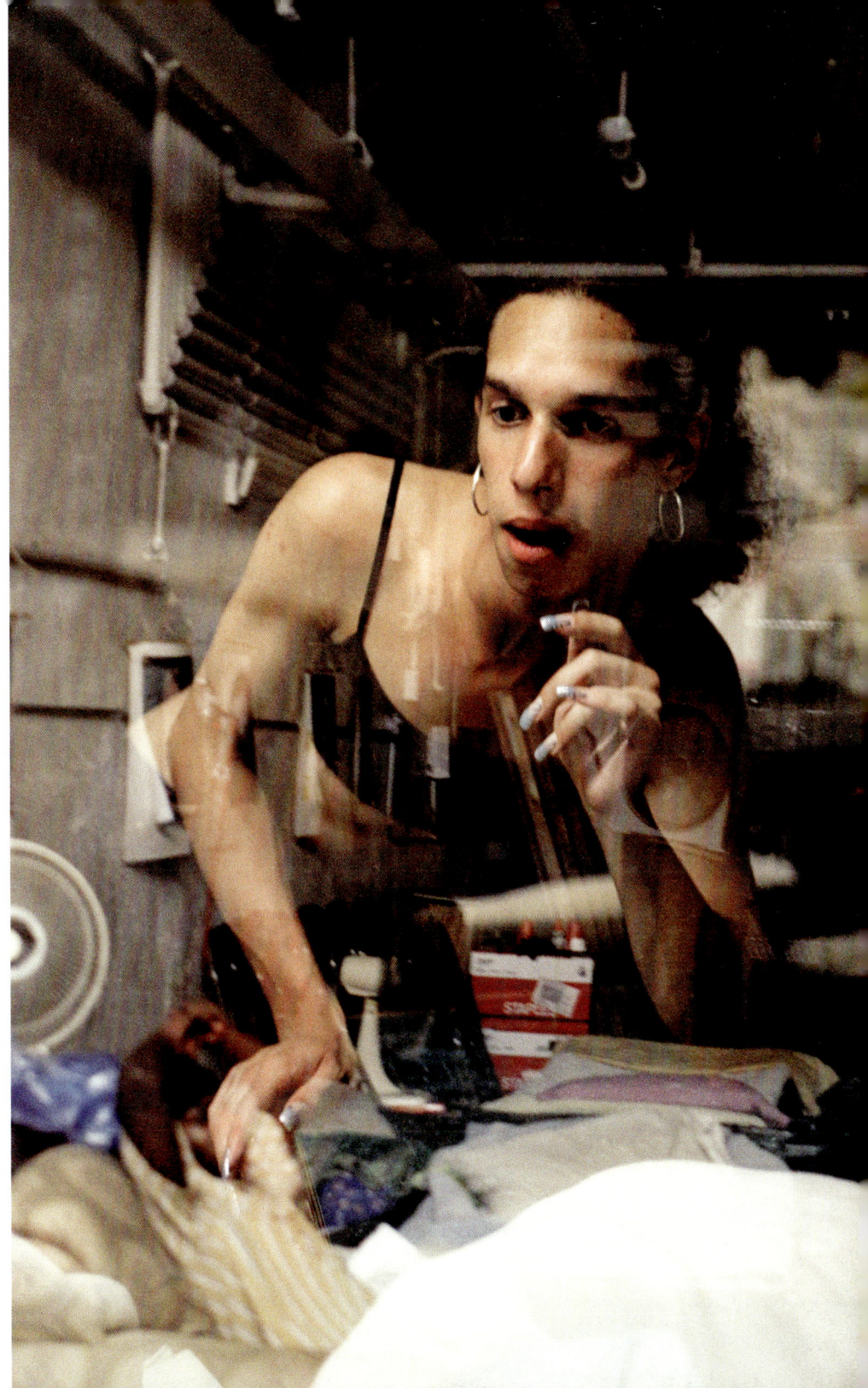

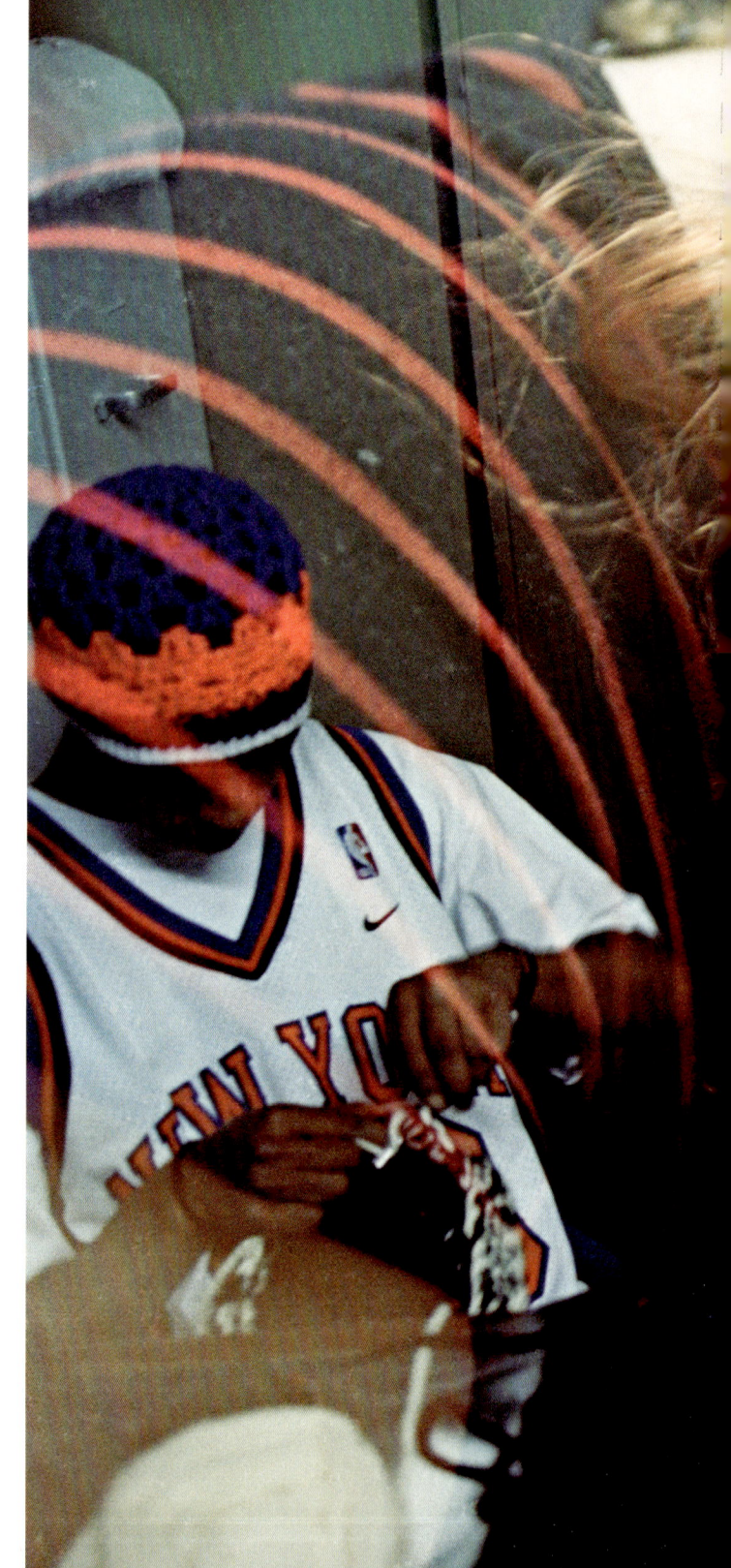

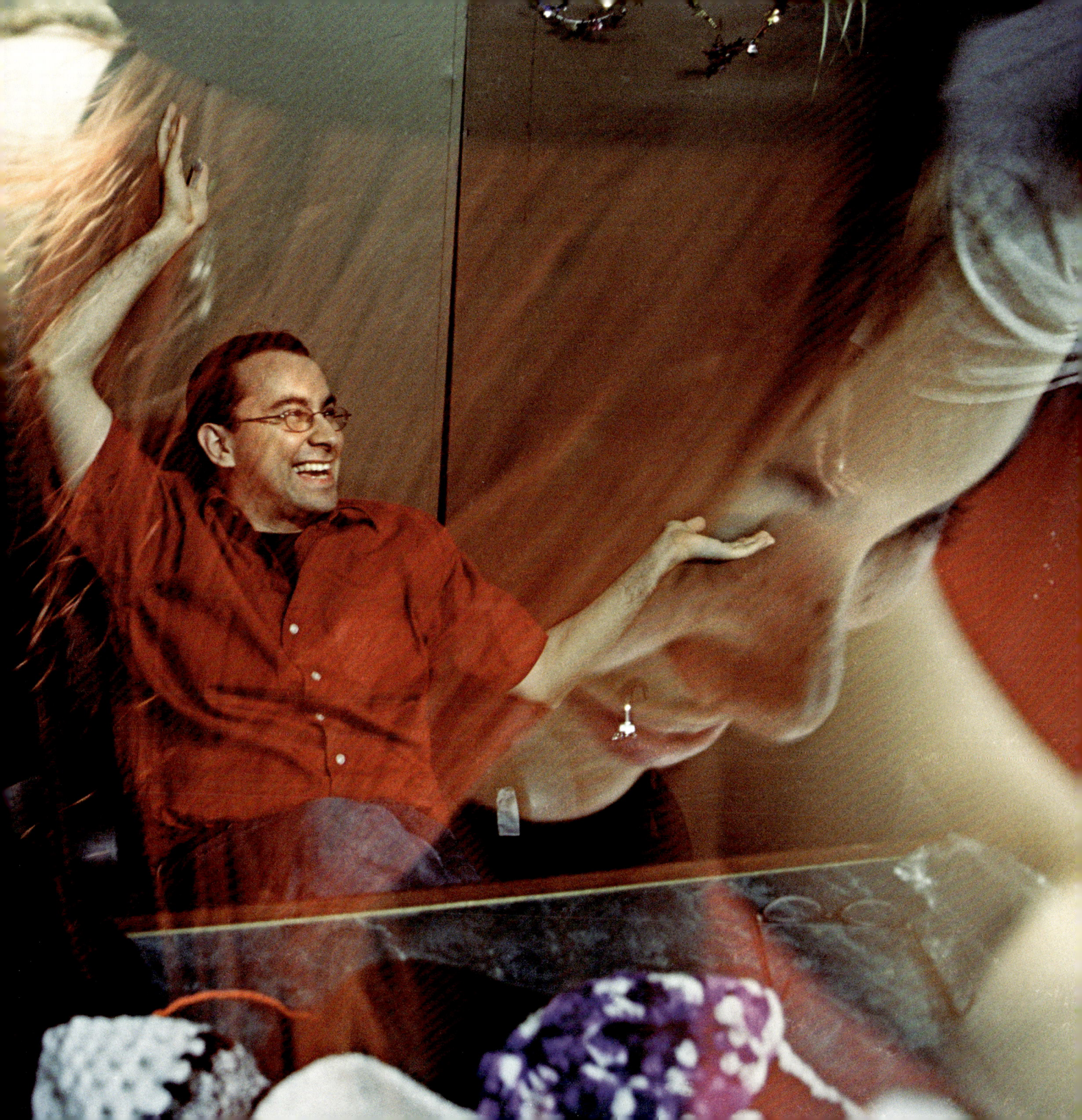

Hey Dad

If i haven't told you
or if you feel i don't
tell you enough...

I Love You
I love you for being the
dad i always wanted... So
when your really really down
pull it out your pocket &
read this.
   'Cauze you may not think
you do enough or mean enough
But to one person (me☺)
You mean the World!!
Thank You  &  I Love You
                 Eternity.

# Biography

At 27 years old, Lucky Stephen Michaels has experienced more than most people twice his age. Born in Ohio, but raised in Detroit, Michigan, Lucky grew up with his three brothers and his single mother in an environment ridden with poverty, surrounded by people who were abusive, involved in drugs, and leaving his family homeless and struggling to survive. By age 18, Lucky had begun taking photographs on a borrowed camera and exploring his blossoming photographic philosophy of hyper-realism. His work captured the odd, harsh, and beautiful life around him and often with an intimate, self-reflective tone. During this time, he attended school at Northwestern Michigan University and received his Associates Degree in Applied Arts.

In August of 2001, Lucky moved from Michigan to New York City where he was accepted into the photography program at Parsons School of Design. Arriving less than a month before the World Trade Center attacks of September 11, Lucky had barely settled into his Union Square apartment when that devastating morning took shape. While continuing his work for school, he volunteered during the overnight shifts of the bucket brigades at ground zero, until growing health problems prevented him from continuing.

Lucky embarked on his first major photography project the following summer when he returned to Michigan to photograph his family. The project, which he photographed over two summers, yielded two full-length photography books, Trailer and Child Support, both of which will be published by Trolley. Selected photographs from Trailer appeared in the 2003 winter issue of Unedited Magazine.

The experience that has shaped much of his current work, including Shelter, began in the spring of 2003, when the Reverend Pat Bumgardner of Metropolitan Community Church of New York, invited Lucky to help open Sylvia's Place, New York's first emergency shelter for LGBTQ youth and young adults. He began working as an overnight counselor, and quickly began photographing the life of the youth in the shelter during his overnight shifts. His personal experiences with the residents of the shelter inspire some of the most powerful images in the project and reflect on a more personal narrative documenting a new chapter of his life. Some of the images from the project are included in the permanent museum archive at Exit Art Gallery in New York.

Lucky continues to work at Sylvia's Place, but no longer as an overnight counselor. He has been instrumental in the creation of the new Marsha P. Johnson Center, a 24-hour drop in center for LGBTQ youth and young adults, and continues to work full-time as the program's outreach director. He continues to intertwine his professional life with his artistic life, always finding new inspiration for his remarkable photography.

# Bibliography

The statistics used in this book were gathered from information from the following websites:

Empire State Coalition, State of the City's Homeless Youth Report:
www.empirestatecoalition.org/
Hunter College School of Social Work:
www.hunter.cuny.edu/socwork/
The National Gay and Lesbian Task Force: www.thetaskforce.org/
PFLAG Pheonix:
www.pflagpheonix.org
Urban Justice Center:
www.urbanjustice.org
Wingspan:
www.wingspan.org/

# Acknowledgements

Shelter Book Campaign Contributors

"Artist"
In Memory of Dad: James H. Hill, 8-1-07

"Editors"
Tom Weise
Hustlaball.com
Richard Skipper
Phillip D. Gibson
Anonymous Donor
Martin Luther King Jr. High GSA

"Printers"
David Beatty
Clare Shipstead
Crispin Sheridan & Brian Puskar
In Honor of David Pratt
Bill Melamed
Matthew Maloney

"Assistants"
Robert Adams & Don Tuthill
Wireless Generation
Daniel Nardicio & Sweetie
Cherry to the kids - its all about you
Crispin & Brian's Wedding Guests
Robert H. Siegfried
Ms Trai La Trash
David Raleigh

# Thanks

In particular I would like to thank:

All of my kids & the kids of Sylvia's Place for not only opening up to me, but for allowing me the chance to tell their stories. Tanino Minneci for being just as dedicated to the shelter, and for all of the work that went into making interviews turn into the stories of our kids.

MCCNY for being my New York family, as well as being a place for all people, thanks for stepping up and practicing what you preach. Rev. Pat Bumgardner, for being a second mother and to the Rev. Troy Perry our founder, Rev. Nancy Wilson our moderator and UFMCC for a lifetime of serving and reaching out to our LGBTQ siblings. Julie Netherland and Kate Barnhart for being supportive of this project.

Carol Fonde, the best color printer I will ever know, thank you for teaching me and encouraging me to keep going every step of the way, and for introducing me to Trolley. Vincent Cianni for being a mentor and role model, as well as Neil Selkirk who also helped hone and edit this large body of work. Lorenza and Tito.

Gigi and Hannah from Trolley for bearing with me and for getting this book done and out to the world.

Jeanette and Papo at EXIT Art. DJ Sammy Jo and his friends for the book launch.

My family in Traverse City, MI, Mum and Robert and all who have no idea what my life is like out here, but keep in touch anyway.

Most importantly to Billy, my partner, for putting up with all the stress that art and not-for-profit can put on a household; good thing we have each other, Theodore, Tattoo, and Vishes Napolean Siegfried-Michaels.

Also I would like to thank Phillip D. Gibson & Soren Anders for contributing to future works and projects.

Published in Great Britain in 2007
by Trolley Limited
www.trolleybooks.com

Photographs © Lucky S. Michaels 2007
Text  © Lucky S. Michaels, Tanino Minneci

Design: www.fruitmachinedesign.com
Text Editing: Hannah Watson, Bryony Harris

A catalogue record for this book is available from
the British Library.

ISBN 978-1-904563-59-4

Printed in Italy by Grafiche Antiga, 2007

191 Shelter